FRANK SKINNER

Born in January 1957 Frank grew up in Oldbury and Smethwick; West Midlands. After various jobs, he performed his first stand-up gig in December 1987 and went on to win the Perrier Award at the Edinburgh Festival. He is currently enjoying success with his own TV chat show.

FRANK SKINNER

by Frank Skinner

ARROW

Published by Arrow Books in 2002

9 10

Copyright © Frank Skinner 2001

Frank Skinner has asserted his right under the Copyright, Designs and Patents Act, 1988
to be identified as the author of this work

First published in the United Kingdom in 2001 by Century

Arrow Books Limited
The Random House Group Limited
20 Vauxhall Bridge Road, London SW1V 2SA

Random House Australia (Pty) Limited
20 Alfred Street, Milsons Point, Sydney,
New South Wales 2061, Australia

Random House New Zealand Limited
18 Poland Road, Glenfield,
Auckland 10, New Zealand

Random House South Africa (Pty) Limited
Endulini, 5a Jubilee Road, Parktown 2193, South Africa

The Random House Group Limited Reg. No. 954009

www.randomhouse.co.uk

A CIP catalogue record for this book is available
from the British Library

Papers used by Random House are natural, recyclable products made from wood
grown in sustainable forests. The manufacturing processes conform to the
environmental regulations of the country of origin

ISBN 0 09 942687 0

Typeset by SX Composing DTP, Rayleigh, Essex
Printed and bound in Great Britain by
Cox & Wyman Ltd, Reading, Berkshire

The author and publisher have made all reasonable efforts to contact copyright
holders for permission, and apologise for any omissions or errors in the form of
credits given. Corrections may be made to future printings.

IF I'M CONSIDERING buying a book, I always take it off the shelf and read the first paragraph. This, I think, gives you a pretty fair inkling as to whether you'll like it or not. So, imagine the pressure I'm feeling at the moment. I suppose this has ended up in the Biography section and you are probably already eyeing up my competition: stuff like 'My Life in Music' by David Hasselhof or 'Fish in my rear-view mirror' by Teddy Kennedy. So, I know I have to work fast. I've never written a book before. In fact I've barely written a letter in the last ten years and even e-mails have become a bit irksome. I quite like text-messaging on my mobile phone, but it's not much of a warm-up for a 120,000-word autobiography. I even had text-message sex on one occasion. It was a long-winded but ultimately rewarding experience. At one stage in the proceedings I asked my fellow texter what was under her pants. The answer took the form of a vivid portrait in words that was three parts Jackie Collins and two parts Gray's Anatomy. I hadn't really expected such a wealth of detailed information. In short, I could almost smell it. Her message ended: 'What's under YOUR pants?' I replied, in all honesty, 'My knees.'

According to my own methods of purchase, if you are still with me at this stage, then the book is bought. Don't imagine this will lead to any falling away of standards. As far as I'm concerned, your outlay has forged a bond between us and I'm going to spend the rest of these pages telling you more about myself than I've ever told a best friend. You see, what I really like about the text-message story is that it's true. I really like true stuff. This is why I never read novels. I'm constantly plagued by the knowledge that they aren't true. If a novel begins, 'Martin lit a cigarette and considered the situation', I'm thinking to myself, no, he didn't. There is no Martin. So, I'm offering you the truth. The story of my life. This throws up a couple of problems.

Firstly, and I am not inclined to false modesty, I find it hard to imagine the kind of person who would be even slightly interested in my life story. I never stood toe-to-toe with Saddam or struck a power-chord at a stadium gig. I'm a nondescript bloke from a working-class family in West Bromwich, who got lucky. I've always been lucky. A friend of mine used to say that if I fell off John Lewis's roof, I'd drop into a new suit, and I know what he meant. On my thirtieth birthday, a mate's girlfriend asked me what it was like to be thirty and 'on the scrapheap'. Ten years later, I was doing a stand-up gig in front of five and a half thousand people, had my own chat show, and was at the core of a national phenomenon when me and two other blokes decided that football was coming home. How did all that happen?

This leads to the other problem. I've read the odd biography and I usually give up after about fifty pages because we're on chapter four and he's still at school. I hate all that early-life stuff. Who wants to know where his grandad was born and that his earliest memory was of staring at a stained-glass window at his auntie's house in Sudbury? By this stage I'm shouting, 'Hurry up and get famous, you bastard, or I'm switching to Hasselhof.' But, as Wordsworth said, 'The child is father to the man', so I feel I *need* to stick in a bit of relevant stuff from my pre-shaving years, just not in a big lump at the front. In fact, I don't see why the story needs to be in any particular order. We're mates now. You'll have to take me as you find me.

I also like books with lots of short little sections, bite-sized to suit the busy lifestyle common to so many people in this, the twenty-first century.

Can I just make a brief point about modesty? I really like modesty. I respect it. Modesty in others draws me to them. A lot of people would regard me as a winner but, for the first thirty years of my life, as my mate's girlfriend instinctively recognised, I was a loser. Thirty years is a long time. I still think like a loser. I still move like one. I'm OK with that. Losers are often very nice people, well, compared to winners.

Unfortunately, the nature of autobiography means I have to talk about myself, at length. I'll have to say 'I did this' and 'I said that'. Sorry. Worst of all, as with the text-message story, I'm going to have to quote my own jokes. Now, as much as I love hearing them quoted by others, it is impossible to quote your own gags without sounding like a tosser. What can I do? I'm stuck with it.

The closest I've previously got to being 'biographed' was getting done by *This is Your Life*. It was a strange dream-like experience. I was doing a gig at the London Palladium. It had been a bit of a stormer and, as I took my bows at the end after an hour and a half of fairly tasty stand-up, I was feeling pretty good. Happily, there was a lot of really loud cheering but then, in the midst of all this, there was a sort of secondary cheer which went up, even louder than the first one. Wow, I thought, they REALLY love me! Turned out the much louder secondary cheer was for Michael Aspel, sneaking on behind me. To be honest, I was a bit startled when, out the corner of my eye, I caught sight of him. Michael and I exchanged pleasantries before I was dragged off to my dressing room and locked in so I didn't accidentally bump into any surprise guests. Meanwhile, they prepared the Palladium stage for *This is Your Life* and, to my amazement, the crowd hung around till 1.00 a.m. to witness the event.

It occurs to me now that this is quite a nice way to structure a biography: the comedian locked alone in his dressing room, waiting to be 'This is Your Lifed', and naturally he begins to reminisce until, 120,000 words later, he is awakened from his nostalgic meanderings by a knock on the door, 'Mr Skinner, we're ready for you now.' And he strides out into the bright light to be greeted by a deafening roar that is less about admiration and more about love. Thus, I tell my tale like the old gal who used to be Kate Winslet does in *Titanic*. As I say, it's a nice way to structure an autobiography. But . . . I don't fancy it.

Something struck me as I sat locked in my dressing room that night. My big surprise shouldn't have been a surprise at all. I had had a phone message in the early hours of that morning telling me that Michael Aspel was going to be at the Palladium that night, and that I was his victim-to-be. It never occurred to me for one second that it might be true. It had, after all, been a strange week on the crazed messages front. On the previous Monday night, I did a gig in Oxford. When I left the building at around midnight, a female fan had written a lewd message

4

in lipstick on my windscreen. It offered me 'anal sex with no complications' if I cared to visit her that night. There was a phone number but the woman was clearly a nutter. I mean, you should have seen the state of her lounge.

Anyway, I barely noticed the phone-message. It never occurred to me that I might be *This is Your Life* material. Why would they be interested in me? (I sense you're already getting fed-up with the modesty thing.) The words 'scraping' and 'barrel' should have come to mind but they didn't. I discovered a few days later that the phone-call had come from a couple of former colleagues from my comedy-club days, Malcolm Hardee and Jim Tavare. Malcolm knew about my special night because he was due to be a guest on the show. He was dropped when the producer heard about the phone-call. Malcolm actually had the cheek to turn up to the after-show party, but he completely redeemed himself in my eyes by performing a commando nerve-grip on Michael Aspel, causing the much-loved broadcaster to drop helplessly to his knees. I have the greatest respect for Mr Aspel but that is what I call comedy. If *This is Your Life* was a live, late-night show it would be the best thing on television. Imagine a long line of ex-lovers, debtors, and discarded ex-friends coming on and haranguing the victim. Or friends and relatives cheerily striding on to talk openly of his surly manner and his various brushes with sexually transmitted disease. As it is, much wonderful stuff was lost in the final edit of my own *TIYL*. I can still see the incredibly professional way in which Michael Aspel smiled and nodded when Jonathan Ross and his wife, Jane, came on and thanked me for introducing them to anal sex.

I should point out that this was a reference to a stand-up routine of mine. Neither Jonathan nor Jane were with me in the untidy lounge. For some reason, anal sex has become something of a leitmotif in my life. Many's the time that I have eschewed the easy pleasures of the main auditorium and, instead, sought out the smaller, more challenging, and ultimately more rewarding charms of the adjoining Studio Theatre. Even if the experience is essentially the same, the mere knowledge that you are in the more exclusive smaller venue seems to make the whole thing more exciting. Many would consider this a private matter but, like the ancient mariner, I feel a strange need to tell my tale.

In fact, I have spent so much time going on and on about the subject on stage and screen that *The Guardian* once described me as the 'Billy Graham of anal sex'. That may be stretching it a bit (to the anal sex enthusiast, something of an occupational hazard) but once, during a stand-up tour, I received a postcard from a man who told me that my lengthy sermon on anal sex at a gig he had attended had triggered a conversation between him and his wife on the way home. While still on the bus, they had resolved to 'give it a bash' when they got back to the house and, after twenty-two years of marriage, they had anal sex for the first time. The experiment was, it seems, a tremendous success. I felt like I imagine a pop star must feel when he hears from grateful relatives that his music has aroused a loved one from a long coma. I have never quite worked out the significance, if any, but on the other side of the postcard was a very formal portrait of Major Yuri Gagarin.

People ask me why I became a comedian. Well, I've been making jokes for as long as I can remember. Not necessarily good jokes but jokes nevertheless. I get endless joy from this process. Whether it's on telly being watched by ten million viewers or small-talking to a stranger in a lift, my greatest joy is to crack a good gag and get the right response. When I still lived in Birmingham, I dated a stunningly attractive woman. I had been seeing her for about three weeks when I finally asked her where she lived. It turns out she dwelt in what was, at the time, a very rough block of flats called Bath Court. I said, in what I felt was a slightly Wildean tone, 'The trouble with Bath Court is that the residents spend a good deal more time in the latter than they do in the former.'

'Where's "The Latter"?' she asked. I knew then that our love could never flourish.

On another occasion, I was wandering around Speakers' Corner with a mate one Sunday morning and we stopped to listen to a bearded man singing the praises of the Muslim religion. Soon he switched to a pretty aggressive attack on Christianity. During this, a black man in a yellow cagoule arrived on a mountain bike. He dismounted and stayed at the rear of the crowd, leaning on the bike. Then he began heckling the Muslim speaker, correcting Biblical misquotations and challenging theological points. The Muslim kept beckoning the heckler forward but he was clearly quite comfortable where he was. Eventually, the exasperated Muslim stepped down from the stage and walked towards the heckler to continue the debate. 'There you are,' I said to my mate, 'if the mountain bike won't go to Mohammed . . .' If a son of mine had played football for England, I don't think I could have been more proud. My mate actually applauded.

This is why I became a comedian. And yes, these two stories show why I love that mate more than I ever could have loved that stunningly attractive woman.

I'm still trying to work out the best approach to this book. I thought I might try mixing the present with the past, so I can tell you what I did today and then chuck in a lump of golden memories. I was out shopping with my girlfriend, Caroline, this morning. When we got back to my flat, there was a man standing in the pouring rain with a big bunch of flowers and an even bigger camera. 'I'd just like to congratulate you on your engagement,' he said. She took the flowers and he started snapping. Caroline is, I think, a very beautiful twenty-three-year-old. This, generally speaking, is a very good thing in a girlfriend. However, I am forty-four, so whenever we are photographed together, I always think of those pictures of Anna-Nicole Smith and her ninety-year-old billionaire husband, J. Marshall Howard: a terrible before-and-after nightmare of what goes wrong with the human face. (Incidentally, I once did a gag about Anna-Nicole, claiming that the film *Tomb Raider* was her life story.) So, any picture of me with Caroline is bound to make me look a bit wrecked. And, I suppose, make her look even prettier.

This, of course, is why prettyish girls often hang around with ugly girls. I remember seeing such a pairing in Samantha's nightclub in Birmingham, back in the seventies. I chatted to the Mr Hyde half of the combo and, after a while, she asked me why blokes always tossed a coin before approaching them. I hadn't got the heart to tell her. Well, not till after breakfast anyway.

Caroline and me have been together for just over six months. She is tall and green-eyed with short blonde hair and a smile that makes me forget to do stuff, like breathe, for example. Sometimes, when she's asleep, I lie and look at her face for ages without getting bored. But she's not willowy and wet like some pretty girls; she's loud, funny and inclined to argue, especially with me.

By the way, I'm not engaged to Caroline, but I bought her a ring that she wears on that finger so I suppose tongues were bound to wag. Still, there we stood, saying 'cheese' in the pouring rain, and me with my hood up looking, in my mind's eye, like the mummified head of Mary Magdalene I once saw in a glass case in a museum in Provence.

I didn't begin my comedy career until I was thirty. People had been telling me I should be a comic since I was about six but, in a way, I already was a comic. I used to perform in the classroom, then in the pub, the factory and now on telly. It's all the same thing: showing off and endlessly pursuing that holy grail, the laugh. You don't need a microphone or a camera. All you need is an audience. Mates, girlfriends, people on buses, anyone will do. It's like an addiction.

Just after my dad died, me and my two brothers had the task of clearing out his house: all his clothes and little trinkets, a lock of my mom's hair, his rosary beads, photographs, the lot. We were being brave about it, but it was a desperately sad process, all three of us frightened we might find the thing that would, without much warning, leave us broken and sobbing. My eldest brother, Terry, was clearing out a cupboard and took out the remains of a cheap ornament that my dad had had an affection for. Originally, it was a bird perched on a branch, but it had got broken and the piece that Terry held up consisted of only the base, a branch, and a pair of bird's feet still clinging on. No doubt, somewhere deep in the cupboard was the footless bird, both pieces put there by my dad with the intention of mending them one day. One of the thousands of loose ends left behind when somebody dies suddenly. I took the broken ornament from my brother, the little feet severed just above the ankle, if birds have ankles. He looked at me but didn't speak. Neither did my other brother, Keith. They looked but they didn't speak. I did. 'Lot 16: Who killed Cock Robin?' I said. We laughed like we used to when we were kids sharing the same bedroom.

Those of you not familiar with the old song, 'Who killed Cock Robin?', will just have to trust me on this one. I always think footnotes are a bit grand.

Anyway, though I feel I have always been a comic, I didn't actually make my stage debut till I was thirty. So, after putting it off for so long, what gave me the kick up the arse that finally made me do it?

If I'm not mistaken, that was this book's second rhetorical question and I'm not sure I enjoyed either of them. They've given the whole piece an 'Anglican sermon' feeling, that I don't much care for. Those of you who enjoy a rhetorical question would be well-advised to make the most of that one. It could be the last. Nevertheless, I'm going to answer it.

It suddenly occurred to me one day that it would be a terrible thing to be a seventy-year-old man and wonder if I could have made it as a comic. To have tried and failed would be bearable, but to have *not* tried. To lie there, pondering what it would have been like, and to know that the chance had gone forever. Horrible! After having these thoughts, I had no choice but to give it a go. Ever since that day, I do a lot of my decision-making with the help of the 'looking back when I'm seventy' test. This has led me to doing my first West End play, taking part in a completely improvised live TV series, and to contracting a venereal disease from a woman I met in a nightclub in Moseley in the late 1980s.

I won an award today. The Variety Club of Great Britain gave me its Comedy Award for 2000. This is fairly amazing because I've been nominated for, I think, fourteen awards in the last twelve years, but never won till now. Well, I won the Perrier Award in 1991, but more of that later. I was once nominated for a National Television Award, for Best Chat Show Host, but

I was filming in Cardiff so I sat alone in my hotel room watching it live on telly. In short, I lost to Michael Parkinson. This, of course, is no disgrace. As a child, whenever I sat on the toilet, I would fill the time, not by reading comics or wiping bogeys on the wall, but by pretending I was being interviewed by Parkinson. 'Of course,' Michael would say, 'shortly afterwards you captained England to win the World Cup.'

'Well, yes,' I'd reply with a chuckle, 'but don't ask me about the three Brazilian girls in the jacuzzi.' (Audience laughter mingles with sound of toilet flushing.)

You'll notice I say 'as a child', thus giving you the completely false impression that I don't do it any more.

Anyway, I hate to admit it, but I got really pissed off about not winning the chat show award. That's the trouble with being nominated. You start wanting it. I'd rather they just left me alone. So, in a fit of luvvie petulance, I turned the telly off and had a bit of a brisk walk around and around the hotel room. When I'd calmed a little, I put the telly back on. As I rejoined the broadcast, they'd moved on to Best Sitcom and were showing a really hilarious clip from *Friends*. Brilliant. Then they cut back to the host, who said, 'And the winner is, *Last of the Summer Wine*.' Suddenly, I felt a lot better.

Being an un-nominated neutral observer at an awards ceremony can be a bit of a laugh, though. I was at the Brits once when Eva Herzigova was presenting the award for Best New Band. She strode onstage in a fantastic low-cut dress and opened the envelope. 'Smashing Pumpkins', she said. 'Hear! Hear!' I shouted. I liked to think that somewhere in the far reaches of eternity, Benny Hill smiled.

Presenting awards can also be interesting. Once, at the British Comedy Awards, in a hall packed with top comics, comedy-writers and producers, I presented the prize for Best New Comedy Show. I was taken aback by the size of the laugh

I got from the line, 'I never watch new comedy shows because I hate that part of me that wants them to be shit.' I believe this is known as the laughter of recognition.

Anyway, the Variety Award for Comedy is just, well, awarded, without any of the nomination nonsense, so I knew I'd won before I turned up. I accepted the award from Dale Winton and explained to the crowd that people once thought me and Dale were engaged, but only because it said so on the door. I felt obliged to do at least one engagement joke because the story about Caroline and me, including photo, was on the front page of this morning's *Daily Express*.

When the show was broadcast on BBC1 the next day, they followed each of my gags with a close-up of Caroline laughing uproariously. It reminded me that a journalist from *Loaded* once asked me to describe my perfect girlfriend. 'A good audience with nice tits,' I rather laddishly replied. It's a funny old world.

Those photographs in the rain appeared again the following day, this time on the cover of *OK* magazine. I didn't look quite as bad as I thought. Nevertheless, there was still more than a suggestion of Princess Diana being hugged by W.H. Auden.

Here goes with a bit of autobiographical information. I was born Christopher Graham Collins, on the 28th January 1957 at 5.15 in the afternoon. My mother, Doris Elizabeth Collins, a slight, dark-eyed teetotaller from nearby Oldbury, gave birth to me in what was then called Hallam Hospital in West Bromwich, Staffordshire, about five miles north-west of Birmingham. My birth certificate says I was born in the town of West Bromwich, in the area of West Bromwich, in the County Borough of West Bromwich. So when people ask me why I support West Bromwich Albion Football Club, I explain that my decision was based on the only criterion anyone should ever use when choosing a football club – geography. You sit with a pencil, a ruler, and a map, identify the nearest professional football club to your place of birth, you buy a scarf with their name on it and that's that.

My dad was John Francis Collins, a heavy-drinking, sports-mad amateur pub singer, with a big chest and a bald head, who came from West Cornforth, County Durham. My dad always told me that he came down to West Bromwich to play for the non-leaguers, Spennymoor United, in the third round of the FA Cup in 1937, when he was nineteen. I'm not sure he actually made the final eleven that day but West Brom managed to win 7–1. That night my dad and some of the other Spennymoor boys sought out a local pub and got invited to a party by a bunch of Oldbury boys. My dad-to-be decided that these boys were a bit dodgy so decided to give them a false name, Len. At the party, he saw this pretty dark-eyed girl and asked one of the Oldbury boys if he knew her. 'Yeah, it's my sister,' he said. 'I'll introduce you.' And my mom called my dad Len till her dying day.

Of course, the upshot of this story is, if it wasn't for West Bromwich Albion, I would never have been born.

When my dad approached that eighteen-year-old girl at that Saturday night party, he couldn't possibly have known the effect his appearance would have had on her. A few years earlier, as my mom maintained to her death, she had had a dream. She was in her bedroom when she heard heavenly music and opened the windows to hear more clearly. As the sun streamed in, she began to make out a group of angels in the distant sky. They seemed to be carrying a young man. As they got nearer, she could clearly see the man's face. It was no one she knew, no one she'd ever met, well, not until a slightly drunk amateur footballer said hello to her at a party a few years later. Shortly after they married my mom sent this story into a newspaper and won two shillings for the Letter of the Week.

Who'd have thought that sixty-odd years later her little boy would still be milking the same story for financial reward?

My dad was what used to be called a man's man. He was sturdy and short-tempered but also very funny, with loads of stories and anecdotes. He would tell me how his uncle, Tom Shanks, had carried a horse across the town square for a bet, and how my grandad, after a disagreement, had hanged a man in a Newcastle pub. He finally allowed regulars to cut the man down when he started to go purple. Apparently, it had been suggested they might cut him down when the man was still only blue, but my grandad insisted they wait till the man had a head like an aubergine.

My grandmother was also a formidable north-easterner. I remember my mom telling me about the shock she experienced when she first met my dad's parents and they were both smoking pipes.

My mom's dad died just as the 1957 FA Cup Final between Man Utd and Aston Villa kicked off. His wife, whose maiden name was, I'm happy to say, Polly Stocking, was the only grandparent I remember. She was a game old bird who lived into her nineties and regularly breakfasted on shepherd's pie and Guinness in her later years. I remember she was rushed into hospital in her late eighties and we all thought this was the end. She survived, and before she left the ward they decided to perm and set her hair as a bit of a treat. After lots of teasing and spraying, they took out the curlers and my gran's hair returned immediately to its natural, Don King-like, I've-been-electrified look. 'It's like me,' my gran explained. 'It's dead but it won't lie down.'

14

I was driving to the West Brom–Crewe game today when my mobile went. It was a conference call, with my sometime double-act partner David Baddiel, and our manager, Jon Thoday, on the line.

Jon Thoday is a chunky, dark-haired man, who looks like I imagine Michael Winner looked when he was in his thirties. He is the boss of Avalon, a company that manages and promotes comedians, and has the reputation, rightly or wrongly, for being tough, ruthless, and downright rude in its dealings with broadcasters, theatre managers, and other employers of comics. I like Jon, though. He is, with me at least, funny and charming, and inclined to giggle in a high-pitched way that belies his scary reputation. I've been with Avalon nearly ten years. A few months after I joined, I walked into their then tiny offices in Litchfield Street, London W1, and found Jon on the phone. 'Fuck you and your fucking attitude,' he was shouting, and then he slammed down the phone with such force that it broke into about six pieces. 'Ah, Frank,' he said, suddenly mellowing, 'I don't think you'll be doing that radio show.' There was a pause, and then we both pissed ourselves laughing.

David Baddiel tells me that the first time he became aware of my existence was when we were both working as stand-up comics on the London comedy club circuit in 1989. I was on stage at the Comedy Store, at that time a basement club in the corner of Leicester Square, and Dave was with a bunch of comics watching the show. I was still fairly raw. I'd been doing stand-up for about a year and a half and was only just starting to get gigs at this much-respected comedy club. It was about 1.15 in the early hours of Sunday morning when I walked on. The crowd were often a bit drunk and mouthy by this stage, but I was having a good time. There was some heckling but, after being a bit scared of hecklers in my very early days, I was now almost encouraging their intervention. It got me thinking on my feet.

There is something of a myth about heckling. It's often suggested that every comedy club has a throng of hecklers making clever, witty remarks that the poor comic is scarcely able to compete with. In fact, I've been doing and watching stand-up comedy for fourteen years and in that time I might have heard three or four funny heckles. Mostly it's drunks shouting 'Fuck off' or just making incomprehensible noises and then falling over.

Perhaps the best heckle I ever received was at a club called the Red Rose in Finsbury Park, North London. There was a blind man, a regular punter, who was in one night just as I was beginning a twenty-minute set. About two minutes in, the blind man shouted, 'Get off, you Brummie bastard. (Pause) Has he gone yet?' I prided myself on being pretty quick with hecklers but a blind man is a tricky opponent. I considered engaging him in friendly conversation for a few minutes whilst, at the same time, holding my hands in double V-signs about six inches from his face, but I wasn't sure the crowd would go with me on this. I decided against shouting, 'Well, at least I can fucking see', for the same reason. In the end I silenced him by trumping his 'You can't attack me because I'm disabled' card by suggesting to him that he was only against me because I was Pakistani. He looked genuinely ashamed.

Verbal jousting with the disabled is, generally speaking, thin ice for a stand-up. I once did a gig at a theatre in Cambridge and had cause, in an improvised moment, to start talking about those people you see who are bent over double with hunched backs and walk along staring at the ground. A man at the back shouted, 'It's called ankylotic spondylitis.' Well, nobody likes a smart-Alec so I asked him how come he knew so much about it. 'I've got it,' he shouted in reply. An uneasy murmur started in the crowd. 'Well . . . ,' I began, fumbling for a way out of this comedy cul-de-sac, 'ermm . . . well at least you'll probably never stand in dog shit again.' The crowd took a second or two to consider this and then, thank God, applauded. I'm not really sure why. Were they being heartless in taking my side against the woefully stooped heckler just because I'd bounced back with a cheeky response, or did they honestly feel that I had shown true compassion by identifying, for the man, a silver lining in his dark, dark cloud?

I have to admit I don't always find a happy way through these dark patches that sometimes occur during audience banter. I was performing at a club in Manchester and casually asked a guy if he had any kids. 'Not alive,' he said. I never like to just ignore an audience remark but this one floored me so I just carried on as if it hadn't happened. Even Homer nods.

So, it's very late at the Comedy Store, I'm on stage, the crowd is lively and David Baddiel, still a stranger to me, is in the audience. Then came the heckle. Now, a lot of comics have set responses to heckles. These, as I'm sure you know, are called put-down lines. It's not really an activity I approve of because the same put-down lines get shared around and I think it's really important that a comic treats each heckle as an individual case. Otherwise every turn is doing 'Don't drink on an empty head', 'Isn't it a shame when cousins marry?' or 'Do your gums bleed once a month?' regardless of the heckle, and the spontaneity, the challenge of dealing with the unexpected, is lost. So, I'm still on stage at the Comedy Store and the heckle comes: 'Don't I remember you from medical school?'

Now, as heckles go, this one was quite tricky. Firstly, it didn't follow the normal heckle-structure of insult from audience, followed by better insult from comic. It was more of a polite enquiry, but still potentially destructive and probably still motivated by bad intent. It sounded friendly but it was designed to throw me. Secondly, you'll be surprised to hear, it was not a heckle I'd had before, so I couldn't even fall back, if stuck, on my own personal heckle-response back-catalogue. If someone says they remember you from medical school, there isn't much logic in suggesting that, as a result of this, they'll never stand in dog shit again. Thirdly, I never went to medical school. Anyway, the exchange went like this,

Heckler: Don't I remember you from medical school?
Me: Oh, yeah. You were the one in the jar.

Dave tells me he joined in with the applause. We didn't actually speak that night, though. Dave was already established on the London circuit and I was just breaking through. There was a fairly rigid pecking-order on the circuit, the general rule being that established comics sat at one end of the dressing room, sharing in-jokes and ignoring the new boys, and people like me sat on their own, giggling nervously at overheard gags they didn't quite get but which the established boys thought were hilarious. I made a vow that if I ever got established on the circuit, I'd always make an effort to make the new boys feel at home. You know, go over and ask their name and so on, maybe even introduce them to the closely knit in-crowd I was now part of. Of course, when the day came that I did get established and accepted, I thought, 'Oh, fuck it. Let someone else sit in "Twats' Corner".' Human nature, eh?

Dave and me (yes, I know it should be 'Dave and I' but I'm trying to find my real voice. I just read what I've written so far and I thought some bits sounded a bit grand) had our first proper conversation in a dressing room at a club called Jongleurs in Battersea. It was during the 1990 World Cup and there was a telly in the dressing room so we could watch that night's Republic of Ireland game. Being of Irish Catholic stock,

I was supporting the Republic. I'd said hello to Dave on a couple of occasions but we hadn't had anything like a proper conversation. He was doing pretty well at the time. He was getting a lot of radio work and doing gigs at all the best clubs. I was sort of world famous in Birmingham and getting on OK in London, but the differences didn't stop there. Dave, or David as everyone called him. Hold it. I found a difference already. In my whole life up till then, I had never met anyone called David who people called David. In Oldbury, he would have been Dave, no messing. And he was Jewish.

I don't think I'd met a Jewish person before. If I had they'd certainly kept it under their hat. Which seems unlikely when you consider how small those hats are. (I'm not totally happy with this gag because although Jews do wear those little hats clipped to their heads, they also wear those big trilby-cum-stetsons which, I imagine, have loads of storage-room for secrets.) I may have sort of known a Jew back in Oldbury. There was a bearded, East-European-sounding local nutter who everyone called Jacob the Jew. I have no idea if Jacob was a Jew (I mean Jacob the nutter, of course, not Jacob, the brother of Esau and the son of Isaac. He was definitely a Jew). The rumour that Oldbury's Jacob was Jewish was definitely beefed up a bit when my mate Ogga saw him on Crosswells Road shouting, 'The Suez Canal: what for?' over and over. None of us really understood the significance of the Suez Canal at the time, but it certainly sounded Jewish to me. I'm not even sure if he was a nutter. This is not always easy to judge. I find, as a general rule of thumb, if you see someone wearing more than two badges, they're a nutter. But that's a personal view-point. I went along with the theory that he was a nutter mainly because it enabled me to pun on the popular foodstuff, Jacob's Crackers.

On a darker note, my dad told me a story of how a Jewish

money-lender he knew of, back in the north-east, had driven a poor woman to put her head in the gas oven because of his cruel interest rates. My dad was not a man to hold back when it came to enforcing a racial sterotype.

Anyway, I know now that Dave is nothing like the nasty Jew that my dad spoke of. For a start, there is no way in the world that he would ever lend anyone money. But he was a bit scary at first. He was more successful, richer, better-looking, trendier and brainier than me, and when he first shook my hand I sensed he knew this as well as I did. In fact, I half-expected him to bring it up, but he didn't. He was dressed in blacks and greys, the way fashionable London people did in 1990. His hair was long on top and short at the sides and he wore little round specs. I didn't know if he actually needed them but I suppose they were easier to maintain than a large flashing sign that said 'I've got a degree', and served the same purpose.

We shook hands in the dressing room and he joined me in watching the Ireland game. At first I thought that at any time he might ask if he could turn over to watch a Fellini movie on Channel Four (I presumed there was one) but he didn't. In fact, he seemed genuinely interested in the game, to the point where he started slagging off Ireland's use of the long ball game and explaining why the Italian and Brazilian systems were, in fact, more efficient as well as more entertaining. This pissed me off. I was prepared to play the newcomer comic role if I had to, but no toffee-nosed, four-eyed Cockney . . . (In those days, everyone from London and its environs was a Cockney in my eyes.) So we had a row about football. And, although we didn't agree, it slowly dawned on me that this trendy Jewish intellectual knew about, and really cared about, the game. I was well impressed. My dad had always told me that I should never trust a man who didn't like football. But if they did, they were alright, you could even forgive them the odd housewife on an unlit Gas Mark 9.

The next time I met Dave was at the Central TV studios in Nottingham. I was doing an Amnesty International comedy special called the Big 30. Dave was doing the same show with his then comedy partner, Rob Newman. When I bumped into them they were standing among their scary-looking management team from the Avalon agency. Rob had a photocopy of the blurb for the back of their new live video and was sitting with a pen, crossing out every 'Baddiel and Newman' and writing in 'Newman and Baddiel'. Dave sat nearby looking depressed. The Avalon team, including their big boss man, Jon Thoday, gazed about them like it was all in a day's work. I said hello and made small talk.

As the day went on, me and Dave got more and more chatty. It's a weird thing when a bloke makes a new male friend. Men of my generation spend about, I would say, forty per cent of their waking hours demonstrating that they're not homosexual. The amount of time I spend talking about football and big tits may be related to this, it's all a bit too chicken-and-egg to work out. Anyway, I sensed I was making a new mate. And a trendy, successful, sophisticated, highly intelligent one at that. And he liked football and big tits. And still no urge to put my head in the gas oven.

The next day I gave Dave a lift to Birmingham in my Citroen AXGT that I'd bought off Steve Coogan. So there's me and Dave driving down the A38 in the thickest fog you could imagine. The sort of fog I thought smokeless fuels had seen off for good. The sort of fog you only usually see in black and white films about Jack the Ripper. The sort that is all around when James Stewart gets into that aeroplane in *The Glenn Miller Story* and says 'It's a little soupy, ain't it.' As we crawled through the gloom past bashed-up cars abandoned on the hard shoulder and distant police sirens, we just talked and talked. The literary merits of John Updike (his favourite) and

Samuel Johnson (mine); The Smiths, The Ramones, being Jewish, being Catholic, American comedians, the films of Woody Allen, Kathy Lloyd, the London comedy clubs, Winona Ryder, Dave's parents, having a girlfriend, marriage, Kathy Lloyd (we talked about her twice), all imaginable aspects of football, the Marx Brothers, *Steve Wright in the Afternoon*, *Monty Python's Flying Circus* – and fog, in all its manifestations. Get on, that's what we did. But I never thought that, in the not-too-distant future, we'd spend five years as flatmates. I was married, for goodness' sake.

Anyway, that conference call. You know, the one I mentioned at the beginning of this section. It turns out that me and Dave are going to be doing our ITV show, *Baddiel and Skinner Unplanned*, live in London's West End. That could be interesting.

Apparently, my mom was told she shouldn't have any more babies. She had lost twins a couple of years before she had me and once told me that she spent weeks having to sit with her legs raised to combat haemorrhaging. Anyway, she had me against doctors' orders. There's a picture of me aged one, sitting on our front lawn in a knitted all-in-one thing. Chubby and smiling with a shock of yellow hair and my hand on my private parts, although as a child, I don't recall them being particularly 'private'. Hey, that's a thought. Do porn stars still refer to their genitals as their 'private parts' long after they've ceased to be in any way 'private'. There could be stand-up material in there somewhere. Mmm . . . maybe not.

That smiling child with his hand on his nob, is he trying to say to the world, 'I find genitals funny, and thus shall I make my living'? I think so. The die was cast. By the way, my hair was yellow because they didn't really have colour photography then – well not in Oldbury – so they'd take the picture in black and white and then the photographer would colour it in. I look like a fucking Andy Warhol painting.

My first memory is . . . actually, one thing that particularly pisses me off about autobiographies is the 'my first memory' bit so I'll keep it brief. My first memory was of me sitting on the edge of my bed saying, 'Well, I'm four today.' Now, unusually for a first memory, the nature of the utterance makes this one fairly easy to put a date on. All the evidence points to it being the 28th of January 1961. Unless, of course, it wasn't my birthday at all, and I was saying it as a gag, just to throw my parents.

My sister's husband, Frank, tells a story of me as a little kid. He was invited to my mom and dad's house by my sister, Nora, so that he could go through one of those nerve-racking meet-the-girlfriend's-parents experiences that all boyfriends must eventually face. He turned up at our little council house in Oldbury, drank tea, and was quizzed by my parents, chiefly my old man. Then I appeared, aged about four or five, wearing a full cowboy oufit and carrying a small plastic guitar. Six Elvis songs later, my future brother-in-law was starting to get a little bored. I couldn't play the guitar, and it wasn't tuned and it wasn't what you'd really call a guitar. My brother Keith had a really nice acoustic guitar with a little photo of Elvis in a sort of circular picture-frame on the front, but I wasn't allowed to touch this. Also, my voice was a little kid's voice, y'know, too high and with a big, audible breath between each line. Apparently, my 'Old Shep', an Elvis song that tells the tale of a dying dog, was particularly mournful. And, worse still, if anyone spoke or even looked away mid-song I cut them down with a look that would stop a charging elephant. Eventually, I allowed a short interval. My brother-in-law moved on to that safest of working-class male subjects, football.

Football was, at that time, an almost exclusively working-class male thing. The terraces, when I was a kid, were all about bad language, the smell of Woodbine cigarettes, a blind passion for your team, and for football in general, in that order. I remember a bloke standing next to me calling one of our defenders a lazy fucker at fairly high volume. Another chap, just in front of us, turned and asked him to curtail his language because he had his young son with him. The swearing man said, 'Look mate. I work in a fuckin' factory five days a fuckin' week, havin' to bite me fuckin' tongue all the fuckin' time in case I say too fuckin' much and get meself into fuckin' trouble. I come here to watch me fuckin' team and be meself and say whatever I fuckin' like so fuck off.' I only remember this speech so well because I've been quoting it ever since, originally because, like most eleven-year-olds, I thought swearing was really funny, but in more recent times because I think it says more about what football means to real football fans than any beautifully written hardback with a weeping Gazza on the cover. The father of the small child didn't look frightened or insulted. He just nodded as if he understood, and carried on watching the game.

So, anyway, my brother-in-law pointed at me, sitting in my cowboy suit, guitar at my side, easing my thirst with a dandelion and burdock before I bounced back for another three or four numbers. 'Is he gonna be a footballer?' he asked.

'No,' said the old man. He slapped the top of our ten-inch black-and-white telly. 'He's gonna be on this.'

England are playing Spain at Villa Park tonight. In aid of Comic Relief, a handful of celebrities are taking a penalty each at half time. Each scorer gets a grand for the charity. I am one of these celebrities. Dave Baddiel is another. Tonight is Sven-

Göran Eriksson's first game as England manager, and there's a full house of 42,000. As half time draws near we, the penalty-takers, are gathered behind the cluster of police in one of the corners of the ground. We wear the blue and white kits of the Comic Relief football team, The Sporting Noses.

I did a tour of West Africa with the Noses back in 1996. It was an amazing trip. I was shitting myself before we set off. I just thought I'd get malaria or go mad because of the side-effects of the anti-malarial tablets, or die of sunstroke or get taken hostage by guerillas or indeed by gorillas. I didn't want to go but I just kept walking until I was on a plane. I once read that Bruce Lee, when he was scared, would say to himself, over and over again, 'Walk on, Bruce', and he would just keep going despite his fear. I walked on. It was worth it, if only for the fact that we all sat in the Sahara Desert one night, gathered around a birthday cake and sang 'Hold me Close' to celebrate David Essex's forty-ninth birthday. David Essex didn't join in, he just smiled his cheeky smile. We played against a series of local teams from Burkina Faso and Ghana, culminating in a thrilling 4–3 victory in Ghana's national stadium in Accra, against the Ghanaian Post Office Ladies Team.

In all of these games, I was shit. In fact, it has always been one of the great regrets of my life that, despite the fact that I love football as much as anyone I've ever met, I have always been shit at it. I was my dad's last chance to produce an England international and I couldn't even get in the school team. In Africa, the locals were clearly insulted by my inclusion in the side. There were even some attempts to return rice and flour, but in the end I was substituted. As I stormed off, my retort to the crowd's catcalls, 'Well, at least I haven't got flies on my face', earned me an official rebuke from Comic Relief.

Oh, shut up, I made up the last bit. But I *was* shit. That

much is true. So at the end of the tour I hung up my boots for the final time. Until tonight.

As the half-time whistle blew, comedian Nick Hancock walked out with a hand-mike to explain the penalty competition to the crowd. He was loudly booed and a chant of 'Who the fuckin' hell are you?' went up. There was a time when people who did stuff for charity were applauded, but this is a cynical age. Besides which, the average fan must be pretty pissed off with celebrities who jump on the football bandwagon and start going on and on about the team they love so much and never fucking watch. Unfortunately, this night, they chose Nick, a truly obsessive Stoke City fan, as their target. Maybe it was just a blanket 'We hate anyone who earns more than us' approach. Fair enough, I suppose. When Dave Baddiel stepped up to take the first penalty, the booing, if anything, increased. Dave looked a bit edgy. He had confided to me as we stood behind the police that he was nervous. I, for some reason, wasn't. Despite a lifetime of evidence to the contrary, I was totally convinced I would score. So, as the jeering got louder, Dave edged forward and put the ball over the bar. He put his hands to his face and the crowd switched to 'You're shit and you know you are'. Merciless.

Then it was my turn. I swaggered towards the penalty spot, and I mean swaggered. I ran the risk of dislocating both shoulders, such was the extent of my swaggering. The crowd had gone through the boo-ceiling. Not only a rich tosser off the telly but also a West Brom fan at the home of local rivals, Aston Villa. I threw back my head and held out my arms with upturned palms like I was in a warm, soothing shower. They booed even more. I pointed at the left-hand corner of the net to signify where the ball was going. I don't know where this arrogance came from. I just knew I couldn't miss. As I walked back to begin my run-up, I could actually see the 'Skinner', on

26

the back of my shirt, on the big screen in the corner of the ground. It was moving with my swaggering shoulders. I turned and began a short series of stretching exercises, just to wind the crowd up a bit more. It worked. The booing and abuse was really, really loud now. I jogged forward and stuck the ball exactly where I said I would. The crowd shut up very quickly. I ran with arms outstretched and stopped in a pose that was less football and more modern ballet.

All my life, I've been a bit of a wimp, really, always worrying about silly things and fretting about what might or might not happen. Strangely, this wimpishness has always been shot through with a mega-self-confidence, verging on cockiness, that gets me through. It's all a bit of a mystery, really. Anyway, this night, the cockiness rose to the surface. How can someone who's always been shit at football suddenly become a can't-miss penalty-ace? After all my shenanigans, if I'd missed that penalty, that crowd would have crucified me. So, I didn't.

When I was still a baby in a pushchair, my mom and dad took me and my brother Keith to Dudley Zoo for a bit of an outing. I sat in my pushchair, gazing wide-mouthed at all the wondrous new sensory experiences that surrounded me. I had on a pale blue cardigan and matching bobble-hat knitted by my mom. Keith, who was about seven at the time, was having a few ice-cream problems so my mom put my brake on to attend to his dirty face. The moment she left me, a chimpanzee bounded towards the bars of his cage, held himself tightly against them and stretched out like a big furry starfish. He quickly fixed himself in this position and then, with teeth slightly clenched in concentration, he pissed all over me. My mom suddenly became aware of the sound of ape-urine against hand-knitted cardigan and turned in horror. At first, apparently, I just gazed around me in confusion, looking, I suppose, to find where this sudden torrent was coming from, but then I began to cry. Either I had spotted the spreadeagled simian and become alarmed by the apparently personal nature of his attack, or perhaps it was just that my eyes had begun to react to the acidity of the steam. Either way, Mom came to the rescue, and although her horror was already turning into not-very-suppressed giggling, she released the brake and wheeled me out of range. She was too busy calming me down to take note of the chimp's reaction. I wonder if he just hung there, watching and dripping, watching and dripping.

Forty years later, I drove David Baddiel and his then girlfriend to Wool in Dorset to visit a monkey sanctuary called Monkey World. Dave likes monkeys and it was part of a birthday-treat weekend for him. The sanctuary takes in a lot of chimps who have been mistreated by Spanish photographers. I don't mean door-stepping and telephoto lens shots of them sunbathing. I mean tourists pay to get their picture taken with the funny monkey and the photographer keeps his little pet in check by burning him with a cigarette and other acts of cruelty.

New inmates of the sanctuary have to spend some time in a separate section with large windows until they get used to the idea of being with other chimps. When we three turned up we began our tour by peering into this new-inmates section at the slightly edgy-looking new boys. You could actually see the cigarette-burn scars on some of them.

Then one of the chimps began to stare at me. I mean REALLY stare at me. He moved closer towards the glass until we stood only inches apart, gazing into each other's eyes. It was so weird that I could hear other visitors comment on it but I didn't want to look away. Deeper and deeper into the chimp's eyes I peered. It was like gazing into the dark, echoing pit of evolution. Could this really be what my relatives looked like? It was certainly what some of them smelt like, but that didn't seem relevant at such a profound moment. And what was the chimp thinking? What instinct drew him towards me like this? I don't know how long chimpanzees live, but in a perfect world this story would end with me recognising the expression of gritted-teeth concentration on the face of the chimp and the whole tale would take on a Daniel-in-the-lions'-den-like feel and would eventually close with me crying once more, for my lost youth, for my lost mother, for my lost innocence, as the piss streamed down the glass pane only inches from my anguished face.

In reality, I have no evidence that this was the chimp from Dudley Zoo. And let's face it, if it had been him, he would have had his own method for putting out the cigarettes.

I was flicking through the Official Elvis Presley Fan Club magazine today when I saw a fantastic advert. There's a book called *Paradise, Suzanna Style*, which has been written by the actress Suzanna Leigh about the one film she made with Elvis. I say 'the actress Suzanna Leigh' but I don't know if she's still working. How long can actors be out of work and still call themselves actors? (I'm getting a lot more relaxed about the rhetorical question thing.) I met Sylvia Kristel, the star of all those 1970s soft porn *Emmanuelle* films, in the summer of 1998. She was a bit full of herself and said to me, 'Hello, I'm a film actress, what are you?'

'Well, by that logic, I'm a schoolboy,' I replied. Happily, she didn't get it.

Anyway Ms Leigh, apparently, tells the tale of filming *Paradise, Hawaiian Style* with King El, or, as the blurb puts it, 'A behind the scenes look at the 60s movie industry by icon actress Suzanna Leigh and the effect that Elvis Presley had on both her career and her outlook on life. A charming, thoughtful text acclaimed by the media.'

Now, being in the memoir business myself, I was very interested by all this. Especially since the book had been 'acclaimed by the media'. I wish they'd supplied more details of this. I'd like to have known who said what on the acclaim front. But best of all, there is a thing on the cover of the book which really made my day. In the top right-hand corner it says, 'Warning! This is not a novel.'

Well, what's all that about? Someone seems genuinely concerned about the possibility of the book being mistaken for a novel and all the ensuing chaos that might trigger. I might persuade my publisher to put something similar on the cover of this. *Frank Skinner* by Frank Skinner. Warning! This is not an A to Z of Leeds.

We lived in a council house in Oldbury. 181 Bristnall Hall Road. Oldbury, as I remember it from my childhood, was a game of two halves. It had a lot of factories. You could smell industry in the air, from the acrid, eye-stinging vapours of the Albright and Wilson's chemical plant, to the seductive, sugary scent of Parkes' sweet factory. In the shadow of these factories lived the workforce, often in council housing, or in poky little terraces that the family had lived in for generations. But Oldbury also had some nicer spots with private houses and cars and caravans in the drive, the homes of the clerk and the middle manager. Bristnall Hall Road managed to combine both. Our side of the road, the council-house side, had barely a car parked on it; there was the odd motorbike and side-car and Mr Feraday's massive lorry, but that was it. The opposite side was all private houses, with cars parked on the street, and in the driveways, where people had had their front gardens tarmacked over for that specific purpose. My dad couldn't drive. He couldn't afford a car so what was the point? I lived in Bristnall Hall Road into my late teens and I can barely remember even walking on that side of the road. I knew my place.

My dad painted a big 181 on the wall of our house that is still there. The house had three bedrooms: my mom and dad's room, my sister Nora's room, and the room that me and my two brothers, Terry and Keith, slept in.

Nora was the eldest, the big sister. She was seventeen when I was born and some of the neighbours thought I might be hers. She was a wild one in her teens, a hairdresser who went in for beehive hair-dos and tight skirts. I remember her practising the twist in the kitchen and getting told off by my dad for staying out too late at jazz nights at the Locarno Ballroom. She had long fingernails and would put a flannel over one and use it to clean my ears. It really hurt and it gave me a life-long aversion to ear-cleaning. I still have dirty ears now. When Nora married, in her early twenties, her husband, Frank, had a car, and they bought their own house. We all felt a bit intimidated. Now she is a member of Halesowen Conservative Party and is always telling me stuff like how she met that nice William Hague and that he was a real gentleman.

Terry is my oldest brother. As a kid he loved drawing, and collecting birds' eggs. He was a good-looking lad with a bit of the early Cliff Richard about him, and soon developed an eye for the girls. He would listen to Elvis and Roy Orbison and Jim Reeves, and worked on building sites as a carpenter. Nowadays, he's a handsome bloke in his fifties. He doesn't draw or go birdnesting anymore, but does impressive DIY and watches endless wildlife programmes. He also likes a drink, and has an endless supply of stories to tell.

Keith is seven years older than me. He was a fat schoolboy and a lean teenager. I remember he caused quite a stir at my confirmation ceremony when he turned up with his long blonde hair and his swinging sixties suit. I once went on a trip from my mom's work to see Danny La Rue in Coventry, and Keith and his friends got some real stares when they refused to stand for the National Anthem. Now he is a chubby, roll-up-smoking angler who has, as he always had, a funny line for almost every occasion.

For the first five or six years of my life, Keith and me shared a double bed while Terry had a single. Thirty years later, when I got Keith a walk-on part in a sitcom I'd written, another extra, an elderly woman whose career highlight had been a stair-lift ad, asked Keith how he got the job. 'Well,' he said, 'I used to sleep with the writer.'

With Keith seven years older than me and Terry five years older than Keith, I think the age-range kept us fairly separate. When I was six, I remember telling Keith that I'd fallen in love with a girl in my class at Moat Farm Infants. She was called Annette and looked a bit like a mousy Shirley Temple. I explained I thought about her all the time, and even mentioned her in my prayers in a 'Make-Annette-fall-in-love-with-me' kind of way. Keith was thirteen and I thought he could offer me some advice, sort of man-to-man. He said, 'Don't be so stupid,' rolled over, and went to sleep. So I never told Annette how I felt about her. She could have been my soul-mate and made me truly happy. As it was, she seemed to develop a crush on Christopher, another classmate, who wore glasses for goodness' sake. Wearing glasses is quite trendy now but in those days it was very shit. Often, a kid who wore glasses would have to wear sticking-plaster over one lens to encourage his weak eye to pull its weight. This seems very primitive now, as if the eyes were seen as riders on a tandem.

Christopher would sometimes, with the teacher's full approval, entertain the class by doing Freddie and the

Dreamers impressions, with himself as the lead man Freddie Garrity, and his stupid, puffy friends as the Dreamers. Freddie was about the only pop star I knew who wore glasses. Annette would gaze adoringly at the speccy git jumping about at the front of the classroom and singing 'You Were Made for Me' or 'Who Wears Short Shorts?'. Whatever happened to the old saying, 'Freddie Garrity breeds contempt'?

Number 181 had garden front and back and we all lived in the kitchen so that the 'front room' could be kept for 'best'. It was empty ninety-nine per cent of the time. I remember it being used on one occasion when Keith brought a girl back. I don't remember her name but Linda rings a bell. She had long dark hair and, most excitingly, wore a see-through blouse which revealed a white bra underneath. My mom, the kindest and most sweet-natured woman I ever met, wrote her off as a slut within about fifteen minutes, an opinion confirmed when she asked the girl what time she had to be home and was told, 'Oh, any time really.' Mistake. She might as well have added, 'because I work quite late as a common prostitute'. But I really liked the white bra. I studied the straps with their metal adjuster-bits, the delicate cut of the cups, the tantalising shadow of her cleavage.

I was about eight at the time. In fact, I was so impressed by Linda's bra and its contents that I was beginning to wish I hadn't carefully taken out the twisted-up newspaper that had been placed in the fire-grate in anticipation of a coal-fire, and mixed in a few fireworks that had been left over from Bonfire Night. (Incidentally, I never celebrate Bonfire Night any more because, with the benefit of education, I have come to recognise the whole thing as a celebration of British anti-Catholic bigotry. Still, more weird religious stuff later.) Keith came out of the front room looking a bit flushed, having lit the fire. Apparently, the effects of the fireworks were, in the context of a council house front room, quite spectacular. I remember him turning on me and snarling, 'Someone could have been blinded.' I must admit I hadn't considered that, but surely it would almost have been worth the pain to have spent the rest of one's life being referred to as Linda 'who lost an eye in a courting-accident'.

The bathroom was next to the kitchen on the ground floor and, for some reason I never worked out, contained not only the bath but also the gas cooker. This wasn't quite the problem you might expect because bathing was not really a big deal in our family. It was certainly not a daily, and for most of us not even a weekly, occurrence. Most of the time the bath was just full of old newspapers and clothes waiting to be ironed. My mom and dad bathed about three times a year. Having a good old wash in the sink was the order of the day. My old man would stand at the sink with the washing-up bowl full of hot water from the kettle. (We had to light the coal-fire to get hot water from the taps. Always a pain-in-the-arse if not in the eye.) He would also have a mug of boiling water for sterilising his old army-issue t-bar razor. He would rub his shaving brush on his little block of shaving soap and then get stuck in. All this was done in a strange sumo-like stance that stopped his trousers falling down, because he had slipped his braces off his shoulders so he could have a good go at his armpits. I'm not sure whether deodorant existed in those days but, if it did, we didn't have any. My dad's only concession to men's toiletries, or 'puff-juice' as most local males called it, was his use of Old Spice after-shave. To be honest, he was actually quite dapper by local standards, my dad. We weren't rich, but he always had a couple of made-to-measure suits on the go. A man called Sammy would come round the house and measure him up and then, after the suit was delivered, Sammy or his son, Sammy (yes, Sammy), would turn up every Friday tea-time for his five bob a week repayment.

Everything was bought by this method, except food. Mom got stuff out of the catalogue, or would buy stuff from a shop and be given a card which the shopkeeper filled in as she made each payment, or she'd use the Provident cheque method. Certain shops accepted Provident cheques, a sort of voucher that you paid for by regular instalments to the Provident man, who also came on a Friday to collect *his* five bob.

There used to be a fashion for finely detailed ornamental china human heads. They were usually things like old sailors or evil-looking Arabs but my mom bought me a pair of these heads which were representations of Laurel and Hardy, and very good ones at that. This was many years later when I was fourteen. I still have the little club card, as they were called, that the shop supplied her with to keep the record of her weekly instalments. The heads cost £1.50 and she bought them over a space of six weeks at twenty-five pence a week. When I think of her making the journey, about six stops on the bus, to that shop, every week, to pay her twenty-five pence, it makes me feel like crying.

When things got a bit desperate, we had to resort to the money lender. He was a fat bloke with a pig-like face, thick glasses and a trilby. His name was Butler. I don't know much more about him than that. But I do know that in the bad weeks, when for some reason or other the money was short, the others got missed but Butler always got paid. Maybe my old man was worried that mom would end up with her head in the gas oven. Imagine the headlines, and having to read them every time you walked past the bath.

All this is true, although I worry that my honesty about my upbringing won't go down too good with my brothers and sister. It's all very well some well-off celebrity going on about how he's risen from rags to riches, but his family might feel all that stuff should be kept quiet. I know our Nora will say I shouldn't be telling everyone our business and 'showing us up'. When I was on *This is Your Life*, my brother Terry got cajoled into telling the story of how, on those occasions when we got the electricity cut off due to non-payment, we managed with candles. My dad would shout at us if we went anywhere near the window because, if the neighbours saw candlelight, they'd guess we'd had the 'electric' cut off and we'd get talked about. Now I live in a posh area of London where everything happens by bloody candlelight and the neighbours take it as a sign of sophistication!

Anyway, Terry told the story and my sister and her husband got upset with me about it, even though I had no idea how the story came out in the first place. I know Nora felt embarrassed, but I was innocent. Her husband, Frank, said I should keep quiet about the poverty thing because I never went short and my mom would have gone without food in her mouth to buy me some silly toy or other. All this is true but, at the same time, working in television and theatre has shown me that most of the people who get on in these professions are middle class and from the south-east. Now I can't help noticing that I had mates who worked as dustbin men or lathe-operators who, as far as I could tell, had much more natural intelligence and common sense than a lot of these privileged southerners. I know from my own experience that it's very easy if you're a working-class person from the provinces to write yourself off as far as achieving anything a bit unusual is concerned. Showbiz and all that stuff seems like another planet, something that 'other people' do. It isn't. If you're running a mile, starting fifty yards behind a lot of the competitors makes it harder but not impossible. My point is, I don't want to shame my family, but I think it's important that people realise that any half-soaked fucker with a bit of luck can end up strolling down red carpets at film premieres and doing TV shows with his name on the titles. You don't have to have a nice accent and a background that involves Enid Blyton, fish knives and rugby union.

So, piss-buckets in the bedroom. Shortly before he became Prime Minister, I interviewed Tony Blair on my chat show. We were discussing working classness and I explained my theory that, of course, when it came to criteria for identifying someone as working class, profession, accent, education, and leisure interests were all important, but the best rule-of-thumb definition is, if you grew up with a bucket in your bedroom, you're working class. Mr Blair looked puzzled. 'Bucket in the bedroom? What for?' I explained that as most council houses had an outside toilet, people slept with a bucket or similar receptacle in their bedroom to piss in during the night, rather than have to go downstairs and outside. I wasn't trying to cast doubt on his socialist credentials but he seemed a bit edgy about this.

Afterwards, Mr Blair's public relations man, Alastair Campbell, asked if we'd take that bit out but we refused. Fair play to Mr Blair. He didn't ask for any veto before he did the interview, and when he turned up, he was accompanied only by Mr Campbell. No fancy entourage, minders or starry demands. I really liked him, and I'd still vote for him, piss-bucket or not. 181 Bristnall Hall Road has an inside toilet now but I remember when the idea to install one, as part of a local council modernisation programme, was first mooted. I suppose it was the late seventies. I remember the bloke from the council sitting my dad down and explaining to him that they were going to put the toilet inside the house. A very serious look came over my dad's face. 'Isn't that a bit unhygienic?' he asked.

It's not a bad question. The bucket-in-the-bedroom method was 'a bit unhygienic' for all sorts of reasons. For a start, sleeping in the same room as an uncovered bucket of piss does tend to get on your chest a bit, and this isn't helped when your two elder brothers go through their 'discovering alcohol' phase.

The most common problem of sharing a piss-bucket with a drunk is that, more often than not, they can't be bothered to pick the bucket up, thus making it a much more difficult target. The end result is a wet carpet, not ideal in a room where you spend a lot of time walking around in bare feet (a phenomenon that could be described as 'beyond the pail'), and, more problematically, a wet bucket-handle, which, it has to be said, is not a pleasant start to the day.

On one occasion when I was about ten, I picked up the bucket to have a nocturnal piss. One of my brothers had been on the beer and the bucket was heavy with about four or five pints of urine. I picked it up, essential in the circumstances unless you have a night-sight fitted, but the handle was soaked. A five-pint-wet-handle combo is deadly, and no sooner had I raised the bucket to waist height when it slipped out of my grasp. Obviously, the spillage potential was enormous but, by what seemed at first a stroke of good fortune, the bucket landed firmly on its base and remained upright. Then came the second tremor. The impact of the bucket landing with such a thud caused the liquid to surge up into a sort of tidal wave and fire a ball of piss full into my unsuspecting, ten-year-old face. Meanwhile, almost certainly at that same moment, some unknown chappie who was born in the right place to the right class of family was using exactly the same principle to create a tequila slammer in a Soho bar.

When I was about five, Terry got very drunk one night and was violently sick into the bucket. The smell of this caused Keith to vomit into the bucket, and the combined smell caused me to vomit into my pillow. I believe scientists call this the domino effect. Sadly, none of us were familiar with the phrase or we could have had quite a lively seminar about the evening's events.

Today is Good Friday. The day we remember that Jesus Christ died a slow, painful death, nailed to a wooden cross so that people like me can gain forgiveness for my endless catalogue of weaknesses, ingratitude and malicious misdemeanours. As a Roman Catholic, I am encouraged by the church to treat this day as one of abstinence and meditative prayer. I must also fast, or at least refrain from eating meat until tomorrow.

This morning, a man from the Bentley car company delivered a midnight blue giant of a car that does seventeen miles to the gallon and retails at £149,000 brand new. I'm not buying the car, or even hiring it. Bentley just wrote to me and asked if I'd like to borrow a Bentley for a few days. It goes back on Tuesday. The idea is that I won't be able to bear parting with it and so they'll make a sale. Essentially, it's what some people call 'a freebie'. In the last few weeks I've had a free video recorder, a free pair of shoes, about a dozen pairs of tickets to music gigs, four free CDs, three free books, and an all-expenses-paid free trip to the UEFA Champions League Final in Milan. A national newspaper even offered me a free holiday to Barbados with my girlfriend on the understanding that their photographer would be allowed to take photos of us in beach-wear and then claim that they had snapped us unawares. That was a bit of an eye-opener. Call me stupid, but I said no. Anyway, such is the life of a celebrity. I lived my first thirty-odd years on the poverty line and no one ever gave me a free anything. Now that, according to the *Sunday Times*, I'm number thirty-six on the list of the country's highest showbiz earners, people are falling over themselves to give me stuff.

I picked up my twenty-three-year-old girlfriend from her job at the BBC and we drove down to Brighton for the weekend. The Bentley handled like a dream and pretty soon we were checking in to our £700-a-night suite at The Grand

Hotel. (I had to pay for that.) The room had a very nice bathroom. It was en suite. It's the rich person's version of the bucket-in-the-bedroom.

Maybe I should feel guilty that this is the kind of lifestyle I have now. I don't. I just feel lucky.

Anyway, I didn't eat any meat today.

When Keith was eleven he went to 'big school', as they called it: Bishop Milner's Roman Catholic School in Dudley. I would have been pushing five when he walked up to the end of the garden to show me his new school uniform. My mom and dad had coaxed him into the full outfit to see how it would look on his first day. It being the summer holidays, I was messing about in the garden. There was a big metal bowl-like thing that my dad used to catch rain-water. He always said that rain-water was much better for the garden than tap-water. However, as we lived close to several factories that pumped out all manner of poison, I'm not sure, on reflection, if he was right. Anyway, at the bottom of the big metal bowl-like thing was a thick, black, unpleasant-smelling silt. The ingredients of the story are starting to come together, aren't they? And guess what. When Keith arrived to show off his new gear, I had just scooped out some of the smelliest, blackest stuff with my little rubber multi-coloured bucket. Before me, in pristine blazer, white shirt, cap, tie, grey trousers, the lot, was my brother. In my hand, a bucket of smelly, black nasty stuff. All these years later, I still have a sense of that moment when I became aware I had a decision to make. I didn't realise till quite recently how big a decision it actually was. The choice was only superficially about whether to tip the bucket over Keith or not. It seems to me now that I stood at the end of that garden at 181 Bristnall Hall Road and, for the first time in my life, I made the choice between comedy and the rest. I could have said I liked the uniform and carried on playing. Or I could have said I didn't like it, or virtually ignored Keith and grunted something non-committal. Compassion, unpleasantness, indifference were all on offer, but somewhere in my head a little light had come on. I looked at this chubby schoolboy in his smart uniform. I saw how proud he was. And I thought, wouldn't it be funny to tip the bucket of nasty stuff over his head.

The trouble with the comedy light is that it blocks out other things, like the consequences light, for example. It's the same light that came on when Sylvia Kristel told me she was a film actress. It's the same light that came on when I had a deep discussion with a close friend about the fact that he was twenty stone and smoking and drinking vast amounts. The conversation became heated and he snapped at me, 'So what if I died of a heart attack? Would anyone really care?' 'Maybe,' I said. 'Especially if you fell on them.' It was the same light that came on when a radical feminist woman that I actually quite liked came up to me at a party and launched an attack on my stand-up act. Parts of it, she said, were 'verging on the offensive'. I should have tried to calm her. Instead I said, 'There's only one virgin on the offensive in this room . . .' She never forgave me. Anyway, I stood there, and I made my choice.

Keith started crying and ran back towards the house. My laughter died down fairly quickly when I remembered that my dad was inside that same house. I stood like a statue and stared at the door that led into the garden. Half of me was thinking that maybe my dad would take the whole thing in the spirit it was intended and not come racing out of the house in a wild temper. The other half of me was toying with the idea of weeing myself with sheer terror. Still no movement at the door. I needed Jesus to appear to me in a vision and say, 'Don't worry. That comic impulse may get you into trouble this time but before you know where you are, you'll be driving to a posh Brighton hotel with a dishy blonde draped over the passenger seat of your Bentley because of it. Oh, and don't eat meat on Good Friday.' Still no movement at the door. Perhaps Jesus had spoken to my dad and told him not to rein in my blossoming comic spirit. Perhaps he had cleansed Keith's uniform, as he did the poor leper after the sermon on the mount. Then there was movement at the door. And my dad came racing out of the house in a wild temper. I stood still like a statue as he came closer. Come on, Jesus. What are you waiting for? My God, my God, why hast though forsa . . . ugh! My dad had surprised me by swooping low at the last moment and grabbing me by the ankle. When he returned to his full height, this turned me upside down and dad was able to return to the house, smacking my legs and arse as he went, without being slowed down by me stumbling and dragging my feet on the floor. It was like a hawk falling upon a sparrow. All down the garden, he smacked and I just hung there. Truly, my world had been turned upside down. From laughter to tears in an instant. I don't know if being upside down does something to your lungs or vocal cords but I was very disappointed with my crying. It sounded breathless and strangled, not at all plaintive, so there was no chance of awakening his fatherly compassion with it. As we reached the house, he flung me through the open door and I landed with a horrible cracking sound . . . on Keith's guitar. You remember, the one with the circular picture of Elvis in the little frame? It snapped like a carrot and Keith's crying went up another couple of octaves. There is a habit, not necessarily a nice habit, that some comedians have. If you make a joke, no matter how funny, they'll try and top it with a slightly better one. I even catch myself doing it sometimes.

I was too young to know it, but this was a sign that God and me had something in common. Despite the fact that there is virtually no laughter in the Bible, God must like a gag. I had done the bucket-over-Keith joke and He had topped it with the guitar.

Tonight, Dave and me opened at the Shaftesbury Theatre in the West End of London. I say the West End of London because some readers may not know the Shaftesbury. Or there may be another Shaftesbury Theatre in another town. My point is that too many people in London think that everyone knows about London or, at least, wants to know about London. I live in London now and I really love it. I get a tingle when I drive over Westminster Bridge at night or stroll through Hampstead on a sunny day, but when I lived in the West Midlands I thought London was an over-priced cesspit full of mouthy tossers trying to sell you fruit or unsatisfactory beer. When I hosted a comedy club in Bearwood, just outside Birmingham, I saw a crowd turn very nasty when a comic began by saying, 'Y'know when you're on the tube . . .'

'No, we fuckin' don't,' some bloke shouted. The comic never really got over it.

Anyway, we opened at the Shaftesbury in the live version of *Baddiel and Skinner Unplanned.* (I think alphabetical order is the safest bet.) This show has a strange history. In 1998 Dave and me went to see the film *Boogie Nights* at the Odeon, Swiss Cottage (yes, in London). The movie was OK but me and Dave got far too many of the writer's in-jokes about porno-graphy and had several moments when we were the only people laughing in the cinema. We soon became identified as not the sort of people you want to share your popcorn with. After the movie we went for a drink in a nearby bar. The most notable feature of this place is that it used to be a Barclays Bank and they've sort of crossed out the 'clay's Bank' bit to make the transformation absolutely clear. So we were in this bar talking about the Edinburgh Festival. The room was crammed with the bright young things of North London nightlife. We were going on to each other about how we loved a lot of the things about appearing at the Festival – the performing, the socialising, the girls – but how we hated some of the other stuff, well, just writing the show, really.

So Dave said why don't we do a show that isn't written. Just turn up and do forty minutes, with us sitting on a sofa chatting to each other, and to the audience, about anything that crops up. We could do it at lunchtime, when not much else is happening and expectations are low, and also charge only two quid. Most Edinburgh shows are between eight and ten quid. That way, if it failed horribly, we'd still have 'Well, sorry, but it was only two quid' to fall back on. We both got very excited about the idea.

When you're a stand-up, you inevitably end up doing the same gags over and over. On a bad night this can seem like a long, over-familiar road stretched out before you. Sometimes it's hard to let a routine go, especially one that's at the top end of the laughter-volume scale. A really strong bit will serve a comic for years but you have to fight this temptation to hold on. It's like children when they reach a certain stage – you have to let them go. If you hold on to a gag too long, you start to forget how to tell it; to forget why it's funny. It becomes stale. The words feel awkward in your mouth. This is the great skill of the stage actor: to say the same words night after night and make them feel fresh every time. There were people doing the Alternative circuit who did the same twenty-minute act, year after year. I'd hear them in the dressing room, complaining about how they'd got bored with stand-up. To the slightly over-excited new boy, it sounded like blasphemy.

I was, at the time, regularly hosting in Bearwood, and other places like the Fleece and Firkin in Bristol and Cheltenham Town Hall. London clubs tend to have quite a large turnover of audience because there are so many places to choose from, but out-of-London comedy clubs get the same crowd in every week so I had to write about twenty-five minutes of new material for each weekly show, otherwise there'd be cries of 'Heard it' after each familiar punchline. This is why it's much easier to be a singer than a comedian. Frank Sinatra never walked on stage to the 'My Way' intro, sang 'And now . . .' only to be cut short by someone calling out 'Heard it'. I remember one comedy club in North London where the regular host never changed his act. After each gag, people would shout 'Again'. I couldn't be having that.

Obviously, some of my weekly twenty-five minutes was piss-poor, but it also threw up some really good stuff . Law of averages and all that. My only problem was cowardice. After a few months doing the London clubs I had put together twenty minutes of stand-up that worked. So why risk taking some of that material out and replacing it with stuff that might not get laughs? It was just asking for trouble. One night I was on at the Comedy Store and Eddie Izzard had just watched my act. He had played Bearwood a few weeks earlier and asked me why I hadn't done some of the stuff at the Comedy Store that had previously stormed it in Bearwood. I explained my fears and he gave me a bit of a speech about risk-taking in comedy.

The thing I admired most about Eddie, apart from the fact he was really funny, was his bravery. I had seen him as a regular host at gigs and his method seemed to be based on composing gags on stage. Just stand there and something will happen. So I started changing my act, sticking in new material, topical references, improvising, and chatting to the London audiences just like I did in the Midlands. I improved about five hundred per cent in just a few months. Good old Eddie.

On a stand-up tour, when I do about an hour and a half, of course ninety per cent of what I do most nights is set material. I can cope with the repetition for a few months, mainly because the buzz I get from the new or improvised stuff gets me through the rest. Not that it's a chore. If it gets stale, I chuck it. It hurts, but it's gotta be done.

What's great about *Unplanned* from a performance point of view is that there is no set material to get through. Dave and I made a rule in that bar never to repeat a gag we'd done in a previous show (that's why we get someone on stage to keep a note of the stuff we talk about. 'The Secretary', we call them), and that bits from our respective stand-up routines are not allowed. Only very rarely do we stray from these rules.

At the same time, from an audience point of view, I sometimes worry about the quality control in these circumstances. Virtually every performance of *Unplanned* has shit bits, those sections that one journalist described as 'the moments between the trapeze'. When I look back on an *Unplanned* show, no matter how well-received, these seem to be the only bits I can remember.

So we decided to try *Unplanned* at Edinburgh 98. Not that it was called *Unplanned* then. The show was listed in the Edinburgh Fringe Programme as 'Baddiel and Skinner return to the original spirit of the Edinburgh Fringe'. I had seriously wanted to call it *This Might be Shit* but Dave felt this was a bit too negative. Incredibly, the shows, on at lunchtime in the 300-capacity Pleasance Cabaret Bar, were stormers. We just turned up and chatted about any old bollocks and people liked it. One day, Dave announced he was off for a session in a flotation tank after the show. He explained that this meant floating in water in a closed container for about an hour. He said this worried him because he could not be in a confined space for an hour without 'having a wank'. This, I explained to the audience, was why the show only lasted for forty minutes. We even had the cheek to close with a song, chosen by a member of the audience from one of the song books we bought on arrival in Edinburgh. Dave sight-read at the piano and I sang. All I needed was my cowboy outfit.

The show sold out every day but, at two quid a ticket, we didn't get too bigheaded. After a few days, various TV executives started appearing in the audience. The next thing we knew, there was talk of *Unplanned* becoming a TV series. I've never been sure if we made the right decision when we said yes.

The Edinburgh show had been a real lark. Now, suddenly, we were having meetings about set designs and which was the optimum size sofa for a wide-screen TV audience. It wasn't really what we'd got excited about that night in the bar in London. To do a completely improvised show was one thing, to do it on national television, LIVE, was something else.

I remember the first show very well. This was it. Live TV and no script. Not even a general idea about topic-areas. Nothing. Dave and me were sitting around backstage and I explained to him that I was feeling a weird sort of stiffness in my joints, and I had a bit of an unsettled stomach. Dave explained to me that this was known as 'nerves'. I hadn't really had pre-show nerves since my very early days as a stand-up. I'd forgotten what they felt like.

It was a twenty-five-minute show with a commercial break. I've never watched it back, I just couldn't, but I remember the first half as one of the worst pieces of television I've ever been involved with. We sat like rabbits in the headlights, trying to remember what funny meant. It was essentially eleven and a half minutes of nothing. And this was the beginning of a twelve-part series. The show was to go out Sunday to Wednesday for three weeks. When, after what felt like about a day and a half, the commercial break finally arrived, I could sense out of the corner of my eye that Dave was looking at me. I didn't look back. I started messing around with the audience; taking the piss out of people, flirting, cracking one-liners, the works. I had one minute ten seconds to remind myself of what it felt like to be funny. Dave sat still and let his usually invulnerable self-confidence raise itself up again to its full height. I did what I needed to do – show off. When the second half started, we were alright. We said funny things, they laughed. The chemistry was there again.

We've done two series of *Unplanned*. It just recently has been nominated for the Rose D'Or and the BAFTA for Best Comedy. Now we're opening in the West End. But if the second half of that first show had been as bad as the first, ITV might have pulled it on the spot, or we might have lost our nerve. Thank God for that commercial break. I knew I was right to move to ITV.

Autobiographies of performers always mention a stage debut, usually with the future classical actor playing a sunflower in a school dramatisation of *The Tales of Beatrix Potter*. My own stage debut was so disastrous that it didn't even take place. I was playing a shepherd in the Moat Farm Infants nativity play. Better still, on the morning of the dress rehearsal, the teacher who was directing the production made me Head Shepherd. When you're five that's quite a big deal. Especially when Annette, the mousy Shirley Temple, was playing the Virgin Mary. This was a real chance to impress her.

The dress rehearsal was going pretty well. I saw to it that my boys watched their flocks like there was no tomorrow. And when the angel turned up we were genuinely taken aback, partly because, in a childlike way, we were aware of her profound religious significance, but also because she knocked a tree over.

Then the scene switched to the stable. Mary and Joseph were sitting by the manger and we were to march on and do a bit of adoring. As head shepherd, I was to lead the other shepherds. The teacher whispered in my ear, 'Go on, and kneel around the baby Jesus.' I passed this on to the boys and then gestured to them to follow me on with a little turn of my head. This is where it started to go wrong. The baby Jesus wasn't actually in the manger for the dress rehearsal. He had just got haloed-up with a bit of wire and some crepe paper and was letting his glue dry in a big crisps box at the back of the set. Lots of people wouldn't have even noticed him back there, but I did. I headed towards him like a homing pigeon, my fellow shepherds following my lead straight past a confused Mary and Joseph until we reached the back of the set and knelt in adoration around the crisps box.

It was an easy mistake to make but the teacher went ballistic. Strangely, she used an identical line of attack to the one my dad had employed after the bucket-of-slime incident. She grabbed me by my ankle and swung me upside down, causing my tea-towel to fall off. However, she had badly misjudged the arc of my swing. As I spun upside down, my outstretched right hand went right up her skirt and touched an area of warm clamminess that can only have been her gusset. The panty-hose was still in its infancy, so inevitably, she was wearing stockings. I could actually feel the springiness of her pubis pressing against her knickers. It was all over in a second but she became scarily upset and began smacking my legs and calling me stupid, over and over again. In a fit of what I realise now was chronic embarrassment, she dumped me down on the floor, told me I was no longer in the play, and then walked out of the rehearsal looking close to tears. Before you ask, this is not where the phrase Shepherd's Pie comes from.

I was confused and upset as I sat on that floor. I could

understand why she took my captain's armband, but to kick me out of the play felt harsh. Also, Annette was looking at me as if I was vermin. If I ever had a chance with her, it had gone. But, most confusing of all, I had handled my first-ever female genitals. I had an awareness, fuelled partly by the teacher's reaction, that this was significant but I wasn't sure why.

This, then, was my first sexual experience – upside down with a woman forty years my senior, and me close to tears because my tea-towel had fallen off. You know, that last sentence wouldn't be a bad quote for the cover of the book. I believe it could be what they call 'a teaser'.

Anyway, forty years later I was interviewed by a journalist about the fact that I was acting in a West End play for the first time. He asked if I'd made a mistake on stage, how I'd felt about it and how the rest of the cast had reacted. I said they'd looked confused and I'd felt a bit of a cunt. I then cracked up at my own in-joke but decided it was best not to explain.

I had a difficult phone conversation with our Nora today. She told me she was 'worried sick about the book' and felt sure I would bring disgrace on the family when I talked about our upbringing. This problem just isn't going to go away, is it? I mean, she's sixty. What if she died of embarrassment and it was all my fault? Or there was a terrible family feud that lasted forever. Now I was getting hysterical as well. Nora lives in a very nice road in a nice part of the West Midlands and I know she's very proud of my achievements, but I'm sure she'd rather my success had come without quite so many nob-jokes and swear-words. But it makes me happy that she's still proud. If her neighbours see anything about me in a newspaper or magazine, they cut it out and pop it through her letter-box. Nora keeps all these clippings of my career. I never keep anything, apart from a crisp packet with Dave and me on it from a promotion we did for the 98 World Cup.

I think it's really sweet that Nora's neighbours go to all this trouble, but the system went a bit wrong when it was in the *Sun* that Frank Skinner's brother, Keith, had head-butted his common-law wife and she'd had to have stitches in the wound. Nora's neighbours dutifully popped this through the letter-box as well. Poor old Nora was mortified, bless her.

Since it was in the press that I was writing my auto-biography, I've heard from three ex-girlfriends asking me what I was planning to write about them. Like I knew. When I agreed to write this book I had no idea that people in my life would get so edgy about it. I can cope with ex-girlfriends, but I *am* worried about our Nora. What are my options here? (Yes, I spotted the rhetorical question.) I suppose if I was the perfect brother, I would give the publishers their advance back and abandon the whole project rather than risk hurting my sister's feelings. Mmmm . . . y'know, generally speaking, I tend to see myself as two people, Frank and Super Frank. Frank is who I am and Super Frank is who I'd like to be. For example, we had a technical rehearsal for *Unplanned* at the Shaftesbury, and at one point I snapped at the woman who is producing the stage show because I felt the rehearsal was a bit chaotic. She looked a little shaken by my behaviour. That was Frank. The next day I sent her an e-mail to say that I thought she was a very nice person and I was very sorry for being so arsey with her. That was Super Frank. Surely Super Frank would feel that Nora's self-respect was more important than any book. Then again, Frank might decide an easy compromise would be to produce a sanitised version of my life. Maybe I could take a few degrees off my swing and have my hand just brush against the teacher's stocking-top rather than thump into her red-hot clodge. If push came to shove, I could airbrush out the piss-buckets altogether. This way I still get the money and mass adulation (my dream is a life-size cardboard cut-out of me gesturing towards a special display case full of *Frank Skinners* by Frank Skinner, in all major bookstores), and a book that doesn't upset any of my friends, family, or former teachers. But what would Super Frank make of that? The old-school rappers used to have a saying, 'Keep it real'. My motives are probably a weird mix of greed, selfishness, pride, meticulousness, honesty and vanity, but I'm sticking with it. Walk on, Bruce.

My dad liked to bet on horse-racing. My dad liked a drink. My dad had a bad temper. I really loved my dad. My dad always said there wasn't one working class, there was two. And we should see ourselves as being in Working Class Division One. Consequently, he believed in keeping up appearances. He was never a man to wander the streets in his working clothes, unless he was going to or from work. Therefore, if he wanted to have a bet on the horses, he would usually get someone else to put it on. Otherwise he would have to put a suit and tie on and once he'd done that he might as well go to the pub and get arseholed. This would almost certainly involve him spending more money in the pub than he was likely to win at the bookies, with his ten five-pence doubles, ten five-pence trebles, and a tenpenny roll-up.

So it was when, one Saturday morning in 1963, he asked my mom to put a bet on for him. Mom said she was too busy and he should ask Terry. Terry claimed he was too busy as well. My dad was slowly inching towards the end of his tether. The bet was never placed. The first horse ran. It won. The second horse ran. It won. My dad's thirst took a turn for the worse and he decided to go to the pub after all.

Even as a small child, I could smell trouble. When Dad

returned at about 3.30 that afternoon, he had sorted out the thirst problem, but his anger at the unplaced bet had grown out of all proportion. Apparently, some of his other unbacked horses had also done quite well. He didn't say much. He took off his jacket and walked into the garden. Keith, my mother, and me decided against following him, but watched him through the window. He stood, centre stage, and took a deep breath. Clearly, he had set himself a task but we had no idea what it might be. Then he sprang into action. The first part of his task seemed to involve pulling down the garden shed with his bare hands. He was holding the bottom of the shed and apparently trying to drag it off its foundations. Bear in mind that the shed contained a work bench complete with vice, plus garden and work tools and, as Keith pointed out, his school cricket bat. Incredibly, the shed slowly began to move. My dad, legs braced and head pulled back till he was looking at the sky, dragged the whole thing into the middle of the garden. We looked at each other in some confusion. I think my mom put her arms around us. Dad's temper took many forms but never before had it manifested itself in landscape gardening. There was another shed, a little smaller than the first. Working-class men in the West Midlands loved a shed. There always seemed to be trucks knocking around the neighbourhood, carrying sheds, sometimes a greenhouse, but usually a shed. My dad was very good with his hands and he had built this second shed from scratch.

He was a great builder of sheds, cucumber frames, chicken houses, chicken runs, goalpost-type structures for runner beans or sweet peas, all sorts, but I never ever knew him to buy any wood, or timber as he always called it. Thus, he was always on the lookout for free stuff. My old man's endless quest for timber lasted for most of his life. Doors and floorboards from derelict houses, wooden fixtures and fittings in skips, any timber he could find. He would wait till it was dark and then tap one of his sons on the shoulder, mutter something about timber, and off we'd go to help him carry it back home.

Anyway, the second shed, which contained other garden tools including the lawnmower, was now making its way to join the big shed in the middle of the garden. I don't think Keith, my mom, or me actually said 'Not the pigeon loft' but I'm pretty sure we were all thinking it. The pigeons, thankfully, were not in the loft; they spent most of the day flying in a close formation which included a strange tumbling movement when, for a second or two, they looked like they were falling out of the sky, then resumed flying normally as if nothing had happened. These pigeons were known as 'tumblers', I presume because they appeared to tumble as they flew.

Once the pigeon loft had joined its fellow wooden structures in the middle of the garden, Dad actually stepped inside the second shed. Surely now he'd finished his re-arranging of the garden the effort had used up his temper, and when, after some calming deep breaths, he emerged from the shed, he'd be ready for a couple of cheese and onion sandwiches and an afternoon nap? Yes. So why had he now emerged carrying a large tank of paraffin? We watched in frozen silence as he prepared the sheds and pigeon loft for cremation. Within a few minutes, all I could hear was the crackling of flames and a child's voice, muffled by tears, saying 'cricket bat'.

My old man stood back and watched what was, it has to be said, a fairly impressive sight. The flames were reaching, I would say, about twenty-five feet and our next-door neighbour, Mrs Weston, said the next day that her lace curtains had singed in the windows. I'll never know at what stage in the afternoon, or how many pints of mild it took, before my dad thought to himself, 'I've lost money because neither my wife nor my son would place a bet for me. What should I do? Oh, I know, I'll make an enormous bonfire of all the wooden structures in my garden. Sorted.'

Coincidentally, it was carnival day in Oldbury, and as my dad purposefully strode past on his way home from the pub families were lining the pavement to see all the colourful floats and people in giant papier-mâché heads. As it turned out, those families who lined the pavement in our road were a bit disappointed because the carnival had to re-route to avoid the two fire-engines parked outside our house. We had a carnival of our own right there in the back garden.

I'm not sure that gambling on the horses really brought out the best in my dad. On another Saturday afternoon, we were watching a very exciting end to a race on the telly. My dad's chosen horse was neck-and-neck with another with only a couple of furlongs to go. Then the TV reception started to go a bit wonky and the picture was replaced by loud interference. At this point, my dad decided to add a bit of loud interference of his own. He picked up the telly and gave it a good yank to rip the plug out of the wall. We all sat looking at the space where the telly had been. It was a warm day and the kitchen door that led into the garden was open. My dad, the ex-footballer, after a short run-up, took a throw-in from the back step and the telly ended up about ten feet up the garden. We all heard the sound of it land and then implode, but no one looked. Dad went to bed. The telly, of course, was rented. My mom phoned the shop on the Monday and explained that Keith and I had been ill in bed, and while she was bravely struggling up the stairs with the telly so we could have some entertainment to take the edge off our terrible illness, she had fallen and the telly had been irreparably damaged. The TV shop, God bless 'em, took pity on the brave mother and sent a replacement telly the next day.

*

Unplanned live at the Shaftesbury seems to be going pretty well, but we had a bit of a hiccup just before the second show. Dave and me got picked up at 7.15 for the show at 8. I sat in the front with our regular driver, Gerry, and Dave sat in the back. When we got in, Gerry chucked Dave the London *Evening Standard*. I don't read in cars. It makes me feel sick. So I was chatting to Gerry about West Brom's promotion hopes while Dave devoured the newspaper. I say 'devoured' because Dave has a flair for speed-reading that, I think, could always get him a job in the circus if the comedy work dries up. I once showed him a very long and complimentary article about me in the *Independent*. After about fifteen seconds, he handed it back. I was pissed off that he couldn't be bothered to read the whole piece and told him so. He got me to ask him loads of detailed questions about the article. He hadn't missed a thing. He'll read a novel in a day, no problem. As I've explained, I don't read novels but, on average, a book takes me about four to six months. In fact, just about the same period I have to WRITE this one.

Anyway, even though Dave was sitting behind me in silence, I suddenly became aware that he was upset. Don't ask me how this works. I was once talking to the Jordanaires, Elvis's backing group for the first half of his career, and one of them said that there was a door at the back of the studio in Nashville which was completely silent. Elvis would occasionally come in through this door, and even though no one heard him enter, the Jordanaires would feel his presence and all turn to greet him. Singing together for all those years must have opened up a few spiritual doors between them. The whole nature of harmonising seems to be about tuning in to another person, and not just musically.

I sang a song with the Jordanaires myself, and it really felt like being gently lifted up and held aloft. We did a song called

'Peace in the Valley' and I never sang it that well before or since. It was as if their voices wouldn't let me go wrong; like those old stories of ghost dogs escorting strangers through dangerous places. The Jordanaires had sung together so many times that their voices had become one. I found myself in the middle of that special place their voices created. Maybe years of doing comedy together has a similar effect. Dave is the ghost dog who's led me through many a nob-joke minefield. *Unplanned* is a very particular bonding process and our previous series, *Fantasy Football*, was another. So, whatever the method, I knew he was upset. An emergency light went off in my head and, as it flashed, it said BAD REVIEW. BAD REVIEW. BAD REVIEW.

My own policy is that I never read reviews until after a project is over. I think good ones make you complacent and bad ones just drag you down. I don't get hung up about reviewers and want them all to get cancer, but one thing that does get me about a bad review is the urge to read it about seventeen times. To be honest, I've been pretty lucky on the reviews front. Dave, certainly during his Newman and Baddiel days, had some really nasty ones. He and Rob were just too cocky and too successful. The critics, especially the broadsheet ones, couldn't forgive them for it. As time has gone by, I've become less bothered by reviews and Dave has, I think, become more bothered. I knew he wasn't enjoying this one. I would tell you what was in it but I won't let myself read it until after the run. When we got to the dressing room Dave was a bit quiet, except when he wanted to read me a couple of bits from the review. I wouldn't let him. I started messing about. Doing silly gags and showing off, just like in that commercial break in the first TV *Unplanned*. Only, this time I was trying to do a Lazarus-job on Dave's confidence.

Dave is an incredibly gifted comic. In fact, 'comic' doesn't really seem a sufficiently all-encompassing term. I'm a comic. I make jokes. So does Dave, but he does a lot more than that. When we write together he has a comic understanding, a comic overview that's exciting to be in the presence of. He just *knows* what comedy is about. Whenever he made directorial points about sketches or other set-pieces on *Fantasy Football*, which he did often, they were always on the button. If he fancied it, he could be a big-time comedy director, no problem. Anyway, all this gives Dave massive self-belief in regard to comedy, but on those rare occasions when he sinks downward, it can take a lot to raise him up again. Eventually, I got a couple of laughs out of him and then he started to join in a bit. By the time the show went up he was ready to rumble. Teamwork.

That night's show was particularly interesting in that there was a bloke in the audience who knew a woman I'd had a one-night stand with several years before. She was a pretty girl and, apparently, a very good footballer. I believe a trial for England was mentioned. Anyway, she stayed the night in my hotel room and we had a long post-coital chat about the merits of playing 4-4-2 and the decline of the orthodox winger. The next day I dropped her off at the station and that was that. But the bloke in the audience was now telling me that two months later she became a lesbian. Of course, I suggested that her thoughts must have been, 'Well, nothing's gonna top that', but, in truth, it was a strange tale. Needless to say, the audience and Dave liked it a lot. I said I should have guessed she was on that road, firstly because she was a lady footballer, and secondly because while I was having a cigarette after, she smoked a pipe.

On the way home that night, I remembered she had told me she was hoping to become a marine biologist. Looking back, it was probably a euphemism.

*

When I was five years old, I developed the urge to shout as loud as I possibly could; to really roar and scream and holler until I couldn't roar and scream and holler anymore. I can still remember the feeling of wanting to do it but knowing that my parents, understandably, would go crazy if I did. This was where having an outside toilet became a distinct advantage. Our kitchen, which operated as a living room, was at the back of the house, with a door leading into the back yard and garden. Just across the yard was the outside toilet. It had no light, so going at night involved a good deal of guesswork. In the winter it was bitterly cold. In the summer, spiders. In the early hours, it was a long scary journey to have a mere wee. Hence the piss-buckets. On a good day there was toilet paper, on a bad day there was newspaper. My dad had, with the aid of some acquired timber, of course, built a sort of lean-to between the toilet and the wall of the house, which housed my mother's 'maid' and tub.

David Baddiel always says that when I talk about my childhood, he becomes convinced that I grew up in the nineteenth century. Here goes. In my early childhood, my mom would wash our clothes with a maid and tub. This tub was a metal barrel about forty inches high with a diameter of about two feet. Mom would fill the tub with water from the kettle and several saucepans, add soap-powder and then stick in the dirty clothes. The 'maid' worked like a pestle in a pestle and mortar. It was basically a broom-handle with a big lump of wood at one end that my mom would grind into the clothes to clean them.

Outside toilets with newspaper, clothes washed outside in a big pestle and mortar. Y'know, I can see what Dave means.

Anyway, about my urge to shout as loud as I possibly could. One night, I went to the kitchen door as if I was off to the toilet. It was dark outside. The air smelt sweet. One wall of the outside toilet was hugged by an enormous honeysuckle bush.

I never really noticed the scent during the day, but at night it was intoxicating. To a five-year-old, it made the back yard a magical place. I walked through that back yard and into the garden. The only light source was from the kitchen window. I could still hear the sound of the telly and the voices of my family. As I walked further and further into the garden, both grew dimmer. It was dark at the end of the garden. I stood still and listened to the night. Distant mumble from our kitchen, almost inaudible traffic sounds. I waited, and even these sounds seem to fade like the stage was being cleared for me. It spooks me out a bit that I can still remember it so clearly. I stood very still. I mean, weirdly still. And then I started. Not with a big breath and an equivalent roar, but with an increasing murmur, slowly reassuring myself that it was OK to interfere with the silence. The sound developed from an 'Urrrrrrrrrrnnnn . . .' to an 'Aaaaarrrrrrrgh . . .' This was the sound I was searching for. Once I'd found it, I let it get louder and louder. I stopped for breath. And then went again with the 'Aaaaaarrrrrrgh . . .', thrilled at how loud it was. I spread my arms and leaned my head backwards into the darkness. I repeated my call about five or six times, then I stopped, very still again, and listened to remind myself what the night sounded like without me. Then I went back into the house. They'd heard nothing over the sound of the television.

The next night I repeated the ritual. It became something I looked forward to and told no one about. Then, after about three weeks, the man who lived next door turned up at our house and explained to my parents that, the previous evening, he had let his dog out 'to do his business' and had heard shouting. In the gloom, he could make out a small figure, with arms outstretched, standing at the top of our garden. My dad asked me about it. I said I just felt like shouting that night. He told me not to do it again. And I didn't. So every night, the neighbour's dog was encouraged to go out into the garden, to stand still in the dark and slowly empty himself while I sat indoors and watched the telly.

I had a meeting with my publishers about the cover-photo for the book. Someone said that, rather than funny, we should go for sexy. I said, 'No. It should definitely be a picture of me.' This, to my disappointment, seemed to be taken as a serious comment. Worse still, I told this story to a colleague and they said, with no detectable irony, 'If you have a long photo session, there's bound to be something useable.' Thanks. I hear that Robbie Williams is currently doing a book. I wonder if anyone said, 'Let's go for unsexy,' and then sweated over the results of that photo session in case there was nothing 'useable'. Perhaps I should have held out for 'funny'. When I see the cover now, I can't help feeling we fell between two stools. The picture, I think, begs the caption, 'My life selling novelty slippers'.

However, I very much like the photo-booth pics on the back. These were taken in September 1973, after I had been to see the Rolling Stones at the Birmingham Odeon. I queued with three mates for eighteen hours in the rain to get those concert tickets. We lay on the pavement in New Street and played pontoon with soaking wet playing cards, and laughed a lot about us deciding earlier that sleeping bags and waterproofs would be a waste of time. At 10.00 a.m. the box office opened and it was all worth it. We were going to see the Stones. They were still cool then. When those pictures were taken, minutes after the gig, I still had concert-ears (you know, that post-gig hissing sound) and, safely tucked into my wallet, the rose petals that Mick Jagger had scattered over the crowd towards the end of the show. I kept those petals for about twenty years, in the same box as the light ale bottle that Ray Davies of the Kinks gave to me at Birmingham Town Hall.

As a symbol of how my life has changed, those photo-booth pics are very apposite. Nearly thirty years after that rainy night on the New Street pavement, I was with Caroline at a charity do for the Peter Cook Foundation. The guests included former Stones bassist Bill Wyman, and Stones guitarist Ronnie Wood. Ronnie's son's band provided the entertainment. The main event ended at about eleven but the band played on.

Meanwhile, Caroline and I, hand-in-hand, went into the ladies' toilets and had fantastic bang-bang sex in one of the cubicles. When we returned, hand-in-hand, there were only about twenty guests and a handful of waiters left in the room, at which point, two Rolling Stones decided to get up and jam. People began getting that I'll-tell-my-grandkids-about-this look in their eyes. Then, even better, they started to play a Stones classic, 'It's All Over Now'. Ronnie Wood was on vocals, but halfway through admitted he didn't know the words and asked if anyone did. When I was fifteen, I sang in a band that played a set which was about eighty per cent Rolling Stones. Of course I knew the words, but I couldn't get up and jam with Bill Wyman and Ronnie Wood. I just couldn't. Then, despite my fear, I could feel myself rising from my seat. It wasn't a sudden burst of confidence, it was Caroline, literally pushing me to my feet. 'Come on, Frank,' called Ronnie. Suddenly, I couldn't even remember what reticence meant. I did 'It's All Over Now', 'I Wanna Be Your Man', and 'Not Fade Away', by which time I was sharing a mike with Ronnie for choruses and holding up fingers to let my fellow performers know when we were going to end, bring in a solo or whatever. We did 'You Really Got Me' and 'Johnny B. Goode' to add a bit of variety. If only I'd had some rose petals! Yeah, it was a special night. I'd have queued eighteen hours in the rain for that, anytime. And jamming with Bill and Ron was pretty good as well.

Incidentally, going back to Robbie Williams, I recently took Caroline to see him in concert. Like all other women in Britain, Caroline fancies Robbie Williams. He is, I have to admit it, an excessively good-looking man. I'm not. I am, on a good day, of very average appearance. I have convinced myself over the years that appearance is only part of the package, and that I can make up a lot of the shortfall with charm and wit, or, in later years, with money and celebrity. The charm and wit supplement has been, at best, a bit hit-and-miss. I have often heard it said that it's possible to laugh a woman into bed, like laughter was some sort of morally acceptable date-rape drug. It just isn't true. Before I started doing comedy professionally, the normal process was I'd meet a girl, make her laugh until she was doubled-up and breathless, and then, when she had composed herself again, she'd say, 'Well, I've had a fantastic evening, now I'm going home with this physically attractive bloke.' The whole 'laugh them into bed' thing is a myth invented by ugly blokes who think they're funny and women who want to pretend that they can see beyond mere physical attraction.

When I was at university, I knew a guy called Mike. He was a really remarkable human being. He was very funny, and so intelligent that other universities were trying to poach him to do a Ph.D at their place. He was a rare combination of very clever and really nice, and not unpleasant in appearance. I once watched him chatting to a girl on a bench in the university grounds. He was turning on the charm to the point where I was nearly falling for him myself. Behind where they sat, there was a bloke digging a hole. He was wearing those jeans and boots that workmen wear. The ones that look as if cement was part of the original design. I mean, he was digging a hole, for fuck's sake. In soil. There was no cement, except on his jeans and boots.

Workmen wear this cement-chic so they can walk into pubs and sandwich bars and greasy-spoon cafes, or sit on the side of the pavement, or buy a can of Coke and a tabloid, and say to everyone there, 'I'm a workman. I am strong, fearless and uncomplicated. Men should fear me and women should worship my muscular lower abdomen.'

The man digging the hole had no shirt on. The man digging the hole had tattoos, largely of the Rule Britannia variety. But the girl on the bench was clearly not swayed by Dr Johnson's contention that 'Patriotism is the last refuge of the scoundrel'. As Mike became more and more interesting, she became more and more transfixed by cement-chic man. She just wasn't listening. Why be laughed into bed when you can be shagged behind a greenhouse by a man who owns every Roy 'Chubby' Brown video? I watched as Mike lost heart. After he'd done his 'Anyway, I'll see you around', and wandered off, the workman began his monosyllabic courtship. Now she laughed. I didn't stay till the end. I imagine they had quick, insensitive sex half a dozen times over the space of a week, he wouldn't use a condom because he considered it unmanly, she fell pregnant, he said it wasn't his problem, her promising academic career was cruelly cut short and her life wholly fucked over. Well, I hope so anyway. And before you ask, yes, of course I was 'Mike'.

The money and celebrity supplement has been much more successful. Back in Birmingham when I was still Chris Collins, I saw myself as being in the top half of what would now be Nationwide League Division One as far as fanciability was concerned. Maybe even in one of the play-off positions on a good-hair day. But certainly not Premier League. Consequently, I sought out women who I felt were in a similar league position. But since the arrival of wealth and fame, I got promoted and I'm holding my own in the top flight. In truth, I don't really need to hold my own anymore. And, incredibly, there are still people who think I'm in show business for the money! The only slight drawback is that I think every woman is just after me because I'm on the telly. I despise them for their shallowness and lack of self-respect and rant at them because they have sold their heart for the dubious rewards of the mercenary. Then I forgive them and we have sex.

Oh, shut up. I'm joking. No, really.

Robbie Williams gives very good concert. Caroline gazes at the big screen with a wistful look and I console myself with the thought that good looks are a positive disadvantage to a comedian. The comedy writer and excellent performance-poet Henry Normal once said to me that he felt my act was greatly enhanced by the fact that I looked like 'I'd been kicked about a bit'. Very good-looking people can never really be funny. Their life is too charmed for them to ever need to develop that wry outlook so crucial to the comedian. If Stan Laurel and Oliver Hardy had looked like Paul Newman and Robert Redford they would have been shit. When good looks come through the door, comedy goes out the window. I turned to Caroline to explain this theory but she didn't hear me because she was laughing so uproariously at Robbie's between-song banter.

It was a good gig, there's no getting round it. Handsome as he is, it's hard not to like Robbie. There's a brilliant song by Jacques Brel, called 'Jackie'. In it, the singer goes on about all the fun he'd have if, for one hour a day, he could be 'cute, in a stupid-ass way'. People who look like me and Jacques can appreciate what a gift that would be, but most people who are 'cute in a stupid-ass way' are too thick to know what they've got. Robbie knows what he's got and he's got it twenty-four hours a day.

When I first met him he was in Take That. We were on the same bill at the Royal Variety Performance. Robbie was friendly and likeable and, even then, it seemed to me, totally aware that he was on a lucky streak and determined to make the most of it. I know because I have similar thoughts. I once gate-crashed a wedding do at a pub in Birmingham and ended up drinking free champagne with a couple of mates. Free drink was rare in those days so I should have been ecstatic. And I did have a great time, but it was ever so slightly spoiled by the fact that the bouncers occasionally looked over at us and I felt sure they were going to ask us for our invites to the party and we'd be in shit. So I drank quicker and quicker while I still had the chance. Ever since I got lucky in show business, I've had a very similar feeling.

I remember giving Robbie a bit of a speech along those lines and telling him to 'just enjoy it'. I suppose I thought the Royal Variety Performance was the perfect place to start talking like an old-school showbiz twat. God forgive me if I, at any time, referred to 'the business'. That would be it. Next stop, the fuckin' Water Rats.

Robbie seemed to take it all in good heart, but if he'd placed any value on my opinion at all, it would have been all spoiled when he saw my performance. I died on my arse. I spent ten minutes cracking jokes to an audience that seemed to be mainly ageing gangsters and their wives. You'd think us nouveau riche would stick together but they hated me. Afterwards, I was in the line-up backstage to meet Prince Charles. As he made his way down the line, shaking hands with Shirley Bassey, Larry Grayson, Tony Bennett, I was thinking, 'What the hell is he going to say to me? I died on my arse.' Eventually, he reached me. As he shook my hand, he said, 'Where do you normally work? Is it in the north?' He said 'the north' with a pained grimace, as if it tasted like dog shit on his lips. I tried to defend my reputation but he'd already moved on to Billy Pearce.

Anyway, like I say, it was a good gig, and then Robbie came on for his encore – and sang 'My Way'! I mean, for goodness' sake. I told Caroline that this was ridiculous; that you have to be a seasoned old campaigner to be able to sing 'My Way'. She just shushed me but I was on a roll. Robbie had finally put a foot wrong and I owed it to ugly blokes everywhere to point this out. And I would have quite liked Caroline to take this opportunity to admit that Robbie wasn't perfect after all, but she was too busy waving her arms in the air and getting the words of the song wrong. So I said to myself, not 'My Way'. You really have to earn the right. What does Robbie think he's playing at? Then, at the end of the song Robbie announced, 'And I'd like to dedicate that song to Frank Skinner, who's here tonight.' I felt so guilty.

I saw him backstage after the gig. We embraced. 'Did you hear the dedication?' he asked.

'Yeah,' I said, 'and what a brilliant version of "My Way".'

Owls, as you may know, are nocturnal creatures. So it was a strange decision by my brother Terry, firstly to get a pet owl, secondly to keep it in a cage that would have been a tight squeeze for the average canary, and thirdly to keep that cage on top of the wardrobe in our bedroom. The owl almost certainly came from a bloke in the pub. In the West Midlands in those days almost everything could be got from a bloke in the pub. My dad's favourites were trays of seedlings. These were the unofficial currency of the shed/greenhouse underworld: trays of soil with little green things growing out of them. He'd bring one home most Saturday afternoons in Spring. On Saturday afternoons, the streets of Oldbury were full of half-pissed blokes carrying trays of seedlings covered in newspaper or plastic bags. And, of course, on this occasion, Terry, with a big fucking owl.

So that was that. Every night, local owls would come and perch on the telegraph pole outside our house and screech stuff to our owl, tucked in his little cage-cum-corset. This would make our owl uneasy and inclined to flutter, had there been room to flutter, which was a little unnerving to a small child. I used to worry that he might escape from his cage, an unlikely event, a bit like someone getting a ship out of a bottle, and swoop down on me in my bed. I had nightmares about being carried out, like a small vole, for a midnight feast atop the telegraph pole.

The owl was a dark mystery to me. Every day, Terry would go to the butcher and buy what was known as 'lights'. These were some sort of unpleasant animal innards that even the local people, who were happy with brains, hearts and faggots, wouldn't eat. The owl gobbled them down like there was no tomorrow. For any pet of ours, this was not a particularly far-fetched assumption.

Eventually, fluttering wasn't enough and the owl started to screech back to his friends on the telegraph pole, so Dad insisted that Terry release him. The cage door was flung open and, with wings close at his sides, the owl slowly squeezed out to freedom.

It said in today's *Daily Mirror* that I'm the highest-paid man on British television. Apparently I get three million a year from television appearances. When I read this, I laughed out loud for about twenty seconds. Not because it *isn't* true. I mean, it isn't true, but so what? If the people in the chart are all exaggerated at the same rate, that still makes me the winner. I laughed because there was something exhilarating about being top of the table. I still feel in my heart of hearts that no one's got a bloody clue who I am, and yet, there I am, top of the raking-it-in league. They say that when the great British actor Sir Donald Wolfit heard that he'd been knighted, the normally sedate man sat on his garden swing with his legs in the air and said, in a cod Midlands accent, 'Ooo! If me mom and dad could see me now.'

I know it's terribly un-English to be excited by money but sometimes it catches you unawares. I was on the dole in 1985, earning £24.70 a week. This works out at just under £1,300 a year. Five years later, I made my first *Des O'Connor Show* appearance and got two grand for eight minutes. Progress, or what?

In fact, I've never really been the materialistic type, but of course it's nice to have a few bob in your pocket. I'll admit that I'd much rather be known as the funniest man on television than the richest, but you can't have everything in life. Sometimes, though, the money-thing isn't so funny.

In the Autumn of 1999, my manager, Jon Thoday, was in negotiation with the BBC about renewing my contract with them. I had just completed the third series of my chat show, *The Frank Skinner Show*, and was keen to sign a contract that would give me a bit more long-term security. ITV were aware that my contractual obligations to the BBC were up and were also sounding keen. My initial inclination was to stay with the BBC, but ITV's offer was well tempting. Part of this allure was financial but, more importantly, ITV's contract offered a variety of projects as well as three series of the chat show, whereas the BBC would only commit to two. So, I was thinking it over. Then something happened which I never would have imagined affecting my career. Des Lynam defected to ITV. The papers started saying the BBC couldn't hold on to their talent and were becoming outdated and unappealing employers. Then the rumour started that I was about to 'follow Des' to ITV. In fact, I was still undecided.

Then the BBC seemed to hit upon a very good face-saving idea. They suggested in a press release that, rather than losing talent because of cheapness or lack of commitment, they were being held to ransom by greedy egomaniac performers. It was a clever switch, and perhaps not wholly inaccurate, but unfortunately they chose me as the scapegoat. Meanwhile, unaware of all this, I was sitting in a cafe next to Wyndham's Theatre in Charing Cross Road, London. I'd just finished a Sunday performance of the play *Art* and was having an iced coffee with some of the company when my mobile went. I stepped outside to take the call. It was Jon Thoday. The BBC had announced that it had broken off negotiations with my management because of their outrageous financial demands. A figure of twenty million pounds was being mentioned. Jon told me he had no idea where that figure had come from. I believed him. I went back and finished my iced coffee, wondering what all this really meant. The next day I found out.

The story ran in every national newspaper. They all had me marked down as a cynical chancer who had got too big for his boots. The twenty million, already an inflated figure, was now being seen, certainly by the tabloids, as all for my pocket rather than as funds to cover the cost of making the programmes. The story led the *Daily Mirror* to run a feature under the heading 'The Pig Issue – you decide' in which they ruminated on who was the greediest person in the world. I won, with a 'Snout Rating' of ten out of ten. Imelda Marcos only scored six. To accompany the feature, the *Mirror* had mocked up a picture of me as Monty Python's mega-fat, mega-greedy Mr Creosote. The article began, 'Is TV comic Frank Skinner the greediest person in the world? That's the question on everyone's lips after the BBC refused his demands for a massive £20 million pay deal.' Within three days, I saw Chris Tarrant, Clive Anderson and Jack Dee all doing 'greedy Frank' gags on telly.

Mind you, I could hardly complain. I was topical, and newspapers and comics do topical stuff. Look at me, I live on topical stuff, especially on my chat show. When Richard Desmond, the owner of such soft-porn classics as *Big Ones* and *Asian Babes*, bought the Express Newspapers Group, I was quick to claim that he now wished to be known as Lord Beaver-book. For all I know, he may have found this extremely undermining. To me, it seemed acceptable. I can only go on my own judgement, and the subject of the gag doesn't always agree. I was at a party once when Posh Spice came over to me and started complaining about how I'd done a gag on *Fantasy Football* about her having anal sex. She also said she was fed-up with me, as she put it, 'caning' her husband on the chat show. I argued my case by saying that her and David were big news and I didn't feel I'd overdone it. I also pointed out that, while David Beckham effigies were being hanged at Upton Park as part of a national hate campaign against him because he'd been sent off against Argentina, I was defending him on *Fantasy World Cup* with a speech that described Becks, unironically, as England's future. She wouldn't have it. Fair enough. I like to see a woman defending her bloke. Even if she's wrong.

I met Becks at a party not long ago. I had just recently played him in a sketch on the chat show. He walked up, looked at me, grinned, and said, 'You must have a bloody good make-up department if they can make you look like me.'

Anyway, now it was the biter bit. And, of course, I felt hard done by. Comedy is my life. Before I walked on stage on December 9th 1987, I had been a drifter. Like a lot of people, I just didn't know what I wanted to do. Most of us, the great undecided, never find out. I got lucky. If anyone could be in my shoes when I'm doing stand-up, or when I'm duetting with Kylie Minogue or Eric Clapton, or riffing on some obscure theme during *Unplanned*, or leading 76,000 people in a chorus of 'Three Lions' at Wembley, they'd know why I'm in it. And it's not for the money. I was an unemployed drunk going nowhere, and then comedy turned up. Here goes, I'll actually say it. Comedy saved my life. Don't tell anyone but I'd have done it all for nothing if I had to.

I didn't even bother to find out what my manager was asking from the BBC because the cash really wasn't a priority. He's a good negotiator and I knew he'd get the best deal. He was very upset, felt he'd been totally misrepresented and was talking about taking legal action against the BBC. I wasn't keen. I thought it was best to say nothing and let it blow over. The following night I went to Teatro, a club on Shaftesbury Avenue owned by actress Lesley Ash and her ex-footballer husband, Lee Chapman.

On the way there, walking up Charing Cross Road, some drunken bloke shouted, 'Hey, Skinner, you asked for all that money and now you've got nothing.' Not so much an insult, more a news report. Anyway, I just smiled. As soon as I got into the club a woman approached me. I recognised her from various media events but couldn't put a name to the face. She went straight into it. 'So, what are you going to do?' she said. 'You've got a PR mountain to climb. Everyone hates you.' I suddenly felt a tremendous clarity come upon me. Now was the time for me to finally speak out on the matter. 'Oh, fuck off,' I said.

I had a couple of cranberry juices and mulled it over. It was the opinions of the quality papers that had really pissed me off. These sneering, toffee-nosed, modern-novel-reading arse-wipes, who'd got where they were by having a family friend at the

Guardian or wearing a significant tie at the interview. How long would *they* last at a fucking comedy club? It's no good quoting Proust and pretending to like football when two hundred people are screaming 'Get off, you cunt'. It's all very well them getting on their moral high horse about money when they've had it all their lives and never got their fingers dirty unless they were playing rugger. Fuck them. Yeah, fuck them. They could mind their own business, or lick my helmet.

These were the calm, reasoned thoughts that went through my mind, sitting in the dark club as the chattering classes chattered on around me. Cranberry juice always makes me tetchy and inclined to generalise. Nevertheless, I felt better when I left. As I crossed Shaftesbury Avenue, two black blokes recognised me. 'Hey, Frank,' one of them shouted. 'Go for that twenty million, man. Make them bastards pay.'

'Yeah. Do it. Do it,' the other one said. I really laughed as we shook hands. I hope they read this and realise how much they cheered me up that night. I think theirs was a very black attitude. I suppose it's why successful rappers wear loads of gold and drive incredibly flash cars. Their black fans seem to love them for it. There's a fantastic LL Cool J track called 'Rock the Bells', with a lyric that goes, 'Some suckers don't like me but I'm not concerned. Six G's for twenty minutes is what I earn.' Here was me feeling guilty about doing well, and there's LL writing rhymes that positively celebrate his high wages. Respect.

I once heard an interview with an American baseball coach. The interviewer said to him, 'You're not a very popular man at the moment, are you?' The coach thought this over, before his reply:

'Y'know, you can spend your whole life trying to be popular but, at the end of the day, the size of the crowd at your funeral will still be largely dictated by the weather.'

Even when I try to mould my behaviour to please others, I often get it wrong. I used to drive a Volkswagen Polo and I remember turning up one day at my brother Terry's house. I always made a point of not talking about doing TV shows or meeting celebs, unless I was asked. I don't want my family to think I've gone all flash. I was chatting about not much and Terry was staring out of the window with something clearly on his mind. 'Have you ever thought about getting another car?' he asked. I looked at him, waiting for the pay-off. 'It'd be really good if you turned up in something like a Cadillac,' he said. And then the *piece de resistance*, and I swear this is true. 'And maybe you could wear one of them silky cowboy shirts.' I'd still blown it. Not flash enough!

At *Unplanned* tonight, someone asked how I could possibly justify getting three million a year. 'Well,' I said, 'you can't put a price on laughter.' They laughed. I think they found the whole thing as ridiculous as I did.

It was a wild night tonight. Someone asked a question about a recent, very grim news story about a man who was ritually sodomised by a bunch of blokes and then murdered. Not an obvious source of comedy, but we went for it. Someone in the audience went on about how many men had shagged him. 'Yes, apparently,' I lied, 'when they opened up the body, he was like a Chicken Kiev.' The laugh began as a scream of horror but then became the sound of people rejoicing in the sheer extremity of the image. I hate comics who try to shock. That's easy, but to say funny stuff that is also shocking, I sometimes like that. It was the I-can't-believe-you-said-that moment. And while the laugh was only just beginning to fade I stood up defiantly, punched the air and shouted, 'That's three million quid's worth, right there!' White-heat laughter.

What joy.

*

As a young kid, I was completely obsessed with Westerns. As I've already explained, I was no stranger to a cowboy outfit, but that was just the tip of the iceberg. There seemed to be about twenty different Western TV series at the time: *Bonanza, Have Gun Will Travel, Rawhide, Wagon Train, Cheyenne, Gunsmoke,* and the rest. I watched them all. This was another strange aspect of my childhood. I never remember any pressure from my parents to go to bed early. It was with some surprise that I discovered at school that the other kids were all in bed for about 7.30. I was stopping up till about eleven on a regular basis. I wasn't being disobedient. Disobedience wasn't really an option with my old man. Nor was it, I think, a case of neglect. It was just that news hadn't reached us that little kids went to bed early. I don't think it's had any real effect on me, except I'm the only person of my age group who remembers *Legends of the West* and *The Braden Beat.*

Anyway, in my Cowboy religion, these Western shows were my daily worship. And I had a Bible too. It was called *Buffalo Bill's Western Annual.* I read it every day. We didn't have too many books in the house but I read like a wild thing. I started school at five and seemed to learn to read almost immediately. It is one of my few acquired skills. I can't ride a bike, ice-skate or ski, and I've only just learned to swim and won't go out of my depth, which also takes out water skiing and scuba diving. I'm a real funboy on holidays. But reading I could do.

I remember my dad relaxing with the *News of the World* once and I started reading out loud over his shoulder, a story of how sex cinemas were becoming more and more widespread, which included a description of one or two of the films doing the rounds. I was halfway through a synopsis of *Sex in the Park* before my dad realised where the voice was coming from. He'd had a drink and I think he'd assumed it was him who was reading out loud. When he finally worked it out, the combination of lewd detail in an innocent child's voice must have been quite scary.

Buffalo Bill's Western Annual, with its colour plates of Daniel Boone killing a bear at point-blank range with an old musket, and a bowler-hatted Bat Masterson gambling on a Mississippi riverboat, was much more appropriate. I quote these examples, but I lost my *Buffalo Bill* many years ago and am relying totally on memory. It's surprising what lingers in the memory, though. Writing this book has opened doors in my subconscious that would otherwise have probably stayed locked forever. Writing the description of my garden-screaming, for example, was quite harrowing. It was like I could actually feel now what I felt then.

I remember the first time I tried magic mushrooms. I guess I was about twenty-five. I was at a friend's house in Edgbaston, Birmingham, and had already been drinking cider and smoking dope all day, which gave me the courage to try the mushrooms. Their effect manifested itself in two specific ways. Firstly, in my head I got a very clear image of an old black-and-white photo from a children's encyclopedia that was knocking around the house when I was a kid. That night, twenty years later, I could see it before me in all its detail. It was a photograph of some sort of microbe-type thing, all circular and emanating light. Up until that point I had forgotten the existence of the encyclopedia, let alone the microbe picture, but I sat on my friend's bed and tried to describe this vision to my mates. For some reason, they were absolutely fascinated. I've been in show business for thirteen years, but I've never had an audience as captivated as they were that night. I believe someone actually said 'Wow!'

The second effect was that my friend played a Fripp and Eno album, and I decided it was the best thing I'd ever heard. I stayed the night at the flat and made the major mistake of listening to it again the next morning. Let's just say I revised my opinion. It is for this same reason that one-night stands are always better if you know the number of an early-hours cab firm.

About five years after that mushroom-crazed night, I came across a copy of the children's encyclopedia in a second-hand bookshop in Quinton. This was remarkable, not just because it involved the re-discovery of a very old, out-of-print book, but also because the merest idea of being in a second-hand bookshop nowadays fills me with horror. For some reason, second-hand bookshops, classical music and Radio 4 all make me think of death. Anyway, there I was. I opened the book, and, after flicking through a few pages, there was the microbe, almost exactly as I had remembered it. Except that it was a picture of the solar system. The circles, the light, all there but scaled down rather than up. I thought this mis-remembrance was really interesting but I never got round to buying the book. The reason for this was even stranger.

As I stood looking at the ex-microbe, I heard a man's voice from the other side of the bookcase. He was chatting to the shop's owner about Nazi war atrocities. He said he had a massive collection of books on this and related subjects, and went on to say that he had been at a party at someone's house recently and their collection was even 'better' than his own. However, he explained to the attentive shop-owner, this 'better' collection was very much enriched by books about Vietnamese war atrocities. He had now resolved to move his collecting in this direction and told the shop-owner to keep back any such books and he would buy them. I was starting to feel a bit uneasy when the conversation was suddenly interrupted by a distorted man's voice, clearly coming out of some sort of radio or walkie-talkie. No, it couldn't be. I peered through a gap in the books. It was true. The war-atrocities book collector was a fucking copper.

Anyway, what I do remember about the *Buffalo Bill's Western Annual* was that I loved it, as I loved all things 'cowboy'. I had a cushion folded over the arm of the settee, which acted as a saddle. I straddled the settee-arm and rode the prairies of my imagination. It sounds tossy but I can't think of a better way of putting it. My mom got very confused when the little girl next door asked her if Davy Crockett was coming out to play. It was the first time I had given a girl a false name. My dad must have been very proud of me – after all, it was a lot more inventive than Len. And I bet he'd never convinced one that he'd died at the Alamo, either.

However, I made the mistake of showing the girl next door my Daniel-Boone-killing-the-bear picture. This sounds like a gag but it's absolutely true. She never brought teddy out into the garden again. Not that I had a musket, but I did carry quite a tasty white plastic rifle. This was where Mr Parkes came in. Mr Parkes lived next-door-but-one where he spent all day sitting outside his garden shed (he only had one!) watching the world go by. Whenever I was out with my rifle, Mr Parkes would stick a matchbox on top of the open shed-door and invite me to shoot it off. I rarely missed. Only quite recently did I work out that he was tapping the door with his foot when I shot. However, what was brilliant about this was that every so often he'd have me miss. I suppose he was trying to give me an early lesson in life.

The little girl who lived on the other side of my house was not really party to my cowboy world. I didn't have much to do with her until one day when she was standing on the fence that separated the two gardens. Land, I had learned from the cowboys, was special. Special enough to kill or be killed for. I told her to get off the fence. She wouldn't. I told her again. Nothing. Couldn't she see the rifle? The first shot was over her head. She laughed. So I fired twice, straight at her. Somehow,

78

I missed. Then I saw a half-housebrick lying in my garden. Half-enders we called them. I put down the rifle and picked up the half-ender. I threw it as hard as I could. Suddenly, she was covered in blood. There was silence, more than you'd expect, and then tears – from both of us. She needed stitches. There were arguments. I was very scared.

But what if I'd killed her? Imagine how different my life would have been. I guess I was too young for prosecution but I'd have been marked for life. Do you think you'd be reading the autobiography of a much-loved, successful, highly paid entertainer who'd killed a little girl when he was five? I don't think so. Even if I'd got that far, the tabloids would have made mincemeat out of me once the story filtered out. Do you really want to laugh at the evil killer freak-kid? Do you want to watch the cowboy murderer pretending he's cured now? My stomach is churning just writing this. She was fine, not even a scar, but what if the half-ender had caught her a bit differently?

Is that what life and death are all about? Who knows which decision is going to be the one that changes your life forever, for better or worse? Like when Roger Milford didn't book Gazza for that first challenge in the 1991 FA Cup Final and Gazza was crippled on the second challenge and England didn't qualify for the 1994 World Cup, or when Jeffrey Archer wrote in his diary: Monday – Stayed in and chatted to my lovely wife, who I'm very loyal to. Tuesday – Spent the whole day definitely not giving money to a black prostitute. Wednesday – Bought this diary.

You never know when you're picking up the half-ender that will change your life. It's a scary thought. My dad never hit me for throwing that stone. He could see how terrified I was. But justice took many forms in the Wild West Midlands.

One night, a few months later, I was playing in the street outside my house. Some of the bigger kids were taking part in this game, which involved leaning a flat stick on the edge of the kerb, placing a stone on the lower end, and then stamping on the raised end to make the stone fly high in the air. I thought I'd give it a go. In fact, I was so enthralled that I stood directly over the stick to get a really good view. I stamped on the stick as hard as I could. There was a loud thud and my mouth hurt. The Wife of Bath, in Chaucer's *Canterbury Tales*, had a gap between her two front teeth, which, the poet says, is a common sign of wantonness. Suddenly, that night, I went wanton. The stone smashed into my teeth and created a gap at the bottom which is there to this day, though it's now more of an upward slant than an actual gap. My lips almost instantly swelled up to about five times their normal size and the kids started calling me Mick Jagger. I walked into my house, holding back the tears. Sticks and stones . . . and Stones.

I suppose my don't-cry policy was based on the cowboy thing as well. Every Western seemed to have a scene where the hero had to grit his teeth while a bullet was prised out of his hide with a Bowie knife. Pain was there to be borne in silence. My teeth weren't really fit for gritting but I stuck with it. Thirty-five years later I was on a ranch holiday in Montana. Yes, the old urges were still there. I'd swapped the settee-arm for a real American quarter-horse and a small group of us were inching our way down the side of a canyon, a steep and scary ride where we had to relax the reins and trust the horses. The genuine cowboy who was leading the party was keeping his eye on stuff. My horse stumbled and was propelled into racing downward through a narrow gap between two trees. My leg was forced against a thick branch which eventually snapped under the strain. The pain was pretty severe and I yelled out in agony. 'Frank,' said our still-totally-cool party leader, 'cowboy-up a little.'

*

If you can't tolerate football, feel free to skip this bit. I have a certain amount of respect for people who don't like football. Even though, as you know, my dad always said, 'Never trust a man who doesn't like football,' I prefer such a man to the dabbler. You know, the one who watches the odd England game and usually claims to support Arsenal. He who hates football is a man who must have experienced football in an emotional way or it would not have triggered such a strong, albeit negative, emotion. The dabbler is a man who has experienced football in a third-gear, quite-like-it kind of a way. This is beyond me. To encounter football is to meet with something big. It requires love or hate. Anything in between is an insult. I hope you will have, up to now, found me to be quite a genial, mild-mannered chap. I think this is a fair summing-up of my general demeanour, but football tends to bring out the mouthy git in me.

Anyway, West Bromwich Albion are in the Division One play-offs. We're only three games away from the Premier League. Trust me, this is massive. We play Bolton Wanderers at the Hawthorns, West Brom's home ground, next Sunday. Sunday is also the BAFTA Awards ceremony, in London, of course. Let me make one thing absolutely clear. If there is a choice between Dave and me winning a BAFTA for *Unplanned* or West Brom winning the play-offs, it's a no-contest. West Brom, or Albion as I would normally refer to them, are the great love of my life. I've loved them literally as long as I can remember. I care about them. I was at a home game against Coventry City in the late seventies when Albion's veteran midfielder, Tony 'Bomber' Brown, stuck one in from thirty yards. I rose to my feet with fists clenched and I remember very clearly thinking to myself, 'This is as happy as it's possible to be.' Of course, women and work have made me elated, but always that elation is slightly scarred by fear of losing, or betrayal, or humiliation or the burden of responsibility. You know, the usual stuff. But Bomber's goal was joy in its simplest, purest form. Forgive me for sounding like Mr Showbiz, but, as I sang on the B-Side of 'Three Lions '98':

> Waiting and wondering till we score,
> Then scream at the sky above.
> So much bigger and better
> Than grown-up games like love.

On the other side of the football-coin, I cried like a baby when Albion got relegated to Division Two. We haven't been in the top flight for fourteen seasons. In all the time I've supported them, they've won two major trophies, the last one in 1968! I don't often use an exclamation mark, but that last sentence really deserved one. If any job had put me through the misery that Albion have, I'd have walked years ago. If any woman had done it, I'd still be in prison. But I remain totally loyal to them. I do not even lust after other teams and commit adultery in my heart. There is a chant that begins, 'We're Albion till we die . . .' This is one of the few opinions I hold that I know I will hold forever. There is another chant that goes, to the tune of 'Land of Hope and Glory', 'We will follow the Albion, over land and sea, and water.' This one, I've never really understood.

Despite all this, I was quite a late starter as far as actually going to the games was concerned. I didn't see Albion play live till I was ten. It was December 1967, the Saturday before Christmas. We were playing Southampton at the Hawthorns and it pissed down with rain from start to finish. My brother Terry took me and sat me on the wall at the front of the Smethwick End of the ground. I had my legs tucked behind an advertising hoarding but I still got drenched, totally, utterly drenched so that my vest was stuck to my back and the blue dye from my overcoat had run into the white cuffs of my shirt. What's more, it was a goalless draw. And, guess what. I was hooked. It remains one of the most exciting days of my life, the best Christmas present I ever had. I became a regular after that and although I miss some games because of work, I'm a season ticket holder thirty-four years later. And counting.

Unfortunately, we live in the age of the celebrity fan, many of whom are phoneys who couldn't, at gunpoint, name three members of the first team. They turn up in the Directors' Box twice a season and get interviewed before the Cup Final to discuss 'their team'. I pay for my season ticket and sit in the stand with ordinary fans like myself. Mind you, before I sound too purist, I love a freebie at away games. Why put money in *their* pockets?

The great thing about being a season ticket holder is that you end up sitting with the same people every week. Some you speak to, some you don't. There is an ageing ex-marine who sits next to me. He goes up for every header and crunches in to every tackle. At first, this got on my nerves. Sometimes he virtually pushed me out of my seat, but I've grown to like it. It reminds me of watching boxing on the telly with my dad. He threw every punch and sat bobbing and weaving on the sofa till the fight was over. I once grabbed a towel and started fanning him between rounds. He laughed, but I'm not sure he was actually aware of his synchronised shadow boxing. It came from somewhere deep down, a dim echo of some three-rounder in a school hall in West Cornforth. A forgotten dream that he could have been a contender.

I think it's the same for the ex-marine. With the right breaks, maybe he could have worn the blue and white. Then there was the old guy to my left, who I once heard shout of an opposition striker, 'I'm glad we didn't have him on the five-inch mortars.' A heckle he'd probably been using for some fifty years. Or the guy two rows in front who always leaves twenty minutes before the end, regardless of the score or the significance of the match. Or the bloke I was next to, leaving the ground after we'd lost 2–0 to Nottingham Forest, following the tannoy announcement: 'We have a message for Mr Martin So-and-so, your wife has just given birth to a baby boy in Sandwell District Hospital.' The bloke next to me said, 'Poor bugger. He's had to sit through this lot and now he's got to go home and make his own tea.' Or the bloke behind who must have read a coaching manual or something similar. He once shouted out, 'Come on, Albion. They're getting us on the second phase pick-up every time. And quite rightly.' I'm all for the first part of this. I mean the 'come on' bit. I can get through a whole match's shouting with just 'come on' said in various intonations: angry, pleading, plaintive, excited – it's so versatile.

Sadly, the rise of the celebrity fan means that it's almost impossible for people like me to talk about football without sounding like a bandwagon-jumper. That hacks me off. The only advantage of Albion's poor record over the last ten years or so is that no one ever accuses me of glory-chasing. Well, not the only advantage. It's also much easier to park.

The much discussed rise in football's popularity reminds me of a similar turnaround in 1977. Before the August of that year, the only other Elvis Presley fan I knew was my sister-in-law, Joyce. At school, my Elvis obsession had me marked down as a bit of a weirdo. Suddenly, he dies and they're everywhere. And telling me they always loved him. Yeah, sure.

As a football fan, I should, of course, be pleased that the game has become so much more popular over the last ten years. Bullshit. When I first started watching Albion, our average attendance was around 32,000, now it's around 16,000. Ergo, football is only half as popular as it was. Full stop. Any other statistics are irrelevant to me.

Anyway, I warned you I might get a bit angry-young-man about this. The fact is, I've grown up with football. I've watched it grow too. For example, when I first went to the Albion there was no segregation of fans. I would stand behind the goal Albion were attacking and then use half time to wander round to the other goal, so I'd still be close at hand if they scored. Not that I saw many goals. Oh, we scored them. Quite a lot. But I only saw about twenty per cent of them. When administrators go on about the safety aspects of terracing, and the supporters' organisations go on about the atmosphere, I really wish someone would mention that the chief characteristic of terracing is that you can't see a fucking thing. As a kid, this was particularly true. Lots of schoolboys brought milk crates to stand on or special little platforms knocked up by their dads, with handles for carrying to and from the game. I used the tip-toe neck-stretching method which is, of course, fatally flawed because everybody tip-toes and neck-stretches at the same time. Thus, the relative heights remain the same. We, the great unsighted, might as well have all made a pact to rest on our heels, relax our necks, and accept our miserable lot.

The game was different then. It was only just starting to become the modern game. When a player got injured in those days, or there was any kind of long stoppage, the other players would lie on the grass and relax while the matter was being attended to. I miss that. I miss lots of stuff. But football nostalgia has also been hijacked by a lot of researcher-assisted Johnny-come-latelys who write stuff about funny haircuts and those little tabs that Leeds used to have on their socks, so I'm leaving it there. Anyway, all I really miss is Albion being in the top flight. The next three weeks might sort that out.

*

One particular memory of Moat Farm Infant School seems nondescript but is, I think, very significant. We had a thing at home – I don't know if it was a family saying or a bit of local street-talk – but if anyone seemed stupid we'd say he was 'as saft as a bottle of pop'. 'Saft', I presume, was a bastardisation of 'soft'. Who knows? Anyway, I was in the classroom at Moat Farm, and we were doing painting. Some kid had a cuddly toy he was showing to me. I dismissed it by saying he was as saft as a bottle of pop and got a big laugh from the surrounding kids. It's the first audience laugh I ever got, and I really liked it. I think I was six.

The more pedantic reader might suggest that, as I (judging by the cowboy-suit story) was something of a show-off, I probably got audience laughs before this, but I just don't remember them. Well, believe me, when it comes to audience laughs, I'd remember. Soon the word went round the class. The phrase was repeated by other kids and got secondary laughs. Soon a crowd of children gathered around my desk, wanting me to say it again. They knew exactly what it was, they just wanted to hear me say it, preferably over and over. It was like being Harry Enfield.

There must have been fifteen kids around my desk. It was the first sense of celebrity I ever got and I really liked it. I said it again, they all laughed. Soon the teacher came over to see what all the fuss was about. She could hear laughs and see I was at the centre of it but couldn't work it out. The desk was covered in newspaper because of the painting, and I had turned some of the letters in the headline words into silly faces, just as an unthinking doodle, no more. She said, God, I remember it so clearly, 'Oh, I see. He's made funny faces out of the letters.' I was outraged. It was the first time I was misunderstood by a critic, and I didn't like it. There I was, setting new standards with my ground-breaking 'saft as a bottle of pop' material, and she thought I was dealing in stupid cartoons. I hit her with my new catchphrase. The kids all laughed. I think someone whooped but I may have embroidered the moment a little. The teacher tried to force a smile but couldn't see what was funny. I remember the expression on her face. I've had two-thousand-seater theatres rocking with laughs, but there'll always be one face in the crowd who has the same expression as that teacher. And what I hate is that all the laughing faces blur out of focus and the only face I can see is that one.

I said at the beginning of this book that I didn't like autobiographies or biographies that went on about the subject's childhood. I hope I've sugared the pill a bit by talking about current, showbizzy stuff as well. It's just that now I come to think about these incidents from my early days, I start to think that stuff about 'Give me a child until he is seven and I will give you a man' is more real than I thought. I now recognise a lot of current themes in my life that, on reflection, seemed to have been planted way back then. Of course, it could be that I'm looking back at insignificant incidents and then imposing meaning on them that was never really there. Why don't you decide?

In the *Unplanned* show, we have an audience-member on stage to document the topics we cover on a white board. As I've said, we call them 'The Secretary'. It's a comedy device, obviously. If the secretary is an interesting character it gives us a whole new avenue for laughs. Tonight's secretary was called Shelley. Turned out that her uncle is Mick McManus. In case you don't know, Mick McManus was one of the most famous wrestlers in Britain in the sixties and seventies. He was one of the bad-guy wrestlers. I didn't realise it until I read an essay by this French writer called Roland Barthes a few years back, but wrestling is a modern-day morality play. It has good guys and bad guys and, most interestingly, the bad guys win quite a lot. Wrestling comes from the same school of realism as Mr Parkes. It would've been easy enough to make good triumph all the time in the wrestling ring, but apart from the predictability factor, it just wouldn't seem true. I know it seems odd to talk about wrestling and truth in the same sentence, but even allowing for the audience's 'willing suspension of disbelief', it still needs to be kind of, well, real.

I used to watch wrestling . . . hold it. I need to make something clear here. When I talk about wrestling, I mean British wrestling in the sixties and seventies. Wrestling that was on ITV's Saturday afternoon *World of Sport* programme and also on most Wednesday nights on the same channel. Wrestling that was commentated on by Kent Walton. Wrestling that included stars like McManus, Jackie 'Mr TV' Pallo, Les Kellett, Billy Two Rivers, Johnny Kwango, Honey Boy Zimba and Adrian Street. What I do *not* mean is American wrestling in the eighties and nineties, where everyone looks like a cross between a body-builder and a heavy-metal star. The mainstays of the wrestling I love were middle-aged rough bastards with beer-bellies and dirty fingernails. The sort of blokes you could see bashing someone's head against a bus stop on a Saturday night in any northern town. To the young me, these men were gods.

Anyway, I used to watch wrestling at two main local venues, Thimblemill Baths and the Hen and Chickens pub. The Hen and Chickens also had a country-and-western evening on Thursday nights which attracted a lot of divorced older women. Younger men, in search of, amongst other things, a nice breakfast, would go there to meet the divorcees. It was known locally as Grab-a-Granny night.

Thimblemill Baths was a great place for all sorts of

entertainment, including swimming, obviously. I remember Keith got arrested there once after a dance. The police claimed he was half-way up a lamppost, calling out encouragement to his fellow rioters. Keith always said he was stitched up. The headline in the local newspaper, the *Smethwick Telephone*, was 'Youths swarm like locusts'. Whenever the word 'youth' appeared in a headline, it usually meant trouble. Terry got arrested for wiping several glasses off the bar in a pub that refused to serve him. The headline was, of course, 'Youth has smashing time'.

Incidentally, one thing I never worked out was how the *Smethwick Telephone* got its name. I imagined the editorial staff, all gathered round a large table, looking at the newspaper, saying stuff like, 'Well, it's definitely some form of communication. Maybe it's a telephone', followed by lots of nodding and muttered agreement. The staff at the *Telephone* were certainly firm believers in the old adage that every picture tells a story. In fact, I wondered if they believed that their readers couldn't actually read at all. For example, I once read a story in there about a man who was retiring from his job in a tube factory. The accompanying picture showed the man, standing outside the factory. Behind him stood several people in overalls, all looking at him and waving, and next to them was a much smaller group in suits and ties one of whom was proffering a large carriage-clock. The non-clock-carriers were also waving. At the front stood the man, waving with one hand, and holding a large tube in the other.

In another story, a girl had passed her A-level geography, and they had her in a mortar-board hat, giving a big double thumbs-up over a map of the world.

However the *Telephone's* finest hour was when a woman from nearby Rowley Regis claimed that a flying saucer had landed in her garden and two little aliens had got out. In the front-page story that resulted, she said she had spoken to the little green men and they had understood exactly what she said. If you've ever met anyone from Rowley Regis you'd know how unlikely this was. Anyway, she told a *Telephone* reporter that she had taken the little men into her house and given them mince pies (it wasn't even Christmas) and then they had left. I know this all sounds like nonsense, but I'll remember the last sentence of that article if I live to be a hundred. It said, 'She watched as the alien craft rose into the morning sky and disappeared, towards Dudley.'

Anyway, I developed my taste for wrestling by watching it on the TV. My number one hero was a bloke called Les Kellett. He always looked about fifty and had a fair old belly on him, but the great thing about Kellett was that he was funny, I mean really funny. One of his favourite bits was to make like he was dead on his feet with no chance of recovery. He would stagger around the ring with his eyes half-open and his opponent would go in for the kill, at which point Les would suddenly recover completely and give the shocked opponent a good hiding. He would also often spit at the referee while talking to him and then pretend it was an accident, or pat his opponent on the back so the man would think it was the referee's signal to break, thus releasing Les from a tricky situation. You might suggest all this was a fix, but so what? If Les was on, I was there, watching his every move and doing impressions of him. If I had to pick my all-time favourite comics, Les would be right up there.

The first time I watched wrestling live was at Thimblemill Baths when I was about eleven. The star of the night was a bloke called Lord Bertie Topham, who arrived in the ring wearing a monocle, top hat and opera cloak, and this was a long time before Chris Eubank. Lord Bertie was accompanied by his butler carrying a crystal decanter of water on a silver tray.

This was a brilliant act for a wrestler: class warfare. He sneered at the audience, called them common and complained about the smell, all in a plummy posh voice. To hammer this home, the opponent, an ordinary-looking bloke, wore his working-classness on his sleeve, and abused Topham in a strong local accent so that the lines were cleanly drawn. We were really desperate that Topham should be taught a lesson, shown that he couldn't treat hard-working ordinary people like that. We were all screaming out 'snob' at the arrogant toff. And then, in a typical example of how the class war goes, Lord Bertie won by foul means. He held the poor Joe Nobody in a headlock while the butler battered his head with the silver tray.

We were outraged but it was too late. The referee, as always with figures of authority, sided with the representative of the upper classes, and Topham left the ring, arms raised in celebration, to a backdrop of loud booing and abuse. The sense of injustice and helplessness the crowd felt as they left that night must have seemed oddly familiar to a lot of people.

Still, the lure of live wrestling lived with me. I spent the evening of my eighteenth birthday at the Hen and Chickens, watching the wrestling. The Hen and Chickens' bills were pretty experimental. They included women's wrestling as a regular feature. I remember there was a big fat bird called the Black Widow, who would greet the crowd with the most elaborate V-sign I've ever seen. It started, fingers pointing downward, at ankle level, and in one fabulous sweeping motion ended with fingers held in the traditional thrusting V, high above her head.

But the women were often disappointing, stretching our suspension of disbelief to the very limit. Slaps clearly didn't make contact, throws received far too much help from those being thrown. The crowd would get restless. I suppose we all knew it was fixed but we didn't want our noses rubbed in it.

They were letting the side down and lots of people were angry at being forced to confront the all-corrosive truth. Once the poison was in the well, we'd be lost forever. I remember, a few years ago, I woke up in the middle of the night and wondered if my religious belief was based on a similar convention. It was a scary half-hour, but while doubt does hurt it also nourishes. I'm talking religious belief now, not wrestling. There's no room for doubt in wrestling. With religion, I find doubt almost reassuring. It shows that I'm still thinking about my faith, still searching, involved in something not completed, but ongoing. But with wrestling, which offers you, at best, only a fragile truth, and is always switching, mid-bout, between real-life and theatre, you need a firm grip. Believe or leave.

The Hen and Chickens may have fucked up with the lady wrestlers but it continued its policy of cutting-edge entertainment by announcing one night that the next bill would include dwarf-wrestling. This had the crowd buzzing on the way out. Unfortunately, one problem with watching wrestling is that the night often begins with a series of apologies for people on the bill who couldn't make it. The excuses were often, to say the least, cosmetic. My own favourite was 'Sorry, Klondike Jake will not be appearing tonight, because he's in Glasgow.' Oh, I see. Fair enough.

However, when one of the dwarves doesn't make it, the one who does is at a bit of a loose end. You can't really stick him in with one of the big boys, so he gets paid for just turning up. I wouldn't be surprised if the management toyed with the idea of pitting him against a big wrestler and staging a slingshot incident to produce a shock result, but, as it turned out, they merely introduced Tiny Tim, as he was called, to the disappointed crowd so we could, well, see a dwarf, I suppose.

Anyway, the next wrestling night they managed to produce

the pair. On that memorable Tuesday night at the Chicks, Tiny Tim's opponent was Little Beaver, 'all the way from Chicago'. Well, it was good of him to make the journey, but strange that he'd picked up a broad Birmingham accent on the way. Little Beaver took off his coonskin cap and the fight began, but the crowd, now finally confronted with two half-naked dwarves, became sullen and ill at ease. Normally, the bouts were accompanied by all sorts of cheering and abuse, but now there was silence in the hall. All you could hear was the dull slap of dwarf against dwarf. Whether it was shock, pity, fear, horror, respect, or a mixture of these, I don't know, but the silence was unbearable.

As the fight continued in this vacuum, Little Beaver, who had set himself up as the bad guy, probably because he was slightly taller than Tiny Tim, gave Tim a totally unprovoked kick up the arse. I never thought I'd go to my grave knowing what sound it makes when a dwarf kicks another dwarf up the arse, but I will. However, the injustice was more than I could handle. 'Pick on somebody your own size, Beaver,' I hollered. A big laugh went up and suddenly the floodgates were open. 'Come on, you short-arsed bastards,' called a black bloke in a smart grey suit to my left. The taboo was broken and soon everyone was joining in. It was the most mediaeval night of my life. At the end, both wrestlers got loud cheers as they passed under the ropes.

I didn't tell Shelley McManus any of this. She was a pretty girl and Dave and me did a bit of comedy-flirting. Shelley said that if it came to a passionate encounter, she couldn't decide which one of us she'd choose. I suggested Dave and me could operate as a tag-team. Just think, if I had told the Hen and Chickens story the Little Beaver jokes would have been thick on the ground.

*

It was the day I nonchalantly sang 'All Things Bright and Beautiful' in the kitchen that my dad resolved to get me a transfer to a Roman Catholic school. 'Listen to him,' he said, 'singing that HYMN.' Never before or since have I heard the word 'hymn' said with such disgust. As far as Dad was concerned, 'All Things Bright and Beautiful' was a Protestant battle-cry, and Moat Farm Infants had taken me as far as they could. It was time to learn about my religion, to take the three C sacraments (Confession, Communion, Confirmation), to recognise that I was part of a spiritual and cultural minority that had been beaten, burned and beheaded by various representatives of the British establishment, but had somehow survived, battered but unbowed. It was time to get Catholic.

I'd been going to Catholic church on Sundays and stuff, but the real combat training had been on hold until now. So, aged eight, I started at St. Hubert's Roman Catholic School on the Birmingham New Road. This was the main road between Birmingham and Wolverhampton, usually referred to as The Wolvo. You couldn't really miss the school because it adjoined St. Hubert's Roman Catholic Church, my family's regular place of worship, which had an incredibly tall steeple adorned with an enormous white cross painted on the brickwork. At that time the parish priest was Father O'Doherty. He was, as you might guess, Irish, but he might as well have been Lithuanian for all you could understand of him. No, actually, that's a bit unfair. You could understand about one word in twenty, so his homilies went like this: 'Ar bara baba baba baba Jesus sappa passa papa, ar bara bara the apostles ba bara baba . . .' and so on. To make things worse, he was not of the opinion that brevity is the soul of wit. His homilies were long. I mean long. My dad always said that Father O'Doherty had to have 'his pound of flesh'. You see, I'm not the only one in the family who liked to quote Shakespeare.

Speaking of which, many years later, just a few months after I'd started driving, I had my first car crash. I inched out of a side-road in my 1967 Vauxhall Viva and slammed into some bloke's Nissan. He leapt out and started going on and on about how I'd nearly killed him and his wife. I explained that he was driving too fast and thus turned my safe manoeuvre into a dangerous one. He went on and on. I was on my way back from Halesowen College where I had just given a lecture on *Hamlet* to a group of mature students. (How did the seven-year-old with the piss-bucket get to be lecturing on *Hamlet*? Stick around.) As the Nissan driver wittered on, my mind wandered back to the Prince of Denmark. The Nissan driver's wife eventually wound down the window and joined in the attack. 'He's right,' she said, sticking up for her husband, 'you did pull right out.' Almost to myself, I muttered, in the words of Hamlet, 'How all occasions do inform against me.'

'Look,' said the Nissan driver, 'there's no need to inform anybody.'

So anyway, I went to St. Hubert's. The school had a house system. Most schools did then. You were put into what they called 'houses', which just meant that each pupil was allocated to a group or house and won 'house points' for good behaviour, good work, promptness or sporting achievements. At the end of each year, the points were added up and the winning house was, well, the winning house. We wore badges with our house names on and it was good early practice for losing and letting other people down.

The houses were all named after Catholic martyrs like More, Fisher, Campion etc. School trips tended to be to Harvington Hall in Worcestershire, where we could squeeze into the 'priest holes' and play at being persecuted. Here, brave Catholic priests were forced to hide out from Protestant oppressors out to get them just because they were saying Mass on the quiet. This might sound like indoctrination to you, but so what?

Catholics are different and there's no getting round it. Go to a Catholic church on a Sunday and you'll see a very special mix of people. Of course there'll be that solid mainstay of all organised religions, the very old, scoring their own house points before the ultimate end-of-term count-up. But then there'll be the special Catholic elements: the chunky skinhead in the Glasgow Celtic shirt; the beautiful dusky maiden of Spanish or Italian descent; the old Irish man with red face and gnarled hands, still smelling of drink from the night before; the trendy young oriental couple in ripped jeans and clubbers t-shirts, the black family with the incredibly cute kids. They're all there. Of course, this doesn't mean that they're all necessarily operating on a higher spiritual plane than other Christians, but they just seem to have more balls about them than the C of E congregation down the road, where bad skin, acrylic fibres and badly chosen spectacles seem to be the order of the day.

Not that anyone in the UK with Christian beliefs could ever consider themselves fashionable. I know it got trendy to wear t-shirts with Mary or Jesus on, or big crucifixes and so on, but that's just externals. (Generally speaking, I'm not keen on this religious-iconography-as-fashion-item thing, but I saw a brilliant t-shirt that had a Renaissance portrait of Jesus on it and said underneath, 'Jesus is Coming. Look busy.' Funny, but also sort of true.)

I tell you, in a society where all manner of once-smirked-upon behaviour like wearing crystals and Feng Shui has become acceptable, only Christian belief can definitely guarantee you the label 'weird'.

I recently spent a week in Italy with a Catholic mate of mine. It was really liberating to be able to cross yourself in the street and kiss statues and stuff without getting stared at. If I'd been with a Protestant mate, I don't think we'd have had as much fun. Besides, how could he have coped with the fashion demands of being in Italy?

In 1990, I went on a whirlwind tour of Sweden with Eddie Izzard, doing stand-up to people whose English was good but not quite good enough to understand stand-up. On our way home, Eddie and me were chatting on the plane and he said he was planning to use his stand-up act to talk about the fact that he was a transvestite. He said he thought it was really important to talk about stuff that's true to you when you're doing stand-up. I agreed with this. It's why I've never been so crazy about character-comics. You know, people who just play a part on stage. I know it can be really funny but, personally, I like to know the person who's up there. I want their opinions and attitudes. It's like Wordsworth said about the poet, he should be a 'man talking to man'. Or woman, obviously. If I want characters, I'll watch a play.

So, we talked about how an audience would react to a comic telling them he was a transvestite and then doing gags about it. We agreed maybe not at the Circus Tavern, Purfleet, but generally speaking, a so-called alternative comedy crowd would probably be fine with it. So Eddie asked me if there was anything close to my heart that I hadn't yet tackled as part of my stand-up act. I suggested Catholicism. We both sat in silence for a bit, mulling it over. Transvestism, yes, but Catholicism? We agreed it was a no-no. They'd never go for that. Too weird. I think lapsed Catholics can get away with talking about Catholicism in retrospect, but only if they take a negative, 'How stupid was that?' approach. Still, I'd rather lose Catholicism as a stand-up topic than burn in hell as a betrayer.

So, St. Hubert's. The teaching staff included two nuns, the older of which was the headmistress, Mother Mary Adrian. My brother Keith had been to St. Hubert's four years earlier and had warned me about Mother Mary. He told me she was the strictest teacher he'd ever known. Mind you, he also told me that he'd put lighted Roman candles under the Nazi soldiers' beds during their occupation of Oldbury.

One day, me and my mate Jeffrey were walking down the school corridor arm-in-arm, singing some current chart hit, when Mother Mary Adrian emerged from a classroom. She was so hacked off she was almost growling. How dare we sing in the corridor? She told us to wait outside her office. We stood there, terrified, underneath the enormous dark-brown wooden crucifix on the wall. Jeffrey looked up at this cross and said, 'He'll help us.' And he meant it. The real, deeply felt, uncomplicated faith of the small child. He liked wrestling as well. So we waited . . . for ages. Soon, Jeffrey was aching for the toilet, but we both knew that if Mother Mary came back and Jeffrey wasn't there, well, we just knew it was a bad idea. So we waited. Maybe she forgot. Maybe Jesus had helped us, although we hadn't seen any lightning or heard a loud bang and resulting scream.

Then she came back. We were tight against the wall like butterflies pinned to a board, looking up at her as she towered over us. She was about four foot ten. I took the initial verbal attack, then she turned to Jeffrey. 'And as for you . . .' At this point, a long jet of urine came through Jeffrey's short grey trousers and Mother Mary had to jump, feet together, out of the way. If this was Jesus's attempt at a struck-by-lightning scenario, it was a bit lame. Mother Mary screamed at Jeffrey but it was too late. Yes, the floodgates were open. Her initial protest was abandoned. In fact, there was a strange moment when she actually waited, in impatient silence, for the piss to stop. She looked at Jeffrey, then at me. I looked at Jeffrey. He was already beginning to cry. For goodness' sake, how much liquid could a small child produce? At last the jet of urine began to curve downwards and stopped. I recall a small after-jet, then silence. And then dripping. And then Mother Mary resumed her attack. He was a dirty little boy and he could keep those trousers on all day and then maybe he'd learn how to behave himself. When we went back to class, the teacher suggested that Jeffrey should change into some PE shorts, but we explained what Mother Mary had said, and the teacher, who didn't look very happy, told us to sit down. And Jeffrey kept his wet trousers on all day.

It was a cruel thing to do to Jeffrey. Even as a little kid I realised that. But like my teacher at the nativity play, Mother Mary got embarrassed and lashed out at the source of her embarrassment. And anyway, in the current social climate, circa 2001, a little old lady being cruel to a schoolkid is quite a refreshing turnabout.

Unplanned has been going pretty well at the Shaftesbury. The crowds have been good and the front of the theatre looks fantastic: two massive photographs of me and Dave, and, in between these, our caricatures above the words 'Baddiel and Skinner Unplanned', all done in neon. This weekend is the end of the run and it's all been worth it, if only for that theatre-front. I don't think of myself as a vain man, but the other night I nearly got myself run over, standing in the middle of the road so that I could see us all over the theatre and reflected in the glass-fronted building across the street.

One night last week, someone from the audience asked me what my favourite TV programme was. It's a toughie, but *Columbo* would definitely be up there. At this point, Dave pointed out that Columbo had a glass eye. I said that it was Peter Falk, the actor who plays Columbo, who had the glass eye. Dave looked confused. To be honest, I had no idea where I was going with this, but on I went. I put it to Dave that, while

Peter Falk does indeed have a glass eye for the purposes of the role, the glass eye plays the part of a real eye. This triggered off a debate in the crowd that I overheard still going on in the pub afterwards. I think that's great.

The next night, someone asked if we could have any super-power what would it be. Dave suggested that X-Ray vision would have its advantages. He started talking about those adverts for X-Ray specs that you used to see in comic books. The advert showed a kid in these specs, staring at his hand and able to see all the bones inside. I confessed that I had discussed this years before in my stand-up routine. I had concluded then that if I owned genuine X-Ray specs, within a couple of months, EVERYONE would be able to see the bones in MY hand.

I went on to say that, best of all, I would like to be able to fly, but if I did I wouldn't do it like Superman. I don't like the one-arm-raised flying style, or even the less common two-hands-raised version. I'd fly, perhaps with my hands folded behind my head, or maybe on my hips, with legs crossed, if I felt so inclined. I demonstrated these various options. Oh, I love my job.

The library at St. Hubert's included a book called *Born Free*, you know, about the woman with the lions and stuff. One day a classmate of mine called Stephen told me and another couple of kids that the book was a must-see. We made our way into the library and stood looking puzzled at each other while Stephen flicked feverishly through the pages. Then he stopped. He looked at us, then at the book, then he showed us. It was a full-page black-and-white photograph of an African tribes-woman shot from the hips up. She stood staring at the camera with a slightly unfriendly air. Stephen was grinning. His eyes had widened. Yes, we'd noticed. The tribeswoman was bare-breasted.

He laid the book open on a table and the four of us just stood staring at it. I mean, for ages. I can still see those breasts even though I haven't seen the book for years. And I absolutely guarantee that it was a picture of bare breasts and not the solar system. We just stared. And then Stephen said, in a slightly hushed voice, 'Y'know, when I see something dirty like this, my thingy goes all stiff.'

Suddenly, eureka! I have never felt so relieved in my life. I thought it was just me. I thought I had some sort of paralysis thing. I looked around and I could see that the other two were similarly relieved. Yes, all our thingys went stiff when we saw something dirty. Hurrah! I could have hugged Stephen for this revelation. We all got giggly and joyous that we'd discovered something universal and important. We even shook hands. We actually shook hands. We were normal. The experience was uplifting in every sense. I'm glad we held back from hugging each other because if Mother Mary had come in and found us all locked in a group embrace, each with an erection, there would have been four other wooden crucifixes on the wall outside her office, and we'd have been on them.

There's a science fiction story about a guy who goes backwards in time and while he's in the past, he accidentally steps on a butterfly. When he returns to his own time, we speak a different language and Britain has a fascist government, all because of the changes he triggered when he stood on the butterfly. Just like I can never know the weird and unfathomable effects the half-ender I chucked at my neighbour might have had on my life, how can any of us possibly predict the consequences of even our most trivial actions on the lives of others?

Could that African tribeswoman have ever imagined that

her breasts would have such a massive effect on an eight-year-old schoolboy on the other side of the planet? She brought me sexual arousal, removed what seemed like very real fears about my health, and gave me a strong sense of belonging and self-awareness, all with one unsmiling flash of her tits. It was a truly important moment in my personal development, all thanks to her. It could also be seen, of course, and not as facetiously as you might think, as another step on my ladder to nob-joke fame and glory. It added a new dimension. We all became firm friends. I guess you'd call it group solidarity.

I thought I'd give you a brief run-down of a weekend in my life. Make of it what you will. Perhaps it will be read by some kid I'll never meet and change his life like the tribeswoman's tits changed mine. I can't imagine that but then, as I say, neither could she.

Friday night. 11th May 2001. If we take our lead from *Ready Steady Go*, the weekend starts at tea-time on Friday. Guess what? I'm in my office at Avalon (y'know, my management company) in Ladbroke Grove, West London, writing this book. I've worked out that I need to write 3,000 words a day to make my deadline. This is slightly scary but I'm starting to really enjoy writing it. Let's face it, I'll probably never write another book, unless I do volume two of this when I'm eighty, so I might as well enjoy it. My girlfriend, Caroline, says she thinks writing the book has made me more reflective, especially about my background. She reckons I've suddenly become very class-aware, more inclined to make casual anti-posh remarks, to whinge about privilege. I need to watch this. I don't like rich, successful celebs who go on about their poor backgrounds. Shit, I've done that big time, haven't I? Well, it's an autobiography. I'm trapped in facts.

I sit in my office, which has a window that faces a brick wall, so I get no hint of the sunny day outside. On the wall, pics of Muhammad Ali, Bruce Lee and Elvis Presley. A photograph of me and another hero, former Albion star Jeff Astle. I go for heroes on the office wall. In the corner, a life-size cut-out of John Wayne. On top of my computer there's a teddy bear dressed as Elvis, a gift from Caroline. There's also a baseball that has the inscription 'The one who complains about the way the ball bounces is likely the one who dropped it', and a little model of my great inspiration, Wile E. Coyote from the *Road Runner* cartoons. He's the one who gets blown up, fried, crushed, and generally badly hurt in his pursuit of the Road Runner, but keeps going. He's the ultimate symbol of endurance, determination and single-mindedness. When I'm writing the book, a TV show, or stand-up, he looks over me. Fuck failure, keep going.

The soundtrack to my writing is an endless wall of hip-hop. Today it was Dr Dre, Snoop Doggy Dogg and the Notorious B.I.G. Throbbing bass lines, and people rapping about niggers, bitches and motherfuckers while I write about garden sheds and schoolboys weeing their trousers. It works for me but I've no idea why. I didn't even get into this sort of music till about three years ago. I didn't like rap. When people tried to win me over, I would say that if I needed bad poetry, I'd buy a greetings card. Then I got drawn in via the weirdest route, French hip-hop. I went out with a woman who was into MC Solaar and 'I Am', both French rap acts, and I got hooked, even though I had no idea what they were saying. Maybe *because* I had no idea what they were saying. It was the human voice as musical instrument, just a good noise, but now I need all those nasty words as well.

At 6.45 p.m. my car turns up. I drive but, particularly when I'm working, I'll often hire a car with driver, and, if he's available, I always book Gerry. Gerry is arguably the most Irish man in the world. He also has more stories than anyone I've ever met, my favourite being the one about when he patented a device for picking up dog excrement. It was called the Mess-Stick, and when he tried to get the pooper-scooper franchise with Westminster Council, him and his friends turned up at the plush council offices to discover that their rivals had all brought plasticine to aid their demonstration. Gerry and his boys had stopped off in Green Park to collect real dog shit for theirs. It didn't help. Gerry is also a Catholic, so that reduces the weirdo factor if I ask him to stop off at the local Catholic church so I can light a candle for someone, or get in the car with ashes on my head.

I like Gerry. I always sit in the front, partly because he's become a mate and it makes chatting easier, and partly because it's bad enough swanning around in a chauffeur-driven Merc without sitting in the back like Lord Twat. We're off to the Shaftesbury Theatre for the last weekend of the *Unplanned* run, picking up David Baddiel from his house on the way. It's a sunny day and the streets are full of scantily clad women. Gerry and me sit in traffic in Notting Hill and two sexy black girls in breathtakingly short skirts recognise me and start waving and giggling. I wave and giggle back. Maybe a vague shadow of the *Born Free* book rolled across my subconsciousness, but if it did, I didn't notice. Gerry points out a white girl in cut-off denims, crossing the street. 'Never choose a new girlfriend in the summertime,' he says, 'because everybody looks good with a tan.' I nod, and remember he gave me the same advice last summer. I think about my own girlfriend, Caroline. She presents an entertainment news show called *The Juice* on Radio Five Live. They record it on Friday afternoons and I'm wondering how it went. She is DJ-ing at a club called Strawberry Moons tonight. We'll probably meet up later. I'm not really sure how I rate as a date. She's a party girl at heart. She's twenty-three, with a taste for strawberry martinis and tequila slammers. I'm twenty years older and I don't drink. The age wouldn't really matter if I drank because everybody is seventeen when they're drunk. Mind you, comedy is definitely not a grown-up job, so maybe I get away with it. What can I do? I can't get younger and if I start drinking again, in six months I'll be living on waste ground with seventeen carrier-bags, shouting, 'I used to be on television.' I don't see how that would help.

Caroline came to a couple of *Unplanned*s early on, but she didn't enjoy hearing me answering questions about my past sex life and the like. I sympathise. I don't feel so good talking about these things if I know she's in the audience. *Unplanned* is about opening up to the crowd, about talking to them like they're old mates, so I have to go for it. Most couples don't hear their partners when they're talking about that stuff, especially not with 1,400 witnesses.

We turn up at Dave's place. He comes out nearly smiling. Dave is not a great one for chirpiness. I ask him how he is, knowing that he will always say 'tired'. Often he will fill this out with additional information like 'I slept like a cunt last night'. We set off and pass more girls. He cheers up a little.

As we pull up outside the theatre, Dean and Bobby, our minders for the West End run, are waiting to greet us. Neither of us need minders in the everyday run of things, but *Unplanned* is essentially a free-for-all and we've had a couple of blokes try to get on stage. They may well have only been looking for a handshake or a moment in the spotlight, but it's nice to think that if they were looking for blood they'd be dealt with.

They say Elvis Presley used to have a revolver tucked in his boot on stage. Obviously, this wouldn't stop him getting shot, but Elvis's priority was that the assassin wouldn't be alive to go around afterwards saying 'I shot the King.' What a fantastic image that is. Pandemonium as a dying Elvis, sprawled on the stage in a blood-stained white flared jumpsuit, fires haphazardly into the crowd where women and children drop all around the fleeing assassin, struck by the King's stray bullets. And the ever-professional orchestra still blasting out 'All my trials, Lord, soon be over . . .' On stage one night Dave asked Dean and Bobby, in their usual front-row, centre-aisle seats, if they'd take a bullet for us. Neither of them seemed outraged at the prospect.

On Fridays and Saturdays we do two shows, at 7 and 9 o'clock. The first one was OK. I won't bore you with the blow-by-blow. The heat has slowed the audience down a little but I like the slightly quieter vibe. OK, it was shit. Dave liked it, but to me there are two kinds of show, shit and brilliant. Ergo, any show that isn't brilliant is shit. It's a tough rule but it keeps you on your toes.

Caroline's old mate Pete was in the audience. He comes to the dressing room to say hello. Pete is a fanatical Watford fan and talks to me and Dave about football, hard-core style. Football is a great conversation fall-back, so he probably didn't like the show and used football to avoid having to confess it. Thus works the mind of the performer. Dressing room visitors are on frighteningly thin ice unless they take an undiluted-praise approach. Anything else will be picked apart by the performer until he finds the most negative possible interpretation of what was said. If you want to drive a performer crazy on your dressing room visit, why not try the old classic, 'Well, you've done it again.' This is a slow burner. The performer might well take it as positive at first, and then be woken in the early hours by all the dreadful connotations that will have been slowly released in his mind.

One that always throws me is when they say, 'Well, how did you feel that went?' If these fuckers are going to come to the dressing room, they can at least shoulder the post-show-critique responsibility and not try to switch it on to me.

An actor friend told me he was once waiting for a backstage visit from a fellow actor and was keen to see what his colleague would say about the performance. Eventually, the fellow actor put his head around the door and said, 'You bastard. Fancy a drink?' That was his only comment on the show. That's one to dissect in the early hours.

The second show was better, but very dirty. No one loves a dirty joke more than me but, in *Unplanned*, the audience set the agenda and tonight they wanted filth. This can get a bit turgid after a while. (Did *I* say that?) Still, big applause at the end and off we stride. Dave and me and a few friends go for a drink across the road. As it's suddenly become summer, people are standing out on the pavement in their shirtsleeves. Dean and Bobby come too, in case we get kidnapped. Or become targets of a drive-by shooting by Ant and Dec.

I invited my doctor tonight, and his young son is telling me at length about why his favourite comedian is Eddie Izzard. Anyway, it's a hot summer's night in the West End and lots of people are saying hello and talking about stuff that was in the show. Then, two men in their early twenties, one short and one tall, approach me. 'Excuse me,' says the short guy, talking to me but pointing at the tall guy, 'I've been asking him to come back with me tonight but he's been staring at you and saying he wants to wait and see if you're interested. Now, I keep telling him you're not going to put out. That's right, isn't it?'

'Well . . .' I'm trying to sound cool. 'Erm . . . no. I'm not going to put out.'

'Thank you,' says the short guy with an air of impatience, 'now will you tell him to come back with me?'

'Right,' I say, turning then to the tall guy. 'I think you should go back with him.' Without a word, the tall guy takes the short guy's hand and they turn and walk off into the night. I think about the butterfly that got trodden on. Did I just change the future of the world? And what about the Catholic church? I just gave my blessing to a homosexual act. Do I have to confess this?

I phone Caroline. She's finished her gig and is on her way home. I say I'll pick up some chips in Camden. We sit on the sofa and eat chips and talk and kiss. She was unhappy with her radio show today. Everyone else liked it. I think she may have caught my 'shit or brilliant' bug. She falls asleep in my arms. She does the breakfast show as well. She was up at 4.20 a.m. this morning. I look at her face while she sleeps. I've got a big surprise for her in the morning. No, I mean after that.

So ends the first day of my weekend. I'm quite enjoying the present tense. There isn't enough of that in autobiographies.

Saturday 12th May 2001. Shortly after we wake up, I tell Caroline my news. I put in an offer on a house and it's been accepted. It's got four bedrooms and a garden and off-street parking and two balconies and a conservatory. It's a big moment. Buying a house instead of a flat suggests that I'm growing up at last. I'm maturing. I'm thinking like a proper adult. She agrees. Then I tell her where it is: next-door-but-one to David Baddiel.

She takes the last bit quite well. Dave once said to me that our ideal situation would be if we had houses next door to each other. Obviously, that would have been ridiculous.

Next-door-but-one is close enough for tea and a chat, but far enough away for Caroline and me to feel, when we hold each other, like there's no one else on the planet. It also means I'll be able to spend lots of time with a plastic rifle, trying to shoot a matchbox off the top of Dave's shed-door. Though, knowing Dave, I have a feeling I'll be missing a lot more than I used to.

So we go and look at the house. It's only a ten-minute walk. We meet Dave in his silver convertible, top down, on his way to buy an evening suit for tomorrow night's BAFTA awards ceremony. You may recall that *Baddiel and Skinner Unplanned* is up for Best Comedy Programme. We won't win. I know this because Bob Monkhouse's son died recently so Bob, who was due to present an award, pulled out and BAFTA phoned to see if we'd stand in for him. They wouldn't have asked us to present an award if we'd won one. Dave is still optimistic. Ish.

Caroline likes the house. So she should at two million fucking quid! And yes, I think that did deserve an exclamation mark. It'll be the first time I've lived in a house that wasn't owned by the council. Ooo, if me mom and dad could see me now. 'Maybe they can,' says Caroline.

I had a dream once. I was walking down the road when I bumped into my mom. She explained that she had been trying to get tickets for her and my dad to go on an open-top bus trip around the Black Country, but they'd sold out. I laughed when she told me. I explained that if her and Dad wanted to go anywhere, I mean anywhere, I'd sort it out. I asked her where she'd most like to go in all the world. 'Spain,' she said. (I doubt that that would have been her choice but dreams are never perfect.) I was delighted. I explained that I'd pay for everything and I'd get them a driver and, well, just anything they wanted. When I woke up I was ecstatic. What a brilliant idea, and so obvious. Why hadn't I thought of it before? Then I realised why I hadn't thought of it before. They were both dead.

My computer has just underlined the word 'dead' with a green squiggly line. I believe this tells me that it is grammatically incorrect. I can't see why. Suppose, I mean, just suppose for a second, that this is my parents' way of telling me that they can see me now. That 'dead' doesn't necessarily have to be followed by a full-stop. Now it's underlined full-stop as well. The hip-hop's stopped. I'll change CDs and move on. Wu-Tang Clan.

Then Caroline and me went shopping. She buys a slinky black top for the BAFTAs. I buy four hip-hop CDs. She buys two Madonnas and a Moby.

The General Election is coming up so there are people on the street trying to tell you how good their party is. As we pass the Liberal Democrat supporters handing out leaflets and stickers, I politely refuse a leaflet. 'Labour scum,' the guy mutters under his breath. I walk on a bit and then ask Caroline what he said. She confirms that it sounded like 'Labour scum' so I go back to check. By now the bloke has moved to the back of the bunch and is looking sheepish to the point where I'm starting to wonder if it was him I spoke to. I get bored and move on. There was a time when something like this would have really wound me up. My masculinity would have felt challenged and I'd either have had a row with the bloke or not had a row and then beat myself up for not sorting it out. Now, I just can't be arsed. Labour scum? I've just bought a two-million-quid house. Maybe he meant New Labour scum.

In fact, I do vote Labour, but only because of some vague sense of working-class duty and the fact that Tony Blair was nice to me and Cherie Blair is Catholic. The bottom line is I'm not really interested. My dad was a classic working-class Tory. His view was that the Tories had been trained to rule; it was the natural order of things. Labour people were too much like us and, as he often said, 'If you beg off a beggar, you'll never be rich.' My mom voted Labour, so one election they came to a deal that they might as well not bother to vote at all because they cancelled each other out. As we sat at home that night, the political correspondent on the telly announced that the polling stations had now shut. My mom turned to my dad with a triumphant smile. 'I voted,' she said. The old man didn't see the funny side.

I leave Caroline to more shopping and head back to watch the FA Cup Final on my stupidly big telly. When I moved into this flat three years ago, the first thing I bought was the big telly. I had that telly before I had tables and chairs. When I watched it, all I had to sit on was the box it came in. You can put up with a lot if you've got a really big telly.

Oh dear, this next section is very bad timing as far as the book is concerned because I just got myself a bit upset about that dream and then the squiggly green line, and now it's 'Abide With Me'. Sorry if this is starting to get like *The Champ*.

One thing my dad insisted on was that we all remained silent and paid attention during 'Abide With Me' which is, of course, the FA Cup Final hymn. Almost certainly Protestant, but my dad was prepared to make an exception for the Cup Final. In the old days, an elderly man in a white suit would stand on a high platform and lead the whole crowd in the hymn. Everybody sang it then. Then football fans changed and, more often than not, 'Abide With Me' was drowned out by people singing 'You're gonna get your fucking head kicked in' and the like. Hymns very much modern rather than ancient. In recent times, though, it's made a bit of a comeback. This year it's being sung by two sexy birds known as the Opera Babes, one in Liverpool kit and the other in Arsenal.

No matter. Whenever I hear 'Abide With Me' before the Cup Final, I think of my dad. I think of his influence on me. I think of how he taught me that football was special. I mean, he gave me a love for all sorts of stuff: singing, boxing, heavy drinking, arguing, but best of all he gave me a love of football. I remember Dave and me sitting watching a nondescript Monday night game on Sky once. We were both having woman trouble at the time, and the game was a backdrop to our morose, frustrated and embittered conversation. Suddenly, somebody hit an absolute pearler from about thirty yards. We both leapt up in the air and whooped with joy. When we sat down again, I turned to him and said, 'Never mind, Dave. We'll always have football.'

'Abide With Me' is still my special little moment with my dad. In recent years, I've been to a few FA Cup finals, usually as part of some sort of corporate jolly. The hymn has been tricky on these occasions. I don't really want to be crying in front of David Mellor and Ed 'Stewpot' Stewart. I've just gone all quiet and stared at my shoes. Now, sitting alone in my front room (I can't believe I call it that), I'm at liberty to cry, but I think the presence of the so-called Opera Babes will take the edge off the moment for me. It doesn't. I cry like a silly kid. Real proper sobbing. I'm trying not to think American-soap-opera thoughts like 'Thank you, Dad', but I do. The song ends, I have a drink of tea, I'm OK. Caroline comes home. I don't mention the crying.

The 7 o'clock *Unplanned* show is shit. I'm glad it's ending tonight. A woman asks the same question three times: 'Why is Frank really sexy but he's not good-looking?' I think there's a very obvious answer to her question but I don't have a bank statement with me.

The post-show visitor is a film director called Mark Locke. I was going to be in a film he made last winter but I wasn't available. I was pissed off. I really liked the script, about a seven-foot boxing shrimp. I was due to play its manager. I know Mark didn't like the show because he doesn't look me in the eye when he says he liked the show.

Dave tells me that Douglas Adams died today. He wrote *The Hitch Hiker's Guide to the Galaxy*. I was introduced to him once and I started singing 'Bright Eyes'. He just looked at me. It's a song from the film *Watership Down*, written by RICHARD Adams. Whoops.

The second show was much better, but I'm still glad it's all over. I'm knackered tonight. And now Dave and me have a 'meet and greet' in the bar. This is where you wander around chatting to people. In this case they're either from the video company who are putting out the *Unplanned Live* video, or from shops who will sell it. They seem like a nice bunch but I start to get a bit dizzy. I think I've been smoking too much. So I slip out and sit on my own in the Royal Circle, watching our set being dismantled and put into trucks by big blokes in t-shirts.

The shows have been great to do. We've had some mega laughs and the old Baddiel and Skinner chemistry has been really bubbling, but I wonder if we've taken *Unplanned* as far as we can take it. The problem is that it really *is* unplanned. Only the other night in the pub, some bloke was going on about how we must use plants in the audience or work out some stuff between ourselves beforehand, but we are very puritanical about it. When I sit on that sofa, I have no idea what we're going to talk about, and I'm sure it's the same for Dave. For TV, this is pretty unique. There are a few 'spontaneous' panel shows on the telly where the teams spend the whole afternoon with the questions and a team of writers. I'm not saying this is bad, especially if it turns out a funny show, but *Unplanned* is totally free-fall, and that makes it balls-on-the-chopping-block stuff.

The great thing about this is that the show requires no preparation whatsoever. The bad thing about it is that you can't improve it by working harder. Everything I've done professionally, stand-up, the chat show, acting, whatever, I've improved by working harder. It frustrates me that I don't have this option with *Unplanned*. So we're moving on a level plain, and I need something to climb. I haven't told Dave any of this yet. No one here knows, but they might be dismantling the *Unplanned* set for the last time.

Jonathan Ross and his wife, Jane, are among the post-show visitors. As are Gerry the Mess-Stick man, and some of his family. All lovely people, but I go home early and wiped out. Tomorrow is the big one. West Brom versus Bolton in the first leg of the play-offs.

Sunday. 13th May 2001. I arrive at the Hawthorns with Phil. He's producing and directing a documentary about Japanese and Korean football which is my next work-project after this book. Outside the ground, a middle-aged woman is selling Baggies Bonanza tickets. There's a draw at half time and you can win a grand or so on a good week. She tries to sell me one. 'I don't need the money,' I explain. It's a slightly dodgy response, I know, but she takes it in the spirit it's intended and smiles. We get inside the ground and I bump into another mate, Lee, who's an Albion fanatic. His friend is explaining how his little boy came home in a Manchester United shirt and wanted to go and play football in it. In the end, Lee's mate had to pull the shirt off the kid, who then headed for the football in tears. Lee's mate said he felt like a heel. I told him he was a hero. He hesitated, then agreed.

However, this triggered off a worry in my mind. I've always felt that you should support your local club and that's it. As I've said before, football teams should be chosen with a ruler and an A to Z. There are no other criteria. But if I have kids, they'll probably be born in London.

Shit.

I won't bore you with a match report. We are two goals up with ten minutes to go. The crowd are loud and joyous. It's like the old days when we were a top club. No one can stop us now. Final score: 2–2.

On the way back to London, in the back of the car, I get changed into my evening suit ready for the BAFTA ceremony. I get a phone call from Robyn, the producer of *Unplanned*. I know the ceremony has started. I know she's there. 'Congratulations,' she blurts out excitedly. I'm stunned. We've obviously won the BAFTA.

'What for?' I say, trying to remain calm.

'Two—nil,' she says. Women have no concept of the phrase 'Latest Score'.

As I arrive at the Grosvenor Hotel, the red carpet laid for the arriving VIPs is still down, but the metal barriers that hold back the excited crowds and the banks of paparazzi are piled up for collection. A couple of stewards sit smoking outside. 'You're a bit late, Frank,' one of them says. I notice that the red carpet is slightly turned up at one corner. I walk into the quiet hotel and follow the signs to the awards ceremony. As I get nearer I can hear distant applause and cheering. I reach the doors of the Great Hall. There is a monitor on the wall. I'm on it. It must be our category. I walk into the hall and walk across to the balustrade at the top of the grand staircase. I can see the floor below, packed with dozens of tables of evening-suited blokes and glamorous-frocked women. It occurs to me that if we win, I can enter the hall down the staircase, like Jimmy Cagney in *Yankee Doodle Dandy*, and just continue to the stage in one sweeping movement. We don't. I hold back on the stairs, and watch Ali G go up to get the BAFTA. He's very funny but, of his genre, not quite as funny as Benny Hill playing the Chinese bloke.

So, there's a weekend in my life, in some ways unusual, in others very typical. Well, I don't often miss Mass on a Sunday. I'm not saying that would have affected the BAFTA result, but two goals in the last ten minutes? I think that could have been avoided with a quick candle.

One of the big changes I noticed when I switched from Moat Farm Infants to St. Hubert's Juniors was the games we played.

At Moat Farm, we did a lot of role-playing games. This led to all sorts of problems on the casting front. For example, if we played cowboys and Indians, more often than not, kids weren't exactly queuing up to be the redskins. OK, you got to whoop and do that thing when you pat your open mouth with the flat of your palm, but that was about it. I always got in a major strop if I couldn't be a cowboy. I took the acting element particularly seriously and wouldn't come out of character, even if kids who weren't playing in the game came and spoke to me. I remember a kid approaching me in the playground and asking if I'd written 'Wolves are Shit' on his duffel bag. I smiled ruefully and said, 'No one said life out here was gonna be easy.' The kid took this as a 'yes' and dead-legged me. Admittedly, this put a damper on my galloping for the rest of playtime, but I cowboyed up and put a brave face on it.

Perhaps I should point out, at this juncture, that the Wolves I refer to are Wolverhampton Wanderers, Albion's local rivals. I was at an Albion–Wolves game once when the guy next to me explained that he would rather do the double on Wolves (if you're not into football lingo that means beat them, home and away) than have Albion win promotion. I don't get this, but when I object, Albion fans tell me it's because I live in London. If I had to live with the Wolves fans every day, I'd understand. But I spent thirty-four years living with them and I never understood it then either.

I know this is getting a bit Albion-hardcore but bear with me. One thing that pisses me off is the amount of Albion chants that are about how much we hate the Wolves rather than how much we love the Albion. I think it's shit if you can only define yourself by your relationship to someone else. It makes them sound more important than you. The General Election campaign is going as I write this and that lot are just the same. Labour can only slag off the Tories and vice versa. If the blurb on the back of this book said, 'Much better than Suzanna Leigh's *Paradise, Suzanna Style*,' you might be inclined to question my confidence in the product.

Anyway, the Albion–Wolves thing does have its lighter side. Former England manager Graham Taylor managed Wolves for a bit. He spent a small fortune on players, still made a terrible job of it all, and ended up back at his old club, Watford. When Albion played at Watford shortly afterwards, our fans sang, to the tune of the old hymn 'Rock of Ages' (y'know, the one that was always 'We'll support you evermore'), 'Graham Taylor, Graham Taylor. Thanks for fucking-up the Wolves. Thanks for fu-u-u-cking-up the Wolves,' and, to his eternal credit, Taylor waved and smiled in acknowledgement. In fact, I think I might have even detected a glimmer of pride in a job well done. In an instant, I completely forgave him for his performance as England manager. Respect.

A few years ago, when Albion were playing at Wolves, the Hawthorns staged a closed-circuit broadcast of the game on a big screen for the Albion fans who couldn't get tickets. Unfortunately, some Wolves fans got in as well and there was trouble. The Albion chairman was so outraged that the club's efforts to stage the screening had been soured, he threatened to stage any further closed-circuit screenings 'behind closed doors'. I'm not sure that he'd completely thought this through.

Meanwhile, back at Moat Farm, I remember causing real problems during one game when I had been forced to play a Red Indian. When the cowboy kids captured me and threatened to kill me, I said I thought it would be a bad idea. When they asked why, I explained, 'Because I am . . . (Yes, I left a pause for dramatic effect. I remember the moment as if it was yesterday) Simon Templar.' I even looked up above my head for an imaginary halo. The cowboys were fucked. They couldn't complain without coming out of character. Suddenly, they'd gone from star turns in a playtime-length Western epic, to bit-players in an episode of *The Saint*. And where was Equity? Nowhere.

As I say, the move to the Catholic school threw up a whole bunch of new games, one of them 'Burn the Heretic', conducted completely in Latin. Just kidding. Anyway, the role-play games disappeared. (The next serious acting I did was twenty years later, when I performed a fortnightly series of fist-clenching, tear-filled monologues about my search for work for various members of staff at the local Job Centre.) The St. Hubert's games could be put into four categories: dangerous, life-changing, very life-changing and incredibly life-changing.

The dangerous games were mainly British Bulldog and pile-ups. British Bulldog, as you probably know, was basically splitting into two teams and then trying to get from one side of the playground to the other while the other kids tried to stop you with sheer brute strength. This game wasn't exactly tailor-made for me. I was always one of the skinniest kids at school: bulbous head too big for my body, arms that joined at the neck, and a chest like a thigh. As a mate of mine said to me a few years later, 'You're built like a gyppo's dog, all prick and bones.'

Pile-ups was a more elaborate game with a carefully considered set of rules. One kid lay flat on the playground, and then about thirty other kids piled on top of him. And that was it. You'd just lie there thinking stuff like 'shouldn't that kid's rib-cage be on the inside of his blazer' or 'I wish I hadn't got a frog in my pocket'. Then we'd all get up, dust ourselves down, and start breathing again.

The life-changing game was football. Nowadays Premiership clubs seem to be signing kids shortly after they develop fingernails, but I don't remember kicking a ball until I was eight. By the time I got to about nine, it was every playtime,

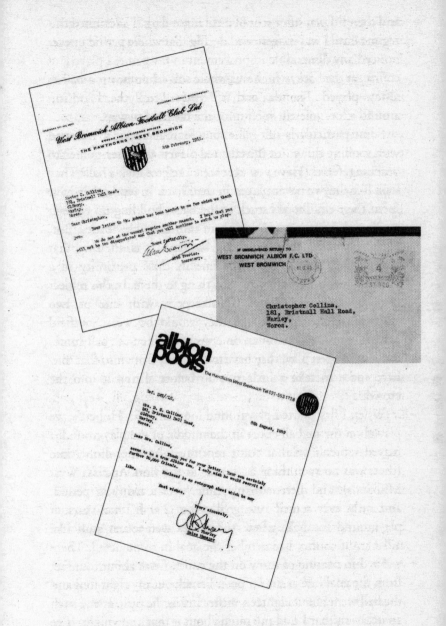

West Bromwich Albion Football Club Ltd

ENGLAND AND REGISTERED OFFICES
THE HAWTHORNS · WEST BROMWICH

5th February, 1969.

Master C. Collins,
181, Bristnall Hall Road,
Oldbury,
Worcs.

Dear Christopher,

Your letter to Mr. Ashman has been handed to me for which we thank you. We do not at the present require another mascot. I hope that you will not be too disappointed and that you will continue to watch us play.

Yours faithfully,

Alan Everiss

A.E. Everiss,
Secretary.

WEST BROMWICH ALBION F.C. LTD.
WEST BROMWICH

IF UNDELIVERED RETURN TO

Christopher Collins,
181, Bristnall Hall Road,
Warley,
Worcs.

---

albion pools

The Hawthorns, West Bromwich Tel 021-553 1758

Ref. DWT/LJ.

9th August, 1969.

Mrs. D. G. Collins,
181, Bristnall Hall Road,
Oldbury,
Warley,
Worcs.

Dear Mrs. Collins,

Thank you for your letter. Your son certainly seems to be a true Albion fan. I only wish he would recruit a further 30,000 friends like.

Enclosed is an autograph sheet which he may

Best wishes,

Yours sincerely,

D.W. Thorley
Sales Manager

and then I'd play after school until it got dark. I continued this regime until I was sixteen, and during that whole period I never noticed any discernible improvement in my game. I played, of course, at the back, which was where shit schoolboy footballers always played. The idea is that if you try really hard and run around a lot, you can spoil it for the talented players.

Some particularly shit schoolboy footballers got so obsessed with spoiling things for the talented players that they trained to become referees. Have you ever seen a referee kick a ball? They look like they've never played in their lives. In truth, they have spent their childhoods stuck at the back, building up enough anger and resentment to last them into their late forties. But, regardless of all this emotional baggage, it is amazing that though they spend so much time in close proximity to a football, it still seems like an alien thing to them. In this respect they are like goalkeepers. Goalkeepers, with one or two exceptions, always look like they would be worse outfield players than any fat woman on crutches. When the ball comes to them in open play, they have to run away from it so that they have space to take a little run-up before slicing it into the crowd.

When I first started playground football at St. Hubert's, we played on the netball court in the middle of the playground. I played football on that court morning playtime, dinnertime (there was no such thing as 'lunch' in the working-class West Midlands), and afternoon playtime, over a two-year period, and only ever scored one goal. One goal in two years of playground football, where the scores were often stuff like 17–15. Of course, I remember the goal in some detail. There was a thin coating of snow on the court. I was about four feet from the goal line at the far post. I stuck out my right foot and the ball went about eighteen inches inside the post. It was such an occasion that I told my mom about it that same night: 'I've had a good day today. I scored a goal at school.' Her reply will live with me forever. 'Ooo! That was lucky.'

Alan Hansen was never crueller, or more accurate.

When you moved up to the top two years, you became eligible to play in the school team. This was my dream. I was hoping to play for the Albion when I grew up. I figured it would be a lot easier to become a professional footballer if, at the interview, I could let it slip that I'd been in the school team at junior school. It would be some sort of seal of approval. The school team at St. Hubert's was picked by the only male teacher in the school, Mr Hartley. We were playing football in PE one day (Oh, yeah, that's another extra three games a week that I didn't score in) when Mr Hartley suddenly appeared. The buzz went round. All the kids were whispering that this was our chance to give him a positive image of our abilities a few months before we became eligible for the school team. Suddenly, the ball was booted high into the air by one of the opposing defenders and I ran to meet it. I don't recall ever heading the ball before so it would have been a big thing anyway, even without the presence of Mr Hartley making it a potential crushed-butterfly moment. The ball seemed to be in the air for ages. I braced myself for the thrusting impact of my headed clearance. The ball hit me in the face and I fell over. Mr Hartley stood looking for a few seconds, and then moved on. If I hadn't been stunned, I would have probably, as a last resort, started looking up for my halo.

I never made the school team at St. Hubert's. As I moved into the top year, we all graduated from the netball court to the big boys' pitch at the top of the playground, next to the school dinner hall. Balls would sometimes get stuck on the adjoining roof and we'd have to wait till the caretaker got them down at the end of term.

Twenty years later I went to a party at my mate Tim's house.

I'd been drinking cider all day and was arseholed by the time I got there. I then started drinking the Greek Pernod-like spirit, ouzo, mixed with Tim's home-brewed bitter. I woke up in his spare room the next morning, with his wife screaming at me. She left the room and came back with a J-cloth and a bottle of Dettol, both of which she threw at me before she stormed out again. Yes, I'd pissed the bed, and being fully clothed, my jeans were a little juicy as well. I walked downstairs, leaving the bed un-disinfected. In the kitchen I strolled straight past a slightly startled Tim and his wife and headed for the fridge. I took out the bottle of ouzo and had what my old mate Shane used to call a 'man-sized swig'. Tim and his wife watched in horror. To be fair to them, it was 8.30 in the morning. I fully intended to explain myself, but I just needed another couple of man-sized swigs to regulate my breathing. This done, I assured them that I had not pissed the bed but, rather, sweated heavily in the night as a result of having slept fully dressed. Tim's wife laughed in what I felt was a scornful way. She said she could smell the piss on me. I took one more man-sized swig and left in a huff. I soon realised that I was on the street, whistle wetted, but the pubs didn't open for three and a half hours, so I walked. By now, the man-sized swigs had topped up the previous day's excesses and I was feeling fairly poetical.

Perhaps I should break off at this point to say something about the drinking element of this story. Some of you might think I sound like a man with a drink problem. Well, we'll come to all that later. Suffice to say that I was no stranger to waking up with a dry mouth and a wet bed.

As I walked my drunken walk, I had the contented smile that one might expect from a man whose piss-soaked jeans are slowly drying off in the bright morning sunshine. Then, either by accident or design, I found myself confronted by the giant white cross of St. Hubert's, so I thought I'd go and have a look at the old school. I stopped to lean on the railings, carefully surveying my surroundings the way sober people never do. From this vantage point I could see the dinner hall and Mrs McGee's classroom where I spent my last year at the school. There was the top end of the playground where we played game after game of football, with ten-year-old me wondering when the late-blossoming talent that would take me through to the ranks of the professional players was going to finally emerge.

And then I saw the roof where all those footballs used to get stuck. I actually rubbed my eyes in disbelief. I'd remembered the wall as being about thirty feet high. In fact, I reckoned that, on tip-toes, I could reach the ball that lay there now.

A similar thing happened to me with an enormous statue of Lucifer I'd seen in the Birmingham Art Gallery. It stood in the entrance hall with its big cock and spread wings, towering above visitors like the Colossus of Rhodes, and gave me one quite unpleasant nightmare. The last time I went to the Birmingham Art Gallery, I met Lucifer again. He's about five feet high and stands in the corner of the tea-room. If I'd been drinking I'd say that this was what life is like. Things that seem big and important and scary and insurmountable at one stage in your life can come to look small and trivial later on. But I haven't been drinking, so I won't.

The very life-changing game was a variation on one of the dangerous games. It was called British Bullsnog. It was basically the same rules as British Bulldog, except the teams were boys versus girls and, rather than wrestle them to the ground, the idea was that one of the assailants would snog the captured runner. If the African tribeswoman could have seen me playing British Bullsnog, I feel she would have said, with no visible signs of emotion, 'My work here is done,' and then walked off, tits out, pot on head, into the distance.

Despite having a big sister, I knew nothing of girls. One day, when I was nine, I was sitting in the classroom casually telling lies. Telling lies is a commonplace amongst children, even at a Catholic school. Don't worry, I've grown out of it. I was saying that I'd been to a sex shop in London – remember I'm nine – and seen mugs that consisted of a big breast with a woman's penis for the handle. Obviously, I didn't say 'penis', I said 'Peter Panda,' but I don't want to confuse you just for the hell of it. Either way, a kid called Brendan soon spotted the fatal flaw in my story and pointed out that he'd seen his little sister naked and she had no Peter Panda. 'No Peter Panda?' I said scornfully, looking round to confirm that everyone had heard Brendan's ridiculous story. A little girl with greasy hair confirmed that Brendan speaketh sooth. I was shocked but, more than anything, embarrassed by my obvious lack of worldly-wise sophistication. If only I'd paid more attention when I was an upside-down shepherd. The greasy-haired girl could see I was crestfallen and clearly felt sorry for me. 'Never mind,' she whispered, 'I'll show you mine at playtime, if you like.'

Lucky old Edith Piaf, who could reach middle age and still, with seeming conviction, sing that she had no regrets. If I live to a hundred, I will always beat myself up for not taking up the greasy-haired girl's offer. And it's not as if I had a sudden burst of Catholic morality or became afraid of the unknown, or decided that football was more important. No, I just forgot. When I saw her again, after playtime, I remembered her kind words and went over to explain my scattiness but she cut me dead and flounced off in the opposite direction. I may not have seen my first vagina but I had had my first taste of playing a game that women of all ages love to play with men. More dangerous than British Bulldog and pile-ups put together, more disheartening than football and more life-changing than

Bullsnogging. Yes, it's 'Guess why I'm upset'. Many's the hour I've spent, at parties, on public transport, even in bed, playing that fucking game.

Looking back, I suppose the greasy-haired girl felt that I had snubbed her vagina, but why couldn't I see it the following playtime? Did she only get it out on rare occasions so I'd have to wait till the next time, whenever that might be, like it was the Halley's Comet of the vagina world? Either way, if Mr Hartley had been going past, I wouldn't have been picked for the relationships team either. Come to think of it, over the years, I've probably proved to be better at football.

As far as the incredibly life-changing games were concerned, there were several, and they helped me to find, at last, a game I was good at, in fact, several games I was good at. You've guessed it. They were comedy games. Pointing at someone's chest and then, when they look down to see what you're pointing at, dragging your finger upward, so it goes in their face. Now, that is what I call a game. I probably played that thirty times a day. In fact, I still play it now. It makes me laugh. I even had my first experience of being in a double-act. This involved perhaps the funniest joke ever. If I could meet the man (sorry, but it just couldn't be a woman) who wrote it, I'd like to shake his hand and thank him. It's the joke when you talk to a kid and, meanwhile, your mate crouches down on hands and knees behind him and then you push the kid over. I've spent hours and hours writing and re-writing gags, but I've never come up with anything to equal that. I would still be using it but it gets dangerous with older people and I can't find a willing accomplice. If Tony Bennett had been up for it, it would have been a great one to pull on Prince Charles during the Royal Variety line-up. But Tony would have been fretting about his wig coming off and the whole thing would have lacked the spontaneity of the playground version.

I just had a meeting about making a documentary about me for ITV. They heard about the autobiography and they thought a Frank Skinner bio-doc might be a goer. Of course, this would be a very good advert for the book so I thought I'd go for it and I made positive noises. Then I kind of forgot about it. ITV are also planning docs on Des O'Connor and Des Lynam, both non-controversial mainstream icons, so I'm expecting a fairly straight 'this happened and then this happened' sort of approach. Then, today, we had a meeting about it.

In the meeting was Jon Thoday, Lee Tucker, the head of production at Avalon Television (he's the fanatical Albion fan I bumped into at the Albion–Bolton game), and the potential director/producer of the documentary, Paul Wilmshurst. I've worked with Paul before on a documentary about Elvis Presley, and I think he's really good. He's got a quirky outlook, and has done documentaries on, among other things, a famous Mafia lawyer and the guy who wrote the cult novel *The Dice Man*. Paul's in his thirties, clean and unshaven, and in his battered combat-trousers and leather jacket looks like the England cricketer Michael Atherton in reduced circumstances.

Jon started talking about ITV's three-doc project with me and the Deses. (What is the plural of Des?) Apparently, ITV's only house-style requirement is that the subject should talk to the camera about their lives. The rest is up to us.

I started talking about things the film might include. I could do a sort of *Unplanned* audience-thing in which people could ask me questions about my life. Paul could interview my family and some people from my past and cut in bits from these interviews at suitable points. I explain the 'Our Nora' problem. It's one thing to have stuff like the piss-buckets revelation in a book, but if it was on national television, it really might kill her. Mind you, I did mention it to Tony Blair on BBC1, but I didn't really relate it to me personally.

All this throws up a distinction which hadn't occurred to me before the meeting. Even though I'm sticking a lot of private stuff in this book, it still seems, well, private. You need to buy the book and open the book and take time to read the book, in order to get right in there. You, the reader, make an investment, financial, intellectual and time-wise. The TV viewer just presses a button. I don't like the idea of all that intimate me just up there like wallpaper. I know a lot of my gags are totally true and, for example, *Unplanned* throws up all sorts of private stuff, but it's a kind of comedy private life. I don't have a problem with talking about wanking or shagging, or stuff a lot of people regard as private, but family and religion, that's something else. This, however, seems to have answered a question I posed earlier in this book. I'll bet porn stars do refer to their genitals as their 'private parts'.

Someone wanted to write my biography a few years back. She was a good writer with a top magazine and I was very flattered. The contract was drawn up, but when the day came to sign, I changed my mind. I just looked at the headings: Family, Pornography, Alcohol, Catholicism, and I lost my nerve. The weird thing is that I've probably revealed more in this book than I would have in hers, but I feel better about telling you direct. Otherwise it has to go through a filter before it reaches you, a filter that might take some stuff out and might put other stuff in. That's why there's no ghost-writer on this book, even though it would have freed up my days somewhat.

I've watched translators on television. An interviewer asks a question that I understand. A translator says something to the subject that I don't understand. I hear the subject give his answer, which I don't understand. The translator gives an answer. I'm showing a fuck of a lot of faith in the translator here. How do I know what's gone on in all the foreign bits?

This is how it works with biographers, and documentary makers.

I asked Paul what he thought the documentary might be like. He said he thought it would be funny and sad. When I asked him why he thought it would be sad, he said, 'Well, because anyone who's spent any time with you knows that you're . . . er . . . well . . . wistful.' The room went a bit quiet. Wistful? What the fuck did he mean by that?

'Well,' I said, 'it's the first I've heard of it.' As soon as I'd said it, I started to wonder whether the tone was, well, slightly wistful. No, no, I'd recognise this tone anywhere. It's called irritated. Oh, dear. For some reason I'd really taken against wistful. But there's a good example. If I was working as Paul's interpreter, I would have translated 'wistful' as 'inclined to be a tortured, self-doubt-ridden, insecure nut-case' and this might not have been exactly what Paul meant. Anyway, I was like a dog with a bone. 'Is that what people say, then? Frank Skinner? Is he the Jewish one or the wistful one?' Laughter, but with a sense of unease.

Then I asked Paul to elaborate on his vision of the doc. He said it could be a bit like that Geri Halliwell doc that everyone was talking about. Of course, the reason everyone was talking about it was that Geri came out of it looking like a tragic cow. At one stage we see her going through the newspapers to see if there are any pictures of her. This got her a lot of scornful criticism. Now that's a worry.

Whenever I pick up a tabloid, I always have a look to see if I'm in it. I even check those '100 Sexiest Guys' things that appear every now and then, and I've never been in one of them, ever. I check the Rich List, Great TV Moments, Quotes of the Week, any old bollocks. I've scanned crossword magazines for my name in answers or clues, and I check those pictures of celebs in the middle of the puzzles in case it's me. I'll even have the occasional glance at the birthdays just in case they've got the date wrong. What's the problem? A local press photographer told me that his editor instructed him to cram as many people as possible into photographs because they'll all buy at least two copies of the paper that week. It's human nature.

I laugh when I read about celebs moaning about the pressures of fame. They want to try forty hours in a drop-forgings factory. I have – fame's better. Whenever a celeb tells you about how the tabloids have been hounding them, the sub-text is always 'That's how famous I am'. I know. My ex-wife has slagged me off in the *Sunday Mirror*, the *News of the World* and the *People*, and I can honestly say I was genuinely hurt and upset on each occasion, but through the tears I was still thinking, 'Two-page spread? That's how famous I am.'

I don't want to let the cat out of the bag but fame is actually very nice. When people ask me for an autograph, they are often very apologetic and say stuff like, 'I know this must be a pain' or 'Sorry to be embarrassing' and I say, 'I'll miss it when it stops,' and they laugh as if I'm joking. These people could be bothered to ask me to write my name on a bit of paper. They'll probably go away and tell their friends they met me. Fucking hell, that's brilliant, isn't it? I meet the odd tosser, but nowhere near as many as I met before I got famous. A lot of people treated me like shit in the old days. Am I supposed to miss that?

Anyway, I tell *you* this but, obviously, if I said it on the telly, I'd sound a bit of a prat. If you're a celebrity, the acceptable way to behave is to say fame is a nightmare and you've got no money really. So I'd best keep my trap shut.

I was listening to the radio the other day and they were talking about how footballers live an incredibly pampered life. Some woman was going on about the fact that they get driven around everywhere, someone organises their plane tickets and passports, all their meals are laid on in hotels that someone else has chosen and booked for them. I thought, 'What's your point?'

I've got a personal assistant called Jenny who organises the paying of my bills, books my holidays, handles my dry-cleaning, buys my cinema tickets, reminds me about birthdays, the lot. Well, obviously, she doesn't do my washing and ironing. I've got a cleaner who does that. Incidentally, some people who have a cleaner say, 'I've got a woman who does,' but if I say that, everyone will just assume that I'm talking about anal sex.

The other day, I went for a quick lunch with Robyn, who produces my chat show and *Unplanned*. Afterwards, we walked up the road to get some fags from the newsagent. On the way, we met a friend of Robyn's. They were going to look at a house somewhere. Robyn suddenly looked distressed that I was now going to the newsagent on my own. I assured her I could manage, they drove off, and I carried on up the road. I was wearing an Hawaiian shirt and bright purple trainers. I suddenly felt like an exotic bird who had escaped from his cage and who would inevitably be torn to bits by the local sparrows, provoked by his colourful plumage. I made it, but when I got back in my office, I felt like I'd been on a bit of an adventure. Pampered? Like a prize poodle. But, again, I wouldn't want to say so on the telly.

Anyway, I thought I'd better sound a bit more positive about the doc. In any meeting, power always goes to the negative person in the room, and I don't know that that's very helpful. I suggested that Paul could film my great-niece's christening. I'm going to be her godfather. He seemed unkeen. He said he was more interested in things that were 'uncomfortable'. My alarm bells were really ringing now.

'Well, what do you want?' I asked, just this side of politely.

'Well, you know,' he said, in a tone of calm-down-Frank. 'I

imagine there'd be stuff about drinking, women, football, about your work and your work-methods.' It reminded me of the headings in the biography that never happened. 'I'm sure you wouldn't want it to be a puff-piece, Frank.' A puff-piece, of course, is media-lingo for anything in the media which is there just to promote or praise someone. They avoid all touchy subjects and dark areas. He was right, of course, that would be crap.

Back in the sixties, British comic Tony Hancock appeared on *Face to Face*, a sort of early television version of *In the Psychiatrist's Chair*. There were a lot of deep and meaningful questions and some people say that it made Hancock become very introspective and self-analytical. I haven't read up on him but I think, basically, he hit the bottle and topped himself. That's no good, is it? I don't want to watch myself on a documentary and start thinking I'm all troubled and interesting.

I've met a few women over the years who have tried to hang the 'broken-hearted clown' thing on me. 'Oh,' they say, 'you're funny, but I know, deep-down, you're hurting.'

'Yeah, OK, just get your bra off.'

Obviously, some shrink-type could read this book and start going on about my relationship with my father and my need to get approval from others and my thinly disguised self-loathing. You buy the book, you can do what you like with it. Use it for a door-stop if it makes you happy. I'd actually prefer that to the psychoanalysis thing, but it's really up to you. I'm not very bothered if people watched the doc and thought I was a bit of a mentaller, but I'm very wary of celebs who are desperate to be seen 'warts and all' on documentaries, like Elton John in *Tantrums and Tiaras*. Actually, that was probably the only ever TV doc to be 'warts and all' and a puff-piece.

Anyway, the meeting ended with us saying we'd all go away

and think about it. I asked Paul how much he would have liked to have filmed this meeting for the documentary. He said, 'A lot.'

The next day Paul phoned my manager and said, in the light of the meeting, he was now twice as interested in doing the documentary. He wants to see the first ten thousand words of this book. Oh, what to do?

When I first arrived at Moat Farm, I had my hair in a long fringe. Two kids from the second year, called Martin and Vincent, decided that it would be fun to call me Beatle, and generally rough me up and make me sing Beatle hits and the like. Martin was a short, mouthy kid with bags under his eyes and a dark crew-cut. Vincent was fat, rosy-cheeked, and very much the brighter of the two. When I arrived in the morning or when I went out to playtime, my stomach would be knotted up with the dread of meeting Martin and Vincent. They were always arm in arm and would approach me, smiling and laughing before going into bully-mode. I had to do a Scouse accent for their entertainment. I loved showing off and entertaining kids but not when it was for all the wrong reasons. It's a feeling I still get today, every time I do corporate entertainment.

One morning I pointed Martin and Vincent out to my mom and she warned them they'd be in trouble if they bullied me again. They looked scared and I was very relieved. The next playtime, I got a double dose for telling on them. I suppose, in reality, this lasted for a couple of months, but to the little me it seemed like a lifetime. But thank God it ended when it did. Shortly afterwards, the Beatles went into their Sergeant Pepper phase, and Martin and Vincent would have killed me because I couldn't grow a moustache. It was a horrible time for me, but it is interesting that, in 1965, I was being forced, against my will, to live the life of a Beatle whereas, up in Liverpool, Pete Best was being tortured by exactly the opposite experience. I should think that bullying has rarely been so 'of its time' as it was in my case. If there are any short-haired albino kids reading this who are being forced to do Eminem numbers every playtime, they have my deepest sympathy.

As I moved up a year or two, the school bully, David, began to take an interest in me. Being bullied by the 'school' bully gave me a certain credibility, but it was still pretty unpleasant. David's approach was fairly standard bullying stuff, arm up the back, Chinese burns, dead-legs, with none of the originality of Martin and Vincent's enforced Mersey-moptop regime. But David was big and, like most big strong people, he had no sense of humour. Everything was done through narrowed eyes and bared teeth. He was really scary.

At this time, I was obsessed with Muhammad Ali. My boxing-fanatic dad plus the whole family would gather around the telly for the Ali fights, and had done since they were Clay fights. I had Ali on my wall and I used to do an impression of him. He was everything I wanted to be – funny, good-looking, and capable of beating people up. Incidentally, I met him a couple of times in the nineties. On the first occasion, he was doing a book-signing (Oh, I've got all that to look forward to) in Sportspages on the Charing Cross Road. He sat behind a desk with his close friend, Howard Bingham. Because Ali's Parkinson's Disease had made his speech very hard to understand, he was muttering to Bingham, and Bingham would converse with the punters. I turned up wearing a Muhammad Ali t-shirt and Ali was clearly very interested in this. He opened his eyes ridiculously wide like he used to do when playing the fool in his glory-days, and grabbed my shirt for a closer look before muttering something to Bingham. 'He didn't get any money for this one,' Bingham explained. Ali signed my book and my shirt (it hangs in a frame in my hallway) and I left feeling like I'd seen the face of God. A few months later, I went to a theatre show about Ali's life at the Mermaid Theatre. Both Ali and his old adversary, Henry Cooper, were there. I was drinking in the bar before when Ali suddenly appeared at my side. I turned and said something that came out as 'Mam mamblee mooha mamali mmmmmm . . .'. I fully expected him to offer me Howard Bingham's business card.

At the end of the play, Ali stepped up from his front-row seat and began sparring with the actor who had played him. It was an astonishing moment. Ali staggered towards the actor with everyone fearing he might fall at any moment, then, suddenly, he did an Ali shuffle and his hands became a blur. It was as if the whole Parkinson's thing had been some terrible hoax. The whole audience was stunned and started chatting frantically about what had just happened. Afterwards in the bar, Ali and Henry Cooper were posing for photographs with the punters. I had mine taken, standing between them. I was wearing a tuxedo and bow-tie but Ali and Cooper had ignored the dress-code and gone for ordinary suits. I was so proud of this picture that I sent a copy to Nora, Terry and Keith. After a few days, I heard from Jason, Keith's son. Having seen the picture, with me in the middle in my bow-tie, he asked in all seriousness, 'Have you started refereeing?'

Anyway, one afternoon, in the playground, David the bully approached me and started shoving me around. Out of the blue, I did what everyone should do at least once in their life, I took on the school bully. I hadn't really done any fighting, I wasn't that sort of kid, but I'd seen a lot of fighting, so I started to dance. 'Float like a butterfly, sting like a bee' is what Ali used to say, and that's what I did. Kids gathered around to watch and I could hear them saying stuff like, 'Why is he bouncing around?' and 'He thinks he's Cassius Clay.' I even remember including an Ali shuffle. David was confused and maybe, dare I say it, slightly afraid. For a few minutes there, I *was* Ali. I could almost hear the crowd. Thus, I beat the school bully, and as I walked away a friend said, 'I think you need to do a bit of work on your footwork.' But no one could spoil my special moment. I looked back at David. His face suddenly looked like he had a heart and a soul, just like I did. I didn't hate him anymore.

I was in a pub ten years later when a bloke at the bar said hello to me. It was David. He was instantly recognisable. He'd grown big and muscular and, worryingly, he had a scar on his throat which suggested that someone had slit it from ear to ear. I decided, early on, that I wasn't going to ask him about this. I shook his hand and smiled, already thinking to myself, 'Don't remember the fight. For fuck's sake don't remember the fight.' After about two minutes of small talk he said, 'D'you remember when we had that fight?'

'No,' I said.

'You must do,' he went on. 'You beat me.'

'No,' I said.

'Yeah, you remember, you had really long nails and you sort of scratched me to pieces.' There's memory for you. I was definitely Muhammad Ali but he thinks I was Edward Scissorhands. Then he said, 'I wonder who'd win if we had a fight now.' I looked at him and wondered if I could still summon up the old Ali magic if it came to it. Before I could answer, though I don't know what that answer would have been, an attractive woman approached us and put her arm around David. Saved by the belle. He introduced her as his girlfriend and I noticed she was pregnant. He became preoccupied with her and I took the opportunity to leave. I saw him a few more times but the subject never came up again. It spoilt things a bit, though. Special moments should end with a nice neat full-stop, not with an epilogue ten years later that just clouds the issue.

When I moved to the big school, bullying left me totally exhausted most days. Well, those first years took some catching. Yes, it's a terrible confession but it's true: when I got into the second year at the big school, despite my previous experiences, I started bullying. I didn't do much physical stuff because I was still as gyppo's dog-like as ever. Generally, we would bully in packs, with me as some sort of sinister court-jester figure. I had a nasty streak in me which I've tried hard to erase as I've got older. I suppose I would spot a psychological weakness in a kid and then concentrate on that. It's something kids often do to each other, but when you can turn it into gags, comedy songs etc, then you can really do some damage. In my defence, my main motivation was to make my mates laugh. The ugly, the fat, the spotty were just my raw materials. Everyone took the piss out of these kids, such is the way of the world, but I found I had a natural gift for verbal bullying, comedy-style. I don't know whether the bullied hated me more than they hated the big kids who carried out the physical element of the bullying, but it must have seemed particularly unfair to be bullied, albeit only verbally, by someone who had trouble opening crisps. At least, as I found with David, if you're being bullied by bigger kids there seems to be some sense of the traditional about it. Eventually, the bullying gang I court-jested for took to carrying thick lengths of electrical wire which we called 'strops'. My own particular strop was known as the 'Black Baron'. We'd uncoil these whenever an opportunity arose and let the bullied have it across their backs, arms and legs. This was the only physical bullying I ever really took to and, although it was fun, it didn't fire me up like the comedy stuff.

My behaviour at that time was very unpleasant in lots of aspects. At one stage, I acquired the nickname Sir Snide. I didn't like that very much. Like my own verbal attacks, it's the true ones that really hurt. During my whole bullying period, I guess it lasted from about twelve to fifteen, I never remember thinking back to how I felt when I was the Beatle boy, or was being terrorised by David. A couple of kids at the big school got transferred to other schools because of the bullying. I wasn't directly involved in either of these cases, but I was a key part of the general bullying environment that existed there.

I sometimes wonder how those kids, who I ridiculed and insulted, feel when they see me doing well on the telly and stuff. Are they outraged by the cruel injustice of it all? I must admit, it doesn't seem very fair to me either. Still, payback time for me could always be just around the corner. I believe it's called panto.

I just went away with Caroline for a weekend in Venice. This is, of course, traditionally the most romantic city on earth but the trip is a bit of a risk for me. I've taken three different women to Venice over the years, and I split up with all of them within three months of getting back. And these were not short fly-by-night relationships. In fact, one of them was my wife. But Caroline and me risked it. We had an idyllic smoochy ride in a gondola and sighed at the Bridge of Sighs and it was lovely. We did have one big row, about whether or not we should have flowers on the balconies at the new house, but we survived. We do argue a bit but we put it down to passion, and, goodness knows, she has a lot to put up with.

For example, I went into pun-overdrive when we got to Venice. The ruler of Venice was known as the Doge. When we learned that there was no longer a Doge of Venice living at the

Doge's palace, I sang 'Who let the Doge out' about fifty times before I got it out of my system. When we saw an incredibly fat woman sitting on the steps next to the Bridge of Sighs, I said that she looked so miserable because she had misheard and was expecting the Bridge of Pies. Even on the flight back, when the captain announced that if we looked out to the left, we would be able to see Luxembourg, I was soon singing 'Pass the Duchy on the left-hand side'. (If you're under thirty, just trust me that that's funny, and ask your mom who 'Musical Youth' were.)

Caroline and me were once walking down Hampstead High Street when a girl from Greenpeace approached us for a please-join chat. I went into joker mode and after about five minutes she looked at Caroline and said, 'How do you put up with him?' Caroline took some imaginary cotton wool out of her ears and said, 'Sorry?' I pissed myself laughing. I think the Greenpeace girl got her answer.

When we got to the top class at St. Hubert's, we had to try out for the school choir. I quite fancied being in the choir. I loved singing and as, traditionally, ninety-five per cent of the top class got selected, I had to fancy my chances. We all lined up at one end of the class and started singing 'Soul of my Saviour'. Mrs McGee wandered up and down the line, listening closely to each kid in turn. When she came to me, she listened for a while and then put her hand on my shoulder. 'We're not American,' she said. I'd blown my chance. She obviously wanted sweet, angelic children's voices and I was trying to be Elvis.

In fact, I've spent most of my life trying to be Elvis. There was a time when I wouldn't have bought an article of clothing unless I could imagine Elvis wearing it. Luckily, white flared jumpsuits were fashionable in the West Midlands right up to the late eighties. I've spent too much of my life with my hair swept back into a quiff, even though it doesn't suit me because my head is shaped like a light-bulb. I've spent too much of my life with sideburns that start about an inch below where my hair stops, leaving a stupid gap at the top. During my last attempt at sideburns, in 1998, the make-up person on *Fantasy World Cup* used to colour in the gap with mascara. Whatever music I dance to, my dancing always comes out like an under-rehearsed parody of Elvis's 'Jailhouse Rock' routine. Every school exercise book, pencil case, duffel bag, even my First Communion card, had 'Elvis' written on it.

I kept an Elvis scrapbook, forced my mom to buy his latest single, learnt the words to all his songs, and not only went and saw all the dodgy movies like *Clambake, Speedway* and, of course, *Paradise, Hawaiian Style*, but whenever the Oscars rolled around, I was outraged when Elvis didn't get a nomination. I really believed in those movies. I really thought life was like that. I thought I could get a job as a barman or a pool-attendant (once I'd learned to swim) and then hang around the club at night until someone asked me to get up and sing a song. Then, within seconds, the whole place would be rocking, and people, instinctively clapping along, would turn to each other, smile and nod. When I left school, it wasn't quite like that.

I went through a wanky poetry-writing stage when I was seventeen. Here's the opening of one of my least wanky efforts:

I'll get you for this, Elvis Presley.
I'll get you for all of those lies.
Where are the women you promised me?
Where are those singalong guys?

It all started because Terry was a bit of an Elvis fan. I slightly hero-worshipped Terry. I remember once copying what order he ate his dinner in so I could be like him. Consequently, I got into Elvis through his influence, but then I became much more obsessive about him than Terry ever was. The big thing that tortured me was that I was blonde, well, blondeish, whereas Elvis's hair was black. This, I believed, was the only significant difference in our physical appearance. My mom wouldn't let me dye my hair and so my non-Elvis colouring plagued me for years. I was thrilled when Elvis wore a blonde wig to play his own twin in the film *Kissin' Cousins*, but I knew, in my heart of hearts, it was only temporary. It sounds stupid now, but this hair thing was a major concern of mine as a child. Many years later I discovered that Elvis's hair was the same colour as mine but he dyed it black. Another interesting life-lesson for me: don't yearn for what other people seem to have because they might not have it at all. The other man's hair is always blacker.

My Elvis obsession continued through my teens, at a time when my friends were all into heavy-metal bands like Sabbath and Zeppelin. Eventually I admitted defeat on the quiff and grew my hair like it is on the photo-booth picture, but I still loved The King. Then, when I was twenty, I got home from the pub one night to find my mom and dad waiting for me with deep concern upon their faces. 'We've got some bad news,' my mom said. 'You'd better sit down.' I was already thinking death in the family. My dad looked anxious but said nothing. 'What's up?' I asked, finally.

My mom took a breath. 'Elvis is dead,' she said.

I didn't say anything. Funnily enough, I was going through my punk stage at the time. I looked down at my multi-zipped jeans that my mom had customised for me. Punk was about rebellion and turning your back on the

Andy Warhol's portrait of me, aged one. To this day, I still smile
when I touch my genitals.

My mom as a teenager. Dad used to call this her 'Russian Spy' photo.

My dad. Ever at home with a whippet.

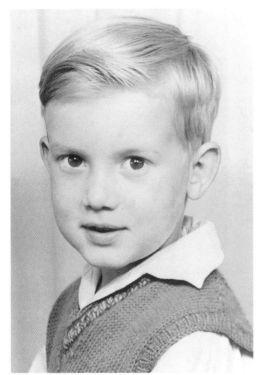

Me, when I was cute.

Me, aged five. (Picture courtesy of the 'Working-Class Wallpaper Museum').

Right: The great love of my life.

Beatle-Boy.

Above: Outside St Hubert's School. My
mom was very late picking me up.

Left: It's a coonskin cap – made by my
mom out of rabbit.

Keith, me, one of
Dad's sheds and the
fence our neighbour's
little girl stood on.

With our Nora.

Aged 15, with my natural ringlets.

During my teens
we didn't have a
camera.

With Shane and some
stuff my dad built.

Fez and me – just
off to the pub.

Dad and me,
both pissed.

When I was cool. My dad
built that fence.

Above: 1976 I honestly
thought this looked great.

In 1978 Albion shirt outside
181, Bristnall Hall Road.

oldies. (Unless they had a sewing machine.) I hadn't played an Elvis record for about four months. I don't think I'd ever gone four days without playing one before. It reminded me of a rabbit called Chubby Checker I owned when I was a kid. My mom and dad were always going on about how I didn't look after him properly, never cleaned him out, missed his meal-times and so on. I went to feed him one day and found him dead, lying in about an inch and a half of his own piss. I felt guilty as hell. Now I had neglected Elvis and he had died too.

I had a cup of tea but rejected the idea of supper. My parents went to bed and I put the telly on to try and get some details, but this was in the days when the telly finished at about midnight. They used to have a thing called *Closedown*, which was usually a photograph of something like 'Sunset on the Norfolk Broads' with a bit of classical music over it. Then a voice-over would come on and say goodnight. The National Anthem was in there somewhere, as well, but I can't quite remember the sequence. Anyway, tonight, *Closedown* was a bit different. They showed a picture of Elvis, I think it was from the sleeve of *Greatest Hits Volume 4*, and they played him singing 'You'll Never Walk Alone'. I never much cared for Elvis's version of this but I cried like a baby. The tears ran down my face and onto my jacket, the right sleeve of which was held on only by safety pins. That's my 1977.

If they'd shown a picture of my rabbit and played 'Let's Twist Again', I think I would have had a breakdown.

I suppose that those of you who are paying attention will be wondering what happened in the second leg of the Division One play-off against Bolton. Fuck off.

*

In 1967, I was sitting in the classroom at St. Hubert's with my teacher trying to get me to think of a one-letter word. 'Well,' she said, 'who is the most important person in your world?' Obviously, she was hoping this line of questioning would eventually lead to me recognising 'I' as a one-letter word. 'Jeff Astle,' I said. Jeff Astle was Albion's star centre-forward of the time. What they now call an 'old-fashioned centre-forward'. He was big, strong, aggressive, and the best header of a football I've ever seen. He wasn't just loved by the Albion fans, he was worshipped. In 1968, Albion got to the FA Cup Final. I couldn't get a ticket so I watched it on our twelve-inch black-and-white telly, with my dad, of course. Astle had scored in every round. In the third minute of extra time, he scored what was to be the winning goal in the final. I can still see the goal going in. Me and my dad went skyward, then I dropped to my knees and kissed Astle as he raised his arms in celebration on our small black-and-white screen. I felt the crackle of static electricity against my lips as the Albion fans sang (to the tune of that part of Camptown Races that's about going to sing all day etc), 'Astle is our king. Astle is our king. The Brummie Road will sing this song, Astle is our king.' (The Brummie Road End is where Albion's most vociferous supporters tend to stand, or, nowadays, sit.)

Twenty-odd years later, I sat with Jeff Astle in a crowded mini-van in Portsmouth while a bunch of lads neither of us had met before sang a variation on the song, 'Astle's in our van. Astle's in our van . . .', followed by, admittedly a less enthusiastic version of 'Skinner's in our van . . .'. Now, how did that happen?

In the early nineties, David Baddiel and me were writing and hosting the TV show *Fantasy Football League*. The show included a pre-recorded segment called 'Phoenix from the Flames', in which we did comic re-creations of great footballing moments, joined by the footballer who'd been involved in the original incident. We did that 'did it cross the line?' goal from the 1966 World Cup Final with Geoff Hurst, Brazil winning the 1970 World Cup with Carlos Alberto, Coventry City's famous 'donkey-kick' goal with Willie Carr, and so on. When the show was first commissioned, we sat down to compile a list of suitable football moments. I was dead keen to re-create a Jeff Astle goal, ever-so-slightly offside, against Leeds United that led to a massive pitch invasion back in the early seventies. I felt that the incident had comic potential, but my main priority was that I wanted to meet my boyhood hero. The filming was set up and Dave, a small film-crew and me turned up at Jeff's house in Burton-on-Trent.

'Phoenix from the Flames' proved to be a very popular part of *Fantasy Football*, but not every footballer we worked with took naturally to the acting element of the job. One old Chelsea star greeted us at ten in the morning, already on his second can of cider, not a method that I could remember from the book *An Actor Prepares*. Dutch defender Ronald Koeman refused to dress as the Milky Bar kid because, as he put it, 'I am not a Gazza', Billy Bremner said yes and then no, as did Paul Ince. The old Celtic player Tommy Gemmel nearly killed me when re-creating a foul of his on the German striker Helmut Haller, and then declared, 'I've had a great day: a few hundred quid, free beer, and I got to kick an Englishman,' and the great Argentinian striker Mario Kempes took one look at the script and said, in surprisingly good English, 'I won't do it. It is just shit.'

But Jeff Astle was a natural. As well as being a nice bloke, he had genuine comic timing and was incredibly keen to help, as was shown when he uttered a phrase that went straight into *Fantasy Football* folklore, 'My wife'll be Gary Sprake.' I had met my hero and he'd come up trumps.

When the second series of *Fantasy Football* was commissioned, Dave and me thought it might be a nice idea to end with a song. We considered singing it ourselves, but decided that Dave and me singing a song could never really capture the public imagination.

Then I remembered something. Back in the early seventies I had bought a single on RCA Victor called 'Sweet Water'. I bought it because the singer was Jeff Astle. Apparently, when Jeff was in the 1970 England World Cup squad, they all went off to record an album and after hearing the whole squad sing, Jeff was given lead vocal on several of the tracks. So what about closing the show with a section called 'Jeff Astle Sings'? The idea was that, towards the end of the show, the doorbell would go and it would be Jeff, dressed in a series of ridiculous costumes, who would then sing a song.

Now, Jeff could sing, but he didn't actually seem to recognise any songs. We once asked him to sing Rod Stewart's 'Sailing' and he said that he didn't know where we dragged these obscure songs up from. His lovely wife, Lorayne, would conduct Jeff from just behind the auto-cue, so he knew when to come in, and he would go for it. It was very funny, but only because Jeff was really trying to do a good job on the song. If he'd deliberately messed it up, it would have been rubbish. He was totally aware that the worse he was, the funnier it was, but he was always trying to prove he could sing really well. When he did, the audience roared encouragement. It became a crucial part of the show, Jeff would sing, and Dave and me would dance behind him.

When Eric Cantona, in an elaborate metaphor about media-attention, spoke of the seagulls following the trawler, we had Jeff come on dressed as a trawler, and we danced behind him holding up photos of Stephen Segal. (We were shameless.) Jeff is from Nottingham. (He always said that D.H. Lawrence had lived in the same street. From the sublime . . .) When an old lady who had been Jeff's next-door neighbour in that street wrote to us saying that she used to scrub his back when he was a baby, we wheeled Jeff on in a tin bath at the end of the show with that same woman scrubbing his back. In our now-established tradition of incongruity, Jeff sang 'There's no business like show business'.

Through it all, Jeff was a real pro. At heart, he was a showman. He had milked the applause as an Albion player and he loved showing off on the telly. He began touring the midlands with his 'Jeff Astle Roadshow', which included him singing, sometimes, alarmingly, done up as Tina Turner, telling gags, and doing a question-and-answer session. Audiences would vary between Albion fans to whom he had always been a cult-hero, and *Fantasy Football* fans to whom he had quickly become one. I know it was a success because my niece, Helen, went to see him and he charged her fifty pence for an autograph!

When Jeff retired from football, he started up an industrial window-cleaning business. When we went to his house to film that day, he had his company van on the drive. On the side it said, 'Jeff Astle never misses the corners'. Up until *Fantasy Football*, non-Albion fans had known Jeff only as the bloke who had missed a sitter against Brazil in the 1970 World Cup. Suddenly, he'd become a TV star.

Hold that thought, I'm about to change the subject completely. I'm writing this in my tenth-floor two-bedroom flat in Birmingham. It's what I like to call Mirrorlands, because I bought it with the money I made from writing a weekly football column for the *Daily Mirror*, a few years ago. It's June 3rd, a sunny day, and in the distance I can hear a brass band playing in the Birmingham Botanical Gardens. As I write, they are banging out a chirpy, rom-pom-pom version of 'Born

Free'. No doubt, those bandsmen can see the smiling, appreciative faces of the assembled punters around the bandstand, but none of them could know that, half a mile away and a hundred feet from ground-level, their music is making me think of African tits and schoolboy hard-ons. I'm sure some of them would be appalled by this news. Still, on this occasion, where there's brass, there's muck.

Anyway, I sometimes worried about Jeff. He would drive down with Lorayne, from Burton-on-Trent, on a recording day, and have to spend quite some time getting his knee-joints operational again. Footballers were often injected with cortisone, in the sixties and seventies, so that they could play through the pain of an injury. The more important the player, the more desperately the club wanted him to play, so Jeff had played through a lot of pain for the good of the Albion. But now the damage was starting to show. Also, a TV show, especially the 1998 World Cup series, which was three or four live shows a week, can be a stressful business. Jeff was expected to learn and perform jokes, songs, and even sketches, that would have thrown a lot of much more experienced performers.

On one occasion, Jeff had to deliver the line 'Thanks for letting me stay in your flat, Frank.' He couldn't get it and the floor manager threw a bit of a wobbly, which was very much not on. This rattled Jeff, and when I took my cue, walked on, and faced him for the next take, he looked at me forlornly for what seemed like an age. I was willing him to do the line and get it right. At last, he spoke. 'Thanks, flat,' he said with a terrible tone of world-weariness. I wanted to hug him. Should I be putting the old war-horse through all this? I know Dave and me dressed up and made fools of ourselves but we didn't really have any dignity to preserve. I had a few guilty moments when I wondered if we were making him look foolish. Well, obviously, we were making him look foolish, but was that bad? Can you still look up to an old war-horse if he's dressed as Tina Turner? The thing was, apart from the fact he was well-paid, famous, and touring a spin-off show, he just loved doing it. Jeff didn't give a shit about dressing-up, and when he murdered a song, he treated it like missing a goal-chance: he'd get the next one.

Offstage Jeff could be a bit of a handful. He was big and strong and would arrive in the canteen keen to tell gags and stories from his week. He would accompany these with a series of digs in the ribs, slaps on the back and bear-hugs, that were very much the habits of a man who didn't know his own strength. But he was a lovable bloke and I could forgive him the odd bruise. Through it all, whether he was dressed as a giant parrot or singing the worst-ever version of Michael Jackson's 'Earthsong', I would occasionally look at him and think of when he would raise both arms to the Brummie Road after yet another goal, or when I would wait with the other kids after training to try and get his autograph (free in those days), or when I kissed my TV screen back in '68. I was really upset when an Albion fan said to me that I had made a mockery of his hero. He was my hero as well, and he'd become a hero because he was fearless and he loved to entertain, and those same qualities had made him a comedy hero on *Fantasy Football*.

So, Jeff and me became mates. He gave me one of his World Cup shirts (imagine how much that meant to me), I was godfather to his granddaughter, Taylar, and I went with him on that trip to Portsmouth.

Albion needed to win at Portsmouth to avoid relegation to Division Two. We won 1–0 and all was well. After the game, Jeff took me to meet his old mate, the then-Portsmouth manager, Jim Smith. Smith, or Bald Eagle, as he was known, sat at his desk, drinking neat whisky and smoking a fat cigar. At the side of his desk was a metal waste-paper basket, and all it contained was about two hundred cigar-butts. We chatted a while and then Jeff and me left the ground. Our hotel was a couple of miles away and I was preparing to walk when Jeff suddenly strode into the middle of the road. A mini-van screeched to a halt and Jeff went over. He had noticed a couple of Albion scarves hanging out of the windows and knew he would be greeted with enthusiasm. 'Can you give me and Frank a lift?' he asked. Of course they said yes, and pretty soon we were on our way with 'Astle's in our van' belting out through the open windows. Back at the hotel, Jeff explained that he often did this and it never failed. This, then, is how Jeff Astle introduced me to Celebrity Hitch-hiking. I told Dave this story, and a few months later we tried it after an England game and it worked a treat, right to our doorstep. Obviously, we risked kidnapping or worse, but a taxi would have been about twenty quid so Dave thought the risk was worth taking.

Jeff and me had a few games of pool at that Portsmouth hotel before heading back to our respective homes. As Jeff played one shot, I heard him gently singing to himself, 'Astle's in our van. Astle's in our van.'

I went to the *Pearl Harbor* premiere on Wednesday night. I wore a shirt with pictures of Japanese warriors on it. As an Albion fan, I am always instinctively drawn to the underdog. I went with a friend, Marino, because Caroline and me had had a big row. In fact, I'm probably the only person who went to the *Pearl Harbor* premiere for a bit of peace and quiet. The invite suggested a dress code of 'Military chic' but I thought the samurai shirt would have to do. Marino had suggested that I wore one of those comedy aeroplane costumes, y'know, with a child-size plane that hangs around your waist, held up by heavy-duty braces. I could, he said, paint it up in Japanese colours and top off the outfit with a kamikaze headband. I explained that I was not going to get big, awkward equipment specially made and then be weighed down and uncomfortable all night, just so I could get my picture in the papers. Who did he think I was? Jordan?

These premiere things always follow the same format. I step out of a Merc, straight on to the red carpet, and the crowds who have hung around for hours to see the stars shout 'Frank. Frank.' But in a way that says 'It's quite nice to see you, but none of us could honestly use the word "excited".' I sign enough autographs to keep up my 'man of the people' club membership. Then it's over to the banks of paparazzi where I try to come up with a pose that will get me in the papers. I go for military salute. I think this is not bad. Those of us who don't have big tits have to try mildly tragic ploys like amusing shirts and relevant hand gestures. Then, of course, there are proper big stars who just . . . well, turn up. Anyway, the salute made it into the *Sun* the next day on the same page as David Baddiel, who arrived separately from me. And yes, he was doing a fucking military salute as well. I should have gone with the plane.

Unlike most of the people I spoke to, I really liked the movie. Mind you, I was raised on John Wayne movies so I like my military history *au gratin*. There seemed to be a John Wayne film on telly every week in the seventies. My dad would often come in, a bit worse for wear, on a Sunday afternoon, and, after flicking through the channels, repeat for the ten millionth time his theory that ITV was 'owned by John Wayne and Derby County'.

I explained to an interviewer after the film that, out of sheer frustration, the Japanese often bombed places they couldn't pronounce. I think she believed me until I mentioned their 1956 attack on Rhyl.

As always at these events, the after-show party had a special VIP section with security men vetting all who entered. Crap as it may seem, I still get a slight thrill when these people recognise me and usher me in with a polite greeting. The exclusive VIP bar is based on the profoundly inaccurate theory that celebrities don't like being stared at. Instead, we all stand in there and stare at each other. Kate Beckinsale, who stars in the film, was there and so was Josh Hartnett. These two form a sort of a love-triangle thing with Ben Affleck in the movie. Josh Hartnett was doing that 'I'll just skulk about unnoticed' thing that celebrities do to make sure they get noticed. I've done it myself, not at a big do like this or I'd just get, well, unnoticed, but I've made it work in Budgens in Belsize Park. Just in case this approach failed, Josh had decided to top off his smart trousers and white shirt with a dark-green woollen hat. This, of course, forced me to completely dismiss him as a human being. Still, he's young. And American.

Caroline e-mailed me the next day to remind me that she was interviewing Kate Beckinsale for her radio show and, as I was too spiteful to take her to the premiere, did anything happen there that it might be good to ask Kate about. I suggested that it might be worth asking her who she would choose if she was in a real love triangle with Josh Hartnett and Ben Affleck. And then to point out that if she chose Hartnett, they'd probably be known as Josh and Becks. I told her she could use this. No greater love hath any man than to give his bird one of his gags. And I managed to do it in a holier-than-thou, 'I'm not one to bear a grudge' way that gave me great satisfaction. She phoned me later to say that Kate had laughed at the gag and described it as 'very original'. I was chuffed. I know that sounds a bit pathetic, but I was worried because I don't often send my gags out into the big wide world on their own. And besides, gags are like children to me and we always like it if people say something nice about our children.

The next day, I got a call from Caroline, during which she happened to say that her producer had cut the gag from her interview because he said it was 'not relevant'. I carefully explained to her that although in this case it was almost certainly an error, even I have sometimes cut gags if they've felt out of place or tacked on. I'll bet I've cut at least three in the last fourteen years. She then mentioned that he had said the gag was 'not funny'. I carefully explained to her that there are a lot of people in positions of power in the media who know fuck all about anything and who should keep their dog-shit opinions to their stupid selves. I asked her if it would have been appropriate to give him a really hard slap in the face. This, I suggested, might have brought him to his senses. Of course, I wanted to scream, 'I bet you fucked up the delivery, you stupid cow,' but I feared it could have been seen as unsupportive. I could tell that she thought I was over-reacting. Maybe you do as well, but what else would you expect from the man who left in the 'where there's brass, there's muck' gag.

I'm going to break off from the story here to explain that this was actually the second time I have written the *Pearl Harbor* section. Last night, I pressed the wrong button on my computer and lost that section and the one after it. It was about two and a half thousand words in total. Having spent a whole morning trying to get it all back by technical wizardry, I have now been reduced to writing the whole thing again, from memory. I ask you to spare a thought for any jokes or wise words that I forgot and are thus lost forever.

Of course, being a Catholic, my first thought when the two

sections disappeared was that it was an act of God. I'm serious. Maybe it's the 'moving in mysterious ways' thing that he does sometimes. I might have actually had a gag deliberately cut by God for some reason that is beyond my mortal comprehension. What a thought. Still, I'm glad he left the Jordan one in. I can't say I would have returned the favour with his Jordan gag, 'So Lot chose for himself all the Jordan Valley, and Lot journeyed east, and thus they separated from each other.' (Gen. 13:11.) It's got potential, but I do feel it needs a bit of work.

In 1968, I left St. Hubert's to go to Oldbury Technical School. Technical schools were a sort of halfway house between secondary modern and grammar schools, aimed at slightly brighter working-class kids who might, with a bit of encouragement, progress on to lower management or even, if they were lucky, the Civil Service. At Oldbury Tech, we wore chocolate-brown blazers and brown and gold striped ties. It was the first time I'd had a school uniform and I quite liked the group-identity it gave us. Only a handful of the first years had come with me from St. Hubert's but I made new friends pretty quickly. There was also a big kid who I knew because he lived near me. I say 'kid' but he was in the lower-sixth and would have been seventeen. He was a big, solid bloke with greasy black hair, and he used to walk home most nights with me and a bunch of other first years. It was quite handy to walk home with a big kid because we would often get trouble from the pupils from Bristnall, the local secondary modern, who resented our technical school status, such as it was. We, in turn, would ambush the kids from Oldbury Grammar for similar reasons. It's odd that the Bristnall kids were invariably harder than us, and we were invariably harder than the Grammar kids. Thus, brains and brawn are dished out, but only the very fortunate get both. I'm trying to think of an example of this rare combination but I can't.

One day, the big kid asked me if I'd ever played billiards. I said I'd seen it on the telly a couple of times but I didn't know the rules. He said that he had a billiard table in his house and would teach me to play. I was really impressed by this because most council houses were pretty poky and I'd never been in one big enough to house a billiard table before. So, a couple of nights later, I went back to the big kid's house after school. As we stepped through the door, I noticed that the house was pretty messy and smelt quite bad. I could hear his family in a downstairs room but he went straight upstairs without saying hello or announcing that he was home. I saw this as a sign of adulthood, and was quite impressed by the idea of being able to come and go as you pleased without having to 'clock-in'. I was also very pleased that their house smelt worse than ours.

We got into the big kid's room, and he gestured towards his billiard table. It was about two feet by three. I looked at the sad, battered little table and felt a bit let down. He could see I was disappointed and passed me a big blue *Encyclopedia of Sport* from a grubby bookcase. I laid it on the billiard table (opened flat it was almost the same size), and began flicking through. Then he asked me if I ever watched 'the wrestling' on the telly. I got excited and started going on about Les Kellett but he didn't really seem interested. He asked me if I knew a wrestling hold known as 'the grapevine'. It rang a bell, but I couldn't describe it so he offered to demonstrate. I was standing at the side of the billiard table and he stood behind me and grabbed the shoulders of my chocolate-brown blazer. I hadn't said I wanted him to demonstrate it and now I felt like I was being bullied. He intertwined his right leg around mine and I could feel his bodyweight bearing down on me. Then he started moving up and down, with his crotch against my bum. He was hurting me and I was frightened by the sound of his breathing getting heavier. Suddenly, I broke free, blurted out 'I gotta go' and headed for the door. I don't know if he followed me. I didn't look back. I virtually jumped down the stairs. I think my feet only touched about three on the way down. I hit the ground, fumbled the front door open, and didn't stop running till I got home.

I can't imagine why God would have made me write that twice.

When I got home, I didn't tell anyone what had happened. I guess there were two main reasons for this. Firstly, my dad, Terry and/or Keith would have killed him if they knew. I don't mean as in 'beaten up', I mean as in 'put in the ground'. I didn't care about him, but I didn't want them to get into trouble.

Secondly, despite the fact that I've ended up as a risqué comedian, my dad could be quite puritanical and we had to mind our language and our subject matter around the house. There was no swearing, not even 'bloody', unless my dad forgot himself in drink, and we weren't allowed to watch naughty stuff on the telly. (Our Nora will love that bit.) Once, in order to watch *The Benny Hill Show*, which was always the big talking-point at school the next day, I had to persuade my dad that Benny Hill was Catholic so he'd feel guilty about switching him off. I remember one terrible occasion when the comedian Marty Feldman did a sketch in which he played a dad telling his son the facts of life. As the sketch developed, getting more and more detailed, the tension in our kitchen got worse and worse. (We lived in the kitchen, remember?) My dad had missed his opportunity to switch the telly off early on and nip things in the bud, and now, switching it off would have left us in a terrible post-squirm void. The sketch had taken over. Marty Feldman was oppressing us in our own home. My mom and dad kept asking me to pass them things and how my day had been and how school was going. We were all totally aware of what was going on but no one could face mentioning it. I wonder how many times my own cheeky TV routines have put respectable families in a similar predicament.

Years later, I was reminded of that terrible Marty Feldman night. My brother Terry liked a gadget and was always at the forefront of modern technology. For example, he was the first person in our family to have a colour telly. I remember walking the three or four miles to his house to watch Albion's Asa Hartford play for Scotland in living colour. When I got there, there was a power-cut and Terry's whole street was plunged into darkness, so I walked home again, not having seen a ball kicked. As I trudged dejectedly down the gloomy streets, I felt I had been punished for wanting to watch the match in colour when we had a perfectly adequate black-and-white telly at home, punished for over-reaching myself. I was as Milton's Lucifer, though I doubt that I made the analogy at the time.

Terry was also the first person in our family to own a video recorder, and the first to go away for an annual holiday. These firsts, however, conspired against him because he was worried about leaving his VCR unattended for a week while he was away. I have to say, it would have been a pretty burly intruder who made off with it. VCRs were still in their infancy and Terry's was about the size of a small bungalow. Anyway, he managed to haul it on to a bus and brought it round to my mom and dad's house. He gave me a crash course in how to operate the mighty brute and then shot off on his hols. My mom and dad weren't exactly at the cutting edge of technology – they were still fighting family pressure to install a telephone – so I became Mr Video-Entertainment. I told them to sit down and I'd go and get them a good film. I toddled off to the only video shop in the area and came back with *On Golden*

Pond. My mom liked a weepie and I knew this would fit the bill because a friend who, years later, confessed that he was homosexual told me he had been shushed for sobbing out loud while watching it at a local cinema. My mom judged a film by how many tissues she got through while she was watching it. I used the same criterion, but for films of a very different nature. Anyway, they loved *On Golden Pond* and I promised to get them something similar the next day.

I had heard that *Sophie's Choice*, with Meryl Streep, was a real tear-jerker so that was the next main feature. Now, I can't face going back to *Sophie's Choice* to check actual quotes, but the following description is as accurate as it needs to be for the purposes of the story. I sat down with my mom and dad that night, and the film began. Early on there was a scene where a young girl was chatting to a young bloke about her various interests. She said, 'You know, what I like best of all is fucking.' I froze. She couldn't possibly have said that, could she? My mom and dad were staring at the screen, unblinkingly, so I presumed I must have misheard. The young girl went on, 'Do you like fucking? I could just fuck all day, couldn't you?' I realised that I was now standing up.

'I'm sorry,' I said, 'I can't cope with this,' and walked past my poor parents who were still staring, transfixed, at the screen. I walked upstairs and sat, shaken, on the edge of the bed. After a few minutes, there was a knock at the door. It was my mom.

'Can you come downstairs?' she said.

'No, I don't want to,' I replied. I could clearly hear the word 'fucking', in an American accent, coming from below.

She said, with a tone of pleading in her voice, 'Your dad doesn't know how to switch it off.' I walked past her and downstairs where Dad was wrestling with the massive bulk of the VCR, while it verbally abused him at his very fireside.

I switched it off and my mom made tea. None of us spoke much. The VCR stayed dormant till Terry, with a slight tan, came and took it away. By the way, I was twenty-six at the time.

When I was in my mid-teens, I knew a few pubs where the landlord would turn a blind eye to my obvious youth, and one Friday night, myself and six school-friends sat drinking in just such a place. We could get drunk on about three pints so conversation would soon get candid, and occasionally reckless. A close friend of mine began to look as if he had something important to say. 'Listen,' he began, 'do you remember that kid in the lower-sixth with the greasy black hair? Well, one day he asked me if I could play billiards . . .' He went on to describe a very similar experience to my own. I decided I would tell my story as well. I'd never told a living soul what had happened. Then, before I could begin, another friend began explaining how the big kid had done a similar thing to him. In the end, it turned out that six of the seven lads at the table had been to see the sad little billiard table in the smelly little house. We laughed at our seventh friend and said it must be bad if even the big kid didn't fancy him, but I knew it had been an important night for us six. It was a bit like the erection discovery in St. Hubert's library. Not so joyous, of course, but it was really good to be able to talk about it at last, and we were all relieved to get it off our chests. We'd all remained silent since the incidents took place.

A few years later I went to a non-conformist church with a friend of mine. Standing at the door when I arrived was the big kid, handing out bibles. He looked me in the eye briefly, and then looked away. I said nothing. I still can't play billiards.

Y'know, I think that was better than the first version.

*

As you may have gathered from my brass-band digression, I've come to Birmingham to write this book. I've got a cute little two-bedroom flat with a nice view and it's good to be back home. I went to Mass at the Birmingham Oratory on Sunday. I've got a soft spot for the Oratory. It's a really beautiful church (Oh, no. The funnyman's getting all weirdo Catholic again) and it's associated with two top-notch celebrity Catholics from the nineteenth century, Cardinal Newman and Gerard Manley Hopkins. Newman was a real cracker because he was one of the country's top Protestants, then he converted to Catholicism. Nice one. Hopkins was a poet who I like a lot but we won't dwell on it or I'll start to sound like a big ponce.

Anyway, that's them summed up. It's very traditional, the Oratory. The priest, I noticed, stood with his back to the congregation, which is something I haven't seen since I was a kid. It died out in the sixties because people felt it was a bit alienating for the ordinary worshippers, but I quite enjoyed it on Sunday. Having the priest at the front of the church, facing in the same direction as us, made me feel like I was part of a team. It felt like we were playing one up front. The priest, who admittedly looked about eighty, was our star striker and it was our job to make sure he got the service he needed. Then I thought that him talking with his back to us was like he was a taxi-driver, driving his fares to heaven. Then I thought I'd better stop thinking of what the priest reminded me of and start concentrating on what he was saying, but this wasn't easy because the old fool had got his back to me.

Actually, I once saw this same priest on a documentary about Catholics and he came over as a bit of a right-winger. I like my priests a bit more on the liberal side, a bit more approachable. My parish priest in London came up to me during the BBC twenty-million-quid furore and whispered, 'Don't let the buggers grind you down.' I can't imagine the

Oratory priest using the word 'buggers' unless it was in between 'all' and 'will rot in hell'. My London priest is also, it seems, quite a heavy smoker and, at the beginning of Lent, he gave a sermon, the gist of which was don't give up something if you will become irritable without it, because then those around you will be doing the penance instead of you. That got him off the hook.

I used to go to a smaller local church in Birmingham called St. Mary's, but I got married there and I'm always plagued by a desire to turn to the congregation halfway through the Mass and shout, 'Why didn't you stop me?' And what would that achieve? People don't like shouting in church. I once went to a Mass in Tottenham, and when the priest was giving Holy Communion this big bald bloke suddenly upturned the dish containing the eucharist – y'know, those little round wafers – and then ran off down the aisle shouting about 'Cranmer in the Flames'. (Just trust me, will you?) As he disappeared out of the back doors, I noticed a couple of burly, Irish-looking blokes go out after him, looking as if they were in the mood for a fairly physical theological discussion.

At the Oratory I bumped into a bloke called Eamonn who used to teach me when I did teacher training. (We'll get there, don't worry.) He used to go to St. Mary's but he explained to me that he had stopped because they had begun to incorporate an accordionist into the services. Sounds like I got out just in time. I knew those acoustic guitars were the thin end of the wedge.

After the service, a very respectable-looking Irish lady took me by the hand as I chatted to Eamonn, and said, 'I love your shows.' She said she watched them all and taped them and sent the tapes to her daughter in Belfast who, she explained, is a psychologist. I found this slightly unnerving, but the Irish lady was very nice and asked me if I might speak at a function to raise money for the Grand Order of Baby Sitters, which is a group that takes sick children to Lourdes. I'll sort something out but I probably won't speak at the function because, to be honest, as you may have already gleaned from this book, and if you haven't, you will, I'm not really a very good Catholic. As well as all the usual sinning stuff, I'm also a divorced Catholic.

So, as far as the Church is concerned, any sexual intercourse I have that isn't with my ex-wife is adulterous, even if I married the woman involved. In fact, that would probably be even worse. The only way a divorced Catholic can satisfy the Church's rules is to remain celibate. I have to admit I haven't done that. I mean, for goodness' sake, the Oratory priest has been on the telly. He must know what the temptations are like. A priest in London once told me he was allowed to forgive me if I'd murdered my wife, but he wasn't allowed to forgive me for divorcing her. Thus, I live my life as a hypocrite. I love the Catholic Church, with all its faults, but it's not too keen on me. Oh, well, you gotta have rules. As someone once said, 'Hypocrisy is the homage that vice pays to virtue.'

I was in a Catholic church in California shortly after Hugh Grant was caught with a receiver of swollen goods. The priest did a whole sermon about the loose morals of 'the Englishman, Hugh Grant' and so, when I got back to England, I phoned Hugh Grant up. I'd met him once when I had been in goal in a charity football match and he'd scored two goals past me. Someone I knew had his number so I rang it. He didn't seem at all bothered by me calling him out of the blue, and described how he could see a group of paparazzi outside his flat through a chink in the curtains. I told him, in some detail, how he had been the subject of a sermon in a Catholic church in California. He seemed quite flattered. I asked him to do my chat show, he said no, and then we said goodbye. There was a time, I'll admit it, when I was too embarrassed to admit that I went to church. Now I'm phoning up film stars to tell them about it.

As I was leaving the Oratory, a young lad approached me and asked if he could have my autograph. I said he could, but not until we got outside the church. As I explained, 'It's not really my gig.'

A question that often crops up in interviews, at dinner parties, or in pubs, is 'What's the first record you ever bought?' Well, I'll tell you, mine was 'Back Home' by the 1970 England World Cup squad. It was in a blue paper sleeve and the label looked like a football. The following week it got to number one in the charts. Now I'm fully aware that, in this book, there have been several 'who'd have thought?' moments. Who'd have thought I'd have been on that telly like my dad predicted? Who'd have thought I'd be the godfather to my boyhood-hero's granddaughter? Who'd have thought I would have lost my virginity to a prostitute called Corky? Oh, sorry. I haven't told you that one yet. But you must admit this one will take some beating. Who'd have thought, when I bought that single by the England football team in 1970, that I'd be writing and singing a number one record for the England football team twenty-six years later? Well, no one, obviously. I, or rather Ian Broudie, David Baddiel and I, even brought out a second version for the World Cup of 1998. Yes, the World Cup, the same event that inspired 'Back Home', and that went to number one as well.

So, having now become positively devil-may-care about rhetorical questions: how did it happen? Well, it was like this. The Football Association contacted Ian Broudie at the beginning of 1996, to see if he'd be interested in writing and performing the official England song for the forthcoming

European Football Championships, or Euro '96 as it was better known. Ian was the voice of, and the brains behind, the Lightning Seeds, one of the country's top Indie bands, and had written a song called 'Life of Riley', which was regularly used as background music for the goals round-up on *Match of the Day*, so there was logic to the FA's choice and Ian was keen.

There was a time when football songs were automatically seen as naff, but New Order's 'World in Motion', England's official song for the 1990 World Cup, had shown that it was possible to write a football song that was classy. Ian, perhaps the most modest pop star ever, was unsure as to whether he could write a football-based lyric – he tended to specialise in bitter-sweet love songs at the time – so he suggested a collaboration with Dave Baddiel and me. Now, whereas the FA's choice of Ian was fairly logical, Ian's choice of us was a bit of a wild-card. He was a fan of *Fantasy Football* so knew we were football obsessives, and he knew we could write gags, but what lyric-writing we did on the show didn't really suggest we could write what one tabloid later described as 'the new national anthem'.

Perhaps our most elaborate lyric appeared on the first *Fantasy Football* video, when we parodied Dean Friedman's seventies hit, 'Lucky Star'. Our version was all about our co-star, Statto. We had written the character of Statto, a football-mad statistics bore, before *Fantasy Football* began, but we couldn't find anyone suitable to play him. A few days before the series kicked off, our producer, Andy Jacobs, said that he had met a bloke called Angus Loughran, who did commentary on the first-half highlights package that they showed at half time on the big screen at Arsenal. Andy said that this bloke *was* Statto, no acting required, and it would be well worth us meeting him.

We met him at lunchtime on the day of our first-ever

Fantasy Football League recording, and he did the show that night. The great magic of Statto (I always think of him as Statto, rather than Angus) was, like Jeff Astle, he had no idea how funny he could be without even trying. Statto was like no one I had ever met. He was the son of the famous classical music conductor Sir James Loughran, and was educated at Ampleforth, the country's top Roman Catholic public school. I met someone who had been with him at Ampleforth and he told me about how one FA Cup Final day, when Manchester United were in the final, Angus, a massive Man U fan, was locked in a cupboard by some other boys so he couldn't watch the match. Thus began, for Angus, a theme of football and bullying which Dave and me continued on *Fantasy Football*. I love Statto. He is a very generous, interesting and entertaining bloke and great company at dinner, only partly because he always insists on paying. But he is, in the nicest possible way, a bit odd. He spends his whole life watching and betting on sport, and will fly anywhere in the world at the drop of a hat in order to do so. We would always rib him about being weird, not having a girlfriend and not seeing personal hygiene as a priority, but he didn't care and he never changed. Now he's a very successful journalist and presenter of horse-racing on the TV, but he'll always be Statto to me.

In order to parody 'Lucky Star', we had to send the lyrics to Dean Friedman for his approval. What sense he made of them, I'll never know. The song began,

> We get letters everyday
> Saying 'Who's that man?
> Is he mental? Is he gay?
> Is he David's gran?
> Is he king of all the spacks?'
> People write in, demanding to know the facts.

163

Whether this convinced Ian Broudie of our lyrical skills I'm not sure, but the FA went along with his suggestion and we were approached to write the words to the Official England Song for Euro '96.

I went up to meet Ian at the Liverpool–Leeds United game at Anfield. David couldn't make it because Chelsea were playing at home that night. He supports Chelsea. (Incidentally, I used to do this gag, 'Me and a bunch of mates went up Chelsea last weekend. Bill Clinton was furious!') After the game, the two of us went back to a dingy little room in a recording studio to talk about the song. Ian played me a melody that he had had kicking around for a while and never put a lyric to. I told him that, as far as Dave and me were concerned, the only idea we'd had was that we liked the slogan on the posters for Euro '96, 'Football Comes Home'. Ian played the chorus of his melody and we agreed it was good but that 'It's coming home' or 'Football's coming home' would scan better than the wording on the poster. Finally, Ian played the guitar and I la-la-la-ed along and I took a tape of that back to play to Dave. Dave and me were new to this sort of thing, but we agreed that the best way to write the song was to say what we really felt about watching England play, and then try and turn that honest reaction into song lyrics. These were our thoughts. We loved the England football team. We were constantly disappointed by their failures. We had seen enough brilliant things from them to feel optimistic about the future. We were sick of hearing people slagging them off. A major football tournament in England, the first since the World Cup of 1966, might just wake up some of the old 1966 spirit in the players and the supporters. We were also very keen to include a reference to a quote by Kevin Keegan when he talked about how proud he felt to play with the three lions on his chest, a reference of course to the badge on his England shirt. We also liked the idea of suggesting the spirit of '66 by a reference to the Jules Rimet trophy. That was the actual trophy, designed by Frenchman Jules Rimet, that England won in 1966. It has since had to be replaced because Brazil kept it for good after winning it three times. A lasting image of that England victory in '66 was the sun catching the trophy as Bobby Moore, sitting on the shoulders of his team-mates, held it high above his head. So we wrote the first verse and chorus.

> Everyone seems to know the score.
> They've seen it all before.
> They just know. They're so sure
> That England's gonna throw it away,
> Gonna blow it away.
> They don't know how to play
> But I remember
>
> Three lions on a shirt
> Jules Rimet still gleaming
> Thirty years of hurt
> Never stopped me dreaming.

The FA later insisted that we change the sixth line to 'But I know they can play' because they didn't want the first verse to be 'wholly negative'.

The second verse continued the theme of disappointment and hope, but this time referred directly to some actual incidents in England games:

> But I still see that tackle by Moore
> And when Lineker scored.
> Terry Butcher at war
> And Nobby, dancing.

165

The 'Terry Butcher at war' line referred to the night England centre-half Terry Butcher got his head split open in a game against Sweden, but insisted on playing on despite the fact he was absolutely soaked in his own blood. We thought this was a brilliant image of English fighting spirit and determination. The FA didn't. They said that any reference to being 'at war' was a definite no-no because, they said, it conjured up images of football hooliganism, the last thing they wanted to think about with Euro '96 approaching. So the line became 'Bobby belting the ball', a reference to a Bobby Charlton goal against Mexico in 1966. Anyway, an added undercurrent of 'Football's coming home' and we were all done. Oh, and a title. We liked 'Three Lions'.

There was still some tinkering with the lyrics in the recording studio. A middle eight lyric was added at Ian's suggestion, and he also contributed to the 'It's coming home. It's coming home. It's coming. Football's coming home' bit. Dave and me were quite keen on just sticking with 'It's coming home' but Ian was very keen that the word 'football' should be in there somewhere. Not a bad suggestion. We recorded the song with all three of us sharing the vocals, and everyone was very pleased with the results. I went through a brief period of thinking it was shit about halfway through the recording process, but that was just me being a bit moody. Everyone was saying it would be a certain number one, but I imagined that people said that after every recording session.

The record was all done and dusted, but then we had to really lay our balls on the chopping-block. The FA asked us if we'd be kind enough to go to Bisham Abbey, the England training camp, and play the song to the England team. Shit. When Ian, Dave and me turned up, the players were having lunch. We had a ghetto-blaster and a tape of the song and we mumbled that we'd play it to them when they'd finished eating. But Paul Gascoigne couldn't wait. He got up from his meal and started trying to operate the ghetto-blaster, very much in the style of a man who had never seen one before. He looked like my dad with the VCR. But it WAS Gazza, so we gave in and agreed to play the song.

I stood up and gave a short speech about the song. Dave and me were worried they might take the negative element of the lyrics the wrong way, and I made it clear that we three were big England fans and were very confident about Euro '96. I explained some of the ideas behind the song and how it had come about. Anyone who knows any modern-day footballers, especially at the top level, will not be surprised to hear that the players actually didn't give a fuck either way. We played the song and they carried on eating. Then we played it again. Then we thanked them and went away. Our next stop was the manager, Terry Venables. We played him the tape in a gloomy, empty lounge area in the hotel, and as he listened, he tapped along with his car-keys on the plastic table-top next to his chair. At the end of the song, he looked up and smiled. 'It's a real key-tapper, isn't it?' he said. Compared to the players' response, it was virtually hysteria.

Then the players were asked about taking part in the video for the song. With a few exceptions, the general reaction was they'd do it, but only if they absolutely had to as part of their sponsorship commitments, and that they'd rather get off home straight away, and couldn't they just sign some more footballs instead. As it turned out, Stuart Pearce, Robbie Fowler, Steve Stone and Teddy Sheringham were absolute stars, and the video looked great. Ian, Dave and me, however, all looked like fat bastards and all three of us went on diets and lost loads of weight afterwards, but the horse had already bolted as far as the video was concerned.

So that was it. We were doing some *Fantasy Football Euro*

'96 specials in a few weeks' time, so I went off to America for a quick holiday. I checked into The Royalton Hotel in New York with my girlfriend of the time, and started to unpack. There was a big bunch of flowers in a vase on the table when we arrived, but this is quite common in fancy hotels. After a while, my girlfriend said, 'Have you noticed that there's a card with these flowers?'

'It's probably one of those "We hope you'll enjoy your stay" cards,' I called from the bathroom. 'It says, "To Frank",' she said. I walked out of the bathroom, opened the envelope and read the card, 'Record straight in at Number One. 55,000 units sold. Jon.' I'd dreamt of having a number one record ever since my first love, Annette, back at Moat Farm, had chosen the kid who did Freddie and the Dreamers impressions. I couldn't get in the choir at St. Hubert's, I'd pissed about in amateur bands but this was it. Number one. Mind you, I wish Jon could have found a slightly more romantic way of telling me than '55,000 units sold'. It sounded like we were selling dishwashers. The following week we were knocked off the top spot by the Fugees doing 'Killing me Softly'. The week after that, we knocked the Fugees off the top spot and went back to numero uno. A few years later, I was lying in bed with Caroline and she told me that she'd been chatted up by Wyclef Jean, the Fugees main man, but turned him down. 'Two–nil to me then,' I said.

So, when Euro '96 started, we were number one. They played the song before the opening game against Switzerland and it was great to hear it played at Wembley. 'This is as good as it gets,' I thought. I was wrong. The second game was against Scotland. I had been quoted in the paper that week, saying that we had written Scotland's next World Cup song. 'It's called Three Games,' I said, so I didn't hang around outside the ground too much. As for the game, we weren't playing too good and, eventually, Scotland got a penalty. Dave and me, sitting just in front of the press box, watched as Gary McAllister stepped up to take it. If he'd scored, England would probably have crumbled and Euro '96, 'Three Lions' and failure would have been lumped together in the collective English consciousness forever. But he missed, or rather David Seaman saved it, and soon Gazza was up the other end scoring a classic and England were on their way.

Then it happened. The whistle went and the players did their usual thing of walking around, shaking hands and swapping shirts. The English fans applauded loudly. They were ecstatic. And the guy who plays the music at Wembley had a brainwave. Why not stick 'Three Lions' on. That weird crowd bit at the beginning kicked in, actually a recording of the Brondsby fans at Anfield done by Ian Broudie on a tiny cassette recorder, and then the piano, the French horn, those samples of commentary, and then the voices, 'It's coming home. It's coming home. It's coming. Football's coming home.' And not just our voices, but also seventy-odd thousand English men, women and children waving their flags of St. George and singing their hearts out. Shit, I'm crying. I don't mean then, I mean now. I can't tell you how it felt. I'm not a good enough writer.

Had you ever heard a football crowd sing 'Back Home' or 'World in Motion'? Had you, fuck. But they were singing this one like I'd never heard an England crowd sing anything before. To stand in front of the press box, perhaps the best view in Wembley, and see the whole place a mass of swirling flags and smiling faces, and to know it was our song they were singing. If I'd never got lucky and found my way into entertainment, if I'd been sitting in a council house in Birmingham watching Wembley sing someone else's song on a rented telly after we'd just beaten Scotland 2–1, I'd still have been ecstatic. But to be at Wembley and for it to be OUR song . . . Well, anyway, it was special.

I was gushing. Sorry, but it's actually quite difficult to describe the most exciting thing that ever happened to you without gushing a bit. A few days later, England beat Holland 4–1, and the crowd were singing the song throughout, no record required. The following Saturday, we beat Spain. The crowd were belting out the song again, all the flags were waving, the sun was shining, and I remember turning to Dave in what had become our regular spot in front of the press box, and saying, 'Have a good look at this, Dave. This is our perfect summer.'

After the games, we were allowed up into the players' bar and would chat with the lads and their proud parents. The players seemed to like the song a lot better now. I think it had grown on them. Gazza told us they always played it on the team coach on the way to the matches. On one occasion the driver forgot it and Gazza stayed on the coach inside the ground until someone found a tape and played the song to him. I know he's supposed to have an obsessive-compulsive disorder, but I was still chuffed.

On another occasion, David Seaman's lovely girlfriend grabbed me at a do and turned to the big man. 'Go on, David, ask him.' Seamo looked sheepish. 'Ask him,' she insisted.

'Frank,' said the England goalkeeper, in his deep Yorkshire voice, 'who's Jules Rimet?'

And then we played Germany in the semi-final. The *Sun* had dedicated the whole of its front page that day to 'the new National Anthem'. It had a picture of Dave and me in our England shirts, with crosses of St. George painted on our cheeks, roaring with excitement. In between us was the scabbiest stuffed lion I have ever seen. He seemed to have eczema all down the front of his snout, and neither me or Dave wanted to get too close to him in the photo session in case we caught something. Perhaps, looking back, the mangy old lion was a bad omen. The headline said 'Three Lions' and underneath that they printed our lyrics, with a large caption that said, 'Here's the words the whole nation must sing tonight.' And they did, with gusto.

And then Gareth Southgate missed a penalty and Germany scored, and Germany won, and England lost. I just stood there and stared at the pitch. I was so sure we were going to go all the way, so sure that this was our perfect summer. I was shocked and completely gutted. I found out the next day that the BBC cameras had cut to me and Dave at the end of the game, and for weeks afterwards people would come up to me, like people do to the family at a funeral, and say stuff like, 'We know how you felt.' I was so sure we were going to win it. Imagine how they would have sung the song at the final. I have, many a time. Football did come home, but someone had parked a big Audi across the driveway.

I'm going to tell you a few 'Three Lions'-related stories, not because I want to say how great I am, but because I want you to know what it was like for me to be part of this phenomenon. It might be just another football song to you, but no matter what I might achieve in my career, I know there'll never be anything else quite like it for me. Maybe it wasn't my 'perfect' summer, but it was fuckin' close.

A few months after Euro '96, the Lightning Seeds played Shepherd's Bush Empire. The place was packed, and as the band left the stage at the end of their set, the lights went down and the crowd began to sing, 'It's coming home. It's coming home . . .' The band walked back out and Ian said, 'I've got a couple of friends with me tonight.' The crowd went mad and we walked out. We sang the best live version of the song we ever did, and there were a few crosses of St. George in the crowd, just to jog our memories.

Dave and me were at a party at his girlfriend's house one night when someone put 'Three Lions' on very, very loudly. Everyone sang along, also very loudly, and pretty soon the neighbour was at the door to complain. He was obviously pissed off, but when Dave and me opened the door, he stared for a bit and then burst out laughing.

Strangely, the German fans also took the song to their hearts and it got to number seventeen in the German charts. When the German team went home with the trophy and appeared on a balcony overlooking thousands of German supporters, at the official celebration of their European triumph, the team sang 'Three Lions'. In fact, Dave and me were invited to sing the song on German television's *Football Review of the Year* in Frankfurt. We spent a long weekend in Frankfurt, and you don't know what a long weekend is till you've spent one in Frankfurt. We did the show in our red 1966 replica shirts and Uwe Seeler, who played for Germany in that final, came over to us and said, with no hint of light-heartedness, 'I don't like your shirts,' and then hobbled off.

Then we sang the song at the BBC *Sports Review of the Year* for 1996. Dave and me turned up for the rehearsal in the afternoon and then we had time to kill before the real event that evening, so Jimmy Hill, a man we had both watched on the telly since we were kids, invited us back to his hotel room. We ordered chips on room service, took our shoes off, and all three of us sat up on Jimmy's bed with our plates on our laps and watched Chelsea versus Southampton on Sky, with Jimmy doing analysis and expert comment throughout.

Finally, there was a Hillsborough Justice Concert at Anfield. That was the last time I sang 'Three Lions' live. It seemed fitting that it was at Anfield, where Ian and me had gone on that first night, and, would you believe it, Dave couldn't make it this time either, because he was on tour. I sang the song live in front of 35,500 fans, not all that well, if the truth be told. That's because I'm not a particularly good singer. Dave is one of the worst singers I've ever heard. Just think of all the great singers and bands that never had a number one record. It's very unfair, isn't it?

In 1998, we brought out 'Three Lions '98'. Essentially the same song but with different lyrics, and with the '96 Wembley crowd joining in on the 'It's coming home' bit, which always gets the hairs going on the back of my neck. 'Three Lions '98' was at number one for three weeks, and we did *Top of the Pops*, which we missed out on with the original song, and there was another brilliant video with us all looking much slimmer. But, to be honest, I wish we hadn't bothered. Respect to everyone who bought the '98 version, but 'Three Lions' was all about a specific moment in time: one hot summer in '96 when England suddenly started playing like winners again, and the crowd had their own, specially written party piece so they could provide the perfect soundtrack.

I'm on page three of the *Sun* today. A lot of people have had to get their tits out to achieve that, but all I had to do was have an argument with my girlfriend. Well, several arguments with my girlfriend. The headline says, 'Let's be Frank . . . it's over', and then, as a sub-heading, 'Rows split Skinner and lover Caroline'. Now, you may have picked up on the fact that there have been a few problems, but you know I'd have told you if we'd split up. You've become my confidante, for goodness' sake. We do argue, though. You know that thing about 'Jack Spratt would eat no fat, his wife would eat no lean.' It's seen as an image of team-work in a relationship: 'The two of them together, they licked the platter clean.' Nice. The thing is with Caroline and me, if I ate no fat, she'd say, 'Oh, well that's typical of you isn't it? You're too bloody good to eat fat, I suppose. Of course, you couldn't tell me that before I cooked it.' If she ate no lean, I'd be saying, 'I can't fuckin' believe that. You'd eat dog shit rather than agree with me on anything. Still, it's alright for you to eat just fat, I mean you don't have to worry about the health thing, what with your heart being made of granite.' So it goes on.

I remember reading somewhere that the poet Milton believed one should be able to divorce one's wife merely by saying, 'I divorce thee, I divorce thee, I divorce thee.' I wonder if my neighbours thought we were performing a twenty-first-century version of this ritual when Caroline stood in the hallway at nine o'clock on a Saturday morning and shouted, with some fervour, 'Fuck off, fuck off, fuck off.' I once screamed at her, mid-argument, 'Your trouble is the only person you're in love with is Caroline Feraday. In fact, that's the only thing we've got in common.' She continued her point, but I interrupted with 'Oh, come on, you've got to admit, that was a good line.' She nodded her encouragement, as if worried about losing her arguing-momentum, and then carried on and on. Great legs, though.

Oh, come on, my mom and dad fought all the time but they still loved each other. Caroline is a gorgeous, bright, interesting, funny woman. And she can cook. And it was her who suggested that I include the sex-in-the-toilet bit in the 'jamming with the Stones' section. How supportive is that? Our only problem is we can't go twenty-four hours without an argument. I was raised on Andy Capp, what d'you expect?

Incidentally, the article was written by a journo called Dominic Mohan who, it's a small world, also did the first kiss-and-tell thing with my ex-wife. That Dominic, he's been with me, man and boy, through all my trials and tribulations. Maybe he should have written the book. He says in the piece that Caroline has 'decided to move out of Frank's £1 million flat in North London'. Caroline sent me an e-mail this morning that said, 'The people in our block will be thrilled when they read that their flats have trebled in price. But not half as thrilled as they'll be when they hear that I'm moving out.' I wrote back to her to say that when I get back there I expect to find nine 'For Sale' signs and a large pile of industrial ear-plugs by the bins. So we're laughing about it. Her main worry was that she thought she looked a bit rough in the *Sun*'s picture of us. She should have seen the lion.

Anyway, that's how famous I am.

You know how I'm always going on about those butterfly-crushing moments when seemingly innocent things can have massive repercussions? Well, what about this. It could be said that Johnny Cash made me an alcoholic. When I was fourteen, my dad took me to my first-ever gig. It was Johnny Cash at the Birmingham Odeon, with Carl Perkins as support. I was chuffed because both of these were Elvis's work-colleagues at Sun Records, and I really liked Cash's voice. Nowadays, I also like Johnny Cash because, all through my career, I've tried to come up with a catchphrase and I haven't managed to find one since 'saft as a bottle of pop'. Which is alright, but not the sort of thing you could open a chat show with. But then I would have said the same thing about David Frost's 'Hello, good evening and welcome'. You never can tell what's going to catch on, can you? And then, if you do find a catchphrase, what's to stop someone else from nicking it? This is where Johnny Cash's catchphrase, 'Hello, I'm Johnny Cash', comes into its own. Anyway, I'm rambling. I saw Johnny Cash and he was great. I was telling my brother Terry about this and he said that he knew a bloke who did a great Johnny Cash impression, and a particularly fine Roy Orbison one as well. Orbison was another ex-stablemate of The King's, so I was intrigued. This singer performed regularly at a pub in Smethwick. Of course, if it was in a pub, I couldn't go, could I? Terry said that he didn't see why not. I was fourteen and it was about time I 'wet my whistle', but it was probably best not to mention it to our mom and dad.

So, the following week, off we went. We nipped in a pub on the way 'for a quick one', so it was sounding like we were going to have more than one. Blimey! I was a bit nervous but also quite excited about the Johnny Cash man. I wore a black plastic jacket that was pretending to be a black leather jacket, chosen because it looked a bit like the one Elvis wore for his 1968 Comeback Special. My hair was greased back and I could, in dim light, probably pass for about twelve. Terry was twenty-six. I had a brown and mild. Not that I really knew what that meant, but Terry felt that it was quite sweet and would suit my schoolboy palate. I tried to drink it like a man, but the fact that I held the glass with two hands slightly detracted from this. I liked being in a pub, though. Considering I was four years under the legal drinking-age and talking in an unnaturally deep voice, I felt very much at home. It saddens me to write this now. I haven't had a drink since September 24th, 1986, and I've never really managed to find anything to replace it.

Though I've never had an onstage catchphrase, I have many little catchphrases that I use in everyday life. If anyone at work says to me, 'Are you happy with that, Frank?', which they do quite a lot, I always reply, 'I haven't been happy since September 1986.'

I like pubs. If you're a non-drinker, a pub is an alien place. You don't have the right to be there. When I was drinking I used to get seriously pissed-off if I was stuck at the bar behind someone who was dallying over half a Vimto. 'Get out of my way, lightweight,' I'd be thinking or, later in the evening, saying. Still, as Richard the Third said, I go before my horse to market.

In 1971, I was yet to learn all this. We drank up. Terry had had two, and we set off to see the man. Musical entertainment in pubs in the West Midlands, and indeed throughout the country, is, of course, in the main, shit. I saw a guy at Guest, Keen and Nettlefolds Social Club, Smethwick, who was doing karaoke before there was karaoke. He had backing tapes of lots of pop standards and he sang along. He even left gaps so that he could do a bit of banter in between the songs. At one point he said, 'And who could forget the magic of Mr Buddy Holly?' and then sang 'I'm a Believer' by the Monkees, thus answering his own question.

On another occasion, in the late eighties, I went to a club in Birmingham, and a singer came on in a blue velvet suit, red patent-leather shoes and a tight curly perm. He went straight into that old Andy Williams classic that goes 'You're just too good to be true. Can't take my eyes off of you . . .' Now it's a lovely song, but what you have to remember is the bit in the middle, after the big brass riff, that goes 'Oh, pretty baby . . .' and so on. Now, that is a big fucking note, and if you want a hope in hell of hitting it, you have to start the song way down deep to give yourself a bit of a run-up. This guy had started high. I mean, too high. He had nowhere to go. All through the verses, there was a terrible tension in the air. I think the crowd, all white hair and bri-nylon, was genuinely concerned for his welfare. You could hear muttered phrases like 'He'll never make it', 'He's gonna do himself a mischief', and 'Someone should stop it before it's too late'.

Finally, we reached the brass riff. The crowd was on the edge of their seats. I actually saw an old woman cover her mouth with both hands, preparing, I presume, to stifle a scream. Only the man in red patent-leather shoes seemed oblivious to the forthcoming carnage. With rhythmic certainty, like the clock in *High Noon*, the last few blasts of brass were sounded, 'Barum-ba-ba-baaaaaa'. This was it. Suddenly, with no warning, the singer thrust his microphone straight at the terrified crowd, and they, myself included, all bleated out an 'Oh, pretty baby' that would have sent a sharp pain through the ears of dogs some three streets away. And it wasn't even as if it was a gag. I'm sure the singer always thrust out the mike at that point, but with a sense of 'I'm a great showman' rather than a sense of 'Chew on that, you bastards'. Judging by his general demeanour, the thought that he, personally, might not have been able to make that note would never have crossed his mind.

Anyway, Terry and me finally got to the second pub and settled ourselves down near to the tiny stage, with me facing the prospect of my second brown and mild. If truth be told, I would have killed for a dandelion and burdock, but I had a vague sense of 'rites of passage', and I didn't want to let myself down. I guess there was an audience of about twenty people in the room, which quickly became an audience of about seventeen because three of them got on stage and started playing instruments. Despite the fact that the drummer, a fat bloke in a pink shirt, looked as bored as I'd ever seen anybody look, I was getting excited.

Then the Man in Black appeared and made his way to the stage. As he grasped the microphone, he said, in an accent which suggested he came from the same part of America as Little Beaver, 'Hello, I'm Johnny Cash.' One woman called 'Hooray!' and my theory about that catchphrase lay broken and discarded on the empty dance-floor. The band played 'I Walk the Line'. To my ears, I have to say, he sounded pretty good, and his Roy Orbison was even better. I remember being impressed by the fact that he had put on dark glasses for the Orbison section of the show. It was an early lesson in the importance of attention to detail. The seventeen people clapped and cheered throughout and the woman who had shouted 'Hooray' did it again when he growled during 'Pretty Woman'.

After the show, the singer mingled with the crowd, which I thought was a nice gesture but, looking back, was almost certainly an example of someone trying desperately to get laid. Terry called him over at one point and said he had liked the show. 'He's a bit young, isn't he?' the singer said, looking at me. Ignoring this, Terry said, 'He's seen Johnny Cash live.' The singer seemed a little dejected by this news. He looked down at the floor and then back at us. 'I don't know why you brought him here then,' he said, and walked away. This was a lesson even more instructive than the sunglasses: if you meet a big fish in a little pool, never, ever mention the existence of the big pool. It's interesting, isn't it, that at fourteen I'd had my first taste of what it's like to face resentment because, through no fault of my own, I was seen as a representative of a glamorous outside world. I always bring this to mind when I make a guest appearance on Channel Five.

Terry, however, didn't like the singer's attitude. We sat and watched, me on my third pint, Terry on about his seventh, as the big fish danced with a woman who had hair like Harpo Marx. 'I bet he's never had intercourse in his life,' Terry said, a bit too loudly. I took a boy-sized swig from my glass, nodded briefly, and then looked longingly towards a bottle of Tizer behind the bar. 'How are you getting on with women?' Terry said to me. I froze. Maybe he'd forgotten I was fourteen, or, more alarmingly, maybe he had an active sex life when he was fourteen and I was about to prove a terrible disappointment.

I was obsessed with girls but there had been no really close encounters at that stage. Some of the girls at school were very saucy. On one occasion, when me and a couple of mates were sitting at the back desk in the physics lab, four of the girls, sitting at the desk directly in front, spent the whole lesson with their dresses pulled right up their backs so we could see their knickers. It was forty minutes of pure joy.

British Bullsnog was far behind me now. We had a game called the Nervous Test. One of us lads would approach a girl, put our hands on her hips and ask, 'Are you nervous?' The reply was always no. Then the hands would move to the waist, and the question and answer were repeated. Finally, we'd arrive at the breasts, the girl would giggle and push you off. Except on one occasion, when I did the test with a girl called Jayne. When I put my hands on her breasts, she just smiled. We were both thirteen. 'Are you nervous?' I asked.

'No,' she said.

'Oh!' I said. I paused. I'd never got to this stage before and didn't know where the game went from here. What I really needed was a manual. In fact I had two 'manuals' when I got home, but let's not dwell on that. I looked at Jayne and she, still smiling, looked at me. By now, my hands had been on her breasts for about thirty seconds. My finger joints were starting to stiffen. (You can do the next gag yourselves.) 'Are you sure you're not nervous?' I asked.

'No, I'm really not,' she said. And now, finally, I came into my own. But I was wearing dark trousers so no one noticed. No, sorry, look, it's very hard for me (I didn't mean that one) to write about something like this without doing nob-jokes. This, like everything else in the book, is a true story but it's starting to sound like a routine. That might be because a lot of my routines are true as well. However, I'm trying to tell you about Jayne and the nob-jokes are getting in the way. But, a nob-joke to me, as Samuel Johnson said of Shakespeare's compulsion to pun or 'quibble', is the Cleopatra for which I lose my world and am happy to lose it.

Anyway, I looked at Jayne and she looked at me. By now I had been holding her breasts so long I feared I was starting to restrict their growth. I had to do something. If we stood like this much longer, the smaller kids would start climbing on us. She raised her eyebrows, encouraging me to speak. It worked. 'And you're definitely not . . .' She shook her head. 'OK . . . right . . . well, thank you very much.' I released her from my grip and shuffled off. When I looked back, she was still standing there, smiling.

But this kind of stuff would be small beer to Terry and, as far as I could see, SMALL beers were not really his thing. The question was still hanging there. 'Well, y'know . . .' I began.

'The thing with women,' proclaimed Terry who, to my great relief, had interrupted me, 'is that if you're nice to them, they'll treat you like shit.'

'Yeah,' I muttered, 'you can say that again.' And, of course, he did. About seven times. He began to reminisce about his youth. He told me that if he turned up for a date and he was on time, he'd nip off for a drink or just walk around the block, so that the girl was facing the disappointment of him not turning up at all. Then, when he showed his face, she'd be really grateful that he'd made it and be putty in his hands. He would arrange to meet on street corners or outside shops to make the wait that bit more unpleasant for them. He would even, he told me, turn up but hide from the girl, have a real good look at the surrounding area, and then go home. The next day he would track her down (we didn't really mix with people who had phones) and ask her what happened. She'd say she was there, Terry would say he was as well, prove it by describing something significant, and then she, unexpectedly freed from the pain of rejection, would be his for the taking. Terry, I should point out, was much better-looking than me. I nodded sagely throughout, and listened to the master. Then, when the brown and mild made me braver, I switched the conversation to football and I was able to join in and contribute my own opinions.

This was the life, sitting in a pub, drinking too much, and philosophising about women and football. I could get a taste for this. All thanks to Johnny Cash.

I had a chat with the publisher today. He said the book is brilliant and anyone who didn't enjoy reading it must be an idiot. No he didn't. I was just trying to put pressure on you. I think he quite likes it so far and he made a few points which I thought I'd share with you.

Firstly, there's more stuff about my dad than my mom. Well, my mom was the loving, selfless, gentle type, and also, she didn't drink, so I guess if she chose to hang out with a loud, beer-guzzling wildman, she must have been OK with him claiming centre-stage most of the time. Mind you, she could be really funny. I was never sure if it was intentional, but she's had me in tears, many a time. Once, I was doing a crossword in the *Daily Mirror*, and reading the clues out loud. One of them was 'Type of penguin', ten letters. I could see my mom thinking it over. 'Mmmmm . . .' she said, 'I can only think of them black and white 'uns.' I laughed for two days.

Another time, Yung Lung's, the local Chinese takeaway, was robbed by two men. They emptied the till and even made the owner, who was called, unsurprisingly, Yung Lung, empty his pockets. I was reading this story in the *Smethwick Telephone*, and commented on Mr Lung's stupidity, because he unlocked his glass door to let in two men who had stockings over their heads. 'Well,' said my mom, 'perhaps he thought they were relatives.'

I suppose my dad was the dominant partner, but my mom hardly handled him with kid gloves. I knew him to have a few minor illnesses in his life – flu, mouth ulcers, athlete's foot – and on each occasion she offered the same diagnosis: 'That'll be the badness coming out of you.' This, and her accompanying smirk, never failed to wind him up.

Secondly, my publisher is worried I sound too happy with my lot and this might piss some people off. Maybe I've talked too much about money, flashy hotels and premieres. Seems like I learnt nothing from my conversation with the Smethwick Johnny Cash.

Anyway, I apologise, but if I moaned about how terrible it is being a TV funnyman you'd all really hate me. I didn't mean to rub it in about the success bit. Listen, my back hurts from leaning over a computer all day, I have lots of fights with my girlfriend and, age-wise, I'm nearer the grave than the cradle. Now that's just going to have to do, for now. If anything else bad happens to me from now on, it's straight in the book.

Thirdly, it's back to the religion thing. I know I'm trying your patience with this but I'm only following orders. My publisher said he'd like to know how my religion now differs from my religion when I was a kid. Well, I tell you, when I was a kid, I believed in God and Jesus and angels and heaven and, basically, I still do. I believed that if I asked God for something and he thought it would be ultimately good for me to get it, then I would get it, and I still do. And sometimes I did stuff because I was scared that he might give me cancer if I didn't, and now I don't believe that. Although I do believe if I miss Mass on Sundays, I might well lose a BAFTA and the Division One play-offs.

The thing is, I don't get these people who believe in God but who don't go with the Virgin Birth or the resurrection and stuff. If you're God, you can do what you like. Look, I'll tell you what. I wrote some prayers about two years ago. I thought it would be nice to have some to say that were sort of specific to me. I'm going to give you a sample or two, in fact seven. It's a very Biblical number. I'm not going to make any comment on them or try and defend them in any way. They weren't written for publication (Oh, no. Of course not) and they're very short. I suppose they give you a fair idea of what my relationship with God is like. This last sentence sounds very wanky but I'm leaving it in. I bet you never thought you'd be reading Frank Skinner's prayers, and not a nob-joke in sight.

1. Dear Lord. When you were down here doing carpentry and stuff, did you know you were God? Did you always know? Did it dawn on you gradually? Did you have flashes of it and did you ever think, 'Whoah! I'm one of them mad blokes who thinks he's God'? You don't have to tell me. It's just that market-traders are all very hard and, when you overturned their stalls, I wondered if you had the old lightning-bolt up your sleeve. And if a very small, human-being bit of you, which hadn't really mingled with your God-bit, was thinking, 'Just you try it, Sunshine.'

2. Dear Lord. If the priest occasionally stopped, mid-Mass, and said 'Any questions?' would anyone have the nerve? Would I? 'Erm . . . yes Father. Should we sympathise with Judas because he was a necessary vessel of betrayal? Without him, Jesus would not have been taken and no one would have died for our sins. In a way, Judas died for our sins as well. Maybe we should celebrate his birthday. Didn't Christ need Judas? Wasn't it a kiss of collaboration?'

'No. Any other questions?'

'Why don't we have a Donkey Derby?'

'Well, now that's a good point . . .'

3. Dear Lord. I think taboo subjects are bad for a relationship. You know what I'm going to say. We need to talk about the hell thing. Now, let me get this right. We fail the course and then you have us tortured forever. Not just till we die. We get teased and toasted for all eternity. When I read about two kids, torturing an old-age pensioner for a day and a half, in his own home, until he died broken and humiliated, I felt like crying. I even thought, 'This is what happens to society when religion isn't a big deal anymore.' Please don't tell me that this is the your-own-image you made us in. Of course, even as torturers, we fall short. We can only keep 'em alive for a day and a half.

This hell thing, it's just not you. You're better than that. Even cattle get it short and sharp. This is the bad thing about working on your own. If only you'd had a team. When you brought up hell at a meeting, you'd have picked up on the raised eyebrows. You'd have gone away and come up with something better. I suppose purgatory was your compromise, but I think that's something you just put in for the Catholics: 'OK, we'll go to heaven but we insist on some suffering beforehand.' Maybe I'm wrong. Maybe I have a corrupted-by-liberalism view of things that has strayed from the truth. Maybe eternal torture is a good thing, but do me one favour. Please don't torture anyone for what they did to me. I forgive them. I'm the forgiving type. I wonder where I get that from.

4. Dear Lord. Sometimes, when I pray, I leave quiet bits so that you can chip in with any epiphanies, bits of wisdom, solutions to problems or one-off money-making schemes you might have up your sleeve. That's an interesting concept, God's sleeve. I imagine it roomy and perhaps slightly flared. Anyway, the scary thing is that, instead of divine inspiration, I might be filling the gaps myself, subconsciously. (PAUSE.) Yes, you're right. Of course it's not me.

5. Dear Lord. Somewhere, in a big pot, there must be a load of Bible out-takes: drafts one and two of the Sermon on the Mount, the extended version of the Good Samaritan story, including some not-so-good things that the Samaritan did, removed to avoid a muddying of his image of general goodness. We really have to trust the editor: 'We could lose that bit about promiscuity being acceptable as long as one's partners are treated with courtesy and politeness.' Some bloke in a night-shirt, crossing stuff out. Oversights, mistakes, whole pages destroyed by the wine-bottle going over, mis-readings, mis-spellings, human error. If, for example, the prodigal's dad had, in fact, killed the *matted* calf, y'know, that calf whose grooming had been neglected as a direct result of the son's absence, then the story becomes even more poignant. The son is then a vivid expression of the way our sins come back to haunt us, as he stands, tearful with guilt, at the sight of the calf's uncombed carcass. So, Lord, forgive us our trespasses, especially if they came about as a direct result of a typo.

6. Dear Lord. Hallowed be thy name, apparently. Which is a bit worrying. Don't get me wrong, it's nice that you're hallowed and everything, it's just that hallowedness can really get in the way of warm, smiley, arm-around-the-shoulder type things, and they mean a lot to me. You see, when I meet human beings who are only just ever-so-slightly hallowed, I'm no good with them. I get awkward and dorky, and they start to think I'm a bit odd. I don't want you to think that. I want you to see my jaunty familiarity as a breath of fresh air. However, it's always in the back of my mind that, on the Judgement Day, you might say, 'Not him. I don't feel he ever truly acknowledged my hallowedness,' and I'd be dragged off, calling back to you that your hallowedness was so fundamental and profound that I'd felt there was no need to up-front it. And some of the more liberal angels would deliberately not catch your eye.

7. Dear Lord. I just want to make it official that I believe in you. I mean, I really believe that you exist and you made everything and all that. Otherwise, your just a device I use to organise my thoughts. Y'know, that last line just fell out of me. I had no sense of contrivance. Maybe it was *your* line, given to me through your divine inspiration. Thanks. Mind you, it was a strange line for you to come up with, if you don't mind me saying. I mean, it's not as if you're trying to communicate to me that you ARE just a device I use to organise my thoughts. If that were true then it can't have been your line because, well, you're just a device I use to organise my thoughts. And a device can't have ideas. Although it does sound a bit like 'divine'. If I hired a clergyman to edit this, then he would be a divine I use to organise my thoughts. Perhaps that's it. You were telling me to hire a divine to edit my stuff and I just mis-heard you. Perhaps you were telling me that I use you like you were just a device I use to organise my thoughts, and that's bad. I should listen more, let you run the prayers a bit, go with the flow. Hold on, I just read that original line again – it should be 'you're just a device' not 'your just a device'. So whose grammatical error is that? I'm not accusing anyone but it's very unlike me to make that kind of slip-up. Anyway, as I say, I really believe in you. And faith is more important than grammar.

Oldbury Technical School was the making of me. Whether the 'me' it made was a good thing is highly debatable. My school-report in the first year was quite encouraging, but pretty soon I was getting 'uncooperative and evasive', 'only works when constantly badgered' and, perhaps most tellingly, 'spends far too much time playing to the gallery'. The class-comic thing had got completely out of hand by this stage. Whilst my professional career began in the December of 1987, in truth, I became a full-time comic during the second year at Oldbury Tech. I did virtually no school-work. Me and a select group of friends just messed about all the time. The school nerds got the treatment, we'd have nicknames and comedy angles on every aspect of their appearances and personalities. One girl had fat legs (a bit like sausages), red cheeks (a bit like tomatoes), and flat tits (a bit like fried eggs). We called her The Breakfast. I wrote comedy-poems and songs about certain kids and teachers, drew cartoons depicting them in various disparaging ways, and was constantly developing my schtick till our gang had their own language and a massive collection of in-jokes.

Now I know lots of schoolkids form these exclusive little sub-groups. It's normal. But I was determined not to let it go, ever. I liked it too much. I think that was one of the reasons I started drinking heavily. Any bunch of drunken blokes in a pub leave behind their responsibilities and emotional commitments and become schoolboys again. I also think it's one of the reasons I went into comedy. As I've said before, it's not really what you'd call a grown-up job, is it? That group of mates from Oldbury Tech have just been replaced by nine or ten million viewers, but I'm still writing jokes and songs and showing off and stuff. I sometimes have that dream that I've got an exam to do and I've done no work for it. I know it's a common theme, based on insecurity I think, but it also reminds me of that time at Oldbury Tech when, occasionally, the grown-up world would intrude into my full-time comedy show.

The drink thing was already starting to happen. My night out with Terry had given me a taste for pub life, and I set out with a mate called Fez to actually get served in a pub without 'grown-up' help. Fez was one of my closest friends. He was tall, chubby, and always looked like he'd just got out of bed. He had a fabulous way with words. It was Fez who once invited me round his house to try his new pellet-rifle with 'Come over and we can dispatch some wildlife.'

We walked into the pub and I, being something of a veteran after my Johnny Cash experience, sent Fez to a table while I went to the bar. I had turned fifteen a few weeks before. The barman looked at me in anticipation. 'Two halves of mild, please,' I said, in a voice so deep that my chin was actually touching my chest. So deep that the barman didn't actually hear me, he just felt the vibration. 'Two halves of mild?' he said, enquiringly. Shit. I hadn't anticipated some sort of question-and-answer session. Maybe, I reasoned, you couldn't actually buy mild in halves. I had asked for something that didn't exist and completely exposed my inexperience. 'Well . . . bitter, then,' I replied. This lack of conviction aroused the barman's suspicions and he asked me how old I was. 'Nineteen,' I said. Eighteen would have sufficed but I was operating on a sort of one-for-the-pot theory. 'I don't think so,' said the barman. I could see Fez looking across anxiously. 'Right,' I said, and strode out purposefully with Fez following on behind.

Then some other mates told me they had found a pub in nearby Langley Green that had made them very welcome. It was called the New Inn on Station Road and was owned by an Indian bloke called Dave. Obviously, he wasn't really called Dave, but this was the West Midlands in the early seventies. English people couldn't be bothered to learn how to pronounce difficult foreign names, so a lot of Asian people just gave up and adopted an English name that was slightly similar. Dave was really friendly and the New Inn became a regular haunt for Oldbury Tech's drinkers. I can't say it was what you'd call a glamorous place. In fact, looking back, it was fairly horrible, but I was soon doing gags and writing songs about the regular clientele.

There was an Indian bloke called Batman (*his* name must

have been *really* hard to pronounce) who had the biggest quiff I'd ever seen and had this thing that he would eat glass for a fiver. I saw him do it once. It was a piece of beer-glass about two inches square. He once paid me and my mate Shane a quid each to throw a brick through the window of someone who'd upset him. We did; and so did our mate, Sammy, but he got the wrong house.

There was a woman who was, I guess, over forty, but wore very short skirts, and eye-shadow like Alice Cooper. She owned a pair of white PVC boots and whenever she wore them I would joke that she had got her 'working-boots' on. There was an old guy we called Alfred the Butler, because he looked like Batman's butler. When I say he looked like Batman's butler, I mean the one in the Batman comic books not the one from the Batman TV series. And when I say Batman, I mean the caped crime-fighter, not the quiffed glass-eater. When Alfred came over to chat, his loose dentures made him spit so much that you had to sit with your hand over the top of your glass to avoid getting a saliva-topping on your beer.

There was a bloke called Ronnie who once held a knife against my throat for about two hundred yards of the walk home because he thought I had informed the police about the whereabouts of his borstal-skipping daughter. I hadn't, but I was being cagey because I kept watch the night before while my mate got friendly with her up an alley. There was Gay Ray, the Sea-Hag, Tommy the Weasel, Trev the Ted and Dirty Violet, who always arrived with at least three black blokes and had a penchant for pissing in the lift at the block of council flats where she lived. Dave's barman, Suki (a sort of a half-way house on the anglicising front), used to sell me beer in the New Inn in the evenings, and then sell me 99s from his ice-cream van when I left school in the afternoons. After several months, he asked me about this. I explained that 'I work there, helping the teachers.' He accepted my story, even though it was wrong on both counts.

Vandalism was another passion. On one occasion after leaving the pub one night, a bunch of us found a pile of newly delivered concrete bollards on a nearby factory car-park. We blocked the road one way by standing three of these bollards half-way across it, and then blocked it the other way by laying three bollards down so that they were less visible than the standing ones. It worked like a dream. A car sped up the road, swerved to avoid the standing bollards and crashed over the other ones so that they became wedged under the car. We hid around a corner, laughing. I always like to think that the policeman who investigated this incident went on to invent the speed-bump. A company working on the local canal had boats with thousands of pounds' worth of equipment on board parked-up overnight. We had a right laugh watching them trying to get it out of the canal the next day.

I think my most enjoyable act of vandalism was in a multi-storey car park in Birmingham. I walked from floor to floor, swinging on the overhead pipes and kicking strip-light after strip-light off the ceiling. They went with a bang, and a cloud of powder from inside the tube that left my boots and jeans dusty-white. I must have done about twenty. I don't know why I did it. I would blame the drink, but I was vandalising before I started drinking. I just did it. Of course, I can't look back on these things without making a damning moral judgement, but although I am loath to admit it, there is something profoundly joyous about destroying an entire bus-stop with a big lump of concrete. Hopefully someone clever will read this section and get me off the hook by blaming society. You certainly can't blame the parents. If my old man had found out he would have killed me.

But always, there were the jokes. I heard David Frost on telly doing a gag. It wasn't a side-splitter but I thought it was quite clever. The joke consisted of him just saying 'Marmite – hopeful pa.' I liked it. That night, my friend Roy came round for me on the way to the New Inn. I sat him down and then said, 'Here's a joke for you. Marmite – hopeful pa.' Roy, a lovely bloke but not the brightest, looked at me and went, in a hollow, staccato way, 'Ha! Haha! Ha!' I wasn't convinced by this reaction and said, 'Do you get it?'

'No', he said.

I said, 'You must do. Marmite – hopeful pa. Y'know.' Roy looked at me blankly. 'Marmite – hopeful pa. Ma, or mother, might . . . have sexual intercourse, thinks a hopeful pa.' Roy stared at me some more, and then smiled.

'Oh, yeah! Ha! Haha! Ha!'

To paraphrase Rex Harrison in *My Fair Lady*, 'By Jove, I thought he'd got it.' So we went down the pub. Later in the evening, I was playing darts and Roy was sitting a few feet away talking to some bloke. 'Here's a joke for you,' I heard him say to the bloke, 'Bovril . . . ,' my heart sank, 'hopeful pa.'

The other bloke stared at him for about five seconds, and then went, 'Ha! Haha! Ha!'

I was telling you what my publisher was saying about the book and I thought that, since we were roughly at the half-way stage, you might be interested to know what I thought of it so far. (It's impossible to hear that phrase without also hearing Eric Morecambe shout 'Rubbish', but I'm going to press on.) Don't get me wrong, I'd love to know what you think of the book so far, as well, but that's not really practical, is it? My guess is that you like some bits but you don't like others. It's OK. I accept that. The problem in writing about my life is that I'm bound to cover my various interests and passions, and the chances of those directly matching anyone else's are fairly slim. How many of my readers are going to be really keen on Elvis, football, Roman Catholicism *and* nob-jokes? Not too many.

I know that all autobiographies are bound to cover areas the reader is not that interested in, but it pains me to think of it. I don't doubt that a lot of autobiographers are so up their own arses that they think anything to do with them is totally fucking fascinating, but I can't really go along with that myself. I know that sounds like a piece of 'Aw shucks' false modesty but I am, as I've tried to convince you previously, quite modest. Honestly. If they made an action-figure of me, on the side of the box it would say, 'Light and bushel included.' The thing is, if there are shit bits, you lot are no help at all. All I get is silence, and as a stand-up comic, silence is my arch-enemy. If there's quiet bits in a gig then something's not working. The trouble with this book-writing lark is I don't know whether there are quiet bits or not.

I could show the book to a few friends and ask their opinion I suppose, but I'm worried that they might see it as a License-to-Edit and start saying stuff like 'Would you mind taking out that reference to me sucking you off while my husband rescued our disabled child from a burning apartment?' Don't worry. You didn't miss that bit, it was just an example. A fictional example, I'd like to point out. But you know what I mean. If I showed it to our Nora, the whole thing could end up as a pamphlet.

I'm still worried about the religion thing. People just don't like that stuff. It's all very well me saying 'I know it's weird but I *believe* that little white wafer actually becomes the body and blood . . .', but you're thinking, 'Yes, it is fucking weird, so stop going on about it because you're embarrassing everyone, including yourself.' And if any religious people actually read the book they'll hate it, partly because of all the dirty bits and

193

the swearing, and partly because they're fucking weirdos who only like the Bible and Cliff Richard.

According to the book-marketing people I've recently met, books like this are mainly bought by women. Now they tell me. If I'd known that I wouldn't have bothered putting jokes in. Hey, just kidding. And anyway, what exactly are 'books like this'?

Oh, fuck it. Whatever happens, at least I'll be able to give my children a copy to stop them bothering me with tedious questions about my life, provided, of course, that they are sufficiently broad-minded. You think I'm kidding, but my vague idea that, on one level, this book would operate as a piece of family history has come into much sharper focus as the work has progressed. Even if it's a commercial disaster it will be a pretty remarkable document as far as my descendants are concerned. Imagine reading a really intimate, detailed account of your dad's or grandad's life and opinions, written by him personally, without any of the usual clouding that comes when communicating with an older relative. None of the 'Perhaps I shouldn't be telling her this in case she tells her mom' stuff from me, and no 'This is fascinating but how much longer can I put up with the smell of piss' from them. If I have kids, one day this book will give them the chance to really get to know me, and how many of us ever really get to know our parents? Even though we are literally made of them, how many people actually try to find out what that 'them' is all about? We often love and care about our parents but, at the end of the day, they are from the Planet Parent and we feel we can never truly communicate with them.

Don't get me wrong, dear reader. I don't want you to feel alienated by this. If reading this book feels like watching someone else's home movies, then I've fucked up majorly. If my children and grandchildren ever exist, I think they'll like this book because I wrote it for you rather than them. They'll get me as a real human being, rather than someone who, like a parent or grandparent, is trying to impress them, or at least make them not dislike me. The fringe benefit for you, the reader, is that I think it would be wrong to tell lies to my descendants, so, consequently, I can't tell lies to you. Of course, maybe I'm reading too much into all this. It feels like a big deal to me but, well, it's just a book. I told this bloke I kind of know that I was writing my autobiography and he said, 'Oh, really. Will it all be about anal sex?'

Be honest. Was this a quiet bit?

And so my drinking continued. By the time I was sixteen, I had graduated to cider. I could actually taste that last line. That's a worry isn't it? Anyway, cider was my drink because I liked the taste and it made me stupid. I was already getting a reputation as one of the heavier drinkers of the bunch. I don't really know why. I suppose the fact that my dad, Terry and Keith were all heavy drinkers made it seem sort of inevitable. And also I really liked it. I liked the fall-about, laugh-till-you-cry, 'Mamma-Weer-all-Crazee-Now' euphoria of it. Getting pissed with your mates. It doesn't get much better than that.

I think I'd better shut up. All this is starting to slow down the wagon to the point where it's starting to look safe to jump off. Eric Clapton told me that if I'd quit drinking through a proper Alcoholics Anonymous programme, I wouldn't still yearn for it now. I saw in the Millennium with my arm around Eric as we sang and he played guitar to 'Auld Lang Syne', at his teetotal New Year's party. I learnt something that night. I used to think that the worst thing about not drinking was being sober when everyone else was drunk. I was wrong. No one drank at that party, and I realised that the worst thing about not drinking was just being sober. Full stop. Still, seeing in the twenty-first century duetting with a guitar-legend took the sting out of it a bit.

I was also getting into music, big-time. I still loved Elvis, but now I was being dragged along to lots of heavy-metal gigs by my mates. Black Sabbath, Deep Purple, all the usual suspects. I guess this started to have an influence on me because I let my hair grow long. As it grew, it sort of fell into waves and ringlets I never knew I had. I was starting to look cool. In fact, I would say that this eighteen-month period, around the age of fifteen to sixteen, was the closest I've ever got in my life to actually being cool.

We formed a band, a few mates and me, which at first was absolutely appalling because no one could actually play anything. We didn't know a chord between us. My mate Tim whose spare bed I pissed years later, had an electric organ and somewhere to practise. Fez bought a bass. Another mate, Mick, got some drums, and we were off. I sang, of course, because I was nearly cool. We even made a tape of this mess and played it to Tim's mom. Tim's family were a bit posher than the rest of us and his mom, I think, slightly disapproved of Tim's grubby friends. 'Well,' she said, having heard the tape, 'the only tuneful thing I can hear is Timothy's organ.' We all giggled because it sounded slightly like a nob-joke and because she was so unashamed in her maternal favouritism. When we said we hadn't got a name for the band, she suggested 'The Timaloes'.

Instead, we went for Olde English, named after my favourite cider. Another mate, Nick, came in on guitar, and we started to actually sound OK. We practised a lot and started to get together a few passable cover versions of rock classics. Then came what, relatively speaking, you might call a turning-point. Yes, we did a school assembly. In calling it to mind, I have just blushed for the first time in about fifteen years. We opened with a slightly painful version of Deep Purple's 'When a Blindman Cries'. Just typing that title makes me laugh. It was one of those sad, slow songs that heavy-metal bands do to prove that they can do sad, slow songs. Next, I read a teenage-angst poem that questioned the whole school thing: 'If I get that bit of paper, will it make me any greater' was my take on the upcoming O-levels, that I'd done zero revision for. Then we closed with 'Jumping Jack Flash'. Basically, we stormed it. Our English teacher, Mr Wilcockson, approached us after and was full of praise. He said we sounded like a cross between the Rolling Stones and Howling Wolf. Looking back, he was probably doing his 'I'm one of those teachers who know about hip music' bit, but we were thrilled. Y'know how, when someone tells you that you look like someone famous, and you deny it and act pissed-off but secretly you're chuffed and you start doing everything you can to look even more like them? Well, that's a bit like what happened to us. Mr Wilcockson's comparison with the Stones made us go a bit crazy and we put together a set that was all Stones except for Steppenwolf's 'Born to be Wild', Sabbath's 'Paranoid' and Free's 'Alright Now'. When I interviewed Sabbath's Ozzy Osborne years later, I told him that when I was sixteen, I was in a band that did 'Paranoid'. 'That's funny,' he said. 'So was I.'

But the Stones were our thing. I did all the Jagger strutting and pouting stuff, and we became, in the universe that was Oldbury Technical School, rock stars in our own right. I remember sitting in the art room, while Jayne (the Nervous Test girl) and her mate teased my ever growing hair into a Roy Wood-like shaggy afro. As they did this, I felt their thighs and bums and neither did a thing to stop me. When we, Olde English, arrived at school in the morning, little girls would be hanging out of the windows calling our names and trying to take our photographs. I remember one first-year girl bravely approaching Mick, our drummer, and telling him she thought he was great. Mick scowled, and said, 'Fuck off, you sparrow-legged virgin' and the girl ran off in tears. And just think, Liam Gallagher wasn't even born yet.

For all this attention, I was, at sixteen, still a sparrow-legged virgin myself. I had gone through a period about three years before when I decided I was infertile. Basically, my first three hand-jobs were literally dry-runs and it seemed that there would be no son with whom to share an 'Abide with Me' on Cup Final day. Then, one night after school, I gave it one more try, in the outside toilet, and the floodgates opened. I actually ran up the garden and jumped up and down cheering for about three or four minutes. Thankfully, my parents never asked. At last, I had become a man. I could feel myself developing an interest in timber.

My sense of what was manly was, of course, a bit askew. I always kissed my mom and dad before I went to bed at night, but on the night of my fourteenth birthday, I kissed my mom and then, when my dad approached me, I stuck out a hand. He paused, smiled, and shook it firmly. I think I saw a tear in his eye, which could have been because he was proud, or could have been because I was really squeezing his hand hard to show how manly I was.

He was lucky. Within a year, the muscles in that hand had developed considerably. I was checking that the well had not run dry, and I was checking it on a very regular basis. On average, about three times a day. In the school holidays, I would often hit double figures. After a while, I started to worry about the religious implications of this. Would I be 'teased and toasted for all eternity' because of my new hobby. That's all it was, a hobby. Why should I be teased and toasted when those kids with unfashionable hairstyles and bad skin, who collected stamps and made model aeroplanes, would almost certainly remain unsinged? One year, I gave it up for Lent. Forty days and forty nights of sheer hell. As midnight struck to herald in Easter Sunday, I whipped up a storm, to a point where it felt very hot and itchy afterwards. The next morning it had swollen to about three times its normal thickness. Believe me, this sounds a lot better than it looked. I took it as a warning, as a punishment, as a sign. And the message was crystal-clear. I must never give up wanking again.

Then I met a girl called Liz. I suppose she was my first girlfriend. She was a slim, Italian-looking girl, with dark eyes, pigeon-toes and a smile that suggested hidden sophistication. I met her in Langley Park, which was about fifty yards from the New Inn. Life was very centralised in those days. Our relationship was largely about snogging, a skill that was still very much work-in-progress as far as I was concerned. I couldn't make my mind up whether it was best to snog with the eyes open or closed. When quizzing some girls at school about this, they said that it was generally accepted that if you closed your eyes you were very passionate. This was good enough for me, so the next snogging-session I had with Liz I did a lot of eyes-shut stuff. However, about half-way through, I decided to check to see if Liz passed the passion-test. I sneaked open an eye and could see that hers were closed. This was good news. After about another five or ten minutes of snogging, I decided to check again. Sure enough, her eyes were shut, but then, suddenly, they opened. I think she had heard the passion-theory as well and was doing some checking of her own. I froze, like a rabbit in the headlights. We just stared at each other, which is actually quite painful from such close range. Eventually, I drew back, winked, gave her a double thumbs up, and then carried on.

Liz gave me my first under-bra experience. I still recall the exciting contrast between the firm, rubbery nipple, and the soft flesh around it. We were under Uncle Ben's Bridge, by the side of the canal, at the time. That night, I lay in bed musing on the ludicrous fact that, in an age when man could land on the moon, you still couldn't buy a headboard with a toilet-roll holder fitted.

That year, a few mates and me went on holiday to Brean Down, near Weston-super-Mare. One night in the caravan, we got very drunk on scrumpy-cider and one of my friends hit Shane over the head with a wine bottle. This sounds dangerous, but Shane was one of the hardest people I ever met. He was a scruffy lad, with a big, beaky nose, and black spiky hair that made him look like a dishevelled crow. When he became a working man, doing felt-roofing, he once fell off a house, arseholed, and turned up at the pub two hours later with his face bloody and pieces of gravel embedded in his head, all set to carry on drinking.

Anyway, that night Shane remained upright, so the other guy hit him again, this time selecting a slightly weightier vodka bottle. I stepped in and managed to calm things down but it caused a bit of a stir on the camp-site. The police were called, but by the time they arrived the storm had passed. When we went home, I carried a blue St. Christopher that I'd bought for Liz out of my meagre spending money. I gave it to her on the Saturday night we got back. She thanked me, told me the postcard I'd sent describing the vodka-bottle incident had caused her mom and dad to forbid her to see me again, and went on to say that, anyway, there was a boy at her school who wanted to go out with her and she liked him better. So that was that. I had been dumped for the first time.

I saw her eight months later and she had stupid hair, so I was glad.

Inevitably, I suppose, it was Nervous Test Jayne who gave

me my first under-knicker experience. We went to a party one night and got a bit drunk. We were both fifteen. On the way back, we snogged and groped like, well, fifteen-year-olds. I went under the bra first. This was the order of things. Her nipples were cold, and when this became known around school (what are you looking at ME for?) she was given the nickname Crystal Tips. I stopped there. Partly because I was scared and partly because she had bad breath and I was starting to lose interest. But she wasn't. 'Would you like to see my new panties?' she asked. To be honest, it was a bit dark for a fashion show, but I didn't want to cause offence so I went with it. She undid the zip on her skin-tight turquoise flares and opened them to show me her knickers. Her smile told me it was lucky-dip time. I slipped my right hand down her proffered pants but it got stuck. During my spell as very-local rock hero, I had taken to wearing two rings on the middle-fingers of my right hand, each with a large letter 'C' so that, on adjacent fingers, they formed my initials, 'CC'. (You remember, Chris Collins.) How cool is that? Of course, I didn't wear them in bed, or their rhythmic clicking would have caused my parents to think that I had bought a very large stop-watch. The rings had now caught on the waistband of Jayne's knickers. Without missing a beat, she reached down, slipped them off my fingers, and popped them in my jacket-pocket. What a girl. I took a breath and then dug deep. What a time to be thinking about your infant school nativity play.

I think Jayne was hoping that we might develop things even further over the coming weeks, but the bad breath had put me off and I avoided her till the summer holidays set me free. At the time, I was not aware that bad breath was often just a temporary thing, perhaps, on this occasion, brought on by drinking disgusting wine. Anyway, I let Jayne slip away, and

when we returned from the summer break she was going out
with a bloke who looked like a parrot.

It was election day, yesterday. Last election, in 1997, I was
working for the BBC as part of their *Election Special* team. My
job was to spend the whole day and, as it turned out, the first
eight hours of the next day flying around the country in a
helicopter, giving a (how did they put it at the meeting?)
'light-hearted and slightly off-the-wall view of the day's
events'. I went to an OAPs' tea-dance and listened, as you
might expect, to the usual OAP mixture of right-wing clichés
and downright silliness, including 'I blame decimalisation',
'There's too many blacks' and 'The weather hasn't been right
since they landed on the moon'. I met a Tony Blair lookalike
and a John Major lookalike, neither of which really did, and I
visited an exhausted Asian couple in hospital, where they had
just had one of the first election babies. All through the early
hours, using makeshift landing sites in fields and jumping into
fast cars, the soundman, cameraman, director, pilot and me
listened to the results coming in on the radio: Portillo's lost his
seat, Labour have gained Grantham, 'it's looking like a
landslide'.

I usually find politics intensely boring. It seems to be mainly
the pastime of men with bad hair who look as if they smell of
tobacco, but on this night – for the first and maybe last time –
politics seemed really dynamic and exciting. There was a
feeling in the air that something special was happening. People
will probably deny that it ever existed now, but there was a
profound sense of optimism and hope that I, personally, hadn't
really felt about anything since I'd stopped drinking. As we
flew from Manchester to London at sunrise, with the three-
man film-crew asleep in the back, I looked down on the light,

fluffy patches of mist covering the dark green landscape below and said to the pilot, 'So, the dawn breaks on Blair's Britain,' and he nodded. Neither words nor gesture had the slightest hint of irony. A couple of weeks, and it was back to the same old bollocks.

Anyway, back to the Oldbury Tech story. In this episode, a moral dilemma, an artistic success, and an academic failure. And probably quite a lot of other stuff that won't actually occur to me until I start writing it.

One day Shane, who by now had left school, and me were out walking when we spotted a wallet on the pavement. He quickly picked it up, and we scurried off to a quiet car park behind the nearby shops to see if we'd got lucky. And, if so, exactly how lucky we'd got. Eighty quid was the answer. We both got very agitated. To try and give you a sense of what we're dealing with here, a pint of cider at the time cost thirteen pence. We discussed whether or not we should do the decent thing and hand the wallet in to the police. I may have had a shorter discussion in my life, but I can't remember it.

As a Catholic, of course, it might have occurred to me that a man has to pay for his sins sooner or later, but I suppose I figured that, with forty quid, I could afford to pay for almost anything. It was a butterfly-crushing moment of massive proportions. I had forty quid to spend, and so did one of my closest friends, but we couldn't spend it on material goods or our parents might have asked difficult questions about our sudden affluence. We only had one choice. We'd have to drink it. The school summer holiday had just begun, so if I was to take advantage of the lie-ins afforded by the summer break, lie-ins that I'd probably need given these new circumstances, I had five weeks to drink two hundred and eighty pints of cider. I didn't bother with the maths, it was party-time.

It was during this period that I started to fall in love with drinking. That was exactly how it felt: ridiculous highs and lows, light-headedness, loss of appetite, and an inability to cope with any prolonged absence from my loved one. Some people drink and some people are drinkers. I discovered, that summer, that I was a drinker. If I'd handed in the wallet, my life might have taken a very different, and probably much healthier, turn for the better. So, if Cash had started the process, cash was about to take it on to another level. Oh, how we drank.

In the midst of this dream-like summer came my O-level results. Much better than expected. I'd got two: Art and English Language. Basically, the only two that you don't need to revise for. I had done no work for my O-levels because I was going to be a rock star and academic qualifications didn't seem very relevant. My parents, being of working-class stock, didn't have much awareness of O-levels and the like and I worked hard to keep it that way. I made sure they didn't get to hear about parents' evenings and stuff, in case someone there let it slip that I was a work-shy, piss-taking little waster who was heading for a massive come-uppance. That could have caused tension at home. They were already starting to get suspicious about my social life. A couple of polo mints on the way home didn't seem to hide my drinking-habit as well as it used to. I hadn't noticed but things were starting to come to a head.

While I was waiting for rock-stardom to hit, I figured I might as well stay at school and relax. I knew if I timed it right, I could avoid having a proper job altogether. The school agreed to let me go on to the upper-sixth provided I re-took some of my O-levels and improved my general attitude. I think the Art teacher had spoken up for me, so I began A-level

Art and A-level English, with O-level re-sits coming up in November. Soon I was in trouble for skipping classes and the headmaster, Mr Lardner, told me that this was my last warning and if I got in trouble again, he'd be forced to expel me. Yeah, yeah, there had been plenty of naughty boys go through the school while I'd been there and I'd never heard of him ever expelling anybody. Two weeks later, in the October of 1973, I was in his office again. A few pals and me had discovered where they chucked the used dinner-tickets when they were done with them, and decided to sell them, cut-price, to the other pupils. Having invented the speed-bump, we now moved on to re-cycling. The one thing we never allowed for was serial numbers. As I walked into Mr Lardner's room, I could hear his secretary typing away in the adjoining office. It was my expulsion note. 'Collins,' he said, 'you're a drifter, and one day you'll drift into something you can't drift out of.' I've looked back on this sentence on many occasions, and wondered if it was as prophetic as it sounded. What was it, in retrospect, that I later drifted into and had not been able to drift out of? Drinking, marriage, comedy, none of them seem to quite fit. Now, if I'd joined the American vocal group The Drifters in later life, this quote would have been a remarkable, almost supernatural, turning-point in the book. As it is, he was probably just talking bollocks, as headmasters are ever inclined to do.

When I returned to the common room to tell my school-mates what had happened, they seemed kind of concerned but I also sensed a bit of 'Oh, well, we can't sit here talking. We've got classes to go to', so I had a cup of coffee from the machine that sixth-formers were allowed to use, and then I walked home. And slowly it dawned on me. What the fuck was I going to tell my dad?

I waited till him and Mom had both got home from work

and then said I had some bad news, and gave him the note. Rather grandly, it said that I had been 'embezzling the school meals service'. It also said I was expelled. My mom started to do a 'I'm not surprised' speech but my dad cut it short by chucking his dirty boiler-suit at me and shouting, 'Here, you'd better put these on and get down the Birmid, with the darkies.'

The Birmid was a local factory that always had the thick smell of heavy industry spilling out of its open windows. It was hard, hot, dirty work for forty hours a week. I think he had hoped that I would be the one who wouldn't have to work in a place like that, the one who would do special, different things, but now that dream was gone. As for the rest of his remark, well, I'm not defending it, but these were less enlightened times and he was very, very upset. I never heard him be impolite to a black or Asian person in all the time I knew him, and he was not a man who worried about offending people he thought needed to be offended. Nuff said.

I considered trying to explain that he shouldn't worry because I was going to be a rock star, but it didn't feel like the right time. That night he came home drunk, obviously having dwelt on the day's events. My mom had gone to bed so it was man-to-man time. After a short speech about his own missed opportunities, he slapped me hard across the face. Fair enough, I thought. It was the last time he ever hit me and we both went to bed with tears in our eyes.

According to today's papers, I'm in a 'shoot-out' with the ex-Chelsea player-manager, Gianluca Vialli, over the house I'm supposed to be buying. According to the estate agent, 'Both seem to like it and it has a 75ft garden, big enough for a kickabout.' Well, that's alright then. Both the *Sun* and the *Mirror* price the house at three and a quarter million. Obviously, two million isn't impressive enough for them. And they've given it an extra bedroom as well. So, what's it all about? Well, I heard through Jenny, my P.A., that the estate agent got a bit panicky when he read that Caroline and me had split up and had asked if this might affect my future plans, so I'm guessing he's using the papers to make me think 'Oh shit, I'd better cast caution to the wind and sign everything quickly or Vialli will get my house.' Of course, it may well be that Vialli really is interested, in which case I suspect Dave Baddiel's enthusiasm about me moving in might now start to wane a little. Either way, that's how famous I am. I'm going to stop saying that because I feel you're no longer taking it in the spirit that it's intended.

In the early seventies, teenagers who needed a job went to the Youth Employment Office. Here they were dealt with by experts who were specially trained to cater for the needs and problems of young people. When I turned up on a Monday morning in October 1973, there was a fat girl making her way to the counter. The YEO woman asked her the sort of job she had in mind. 'Well,' said the fat girl, 'all my life, I've wanted to work with animals.'

'Yeah,' said the woman, 'well we don't get many jobs like that, but they need a checkout girl at Woolworths. Here's the details. Next.' The fat girl waddled away, looking slightly shaken and clutching an official-looking white card in her chubby hand. Her butterfly had been well and truly crushed, but no wonder if *she*'d stood on it.

Then it was my turn. I explained that I was in a band and so I just needed a job that would tide me over till we got established. The expression on the woman's face made me wonder if I'd accidentally said 'Eat my nob-cheese' instead. She said that someone, as she put it, 'with your qualifications' should be taking the 'job-market' a bit more seriously. With my qualifications? That was the thing with growing up in a place like Oldbury. You get two O-levels and people start eyeing you suspiciously, like you were some sort of Stephen Hawking figure. I felt that the photographer from the *Smethwick Telephone* could have turned up at any moment with an easel, palette and artist's smock. Incidentally, one night on stage at Birmingham Town Hall, I asked if anyone in the audience knew why the paper was called the *Smethwick Telephone*, and one bloke said, without a trace of humour, 'Cus it's from Smethwick.' Anyway, the YEO woman said that there was a vacancy at Hughes and Johnson's Stampings. I was very familiar with Hughes and Johnson's and it had one major plus-point. It was literally next door to the New Inn. I almost tore the card when snatching it from her hand.

When I turned up for my interview, the personnel manager said that, as I had O-level Art, he supposed I could draw a straight line, and gave me a job in the drawing office. I had never done anything approaching a technical drawing in my life, but no one seemed to care. I started on the following Monday and fucking hated it. We had to do an eight-hour day, for goodness' sake, not including lunch. I got home that night and my dad asked me what I thought of my first day at work. 'Horrible,' I said.

'Never mind,' he said consolingly, 'tomorrow will be better.'

'I know,' I said, 'I'm not going.' And I didn't, but by day three I had got over the shock and it was literally back to the drawing-board, staring at sheets of tracing-paper, pretending I knew what I was doing.

The drawing office was separate from the other offices, even closer to the New Inn than the rest of the factory. On the other side was Harrold's the newsagents. The owner, Edward Harrold, was known locally as Teddy the Paper-Chap to adults, and The Beano Man to kids. He always wore the same long grey coat and wellingtons, and his baggy black trousers were cut off where the wellingtons started. If you got up close when he was on his bike, you could see that his legs were so filthy that they were the same colour as his wellingtons. Throughout my childhood and teenage years, I never knew him to change those clothes, and he was too stingy to employ paper-boys so did all the deliveries himself. You would see him delivering daily papers at four in the afternoon and evening papers as late as ten at night. Every morning, his sister, Ivy, served newspapers and fags whilst breakfasting on lard sandwiches at the counter. Eventually, word went round that the Harrolds' dirty old shop was full of money. Someone broke in and gave them a bashing. I turned up for work one day and the shop was closed down. The policeman on duty said they had found boxes of money in there, much of it long since gone out of circulation, and brands of cigarettes that no one had seen since the war.

It wasn't a great area for brother and sister partnerships. I would occasionally stick a couple of quid in the local post office, run by Sidney Grayland and his sister, Peggy, in anticipation of a lads' holiday we were planning in Burnham-on-Sea for the following summer. I turned up with my two quid one Thursday and found the post office closed. A criminal known as the Black Panther had broken in during the night, beat poor old Sid to death, and tied up Peggy so tightly that the ropes had to be surgically removed.

I was a less obvious target for attack. My first wage packet was £14.50. I gave a fiver to my mom and drank the rest. The combination of boring job and money in my pocket did wonders for my thirst. For the first fourteen months at Hughes and Johnson's, I couldn't remember past 9.30 on any night. I never remembered leaving the pub, or getting home, or anything in between. If the police had said it was me who raided the newsagent or tied up Peggy Grayland, I couldn't have put my hand on my heart and sworn they were wrong. When I got too bloated to drink more, I'd put my fingers down my throat and make some room, and I woke up covered in cuts and bruises with no idea where I got them. I was seeing a very nice girl but she dumped me because I had arranged to meet her on New Year's Day and didn't show. The truth was, I decided to have a quick pint with my dad on the way to my one o'clock rendezvous, and woke up on my sofa at four. Apparently, Dad and me had both been chucked out of the pub for singing. I didn't actually remember it myself.

Maybe all this drinking is normal teenage behaviour, I don't know, but the thing is, it was fun. 'Fun' is not a word I often use because it's been completely hijacked by local radio DJs who apply it to things that are definitely not fun. There are fun-runs and fun-pubs and fun-days, and they're all shit, but getting drunk every night is fun. Well, sort of.

Anyway, what fun there was started to go a bit sour. I got chucked out of the band because I was turning up pissed to rehearsals, and they changed the name from Olde English to a name I can't remember but which, inevitably, had something to do with Tolkien. This, of course, meant I could never go back. I have an aversion to all things children's literature. Any adult who reads Tolkien, Pooh, Harry Potter and the rest, is a worry to me. I didn't read children's literature when I was a child so I'm damned well not going to read it now. It's for kids. Look, they don't read hard-core pornography, I don't read their stuff. That's the deal. Either way, I was out of the band.

Then I was in church one Sunday morning when my heart suddenly started pounding and I could barely breathe. I walked out, mid-Mass, and staggered home. It was raining, and I thought I was going to collapse and die right there on the wet pavement. I saw a doctor the next day and he told me that if I carried on like this I'd be an alcoholic by the time I was twenty-one. This would have been fine if I was a rock star, but for someone who works in a scabby drawing-office between a newsagent where people eat lard and a pub where people eat glass, it was just pathetic.

The doctor gave me some tablets and told me not to drink with them. I went to the New Inn and ordered a lemonade. An old black guy came in, a regular who, like Teddy the Paper-Chap, also wore wellingtons all the time, but combined them with surprisingly elegant suits. On one occasion he had brought a saxophone into the pub, so my mates and me presumed he was some sort of jazz player. From then on he was known as Duke Wellington. Anyway, he asked me about the lemonade and I explained about the tablets. 'Well,' he said, 'it sounds like whatever you needed that was in the booze must be in them tablets as well. So you might as well just drink the booze.' It made perfect sense. I ditched the tablets and went back to the cider. However, I did cut down somewhat and started just getting drunk instead of very drunk. I had been treating life as if it was a limited-overs game, whereas, really, it is a five-day test match. Getting drunk instead of very drunk was a much more pleasant way of carrying on and I stuck with it for some time.

'My battle with the bottle' stories are always very tedious. I carried on drinking until I was thirty, so I won't go on about being drunk unless it's really relevant. You can safely assume that, during the next thirteen years, any incidents I describe usually involve some degree of drunkenness. You don't need to hear the details and, besides, it's starting to make me thirsty. I mean, you know, thirsty.

*

Being that, at the present time, I'm incarcerated in a tenth-storey flat in Birmingham, writing all day, the 'Today, I did this . . .' elements of the book are starting to get a bit tricky to write. When I look back at the book, I don't think I'll see the Vialli section as a highlight. Anyway, my point is that the more observant readers will have noticed that I – fairly accidentally I must admit – have put together something of a structure for the book which alternates a sort of journal comprising a description of my current experiences with a chronological autobiography telling what happened in my past. I didn't set out with this as a definite structure, but I thought it would help you because celebrities' pre-celebrity lives aren't necessarily all that interesting to read about and I hoped regular helpings of showbiz-glitter would help you through it.

As it turns out, I've let myself get a bit wrapped up in my past, and although I like doing the journal I don't want to make a rod for my own back on the structure front. I have found myself thinking, 'Well, I'd like to put three journal bits together here, or have two consecutive past-life bits there, but I'd better not because they won't like it if I mess with the structure.' Well, fuck off. From now on, they happen when they happen, and if I don't like that I'll change back.

I was in a pub one night with some mates who told me they'd seen some prostitutes standing on a street in the Balsall Heath area of Birmingham. They'd pretended to be punters and asked how much it was for sex. 'Five quid,' was the reply. None of us could believe it was so expensive. I'm not kidding. Remember, this was the early seventies. It was over a third of my weekly wage, and for what? Some old tart from Balsall Heath. If I spent a third of my weekly wage now, I could probably shag Fergie. Anyway, one mate, I suppose I better not name him, said he'd got a fiver and he was considering a late-night drive. A few of my mates were starting to get cars now. I was even having driving lessons myself. But tonight, though I didn't know it, I was heading for a lesson of a very different kind. (I feel there should be some dramatic 'da-da-daaaaaa' music at this point. If only this was a CD-rom.) I put it to my mate that he might have the fiver but he didn't have the guts. In a dramatic gesture that would not have been out of place in an episode of *Maverick*, he slid the fiver along the table towards me. 'Woooooaaaah!' went the crowd. I felt my stomach implode, but I cowboyed-up. 'Gooo onnn!' went the crowd. I picked up the fiver. Much cheering ensued.

At this point, I must say that the following story is profoundly grim. A young man's first entrance into the world of what the local radio DJs call 'bonking' should be, one feels, strewn with rose petals and shot in soft-focus, but this particular encounter fell a long way short of mystical. I actually had rose petals with me. I still carried the ones Mick Jagger had scattered on me at the Odeon, but I would not have liked to squander them on a night like this.

And the challenge had come quite early in the evening, so my focus was still unnervingly sharp. What I'm saying is, there's still time to pull out and skip to the next section. If you continue with this one, don't come crying to me.

Here goes. I drove with my unofficial sponsor to the street where he had spotted these women. Sure enough, two of them were on the prowl. On the way, I had dropped some very heavy hints that there was still time to back out, we could nip in for a drink somewhere, he could have his fiver back, and no one would be any the wiser. But no, he was determined that the challenge should be met. I had never done anything remotely like this before but reckoned I knew the type of thing that was said. We pulled up and I wound down the window. It was, as far as I could tell, the more attractive of the two women who approached the car. This was probably the last good news of the night. The other, a tall, broad-shouldered white woman with afro hair, reminded me of the cartoon-character Hair Bear. I was already scared as it was. If she had approached the car I would have been worried that she might possibly overturn it in a fit of pique. The approaching whore, also a white woman but with straight, jet-black hair, was probably in her early thirties. She wore so much make-up it was hard to tell. This was how our exchange went. Throughout this conversation, she chewed what I hoped was gum.

'Yeah?' she said.

'I wondered if you might know where I could find a good time.' Suddenly, I had become a nineteenth-century gentleman, leaning out of a hansom cab window as he once more gave in to his secret vice.

'No,' she said, as if surprised by my enquiry. Perhaps she had taken me literally and thought I was trying to use her as some kind of late-night Entertainments Officer. If I'd thought my mate would have let me off, I would have said, 'Oh, well, sorry to bother you,' and wished her a respectful good night, but I knew he wouldn't swallow it. Which was more than I could say for her. So, I persevered.

'Oh, really? I thought you would.'

'Look,' she said, impatiently, 'd'you want business?' Now, whereas I felt that my euphemism had got a disarming jolliness about it, hers, well, it just made the whole thing sound sordid.

'Erm, yeah,' I said, loath to share the metaphor.

'Ya got five?' she asked. Every element of my being wanted to say 'I dunno, I've never measured it', but she really didn't look like a woman who enjoyed persiflage.

'Erm, yeah.' What a time to develop a catchphrase.

'Come on,' she said abruptly, with an air of 'There's work to be done.' I stepped out on to the street, with my mate explaining that he was going to just pull round the corner. I think he meant the car.

My new friend opened the front-door of a terraced house and I followed her in, taking one backward glance at Hair Bear. I must have been hysterical by this stage because I actually said, 'Are you gonna be alright out here on your own?' She looked back at me as if I was an inanimate object. I paused to wonder if a more inappropriate thing had ever been said. And then I entered the whore's lair.

It was a small room with a tiny, dark-blue three-piece and, surprisingly, a rather enticing coal-fire. She turned and held out a hand. Maybe she always liked to begin proceedings with a hearty handshake? 'Got the money?' she asked. She was obviously used to having it up-front, so to speak. I handed over my mate's fiver. I have to say, I had liked her better in streetlight. Under a harsh, bare light-bulb she looked like Cher's six-month-old corpse. Still, I didn't feel it was my place to suggest a lamp-shade. She put the fiver in the pocket of her long denim coat. In fact, she was all in denim, with matching jeans and waistcoat. It was going to be like fucking one of Status Quo. She took off the coat and hung it on the chair. Then popped open her waistcoat, which had studs rather than buttons, to reveal small naked breasts and a pot-belly that had so many stretch-marks, it looked like a grey slinky. I would have walked out there and then had it not been for the coal-fire.

I produced a condom from my pocket. 'D'you want me to wear this?' I said. I'd been carrying it around, just in case, for about two years. 'It's up to you,' she said. Well, I was in two minds, really. There would have been something satisfying about just sneaking in so close to the 'Use By' date but, on the other hand, I had never actually put one on before and I was worried I might come across as slightly gauche. 'I won't bother,' I said. Stifle that shriek. This was the early seventies, before Aids was invented. I was only risking old-fashioned ailments like syphilis, gonorrhea or trench-foot. Besides, there was no sign of a waste-bin and I didn't want to put the fire out.

She kicked off some unpleasant sandals and removed her jeans and pants simultaneously. She had very little sense of the dramatic. However, I was able to peer down into the jeans as she held them in front of her. This was an error. I won't upset you with the unpleasant details but let's just say that, judging by her pants, her arse was a very heavy smoker. Now, I'm no snob, but you would think that someone whose job involved working with the public would have had a tad more pride in her appearance. She was just filthy. As she stood naked before me, I could see white lines down the length of her inner thigh where some indefinable fluid had run down her legs, cutting its way through the grime. (Don't you wish you'd skipped this when you had the chance?) She sat on the floor, with her elbows on the seat of the settee, and spread herself in anticipation. A blind man would have presumed that someone had opened one of those tins of salmon rescued from Scott's Arctic expedition. I dropped to my knees, hoping that I could get underneath the smell, the way people trapped in burning buildings get underneath the smoke, but there was no escape. I noticed that she had 'Corky' tattooed on her thigh. 'Is that your name?' I asked. 'No,' she said, 'it's a nickname.'

'Oh,' I said, wondering if perhaps she was a lover of fine wines.

I undid my powder-blue flares and revealed myself to her. She looked at it the way Imelda Marcos might have looked at a pair of supermarket plimsolls. With a bit of manual assistance from her and a nostalgic flashback to four girls' bums in a physics lab from me, the deeply unsatisfactory deed was done.

This was an even worse experience than you might imagine. Half-way through, the door, presumably leading to another room, began to rattle. I heard children's voices. 'Hey, come away,' a woman's voice said. 'Corky's got a gentleman in there.' This truly was the nineteenth century. I felt sure that at any moment the woman would tell the children to get back up the chimney. But I heard no more.

Her part played, Corky began to thaw somewhat. In fact, she became what I would almost describe as chatty. 'What's a nice bloke like you doing in business?' she politely enquired. I had to admit that I was starting to favour her euphemism over mine. I explained that it wasn't my fiver. It could be my imagination but I think she looked a bit hurt.

'You should come over to my place in Aston,' she said. 'I've got all sorts of equipment there.' Hopefully, she meant soap and water. She even offered me use of what seemed to be the communal J-Cloth to clean myself up. It lay at the side of the hearth, and looked like it might scurry for cover when she reached for it. As she picked it up, it crackled in her hand. I declined. She gave herself a quick wipe-round and put it back to dry. Finally, she explained to me that, for eight quid, I could have her and her friend outside, for a threesome.

Now, I love a bargain, but in the end I declined. Although I did imagine with glee sliding the eight quid across the bar-room table towards my mate. As I left, I shook Corky's hand and actually said, 'It's been a business doing pleasure with you.' I don't think she got it. Or maybe she'd heard it before.

I spent the next two weeks having to tell this story to my friends, which is why I remember it in such grim detail.

When I got back that night I went for a piss, and suddenly, when my once-virgin nob emerged, that tin of Scott's Arctic expedition salmon was opened once more. No wonder Captain Oates went for that walk.

*

At seventeen I started to get a bit disillusioned with the Catholic Church. It was the usual stuff. I wasn't convinced by their views on contraception, masturbation, divorce, or even homosexuality. I single out the last one because up until my mid-teens I had, like everyone else I knew, felt that moes, as we called them, were worthy firing-squad material. By the way, the term mo was, as you may have guessed, an abbreviation of homosexual. I had assumed that it was a common expression but think now that it may have been exclusive to our area. This was made evident when I did my first-ever paid gig at London's Comedy Store and told the audience I had just been to see a fabulous gay musical entitled *Five Moes Named Guy*. The audience just looked at me. (You know, I'm having the same problem with the plural of 'mo' as I did for the plural of 'Des'. Should there be an 'e'?)

My view on moes had changed totally after watching a TV drama called *The Naked Civil Servant*, featuring John Hurt as Quentin Crisp. For the first time, it occurred to me that moes could be witty, clever and likeable. The anti-mo characters, on the other hand, were all ignorant and humourless. I know people slag telly off and say it's mind-numbing and low-brow, but I believe that watching that drama made me a better person and its influence has stayed with me. I even wrote a gay anthem called 'Marmite Soldiers'. That's a joke. I never said I'd stopped doing gags about them.

Anyway, these sort of objections to Catholic teaching were fairly widespread. My other doubts were a bit more hardcore. Papal infallibility, the concept of purgatory, transubstantiation (oh, look it up). These were more technical problems. My mate Tim's family were Christadelphian, and I started to get interested in that. I even toyed with the idea of switching to the Church of England, though I wouldn't have been seen dead in a purple crimplene safari-suit. I hadn't stopped believing in God but, putting it simply, I was uneasy about the power, riches, grandeur and resulting attitudes of the Catholic Church, and felt that wasn't what religion should be about. I imagine similar doubts occasionally run through the minds of people who support Manchester United.

So I stopped going to Mass and announced to my parents that the Catholic Church was hypocritical and un-Christian. If you don't come from a Catholic family, it'll be hard for you to understand the upset this caused, but what did I care? I was young, idealistic, headstrong and, of course, drunk. So the Catholic Church and me parted company.

Meanwhile, Tim's family were very keen for me to join their lot. I suppose they thought my conversion might bring Tim back to the fold.

I was with Tim one night, driving down Broad Street, one of the main roads that lead into Birmingham City Centre. Well, he was driving. My attempts at getting a driving licence had come to an emergency stop a few weeks before. I had done my driving test in nearby Quinton. About two minutes in, having just turned the corner from the Test Centre, I stopped at a zebra crossing to let people cross. So far so good. I took off the hand-brake (hand-brake at a zebra crossing! That brings back memories) and set off again, but suddenly there was a loud bump and an old man was on the bonnet, his terrified face about three inches from my windscreen. The examiner yelped in horror like a puppy that's had its foot trodden on, I braked, and the old man slid back on to the road. Obviously, all these things happened more or less simultaneously. 'I couldn't help that,' I snapped at the examiner. 'He just dashed out.'

'Dashed out?' said the examiner, in a voice that would have hit the 'Oh, pretty baby' note with ease. 'He's about seventy. He hasn't dashed anywhere for thirty years.' By now, the old man was limping away – I think I heard him say 'young fool' – and the examiner got out of the car to call him back. I suppose there were forms to be filled in, but the OAP was having none of it. He muttered something about not wanting to get involved and hobbled off. The examiner reluctantly returned to the hot-seat, I took a breath and drove on. You would think that the examiner would have stopped the test there and then, but he didn't. He had me doing three-point turns and reversing round corners, even an after-the-horse-had-bolted emergency stop. It says something about my naturally optimistic view of life that by the end I was starting to think that I might have just sneaked it. I didn't. And I was so disheartened that I didn't drive again for ten years. If that old guy hadn't stepped out, I might have passed my test, bought a car, had my drinking legally restrained, and led a very different life. At the same time, I might have passed my test, bought a car, carried on drinking, and ended up killing myself and a number of innocent fellow road-users. But I failed, and slid across into the passenger seat of life.

As Tim, all after-shave, leather bomber-jacket and signet-ring with the family crest on, drove down Broad Street in his blue Mini Clubman, he broke the news that his mom had set up a date, for me and him, with a couple of nice girls from the Christadelphian church. I explained that I had no intention of going on a date with two 'my vagina's a closed book' girls from his mom's church. Tim was pissed off by this. 'Oh, you really get on my nerves sometimes,' he said. He leaned back, over the seat, and started steering the car with his knees so he could punch the ceiling in frustration. We were doing between 50 and 60 mph, and I watched as the car headed towards the central reservation. This was about nine on a Saturday night.

I remember saying, 'Watch that fuckin' pylon' (I thought bollards were called pylons) as we ploughed through a bollard, uprooted a grey-metal lamppost, and overturned so that the car was skimming down the street on its side. Neither of us wore seatbelts – we thought they were for puffs – and I remember lying against the side window, watching sparks hitting the glass as the door-handle ground against the road surface. When the car finally juddered to a halt, right opposite the statue of Birmingham's industrial founding-fathers, Watt, Boulton and Murdoch, Tim's eight-track came on. It was Deep Purple's 'Highway Star', the first line of which is 'Nobody's gonna take my car, I'm gonna race it to the ground'.

Tim, who had slid down on top of me, pushed open the driver's door directly above us, and we climbed out. Loads of Saturday-night revellers came running over and we stood on top of the car, doing a gesture of celebration that no one seems to do anymore. It consists of interlocking your fingers to form one big fist and then shaking it either side of your head. We stood there, relieved to be alive and unhurt, like two astronauts who had just clambered out of an Apollo capsule. We were so excited we danced on the car for a bit, and then ran off into the city centre to get drunk, leaving the written-off car behind us. Incredibly, apart from an admonishing letter to Tim from the police, no further action was taken.

That could easily have been that. If we'd been going slower, we wouldn't have had the momentum to uproot the lamppost. The car would have stopped and Tim and me would have gone through the windscreen. So, the moral of this story is drive faster. Seriously, though, it was close. Looking back, I would have hated to have died not-Catholic.

Hughes and Johnson's was doing my head in. I'd been there for two years. My fellow drawing-office worker had gone and I was left solely in charge. I sneaked my guitar in and spent my days learning Bob Dylan songs. He was replacing the Stones in my affections. Elvis, of course, was an ever-present. No one seemed to care if I was busy or not. Because my office was separate from the rest, I was able to turn up late, and did so on a regular basis. I once had two days off, and when I returned I realised no one had noticed. But I was bored, bored, bored. Of course, there were laughs as well. I was spending more and more time in the factory, measuring broken pipes and stuff. It was a strange place, with massive hammers banging red-hot lumps of metal into shape. It was loud and scary and everyone who worked there was deaf and had three fingers. I remember a driver up from London remarking on the fact that the factory was a bit out-dated. He was amazed, for example, that it had soil floors. 'All that's missing is the three-cornered hats,' he said.

Then there was Joe. Joe was a labourer, about six feet tall and with the look of a young Spike Milligan. He was a friendly chap but not, to be honest, the brightest lamp in the shop. His wife, who I'd seen in the New Inn a time or two but not always with her husband, had just had a baby, and she nipped into the factory one day, needing to see Joe about something or other. Everyone likes a baby, and even the biggest and toughest men came over to wiggle what fingers they had left at the new arrival. I mean the baby, not the wife. Soon, there was much muttering among the ranks. Well, actually it was not so much muttering as slightly reduced shouting. Muttering would have been pretty pointless amongst the thudding hammers, especially if you're deaf. The big topic of conversation was Joe's baby. It was very obviously of mixed race, a fact that Joe had mentioned to no one and didn't refer to even when the baby was being shown off. Joe and Mrs Joe were both white. Eventually, after wife and baby had left the premises, one of the freer spirits among the work-force asked Joe whether it bothered him that his wife had given birth to a baby that was obviously not his. Joe looked puzzled. 'What d'you mean, not mine?' he said.

'Well,' said the slightly deflated worker, not used to hampering his communications with diplomacy, 'he doesn't look like you.'

'D'you mean the colour?' asked Joe. The not-quite-so-free-spirit-now nodded. 'Oh, I asked me wife about that.' We all held our breath. 'Apparently it was them iron tablets she took when she was pregnant,' he explained. Thus, Joe, his wife, and their medical phenomenon of a child stepped straight into local folklore.

But Hughes and Johnson's was still doing my head in. I'd fucked up at school, I realised that now. My mind felt like Terry's owl, restricted and yearning for flight. I went to my mom and dad and asked them if they'd help me out financially if I quit work and went and did some O- and A-levels, full-time. My mom, understandably enough, pointed out that I'd never done any studying when I was at school so why should I start now? But my dad surprised me. He said everyone deserved a second chance, and if it was what I wanted to do, he'd help me as much as he could. So I did it. I turned my back on Hughes and Jack's, as it was known, and started my course at Warley College of Technology.

However, despite the fact that my mom and dad were bunging me a few bob, I had to supplement my earnings by doing some more factory work, this time as a labourer. Firstly, my mom got me a job at the glass factory where she worked. Her job was putting those glass slides they use on microscopes into little cardboard boxes, with a slice of foam-rubber to stop them moving about. She did this eight hours a day, five days a week. My job was to keep the women supplied with glass, tidy up, and do what I was fucking told. The worst bit was having to dump the scrap glass. I'd load a wheelbarrow up as high as I could, then tip it down a hole in the floor. I'd then run for cover, because as soon as the glass hit the skip several floors below, it would send up a massive cloud of glass-dust that, I suspected, wasn't that good for inhaling.

Then I worked at a local furniture factory, just around the corner from where Kevin Rowlands, the main man for Dexy's Midnight Runners, lived. My main job here was to smash up perfectly good tables, bookcases and three-piece suites and burn them in the furnace. Don't ask. I didn't. I quite liked this. I'd let my old vandalism skills get a bit rusty and this was a chance to sharpen them up a bit. In fact, I loved smashing and burning so much that I did what everyone thought was impossible and set the furnace on fire. Fire-engines were called and there was all sorts of commotion, and it wasn't even Carnival Day. I was taken off furnace-duty for good after that. It was at the furniture factory that I perfected the skill of eating my sandwiches while I worked so I'd have a whole lunch hour dedicated purely to boozing. I found that four pints of cider made the afternoon whiz past that little bit quicker. I worked with a bloke called Gary, who became a good mate. We'd spend the whole day talking about music, and he'd make me compilation tapes of his favourite acts, Iggy Pop, Velvet Underground and The Electric Chairs. It was the summer of 'Come on, Eileen' and we'd often belt it out in the afternoons if there were no bosses about. I wonder if Kevin ever heard it in the distance.

At college I started, for the first time in my life, to actually do some work. I felt like I had to make the most of my second chance. I found that I really liked the English literature stuff, and even read one or two of the course books. Not the novels, of course. I preferred Coles Notes, the 'handy study guides'. Coles Notes were like novels for people who had other stuff to do. And I had other stuff to do. I'd met a girl at college and we were spending lots of time together. If you ignored the fact that she was spotty, she looked a bit like a young Glenda Jackson. (Have you noticed that a lot of the people I've known looked like a version of somebody famous? Strange.) I had a real thing about Glenda Jackson. I used to have *The Music Lovers* on video and watched that scene with her on the train, over and over. Now, coincidentally, she represents my area of London in parliament. There can't be that many people who've had a wank to their local MP. (Now I'm going to get loads of letters from men who live in Kensington and Chelsea.)

I don't think I should name this girl, so I'll call her Glenda. Her and me got very physical but she drew the line at penetration. Of course, I didn't tell any of my friends this. I said we were banging away like a shit-house door in a gale, and tried hard to make this dream a reality. I really wanted a relationship that was like the movies, preferably *The Music Lovers*, but they always seemed to turn out weird. I was around Glenda's one night, snogging her on the settee. I had my arms inside her open shirt, and she had one arm around my waist, one in my lap, and was running her fingers through my hair, in a very sensual way. After about ten minutes of this, it began to dawn on me that what she was doing actually required three arms. I looked up and Glenda's Down's Syndrome sister, who I didn't even know existed, was playfully massaging my scalp. No disrespect to her, but after she was chucked out I had to sit down, have a couple of cans, and slowly pull myself together before I could laugh about it with Glenda.

Not long after, we went to a dance where I introduced her to my mate, Duck. Duck, on leave from the army, was something of a ladies' man. Now, in my experience, anyone who can be accurately described as a 'ladies' man' can also always be accurately described as a complete cunt, but Duck was, surprisingly, quite a nice chap. (And I'd have to say, if pushed, that he looked like a cheeky version of Paul Reaney. Oh well, one for the football fans.) Nevertheless, nice chap or not, he made a play for Glenda that night. Perhaps I slightly blotted my own copy-book by getting up on stage when they played 'The Stripper' and doing a very drunken striptease which culminated not only in a lot of unashamed nob-exposure but also in quite a lot of nob-stretching and wiggling as well.

You would have thought, would you not, that this would have made Glenda love me even more, but who can predict the whims of a woman. Duck whisked Glenda off her feet while I stretched and wiggled, and saw her the next night, behind my back. Having been tipped off by friends, I confronted him about this. He admitted everything and offered to let me hit him as hard as I liked, in the face, because, as he explained, 'it will make us both feel better'. If Glenda had made me a similar offer I would have gone for it but I could not bring myself to hit a mate. So we shook hands and he bought me a couple of ciders. Then, after some banter, he said to me, in front of about ten mates, 'Mind you, you could have told me she was a virgin. I got blood all over my brand-new sheepskin.' Much jeering and laughing followed. Duck had been away in the army during the course of my lying so he just looked confused. What I couldn't achieve in three months, he had managed in an evening. 'I must join another band,' I thought to myself.

A few weeks later, I was round my mate Nick's house when he stuck on a new album he'd just bought by an American band called The Ramones. When I heard the first track, 'Blitzkrieg Bop', the hairs went up on the back of my neck. There and then, I decided I wanted to be in a punk band.

This was 1976 and punk was only just starting to filter through to the provinces. I used to read about it in *NME* every week, usually accompanied by a picture of Siouxie Sue in black PVC. Essentially, that was all I needed to know. Then I saw an advert in the Birmingham *Evening Mail* saying that a punk band was looking for a vocalist. I phoned the number and we arranged to meet in Yates' Wine Lodge on Corporation Street that coming Saturday night. The punk band were two brothers called Paul and Alan, a drummer and a guitarist. They suggested an immediate audition so we stepped out on to a busy Saturday night Corporation Street and I sang an a cappella, full-volume 'Blitzkrieg Bop'. When I'd done my final 'Hey ho, let's go', they smiled and offered me the job.

We rehearsed in a church hall in the Yardley area of Birmingham. One number involved me reading a passage from *The Black Panther Story*, a book about the villain who had done over that post office near Hughes and Jack's a few years before. The chosen passage described the Panther killing some innocent night-watchman at the nearby Dudley Freightliner depot. In court, the Panther claimed his shotgun had gone off accidentally, twice. As I read, in a punky, ranting-poet voice, the boys blasted out a punk-instrumental version of Roy C's 'Shotgun Wedding'. One night it got so loud the neighbours complained and a police constable came knocking at the door. He decided to do the community-policing bit and got quite chatty. 'Have you done many gigs?' he asked, thus demonstrating that he knew the lingo. Sadly, he pronounced 'gigs' with a soft 'g', and punk bands didn't really do 'jigs'. Still, he was very nice, and didn't seem at all fazed by the fact that the drummer was wearing a Nazi uniform.

I started going to loads of punk gigs. 'Anarchy in the UK' had just been released, and me and my mate, Fez, went to see the Sex Pistols in Bogart's, a poky little cellar-bar on New Street. Word had got round about the Pistols and the place was jammed. Paul and Alan were in there somewhere but Fez and me were not about to give up our spot at the bar to go and find them. We waited and waited but still no Pistols. Bogart's was only licensed till 10.30 and it was already nearly twenty past nine. Fez and me were resisting going for a piss because it was so hard to move, but eventually Fez gave in and disappeared to the bogs. It took him twenty minutes to get there and back.

I wasn't having any of that. I reached over the bar and managed to grab an empty lemonade bottle without being seen. In the crowd, it was easy to piss in it unnoticed, so I pissed till the bottle was full and then replaced it.

Shortly afterwards, a very big bloke with a moustache ordered a pint of lager and a glass of lemonade. Fez and me watched in silence as the barmaid picked up my bottle of piss and filled a lady's glass from it. One side-effect of heavy drinking is, of course, that your piss loses its normal yellowy colour and becomes clear. Tash-man passed the glass to his, I have to say very pretty, girlfriend, and she had a girl-sized swig. She turned up her nose, said something to Tashy, and then he took a swig as well. El Tasho turned to the barmaid and said, 'This ain't lemonade. It's just warm water.' At which point the barmaid took a swig as well, and then offered it to a second barmaid for verification. The second barmaid agreed with the Tash-meister, and they opened another bottle. Fez and me were crying with laughter but we had to hold back in case Johnny Tash got suspicious. Was this, I asked Fez, what people meant by a night on the piss?

At ten, the Pistols finally showed. This was their original line-up, with Glenn Matlock on bass, rather than Sid Vicious. They were so loud in the small basement room that Fez and me put cigarette-ends in our ears to take the edge off the volume. A half-hour set and they were done. As they left the room I stood cheering wildly. Johnny Rotten grabbed my hand, shook it and said, 'Thanks mate. They won't let us play anymore.' I know it's not very punk ethicish, but I was really thrilled that he'd spoken to me and shook my hand.

Twenty years later, we had him chucked off *Fantasy World Cup* during the commercial break because he was being such an arse. As soon as I got home after that incident, I put on the Pistols' 'God save the Queen' to make sure it wasn't spoiled forever. It still sounded great.

The place to see punk in Birmingham was Barbarella's nightclub. I was down there most Tuesdays, Fridays and Saturdays for the punk nights. I saw The Clash, who were brilliant even though there was a bloke at the back, with long hair and glasses, who kept shouting, 'Oh, why don't you play a diminished chord?' Incredibly, The Clash were supporting a local rock band called Suburban Studs, who had jumped on the punk bandwagon. They were so bad we had to ice them off, that is, throw handful after handful of ice-cubes at them until they went away.

I never got through these gigs sober and was often woken by a bouncer, standing over me as I sat, face flat on the bar-table. I'd look up and people would be sweeping up and washing glasses, and I'd creep out and stagger the four miles home. This was fine if I paced my drinking so that I was still conscious for the band, but sometimes I got it wrong. I slept through Billy Idol's Generation X two nights running. I didn't make it home at all the first night. I woke up at about 8.00 a.m. on a grass verge near the very busy Five Ways Roundabout. No passer-by had bothered to find out if I was alright. They probably thought I fell out of a fuckin' aeroplane.

Anyway, the punk band never really got past the rehearsal stage, so I drifted away. They stuck with it, became the Prefectz, and got quite a following on the punk circuit. The last time I saw Alan was in Barbarella's. Elvis had just died and he said he wasn't bothered. We never spoke again.

I was happy at college, and had made a lot of new friends. One of these, an albino kid called Smithy, like me had become obsessed with kung fu films. Bruce Lee, of course, was our hero, but we really liked the obscure films as well, stuff like *Deaf-mute Heroine* and *Kung Fu the Head-Crusher*. We'd spend hours reciting dialogue from the films and talking like we'd been badly dubbed. My mate Tim and me even went to a place that advertised itself as a School of Kung Fu to find out if we could get lessons. The bloke at the school told us that if he taught us, after six months, we'd not only be killing-machines but also 'able to run to, say, Bristol, without getting out of breath'. Which, I suppose, would be perfect if you wanted to kill somebody in Bristol. We didn't sign up because he never looked at us throughout the conversation. Instead, he gazed into the mirror, blow-drying his hair.

I actually owned one of those kung fu stars, y'know, a flat metal star about five inches across, with razor-sharp edges for skimming at enemies. I got a mate from Hughes and Jack's to make one specially for me. He even put pretend Chinese writing on it and stuff. I used to go to Langley Park to practise my aim but a bloody dog ran off with it. Mind you, it was in his back at the time.

I made the last bit up. Honest.

I was the cabaret at the Waterstone's annual dinner last night. Waterstone's is, of course, one of the biggest booksellers in the country. Part of writing a book, I am discovering, is meeting a lot of people who sell books because then, for some reason, their shops will sell more of your book than they would have done if they hadn't met you. My publishers are very keen on this process, but I can't quite see it myself. The logic, I'm told, is that a manager of, say, Waterstone's in Leicester meets me, and a few months later when the book is about to come out, she sees a list of potential books to stock and thinks, 'Oh, I've met him. I'll order loads of his book and put it on very prominent display and actually pressure customers into buying it by saying stuff like, "What's this you're getting? *Captain Corelli's Mandolin*? Why are you buying that? I've never met Louis de Carbonari, or whatever his stupid name is. You wanna buy that Frank Skinner book. I spoke to him for forty seconds in a London hotel. Wait there and I'll go get it for you."'

Of course, this would be lovely, but I just can't imagine that it works like that. If it does, the rep who handles the Penguin Classics is on a bit of a hiding to nothing: 'Hold on a minute, Erasmus, Gustave Flaubert, St. Ignatius Loyola? But, I haven't met any of these.'

Anyway, I went along to the dinner and agreed to do a bit of stand-up. Apparently, this really helps as well. Unless, of course, you die on your arse, in which case the manager at Leicester will be saying stuff like 'Don't buy that. I saw him do stand-up once. He was shit.'

When I got to the dinner, there were several other celebrity authors wandering around getting met. I saw World Cup hero Sir Geoff Hurst, quiz-show host Anne Robinson, ex-boxer Chris Eubank, ex-rugby player Jeremy Guscott, and former *Old Grey Whistle Test* host 'Whispering' Bob Harris. Whispering Bob gave a short speech in which he described the event, as far as the celebs were concerned, as being a 'turn-up for the books'. A good line, I thought, but no one seemed to get it. Perhaps I'd taken the edge off Whispering Bob's speech by shouting 'Speak up' just after he began. If I'd failed at comedy, I think I could have been quite happy as a heckler.

There was a brief awards ceremony, with categories like 'Best outlet with a turnover of over ten million pounds', and Anne Robinson presented an award. She chose this moment to, I suppose you'd call it rally the troops. She said that she was going to work very hard to sell her book and she felt sure that 'if we all pulled together' it would be a big success. It seemed to me that Anne fully expected the Waterstone's lot to be surprised and impressed that she was offering to help sell her own book. Perhaps they were, but I didn't fancy this 'we will fight them on the beaches' approach myself.

Then came my bit. I walked on stage and stood under the enormous 'W' that provided the backdrop. I stared at it for a while and said, 'Welcome to Frank Skinner's A–Z of Sex. Tonight,' gesturing upward towards the W, 'my own personal favourite.' OK, it *was* a wanking joke, but I had to wait about three or four seconds for the laugh. Too complicated for an opener, or just not very funny? Either way, I proceeded, and by the end of the half-hour (I'd been asked to do fifteen minutes but got slightly carried away) it was a job well done. I had one sticky moment when I suggested, following the success of Stephen Fry reading *Harry Potter* for eight and a half hours on Radio 4 last Boxing Day, the station were now looking for a children's book that would last for the whole of the Christmas period. I said they'd settled for *Stig of the Dump*, which isn't really long enough but they'd solve the problem by getting Stephen Hawking to read it. This got a few laughs, but also a few bad-taste noises. I knew this was on the cards but my logic had been, 'Fuck it. It's about books so it's in.' Anyway, it was a minor blip and didn't seem to do too much damage.

When I'd arrived, earlier that evening, one of the organisers had asked me if I'd mind introducing Chris Eubank after my set as he'd like to do a poem. Of course, introducing someone at the end of your set is always heart-wrenching because, as you leave the stage, you can never be sure how much of the applause is for you, and how much for them, but I agreed to endure this uncertainty and introduce Mr E. Also, to be able to say that I had played even a minor part in a Chris Eubank poetry recital was more than I could resist.

So it was that the former WBO Super-Middleweight Champion of the World stood before four hundred non-paying guests at the Waterstone's annual dinner and recited, from memory, Henry Reed's 'Naming of Parts'. There was a time when most ladies and gentlemen of any worth had at least one poem at their disposal that they could recite by heart. This tradition of recitation has largely fallen by the wayside, but I hereby witness that, on Monday, June 11th, 2001, at the Novotel, Hammersmith, former bruiser Chris Eubank brought it back with a bang. All boxers are brave, but to recite 'Naming of Parts' at 11.20 p.m., to a bunch of away-from-home bookshop-managers, all gazing longingly at the Penguin-sponsored free bar, is something else.

I recognised the poem from the 'War Poets' anthology I studied at Warley College. It describes a young soldier, standing, transfixed by the natural beauty of the landscape while his superior officer explains the various parts of a rifle. Chris played both parts, making the officer gruff and abrupt and the young soldier dreamy and effete. Some of the book-sellers grew restless and there was even some barely suppressed sniggering. But I was mightily impressed, even though it's debatable whether Chris Eubank should choose to recite a poem that includes the lines:

> This is the lower sling swivel. And that
> Is the upper sling swivel, whose use you will see
> When you are given your slings.

It certainly saw a few hands covering pint glasses in the front row, but his performance was word-perfect and from the heart.

I didn't get a chance to speak to him afterwards, but I wondered if he was aware of those people who were sniggering. If I'd asked him to describe them, he may well have disproved the oft-cited fact that there is no word in the English language that rhymes with 'month'. Nevertheless, so inspiring to me were his efforts that I have since resolved to learn, by heart, Gerard Manley Hopkins' 'The Wreck of the Deutschland' as a tribute to a man who I can now honestly say is 'Simply the Best'.

As my story moves through the late seventies and into the eighties, we reach a fairly significant turning-point in the book. Frankly, I'm starting to lose faith in your attention span and reckon it's about time we got me moving into the world of comedy. I said at the start that when I read a biography or autobiography (usually a biography. I don't read many auto-biographies because you don't get enough vicious attacks on the subject), I always spend the first chunk of the book shouting 'Hurry up and get famous, you bastard', and now I find I've fannied around in my wilderness years for far too long. I could go back and hack out some passages, but I have written this book through the course of a crippling national foot-and-mouth epidemic and I've seen enough carnage for one year. Furthermore, I was completely arseholed for almost all of my twenties, so my memories of that period are, at best, intermittent. Many's the pop-quiz I've sat out of when confronted with questions about the eighties. Therefore, a quicker-than-usual move through this period of my life could be something of a blessing for all of us.

So, what I'm going to do is fast-forward through my twenties, stop and settle a while at what I regard as absolutely key points, then move on. It is, I'll admit, an approach largely inspired by watching a massive amount of pornographic videos when I lived with David Baddiel.

Fear not, I'll be hob-nobbing with Bob Monkhouse before you know where you are.

I was woken up by my radio-alarm at eight this morning. I have it tuned into Five Live so I can hear Caroline doing the traffic reports as I shower or drink tea. I was fast asleep when it kicked in, so the voice talking about horse-racing took a while to reach me. He was saying something about the Two Thousand Guineas being a very big horse race. In my semi-comatose state, I wondered why, if it is such a big horse-race, they don't call it the Two Thousand Whinnies. I smiled to myself, and began drifting back to sleep.

Then, a few minutes later, I drifted awake again, and heard a reference to the TV show, *Who Wants to Be a Millionaire?* I hadn't moved. My eyes were still closed. It occurred to me that a desperately dull quiz show could be devised in which the winner, rather than be given a cash prize, is set up in a small hat-manufacturing business. It could be called *Who Wants to Be a Milliner?*

Two elaborate puns and I was still more or less asleep. Imagine my inner turmoil if I'd never found an outlet for all this rubbish. I might have become that most tragic of figures, the office-joker, forwarding amusing e-mails, sending Wicked Willy greeting cards, and referring to myself as a prankster.

I left Warley College of Technology with a total of five O-levels and three A-levels (a 'B' in English but only 'E' for Sociology and General Studies) and went to Birmingham Polytechnic to do teacher training. Like virtually everyone else on the teacher training course, I had no desire whatsoever to be a teacher but couldn't think of anything else to do. Slowly, the others seemed to grow into it and soon people were marching around carrying overhead projectors and doing things with crepe-paper. I wasn't. I had a five-week teaching practice in a local junior school during the second term, and it was one of the worst experiences of my life. Elvis Costello was in the charts with 'Oliver's Army' at the time, and every morning as I passed through the school gates I would sing to the other student-teachers walking in with me, 'And I would rather be anywhere else than here today.'

The kids were all cunts, and I became so desperate I even grew a beard to try and hide behind. This, combined with my poor performance, gave the school's headmaster a fairly negative impression of me. When, thank God, the teaching practice finally ended, he called me into his office and said that he feared if I didn't sort myself out, he could imagine me ending up as a tramp. My closing speeches from disappointed headmasters were getting ever more bleak.

Still, I battled through to the end of the first year, and during the summer holidays, I resolved that I would work much harder in future and really try to turn myself into a good teacher. Thus, it was with new-found purpose that I strode into the polytechnic on that first day of the second year. I managed to sustain my fervour until, as I stood eagerly awaiting my first class, a lecturer took me to one side and asked me if I'd received the letter telling me I'd failed the first year, and was therefore off the course. I hadn't. She looked guilty, said sorry, and walked away. I walked, crestfallen, into the Junior Common Room, sat down on one of the yellow-plastic-upholstered benches, and wondered what the fuck I was going to do with the rest of my life. All the support, financial and emotional, my parents had given me, all my dreams and hopes of doing something significant, had come to nothing. I sat on my own and drank a cup of coffee from the machine, just like when I was expelled. Was it going to be another night of boiler-suits and slapped faces?

Then I was aware of someone standing over me. I half-expected it to be some bloke with a big scythe, but it wasn't. It was the same lecturer who'd told me about the letter. She said that, although I had miserably failed every other section of my course, I had passed the English Literature component with a straight 'A'. Therefore, two of the lecturers had put forward the suggestion that rather than be booted out, I should be transferred to the BA (Hons) Degree in English. However, she explained, there were a couple of large problems. Firstly, local authorities didn't give out two first-year grants, so I'd have to live on nothing for twelve months, and secondly, the bosses of the English department might not accept me on the course. It all sounded very dubious, but I was in the gutter and any helping hand, no matter how slippery, would have to do. It also meant I could delay telling my parents about another miserable failure. If the transfer happened, I could say it was my choice. So, I went home, and when they asked me how the second year had started, I said, 'Really well.'

The next day I went to see the Careers Officer at the Job Centre in Aston. I don't recall his name but it was something double-barrelled. After a five-minute chat, he told me he couldn't think of any organisation that I would be an asset to, and he felt the only advice he could offer me was to stay on the dole as long as I possibly could. It wasn't quite the morale-boost I'd been looking for.

A week later, with me still pretending that I was going to college every day but actually chilling out with an unemployed mate, the English department agreed to let me transfer. The next morning, I phoned my local authority and asked them if

I could have another first-year grant. The woman there said that was very unlikely, and the only time it ever happened was if someone was transferring from a four-year course to a three-year course. 'How long is the course you are transferring from?' she asked. The answer was three years. 'Four years,' I said. 'Oh, well. That's alright, then,' she said.

A few days later, my first term's cheque arrived in the post. No one had bothered to verify my claim. They just stamped the request and sent me the money. I joined the BA (Hons) English course, read all the books I'd never read, discovered all the writers I'd never heard of, felt my mind expanding day-by-day, and finished up with the highest marks on the whole course. The following year I went to Warwick University and got a Master's Degree in English Literature. I'd had my third chance and I'd fuckin' taken it. And neither my mom and dad, nor my local authority, ever knew the truth.

At the risk of sounding like a complete berk, studying English literature really changed my life. I went through all the stupid student-things, like letting the beard go totally wild so I looked like I should be in an Irish folk band, wearing army-surplus gear, and even, for a spell, going a bit left-wing. But, more importantly, I started thinking about things differently. I had always been obsessed with words. I'd repeat some phrases over and over just because I liked the feel of them on my lips: a quotation from a Nazi leader, 'When I hear the word culture, I reach for my revolver'; a bit of stray snooker-commentary, 'the game of chess played on the green baize'; or a sentence from a letter to a pornographic magazine, ' "Guess you'd like to handle these floppy old tits of mine," she said, swinging them to and fro in a massive display of succulence.' I started thinking more and more about turns of phrase and use of vocabulary. Having read my prose, you may find that hard to believe, but my obsession with words was not entirely fruitless.

It enabled me to slowly become that most heroic of men, the poetic drunk. I was at my happiest leaning on a bar, foul-mouthing, philosophising, and free-associating with a bunch of cronies.

Mind you, not all the side-effects of a literary education are good. After my success in my first degree, I had a massive burst of self-confidence that was perilously close to cockiness. One night in the Duck Inn, my regular haunt, I had a debate with a very hard bloke I knew called Duncan. I suggested that, given my superior intellect, it was very stupid of him to challenge my opinion. He beat the shit out of me, and the next day I looked at my bruised face in the mirror and said out loud, 'You deserved that, you arrogant bastard.' I went up the pub, thanked Duncan for saving my soul, and bought him a pint. I'm not sure he ever understood, but I have no doubt that beating pulled me back from the brink of lifelong cuntiness. Maybe they should bring back flogging.

One non-academic milestone that occurred at Birmingham Poly was that I wrote and starred in a comic play, as part of the poly's 'D.H. Lawrence Week' celebrations. It was called *Sadie Chatterley's Lodger*, a kitchen-sink comedy in which I played Lawrence as an amorous Jewish lodger, chiefly because I'd been to a Vicars and Tarts party as a rabbi a few weeks earlier and still had the costume. The play began with a prologue, sung by me in George Formby, cheeky-wink mode, complete with ukulele. It had the same tune as 'When I'm Cleaning Windows', and included references to Lawrence's Oedipus-complex and various risqué episodes from his novels.

> Here's a song I love to hum
> About a lad from Nottinghum
> A nice boy and he loved his mum,
> David Herbert Lawrence.

In the books of his I've got
The characters are really hot
And showing everything they've got,
David Herbert Lawrence.

The Rainbow seemed a nice book, I'm afraid I spoke too soon,
With big fat pregnant women dancing underneath the moon.

Nude men wrestling by the fire
Temperatures get higher and higher
It certainly made me perspire.
David Herbert Lawrence.

Typical undergraduate drivel, but I liked being up there getting laughs. The play itself was pretty disgusting, including a sex-scene with Sadie's neighbour where I tell the audience, mid-shag, I'm thrilled because she's a virgin. Then she turns to them and explains that she's still got her tights on. Still, it stormed it, and afterwards a lecturer told me he'd never seen anything that 'adhered so strictly and consistently to bad taste'. Signs of things to come, I suppose.

Anyway, with two English degrees under my belt, the way forward was pretty obvious. I went on the dole for three and a half years.

I just got into Northern Seoul today. I don't mean I'm spending my weekends at the Wigan Casino. I mean I'm in Korea. I'm going to be making a documentary about Korean and Japanese football when I've finished this book, so I'm out here with Phil the producer/director and Bernie the assistant producer. Phil, mild-mannered in thick spectacles, looks like a very brainy twelve-year-old, but has made loads of documentaries and you get the feeling he really knows what he's doing. Bernie is blonde, business-like, and probably in her thirties. If I'd seen her in a bar, I would have said she was cute, but I don't think she's the kind of woman who'd really enjoy that adjective. They're both good company, though, and I've been looking forward to the trip. We're doing a bit of a recce. I didn't find out how to spell 'recce' until very recently, and now I find myself on one. I must be careful not to find out how to spell 'heamephrodite'.

Sorry, I'm just trying to work out what tense I'm writing this in. There's a temptation to write these journal-bits in Present Tense but I'm going to switch back to Past Tense now. I think it's a bit classier.

Having met up with Phil and Bernie, who've already been here for a week, we went out to meet a couple of English guys, Brian and Mike, who've been living in Korea for about twelve years. They used to be journalists but now they do PR, including helping with Korea's World Cup bid. We had a traditional Korean meal, with bowls and bowls of pickle-type stuff, and a bit too much sitting on the floor for my liking. When we'd finished, I limped outside and noticed that the barber-shop across the road was still open. It was nearly midnight. Mike explained that barber-shops in Seoul are a bit unusual. The barber asks you if you need any special services, and if you say yes, he steps out of the individual booth that the chair is in, and a young woman comes in and masturbates you.

No, I didn't. In fact, there seemed something very odd about the whole concept of what I suppose you'd call the barber's hired-hand. I wonder if being in a barber-shop influences her approach to her work? I wouldn't want to be masturbated by a woman who was saying stuff like, 'D'you see the match last night, sir?' or asking me where I was going for my holidays. And I'd be very uneasy at the end, when she held up the mirror for me to see the finished job from various angles, with me having to go 'Yeah, that's great, that's very nice' before she moved on to the next one.

My mate Fez had already had a little spell on the dole, and had upset the Social Security people at his initial interview by turning up drunk and asking, across a crowded waiting room, 'Excuse me. Is this where you get the free money?' This approach, refreshing in its honesty, I thought, didn't go at all well with the Social, so I decided to play it straight. I went to the Supplementary Benefit Office in Smethwick, took a numbered ticket from the machine and waited my turn. My plan, brilliantly conceived by my Careers Officer some years earlier, was to stay on the dole for as long as I possibly could. I even left home and moved into a horrible bed-sit so I wouldn't be under any parental pressure to find a job. I'd worked my balls off academically for four years, and was now trained to use my spare time constructively. I thought it might be nice to take a few years off to read some books and get drunk. All I needed was a few bob to keep me going.

On the staircase leading to the Benefit Office, someone had written in black felt-pen, 'Cheer up, money isn't everything'. It made me laugh every time I passed it. The waiting room at the top of the stairs wasn't so funny. I was surprised to discover that some of the people there were actually looking for work. I couldn't quite get my head round that. The waiting room always had loads of kids running about and getting inter-mittently screamed at by chain-smoking young women in laddered tights, who, apparently, didn't own any shampoo. The men fell into two groups: the younger ones, with tattoos and lumberjack coats, also chain-smoking, mainly roll-ups, and the middle-aged, who had always worked but had fallen victim to international economics, and other stuff they didn't understand. These guys always wore a suit and tie for their appointment, as if to say 'I shouldn't really be here. It's just temporary, I'm sure.' Over the years, I watched their suits and their optimism slowly grow threadbare. Most of those men never worked again.

I, on the other hand, was living the life of Riley. My housemate, Paul, was a manager at the Triangle Arts Centre in Gosta Green, Birmingham, and I started doing a bit of voluntary work for them. Basically, they paid me in cinema or theatre tickets, so most nights I'd nip in their canteen for some ethnic food, catch a Beckett play or a Japanese movie, and then get pissed and talk about women and football in the pub next door.

The government paid my rent and gave me £24.70 a week to live on, but this was no good to a man of my thirst, so I did lots of shit cash-in-hand jobs on the side. Obviously, it was my intention to declare these earnings, but alcohol has a terrible effect on the memory. When I wasn't at the Triangle, I spent my time on Birmingham's Hagley Road, either at the Duck Inn, or about fifty yards away at the Garden House pub. Life was simple. I never made any social arrangements. I knew that in any of these three places there would always be people I knew, and lots of drink to be drunk.

I had been going out with the same girl, Sally, since the first year of the English course. She was my first-ever posh girlfriend, short, dark and curvy. I liked her accent. It made her sound cultured and proper, which, in some ways, I suppose she was. Our relationship worked in a very similar way to that of Lady and the Tramp. As a boyfriend, I wasn't a very easy gig. Once, after a particularly heavy night, I pissed the bed with her in it. I woke up the next morning and tried my stock excuse, 'Phew! I was really sweating last night', but her sniffing and

243

suspicious looks told me that it wasn't going to work. 'I don't think this is sweat,' she said.

'I know,' I said. Then, trying my best to look pained and hesitant, 'I think you've pissed the bed.'

Ten years later, during which time I'd incorporated this story into my stand-up act, she turned up at my dressing room after a gig at Leicester's De Montfort Hall and had a go at me for what I'd done. She'd had a slight doubt in her mind ever since that damp awakening, but my re-telling of the story on stage that night had finally put things straight. Of course, if I'd known she was in the audience, I would still have blamed her.

Sally also had to cope with a particularly weird period of my life when, at the age of twenty-eight, I became slightly obsessed with South African runner Zola Budd. I used to cut pictures of her out of the papers and even started going to athletics meetings where she was running. I eventually wrote her a steamy letter explaining my devotion, and she sent me back a signed photo that said 'Thank you for your interest, Zola Budd'. What a flirt! Looking back, I can't work out what I saw in her. Maybe it was the bare feet. This was at a time when – certainly at the Triangle – it was frowned upon to eat South African apples, so wanking off to one of their athletes was definitely a political no-no. Perhaps that was it. She, like the apples, fell into that most alluring of categories, forbidden fruit.

Meanwhile, bed-pissing, sherry for breakfast, dancing and singing 'The March of the Siamese Children' with my pants round my ankles in front of Kenny Ball and his Jazzmen, after they had dropped in at the Duck one Sunday lunchtime, all seemed like normal behaviour to me, but the hangovers were getting worse and lasting longer. I had made that most dangerous of all discoveries for the drinker, 'the hair of the dog that bit you'. This is when you drink to get rid of your hangovers. I would keep a large bottle of sherry on my bedside table for this express purpose, having several man-size swigs, most mornings, even before I got out of bed. When I say large bottle, I used to buy what they called 'loose sherry', which was served from a plastic barrel at the local grocers, so you had to take along your own bottle. I would usually take a two-litre one that had originally contained Pineappleade. It stopped me getting edgy about the prospect of running out. I have got there at nine in the morning when there has been three or four people queuing with their bottles, waiting for the shop to open. I remember saying that they should open a special twenty-four-hour off-licence for alkies, that just sold Special Brew, Thunderbird, loose sherry and cider. It could be called 'Desperate Measures'. Of course, whether I actually was or, indeed, am an alkie, I don't know, but I think it's fair to say that I had what you might call a 'drink problem'.

On my second day in Seoul, I went off to see the Korean Mr Keepy-Uppy. Keepy-Uppy, as you may know, is the art of keeping a football off the ground for as long as possible by bouncing it from foot to foot, up on to the thighs, the head, catching it in the nape of the neck and so on. Robbie Williams, the rich, good-looking, very talented singer, is good at it. That's fair, isn't it? Needless to say, I'm shit at it, but happily, I was to be just a spectator on this occasion. The Korean Mr Keepy-Uppy, Hur Nam Jin, was giving an exhibition of his skills at a trade fair in downtown Seoul.

There is something heroic about the story of Hur Nam Jin. He was a promising footballer, expected to turn pro, when a terrible injury halted his career. Several of his amateur team-mates progressed into the professional game, and it was surely his cue to become a disenchanted, hobbling misanthrope, wincing at the mere sight of the sports pages and ending up swinging from a light-fitting, with a bottle of scotch and a melodramatic note left on a nearby table. But no, instead of drink, Hur turned to Keepy-Uppy. It was less of a strain on his injury than playing in a proper game, and he started to practise day and night, like Bruce Wayne weightlifting and studying chemistry as he trained himself to become Batman. Now Hur holds the world record for Keepy-Uppy. He Keepy-Upped (I believe that is the verb) for eighteen hours and twelve minutes, including, he pointed out through an interpreter, eight hours of heading. I was very determined, when I arrived in Korea, not to start doing a lot of gags about people's odd-sounding (to me) names or asking if they had a TV medical drama called *E.L.*, but when the interpreter introduced me to Mr Keepy-Uppy and said 'This is Hur', it took a gargantuan effort for me to not say 'Who's Hur, the cat's mother?'

Mind you, jokes about domestic pets are also a bit of a no-no in Korea. The Koreans are slightly touchy about references to their tradition of eating dogs. Brian told me, during our traditional meal, that he was pissed off that someone had suggested that a country that ate dogs was not a suitable venue for the World Cup. He pointed out that no one had moaned about the French eating horses when the 1998 World Cup was being discussed. Considering that as a result of sitting on the floor for an hour and a half, I had become completely paralysed from the waist down, I didn't give a fuck either way, but I don't really see the difference between eating dogs and eating cattle. In fact, when you consider that you never see a picture of a little kid in the paper who had to have fifty-six stitches in his face because he was attacked by his neighbour's cow, you can't help but think that dogs, as a breed, deserve to be scoffed more than cows, pigs or sheep do.

Either way, Korea is not a country where 'Man Bites Dog' is

news. Bernie told me that the Korean footballers eat dog before a game to improve their stamina. I'm surprised that the team-name 'Rovers' isn't more common.

Anyway, I took my seat in front of the small stage in the corner of the trade fair hall, and waited for Hur's exhibition. After an exciting film-montage of great moments from previous World Cups, two very sexy Korean girls in matching outfits walked on stage. I suppose if you're known as Mr Keepy-Uppy, girls will inevitably come flocking.

Then, after their introduction, out came Hur in his footie kit, and the tap-tap-tap of ball against boot began. Soon it was ball against thigh, shoulder, knee and anything else that wouldn't constitute hand-ball. This man didn't DO keepy-uppy, he WAS keepy-uppy. He rolled on his back, did hand-stands, and circled the ball with his foot while it was in mid-air, like a kid drawing circles with a sparkler. He had re-defined keepy-uppy into an art-form. I could feel tears in my eyes.

Then suddenly, he stopped, and the large crowd of business-types who had gathered round screamed and applauded like crazy folk. I was as loud as anyone. I was elated and emotional. I loved Mr Keepy-Uppy. And then he stepped forward and offered me the ball. I felt like someone had hit me hard across the shoulders with a cricket bat.

Somehow, the ball was in my hands. I walked towards the small stage. Here I was, the unofficial representative of the home of football. The crowd fell silent. You could have heard a Hur Nam Jin drop (Korean rhyming-slang). I stood on stage, holding the ball and facing maybe two hundred ladies and gentlemen of the Korean business fraternity. Still silence. I could feel my palms, my thumbs, my fingers clammy against the plastic covering on the thirty-two little leather panels. So much of my life, personal and professional, had centred around football and now, once again, I had to confront the fact that our relationship was purely platonic.

The crowd were starting to look puzzled. Mr Keepy-Uppy himself gestured subtly for me to begin. I took one last look down at that hand-stitched, inflated symbol of my physical inadequacy. (I'm talking about the football.) On one of the panels, it said 'Made in Vietnam'. It was a name that, throughout my childhood, had been associated with anguish and shame. I took a breath and lobbed the ball into the air.

Whenever I kick a football, I always think that something will have happened to me since the last time I kicked one that will suddenly have made me a much better player. This is probably because I fantasise about being a great footballer so much. Whenever I'm on the toilet, I imagine that I'm Chris Collins who started playing for West Brom when he was sixteen, stayed there for ten years of glory, and then moved to Barcelona FC for another ten-year stint and another mountain of silverware. I then moved back to Albion for six years and at the age of forty-two returned to Barca to see out the twilight of my career. I have a clause in my contract that prevents me from being picked for either side if they meet each other in European competition because I love them both so much. Currently, in order to sustain my career for as long as possible, Barca use me as a sort of pinch-hitter, only playing me when absolutely necessary, and taking me off after I've banged in a quick hat-trick. There was a mid-season scare when I was crippled by a vicious tackle from a Real Madrid defender, since forced into exile by threats from Barca fans who regard me as their adopted son. However, I made a miracle recovery and clinched the Spanish title by coming on in the second half and scoring three goals against Real at the Nou Camp.

Meanwhile, I arrived on the scene too late for England to qualify for the '74 World Cup but, since then, I have acquired six World Cup winner's medals. My domestic honours are too numerous to list. I have no qualms about playing against Spain because I consider myself an adopted Catalonian. I speak the language fluently, and am generally regarded as the greatest player of all time, but am sometimes condemned for my arrogance and womanising. When I leave the toilet, I'm me again. And no, tragically, I'm not joking.

You know, the last time I kicked a football in the real world, I scored that penalty at Villa Park. Maybe it was a turning point. If I believe like I believed then, I know that anything is possible. If I just believe.

I kicked the ball twice with my right foot and it spun off into the crowd. They returned the ball and I tried again. Sort of three times this time, but the last one came off the outside of my knee. The crowd looked shocked and confused. One of the pretty girls said something into her offstage microphone. Mr Keepy-Uppy looked slightly wary, like he was afraid of catching whatever it was that I'd got. Everyone's face seemed to say 'We were having a really lovely time and now the white guy has spoiled it.' Then I noticed Bernie, sitting amongst them. She seemed much less business-like than usual. In fact, I would go so far as to say she was pissing herself laughing.

Then a Korean volunteer stepped up. He looked about nineteen and was wearing wholly inappropriate shoes, sort of zip-up platform boots. He tossed up the ball and kept it in the air for about thirty touches. The crowd cheered. The world was a lovely place again. But not for me. Mr Keepy-Uppy's manner had now gone from horror to pity and he was trying to engage me in a game of head-tennis. I headed three high over his head and one down at his feet before he gave up. He had started to look scared again, like I was a virus that might get into his keepy-uppy computer. He suddenly gestured towards me, the way a pretty girl in a sparkly leotard might gesture towards a conjurer who had just performed a breathtaking illusion. The crowd instinctively applauded. I decided on an ironic bow. This being Korea, of course, they all bowed back.

As I looked for a place to hide, the interpreter came across and explained that the pretty girl's comment into the microphone was 'The handsome foreign gentleman is having quite a difficult time up here.' This made me feel slightly better. Handsome but shit. It was like being in a boy band.

As I left, a PR man from the sponsors presented me with a football. He did so with the kind of facial expression one might adopt when presenting Peter Stringfellow with the Complete Works of Shakespeare. I just wanted to die.

As I neared thirty, strange things began happening to me. There was something about the big Three-O that made me start to wonder about what I was doing with my life. It seemed to be happening to a lot of my mates as well, as we all headed for this grim milestone together. They started wearing trendier clothes, dumping their girlfriends, changing their jobs and, of course, doing sit-ups. I think we could all hear the shovel hitting the soil.

I finished with Sally. She was living in London by then, which suited me because absentee girlfriends don't get in the way of a man's drinking habits the way ever-present ones do, but I felt I had to move on. I got the train from New Street to Euston, and the tube to her flat. I walked in, told her, and walked out. I got on a tube and caught the next train home. I was in London for less than an hour. It's a lousy way to end a six-and-a-half-year relationship. But, what's the nice way?

Over the last few years, my reading habits, Samuel Johnson, Auden, Tennyson, Shakespeare and Gerard Manley Hopkins, had started to move in other directions. I was reading stuff by and about Lenny Bruce, the dead American comic. I didn't get all the references, and it wasn't as funny as the Two Ronnies, but something about it really touched me. I liked his honesty, his use of language, and his sexual frankness. It made me think that a stand-up comic could do more than tell jokes about an Irishman going into a pub, he could talk about himself. I was half-way through Bruce's *How to Talk Dirty and Influence People* when I was in the Duck one night, and a bunch of us were hovering round a couple of girls we hadn't seen before. One of them said, 'Wow! You're all very chatty aren't you?'

I said, 'Yes. But chatty is what men become when they sense the possibility of a quick shag.' The girls got pissed off and left, and then my mates got pissed off as well. But I felt exhilarated. It was so true. Of course, I knew it would blow my chances with the girls but I think I liked saying it more than I would have liked the quick shag. To me, it seemed like Lenny Bruce would have approved. I'd said funnier things in my time, but this was something else. I liked cutting through the bullshit. I think maybe I'd stood on another butterfly.

During the same period, my reading was also becoming very Roman Catholic. An interesting combination, Jesus and Lenny Bruce, but they both seemed to do it for me. Clearly, something draws me towards Jewish men who have a way with words. (Even ones that support Chelsea.) The fact was, on the religious front, I was getting a mega-urge to rejoin the Catholic Church. I dreamt of incense and 'Soul of My Saviour'. Actually, speaking of dreams, I had a dream during this period that was as vivid a dream as I've ever had. In fact, it still seems sunlit and crystal-clear as I think of it now. I was clambering up a steep mound of soil. I could smell its soiliness. The surface fell away from under my hands and feet as I struggled upwards. Standing on top of the mound, as if on a cliff's edge, was a tall, slim male figure that I knew was God. He wore a black suit, a black stove-pipe hat, and a white shirt. He looked like Abraham Lincoln, black beard but no moustache. As I clambered nearer, he leant forward and said, 'I'm already here.' I noticed he had very bad teeth. That's it. One for the dream-analysts, I guess. I can see the struggle for religious certainty. I can see Lincoln, 'Honest Abe', as a symbol of truth, but I don't get the bad teeth. Maybe a suggestion that even God has imperfections? As for his words, oh, I don't know, I've never really worked it out, but I suppose it means something like stop splashing about and just float for a while. Or, alternatively, you don't need organised religion – the man looks like a Bible-belt preacher with that outfit and facial hair, but his teeth suggest corruption. You don't need churches to find God because he's already here. But then why does the corrupt preacher get that line? Oh, I just don't know. I once dreamt I was having sex with the tennis star Virginia Wade, and she turned into a blue-perspex pyramid. Answers on a postcard.

Anyway, I started reading lots of books about Catholicism. I'd made quite a fuss about leaving the Church and it had caused big family disruptions. I'd feel a bit of a prat being seen to return after all that, so I tried to talk myself out of it. I read any anti-Catholic book I could get and chucked in a few pro-ones just for a bit of texture. I felt sure the urge to return was just a result of indoctrination at an early age, and insecurity and weirdness as I approached thirty. But the urge wouldn't go away. I started going to Mass, but just sitting at the back and not taking Communion. Communion was for the proper Catholics. I was just an observer.

I read a book by the theologian Hans Kung, who had pissed off the Church with his unorthodox views. In this book, Kung said that he felt the Catholic Church was on the right road to truth but it went down the odd unhelpful cul-de-sac on the way. This was similar to the conclusion I had arrived at

Just finished my finals, 1981. In foreground the second great love of my life.

Shaving gets dangerous when you drink a lot.

Sadie Chatterley's lodger, 1981.

I wanted to be Che Guevara.

Three and a half happy years on
the dole.

Twat.

Someone said 'It's MURDER backwards', but that's never been my experience.

Perrier Award winner 1991, with Madame Cynthia Payne.

THE
ST. ANDREWS
FESTIVAL

1971-1993

Have jokes, will travel. Here's me thinking 'maybe it's about time I started combing it forward.'

Me, ten months after
getting married.

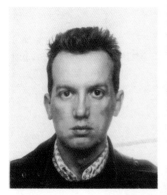

Mom and Dad – 'If you die on the
Sunday...'

Heavy Revie. The great lost sit-com.

The third great love of
my life.

An early 'Fantasy Football' publicity shot. Notice that success has gone straight to my belly.

With Conleth Hill. The stars of Channel 4's *Blue Heaven*.

Dave and me on Vic Reeves' Farm.

Left: Three Lions '98. Make your own World Cup with one small melon and one large bucket of custard.

Man in West Brom shirt lifts Premiership trophy. You might never see this again.

Left: How to avoid relegation by positive thinking.

Jeff Astle, me, Dave and Statto. Fantasy Football 1998.

My dream come true – with Jeff Astle at the Hawthorns.

Below: My early career as a boxing referee.

'You changed the world, man' with Elvis's guitarist, Scotty Moore.

With Dave Hebler and the shirt.

Jon Thoday and Richard Allen-Turner, shortly after they killed Jack the Hat.

Right: Yes, I would. But only as an act of class warfare.

As Eminem, with the Skinnerettes.

myself. I felt it was a good enough reason to go back, so I went and saw my local priest, Father Stibbles. I chatted to him about the last twelve years of my life since I had left the Church, my doubts, my opinions and so on. Towards the end of the conversation, he started to mutter and began making the sign of the cross. It slowly dawned on me that, for the first time in twelve years, I'd been to Confession. The next day I went to Mass. Being midweek there were about fifteen people there, and I took Communion. I was back. It was the 5th of June, the Feast Day of St. Boniface, the patron saint of brewers.

Then, the biggest change of all, on September 24th, 1986, as I approached thirty years of age, I quit drinking, sort of accidentally. I got flu. I couldn't drink for five days. I hadn't been that long without a drink for ten years, and I thought I'd see if I could do six days, and then seven . . . There was no flash of light, no pledge with hand raised, no vision of St. Boniface pulling a fast one on his devotees at the brewery. After a whirlwind of boozing, the end was still and undramatic.

I must admit, in recent months I had replaced the bottle of sherry on my bedside table with a bottle of Pernod. This had made me wonder if things were getting out of hand. One morning I had called my doctor away from his crowded surgery because my hangover was so bad I couldn't breathe. I couldn't even swallow the Pernod, for goodness' sake. I suppose it was now or never.

As soon as I had gone a few more days without drink, I started running. Every morning, the ragged, shambling stagger of the reformed drinker, pale-faced, sweating, gasping for air and crippled with the stitch. My route included one particularly nasty hill and, as I approached it, I imagined my old drunken self closing in right behind me and cussing loudly as he just about managed to climb up on to my back. Day after day, I took on that hill, weighed down with this imaginary piggy-back burden of past excess.

I ran because I had to have something I could get weird and obsessive about to distract me from the drink, something that couldn't co-exist with my former lifestyle and so would prevent me from returning to it. Of course, my return to the Church had inevitably made me think of personal reform and renewal but, as far as this new obsession was involved, it was Zola Budd, not the Pope, who was my saviour and spiritual guide. I ran because Zola ran, and because I ran, I didn't drink. My return to the Church may have saved my soul, but it was Zola Budd who saved my life. She was the mermaid who led me away from the rugged rocks. Soon the run became eight miles a day, and the stagger gradually grew into a stride.

My friends didn't take my new-found abstinence very well. 'Come on, have a drink.' That was all I heard, over and over again. Even though some of them admitted, to my complete surprise, that they had become inclined to avoid me when I was on a heavy session, the new me seemed to arouse suspicion and uncertainty in them. I had broken the drinker's code by deciding not to go down with the sinking ship.

I had previously switched from heavy industry to academia and I would go on to become a TV celebrity and move to the bright lights of London, but none of this estranged me from my old mates the way that giving up drinking did. I carried on going to the pub and hanging out with them, but it was different. Although the old me could be a bit of a nightmare, I think they still missed him. Sometimes, so did I.

Heavy drinking is about massive highs and corresponding lows. To not drink is to travel that long straight line in between. I don't miss the lows, but even in a job where thrills and excitement are fairly plentiful, nothing has ever really replaced the unmitigated bliss of being completely arseholed.

Like that little kid who had shouted loud in the dark garden, I found myself back in the warm, brightly lit kitchen, but this time my incarceration was self-imposed.

But, within a year, I was doing my first-ever stand-up gig. I was entering a world that meant working in pubs every night, where someone always wanted to buy you a drink, where the obvious preparation for standing in front of a room full of indifferent strangers and trying to make them laugh was a bit of pre-gig Dutch courage, and where the obvious accompaniment to post-gig celebration or despair was another five or six glasses. If my old self had climbed down off my back and gone into that world instead of the new me, he wouldn't have lasted twelve months. Of course, I say all this in hindsight. When I gave up the drink, I had no idea that I was preparing for a brand new obsession. And it was going to last a lot longer than Zola Budd.

I went to a K-League game tonight, Taejon Citizens versus Harpong Steelers. As I walked to the ground, I thought I'd stop for snacks. None of the food looked very familiar so I decided to go for a small bowl of crinkly nuts. This seemed like the safest bet. They tasted pretty unpleasant but needs must. After some investigations, they turned out to be glow-worms. I managed to keep my composure and even managed to muster a 'light snack' joke.

The ground was pretty impressive. Unfortunately, there was hardly anyone in it. I stood with the Taejon Ultras, all two hundred of them. They are known as the 'Purple Crew', and they were very much in the news this week because last Saturday they staged the K-League's first-ever pitch invasion. Well, one of them did. But it caused quite a stir. The ref, who'd brought about this encroachment by accidentally sending off

255

the wrong player, was sacked and there are threats to fine the Citizens club, so I was in the eye of the storm tonight. Me, a couple of drummers, a hundred and fifty slightly pissed Korean blokes and about twenty schoolgirls who joined in with the chants, like English schoolgirls joining in with Bob the Builder's song, and screamed every time there was a goal-mouth incident. The attitude, generally speaking, was a bit different from a British 'end'. When Taejon went a goal down, the interpreter explained that the resulting chant from the Purple Crew was, in translation, 'It's OK. Don't worry about it.' A lovely gesture but I can't really see it catching on at the Albion.

This was followed by someone setting off a purple smoke bomb. Well, it was more red than purple but the thought was there. I have to say, it was a particularly unspectacular moment. One bloke held up the smoke bomb and the, shall we say, maroon smoke slowly poured out. It seemed to bring with it a sort of acid snow that fell 'deep and crisp and even' on the Purple Crew's heads. The two schoolgirls standing on their seats in front of me seemed particularly pissed off by this and kept interrupting their carefully co-ordinated clapping to pick particularly hot bits out of their hair. I think we were all happy when the smoke finally stopped spewing forth. Even the bloke who'd held up the bomb laid down the still smouldering casing with an expression that said, 'I'll be glad when I've used these up.'

Then the Purple Crew showed their dark side. Harpong scored again and, with the interpreter having gone to the toilet, I was left to presume that the ensuing chant was something along the lines of 'Oh, well, these things happen.' Then Taejon scored, but the ref disallowed it and all hell let loose. Well, not ALL hell, more like a very small section of it. The drummers and their friends had arrived at the ground with several crates of blue Gatorade, which seemed to be for communal use. I had wondered if the red smoke bombs were deliberately chosen to make the Gatorade look purple. Now, the still-full one-litre plastic bottles became missiles. The Purple Crew started chucking them on to the pitch and surrounding running-track, and one bloke chucked his training shoes as well. Even one of the schoolgirls went crazy, and after a particularly high scream which must have set dogs barking in restaurant kitchens all over Korea, she threw her mobile phone on to the running track.

A fat senior-steward-type came out to try and quieten the mob, but they began chanting and pointing at him. I hoped that they were singing 'Who ate all the glow-worms?' but I don't suppose they were. Eventually, he managed to calm them, partly by the use of placatory hand-gestures, and partly by picking up the schoolgirl's mobile and the training shoes and passing them back through the perimeter fencing. I thought this was very reasonable, but then it went a bit silly. A second steward turned up with a supermarket trolley and began gathering up the Gatorade. When he'd done, he came up to the fence and slowly handed back the bottles that had survived the impact. One of the drummers forsook his instrument to help.

Meanwhile, Harpong scored a third, and the Crew started to get very encouraging again, feeling, perhaps, that they had neglected their duty during the user-friendly riot. At the end of the game, the Taejong players came up to the fence looking distinctly apologetic, and did a very well-synchronised bow to the fans. We all applauded their 3–0 drubbing at home, and that was that.

After the game I was introduced to one of the Taejon board of directors, who presented me with a mini-football with the Taejon badge on it. Clearly, word had got round that, when it came to free footballs, the best bet was to give me something slightly ornamental.

Fasten your seatbelts, I'm about to get a bit experimental on the chronology front. I had met a bloke in a pub who worked at the nearby Halesowen College. He said he could get me some work doing a bit of part-time lecturing. I was still boozing at the time and was worried that this sounded a bit too much like a proper, responsible job, not really suited to a drinking man. Then he explained that it was fifteen quid an hour and I started to weaken. That was twenty-odd pints, so I said I'd give it a go, thus crushing two very big butterflies in one go. If we move forward to late 1987, I can show you the butterflies in very close proximity.

Butterfly Number One was a dark-haired sixteen-year-old girl, dressed all in black, sitting in a college corridor. She smiled. I smiled back. Above her head was Butterfly Number Two. It was a dayglo-orange poster for a charity gig in Birmingham.

The poster said:

Mitchells and Butlers presents
An Evening of Alternative Entertainment
Featuring . . .
Earl Okin
Andy Feet
The Nice People
Chris Collins
At The Portland Club, Icknield Port Road
Wednesday 9th December. 7.30 p.m.
Door Charge £6.

This was to be my first ever stand-up gig. The girl in black was to be my first ever wife. I think we need to go back a bit further still. Don't panic, it's all under control.

I'd started working at Halesowen College of Further Education, to give it its full title, in September 1985. At that time, no formal teaching qualifications were required in FE colleges, so anyone hanging around the building come September was likely to pick up some lecturing work here or there. I started off teaching engineering students how to write letters (I think we got as far as 'J') and was soon doing a General Studies class where the students and me just talked about what we'd seen on telly that week. This was listed on the timetable as 'The Media'. Unlike my terrible time on teaching practice, I quite took to lecturing. I was more confident after my academic success and the students were all at least sixteen, which meant I could talk to them on a more adult level and even shag some of the prettier ones. I suppose I was the young, trendy lecturer that female students often go for. Of course, in reality, I was neither young nor trendy, but, luckily, the other lecturers managed to make me seem both. In the country of the bland, the one-eyed man is king.

I had a few liaisons with female students. This is not as bad as it sounds. Several of the female students at Halesowen were of a similar age to me, or even older. Obviously, I didn't shag any of them but I just thought I'd mention it in order to mislead you.

Anyway, a far more significant relationship was one I struck up with a twenty-stone man with long curly hair, brown-tinted spectacles and a Viva Zapata moustache. His name was Malcolm Bailey. He was a big bear of a bloke who had a love–hate relationship with most of the students and staff. He was blunt, opinionated, liked a drink and a smoke, and constantly took the piss out of everybody. I liked him and we got on really well. Malcolm was head of the college drama department and directed quite a few plays. He was planning to take Ron Hutchinson's play *Rat in the Skull* to the Edinburgh Fringe Festival in 1987 and asked me if I'd like to be in it. I was to play the part of a nasty, right-wing London copper who's trying to stitch-up various suspects. I thought it sounded like a good laugh so I went for it. In August of 1987, Malcolm, the other three members of the all-male cast and me headed for Edinburgh in a hired white van.

By now, I had a new girlfriend, Celine. (I've changed the name. The rest is true.) She was tall and busty with cropped peroxide-blonde hair and a wardrobe that was almost exclusively black. We used to listen to the Smiths a lot. I'd kissed her goodbye and told her I'd see her after our play had set the theatre world on fire.

We totally bombed. The play was alright but no one came to see it. Well, we probably averaged about five people a night. After the performances we'd go and see other shows and generally soak up the Festival vibe. One night we went to a venue called the Pleasance. This was to become a special place for me. The show that night was called the 12.12 Cabaret, because it began at twelve minutes past midnight. I'd never seen any so-called alternative comedy in the flesh before, but by about half past midnight I'd decided what I wanted to do with the rest of my life.

The compere that night was called Ivor Dembina. He was funny and did a lot of ad-libbing with the audience. I remember he christened one bloke 'Foetus', and kept on going back to him for endless digs and put-downs. He introduced an American act called Ray Hanna who did really slick one-liners and played keyboard and sang funny songs. (Coincidentally, Hanna went with Eddie Izzard and me to Sweden years later, and then returned to Edinburgh with a one-man show about

Lenny Bruce.) I was too shy to speak to either of these guys afterwards, but I really wanted to tell them they were brilliant and I wanted to be like them.

I spent the next day in a daze. I told Malcolm I'd decided to become an 'alternative comedian' and he said, 'Yeah, but you'll be shit.' Then he smiled. It was about as encouraging as he ever got. So the next night I went back to the 12.12 to get another man-sized swig of my new obsession. This time the compering was done by a double act, two energetic, fresh-faced student-types who, again, were really funny. They were called Black and Baddiel. Yes, THAT Baddiel, with a pre-Newman partner from Cambridge University. Again, I would have loved to speak to them afterwards but, well, this is another problem with not drinking. Stone-cold sober, I was uneasy about initiating a friendly chat with two relatively unknown comics, but when I was drunk I was perfectly at home dancing in front of Kenny Ball and his Jazzmen with my nob out.

The following night I went to see Julian Clary, or The Joan Collins Fan Club as he was then known. I'd heard that he got someone out of the audience to sing 'I'm Gonna Leave Old Durham Town' so I deliberately sat near the front and laughed a lot. Sure enough, I got chosen and stood on stage in my first-ever professional comedy show as Julian Clary's straight-man. (Leave it.) As he handed me my script, he whispered, 'Don't be nervous. You won't be humiliated.' I bet he's used that one before. No, it was sweet, but, of course, I was loving being up there. I delivered all the lines enthusiastically and enjoyed the applause as I left the stage. It was also a nice change, after the play, to gaze into an auditorium that didn't look like a very orderly furniture exhibition.

Meanwhile *Rat in the Skull* crawled on to the end of its run and we left Edinburgh, driving past a few of our already-tatty photocopied posters flapping in the August breeze. The mood inside the hired white van was a bit more subdued than when we'd arrived. Nevertheless, I had decided I was going to come back the following year, this time as a comic.

On the way back, I got Malcolm to drop me off in Nottingham. I was due to meet Celine at a party there and stay at her aunt's for the night. We danced and kissed and ended up in bed together, naked. I'd bought her a stick of Edinburgh Rock. It doesn't sound much, but her birthday was coming up and I'd just spent ten quid on a pair of earrings she'd said she liked, so don't go thinking that I was holding back on the financial front.

Anyway, I sat in bed with Celine, telling her how I was going to set the comedy world on fire, but she seemed troubled by something. Eventually she looked at me and said, 'Y'know, this is really hard.'

'It's rock,' I said, 'it's supposed to be hard.' (That sounds like a routine, but it really happened that way.)

'No,' she said. 'I mean I've got something hard to tell you.' I listened. 'There was this bloke in the pub who kept asking me out. In the end, I went just to shut him up.'

I could see where this was going. I immediately got out of bed and put my pants back on, thinking, 'Well, you won't be seeing that again, m'lady.' Then I got back into bed, and she went on to explain, in more detail than I needed, how she had fallen for this guy. I suddenly remembered that I had spent ten quid on a pair of earrings for this woman, and I started to laugh at the grim irony of it all. I deliberately made the laugh arch and pronounced so she'd ask me what I was laughing at. She did, and I was able to do a sort of 'Well, what a mug I was . . .' speech, during which I adopted various body-shapes that made me appear tragic and mis-used. As planned, she was over-whelmed with guilt. 'Oh, tell me how much the earrings were and I'll buy them off you. Oh, please.'

'Twelve quid,' I said.

They say you come away with something from every relationship. In this case, two quid. But years later, I incorporated the earrings thing into a storyline for a sitcom I wrote, so even more good came out of it. When I bid Celine farewell the next day, I said, 'Have a nice rest of your life': I was still playing it like some sort of Hamlet-figure. Thus, I found comedy and lost my bird. She had dumped me for a double-glazing salesman called Kevin. (In this case, it seemed a shame to change the name, so I didn't.)

When I got home to Birmingham, I decided to book my space for the following year's Edinburgh Festival virtually straight away. This was about six months earlier than people usually booked venues for Edinburgh, but I didn't know that at the time. There was a company in Coventry called Tic Toc, who I knew ran a venue at the Festival, so I phoned them up. I explained to the bloke that I was a comedian called Chris Collins and I wanted to hire a room for Edinburgh '88. He asked how long the show was. I hadn't even written one gag yet, so it was a bit tricky to estimate. 'Oh, about an hour and a half, two hours should do it,' I said.

'Look,' said the bloke, 'no offence, but I've never heard of you. Even the big acts only do an hour.'

'OK,' I said, 'I'll do an hour.' He explained the cost and it turned out that the good time-slots were all too expensive for me. It'd been a year since I quit drinking and I'd managed to save four hundred quid during that time. All that would buy was a lunchtime slot, 12.45 to 1.45, at the 100-seater Calton Studios. I agreed. I wrote the cheque, and sent my life-savings to a company in Coventry so that, in ten months' time, I could perform an hour of comedy at the Edinburgh Festival. I had the venue, now all I needed was the show.

I should probably point something out at this stage. I had

no fucking idea how to become an alternative comedian. The normal procedure, it turns out, was that you did what were called 'open spots' at London comedy clubs, and you carried on doing these, about ten minutes each and unpaid, until some club owner or other offered you a paid spot. Once this had happened a few times, if you went well, other paid work would come in and you'd begin to build a reputation on the comedy circuit. Then, usually, you and two or three other up-and-coming comics might get together, share the cost of a room in Edinburgh, and put on a show in which you did fifteen or twenty minutes each. If this went well, the following Edinburgh you might risk a two-hander with just one other comic, and if *this* was a success, finally, maybe after another two-hander combination at the next Festival, you might bite the bullet, take the ultimate step, and try doing an hour on your own. The whole process normally takes between three and six years, sometimes much longer. I was going to do the hour show having never worked as a professional comic in my life. Not because I was brave, but because I didn't know any better.

I even toyed with the idea of writing loads of stuff, but not actually trying any of it out in public until I opened in Edinburgh, an approach that was not so much 'in at the deep end', as 'in at the shallow end, but off the top diving-board'. Just write the show, practise in front of the bedroom mirror so I know it lasts an hour, and then do it. Malcolm, having listened, mouth agape, to this plan, suggested that it might not be a terrible idea to try doing a bit of comedy beforehand. I wasn't sure it was necessary but I thought I'd give it a go, just to be on the safe side.

I feel that I shouldn't go any further with this until I've offered some sort of definition of 'alternative comedy'. Bob Monkhouse once said to me that alternative comedy is the same old jokes but no one's shaved. This is funny, but not true, and is therefore not a bad example of the difference between alternative and mainstream comedy. I'm not saying that all alternative comedy is true, but it is, or was when I started doing it, generated by the comedian for the comedian. What was said on stage roughly represented that comic's view of the world. For example, I used to do a routine about taking a woman I'd met in a pub back to my flat, and being slightly non-plussed when I asked her if there was anything she'd like me to do, and she said she'd love it if I'd lick honey off her breasts. I continued like this:

Well, frankly, I wasn't keen. And, anyway, I'd only got lemon curd. And if you put that on nipples, it looks like acne. So I said, 'I'm sorry, I don't fancy that much,' and she said, 'Oh, for goodness sake. I've got just the thing for you.' And she reached into her carrier-bag and took out some newspaper, and when she unwrapped it, she had a dozen oysters. She said, 'You have twelve of these and you'll be able to satisfy me all night.' Well, have you ever tried oysters? Oh, my God. Honestly, it's like licking phlegm off a tortoise. I thought, 'Twelve of these and you'll be able to satisfy me all night?' No fuckin' wonder. After twelve of these, oral sex is gonna be a piece of piss. If you'll pardon the pun. I tell you, after twelve oysters, oral sex is gonna be like the fucking sweet trolley turning up.

Now, I chose this short routine, more or less at random, in order to make my point about what I regard as 'alternative' comedy. Classically, so-called alternative comedy would have been a bit more worthy. They all slagged off Thatcher and bleated about Nicaragua, but my stuff was never political.

However, the reason both strands qualify as alternative comedy is because they are both reflective of the comic's world-view. Political comics, like Mark Thomas or the American Will Durst, do stuff about politics because they are interested in it, and therefore spend a lot of their lives reading, thinking and talking about it. Quite rightly, this is reflected in their acts. That's why I do jokes about licking women's tits and vaginas. Their material is very different from mine, but we all believe that comedy should be true, in that it should reflect the attitudes and opinions of the comic. When Frank Carson says 'A fella went into a pub' etc, it's often very funny, but it doesn't tell us much about Frank Carson's world-view. There might be fifty other comics telling that same joke. They can't all think and feel the same. I don't just want the jokes, I want the man behind the jokes. That's why, as I said before, character comics leave me a bit cold.

As you may have already begun to suspect, whenever I try to analyse comedy I disappear up my own arse, but here's a look at the oysters routine that says why, apart from the fact that it's written by the performer, I think it's 'alternative' comedy rather than mainstream.

Firstly, it's a bit too rude for mainstream. Mainstream comedy tends to go for cheekiness but not graphic detail. Graphic detail is a bit too true for a mainstream crowd. The usual criticism that mainstream comics aim at alternative comedy is that it's 'too crude' or 'blue'. 'Dirty' comics, such as myself, are just going for the 'easy' laugh. This is all a bit misleading. I agree dirty jokes that aren't funny are bad. I also think that clean jokes that aren't funny are bad, but, I'll admit, a bad dirty joke suggests that the teller might have been hoping to get a laugh merely at the mention of swear-words or rudeness. In my experience this doesn't work. Occasionally, and unfortunately, an audience will laugh simply because something dirty has been said, but they won't laugh for long if that's all that's on offer. Audiences are not that stupid. Anyone who thinks there are 'easy' laughs to be had should try doing a bit of stand-up.

I like funny comics. Clean, filthy, political, slapstick, surreal, the lot. I am quite a dirty comic but a clever dirty joke is a beautiful thing. For example, here's a gag I was doing in my early days:

I have to admit, I don't like condoms. I hate that moment, after sex, when you look down at yourself, and there's a pink, wrinkled condom, just hanging there. I hate that. Especially if you weren't actually wearing one when you put it in. (LAUGH.) Oh, it can happen, you know. Those ribbed ones will stay there for months. It's like knocking a fuckin' rawlplug in.

That is a dirty joke, but I'd defend it because I believe it to be funny and well-constructed and quite clever, if you'll excuse me saying so. If you find the joke offensive, fair enough, but that is to condemn it because of its subject matter rather than on its comic merits, such as they are. There is no comic hierarchy based on clean and dirty, only on funny and un-funny. Champions of mainstream comedy are always going on about how political correctness has killed comedy, but the anti-smut thing is also political correctness, just someone else's interpretation of 'correct'.

I was once compering a gig and I did a short routine about the difficulty of masturbating while watching a dirty film on television rather than on video. The dirty bits are often quite short, and you never know exactly when they're coming up, so you have to sit in a state of preparation, 'not rigid, but rubbery', to give yourself a bit of a head start. By the time that dirty bit comes, 'you need to be half-way up the runway'. That's your only chance of making it. I went on to explain how I'd got myself into this state of preparation when Channel Four kicked off its new documentary series, *Censored*, a collection of previously banned TV films described by the broadcaster as 'Television they said you should never be allowed to see'. As you can imagine, I was all set and raring to go. 'Now, I don't know if you've ever tried masturbating to a fifty-five-minute documentary about the miners' strike . . . but it's not easy.'

It might not be top-drawer comedy but it got a few laughs.

However, the next bloke I introduced at the gig was very much from the mainstream circuit. He glared at me as we passed on stage, apologised to the audience, and said he wished to totally disassociate himself from the filth I had just uttered. 'Anyway,' he continued, 'these two niggers went into a pub . . .' Different taboos, that's the thing.

Where was I? Oh, yeah, the oysters. I would say that that routine not only reflects, in some ways, my world-view but, furthermore, is, if you want to go look for it, quite political. Also, and I'm playing with fire here, I think that one of the reasons I've done alright as a comic is that I'm a working-class bloke who got educated and worked in an arts centre. Though I may sound anti-mainstream in some of my above remarks, the fact is that I dislike any kind of restraint on a comedian's work other than his own personal morals. I reckon I'm probably half-alternative, half-mainstream, half-university, half-factory. I'll show you what I think I mean, though I should warn you that this view of my stuff as 'alternative mainstream' has only just, this minute, occurred to me, so we walk hand-in-hand along a rickety bridge that I'm very much still building.

Firstly, the woman in the routine is independent, innovative, and inclined to be the dominant partner. She is much more sexually liberated than me, happy to use any aid to sexual pleasure, be it the product of the mighty ocean or the humble bee. In fact, she sets a sexual agenda I find threatening and altogether more sophisticated than anything I might come up with. The fact that I only have lemon curd to offer makes me sound small-town, domestic, cheap and old-fashioned. The oysters represent sophistication. Rather than embrace their differentness, I am repelled by it and seek familiarity in still more small-town comparisons, tortoises and phlegm. All this is pretty alternative stuff. No bimbos or brash male behaviour here. She is Madonna, I am Jack Duckworth.

Then it turns. Having firmly established the alternative credentials of this encounter, I am now able to make a Bernard Manning-like point: that men don't like giving women oral sex because it often doesn't taste very nice. However, the point is made in a very non-confrontational, docile fashion. I think about the oral sex comparison but there is no evidence that I voiced it to her. Thus, it can be concluded that she continued to dominate, and that I did give her oral sex, be it from motives of fear or compassion, neither of which enhance my macho credentials.

Interesting, but, essentially, bollocks. I wrote the routine because I thought it was funny. Everything else is incidental. Now, can someone fetch me a step-ladder so I can get out of my own arse?

Today, Phil, Bernie and me went to the Seoul Stadium, where they'll be playing the opening game of the 2002 World Cup. The stadium isn't quite finished yet, so we had to wear hard-hats. We wandered around the press box and had our photos taken on the running track. It was thirty-six degrees in the shade. Throughout the trip, the stadium's technical people were testing out the sound system by playing, very loudly, over and over again, that Tom Waits song that goes 'And the small change got rained on, with his own .38. And the small change got rained on, with his own .38.' It echoed around and around the empty arena. God, it was hot.

So, it was to be my first gig as a stand-up comedian. December 9th, 1987, at the Portland Club in Birmingham. Malcolm had decided he wanted to be a comedy promoter, so he got together a few local acts and a couple of turns from the London alternative circuit, Earl Okin and The Nice People, and staged a charity gig, sponsored by Mitchells and Butlers, a local brewery, at the Portland Club in Icknield Port Road. It was an ugly red-brick building that, among other things, was the home of the Birmingham Anglers Association. The idea was that I would compere the gig, free of charge, obviously, and I was very excited. Today, the Portland Club, tomorrow . . . Malcolm, of course, had a period of much-verbalised doubt about my role in the event, wondering aloud whether I was up to it, but, having pulled two or three legs off my psychological spider, he finally said I had the job. Thus, I began my preparation. Without wishing to sound like a twat, I had been getting big laughs from my mates for as long as I could remember, and I didn't see why this audience should be any different.

There was a show on TV at that time called *Saturday Live*. It was more or less the only place people from outside London could see alternative comedy. I remember being utterly convinced that once word had got round of how brilliant I was, I would almost certainly be on there the following week. I

SATURDAY, 23rd APRIL
8pm at 'THE BARTON'S ARMS'
HIGH ST, ASTON (BUSES 33, 51, 52 FROM CITY CENTRE)

HO! BLOODY
HO! Enterprises present
AN ALTERNATIVE CABARET
featuring: **SHEILA HYDE**
"One of the best female comics around"
- City Limits

Your Hosts - **RedMaN GreeNMaN**
Local lads croon & chant, strum & rant
with **CHRIS Collins** - The rockabilly
Charles Hawtrey
plus

TICKETS:
ONLY
£1·50 ON DOOR
£1·00 IN ADVANCE FROM PUB
HO! BLOODY
HO! H.Q.- Tel
533 4856

"Buy TWO:
GET ONE FREE"
SONGS from swinging
solicitors
AND SUPRISE GUESTS..

don't know how I imagined that word of a crappy gig in Icknield Port Road would reach the ears of the comedy intelligentsia in London, but I did. It scares me when I look back and think about that. I mean, I was thirty, for fuck's sake, not some stupid kid. At least when I'm banging in goals for Barcelona I know it's just a fantasy. But this was something that I honestly thought would happen.

I had spent the previous weeks trying to remember funny things I'd said or done in the pub, writing them down, and then working them into little routines I could do in between the acts. For example, sometimes when I was out with my mates, I would pretend that I was about to do a massive sneeze and start frantically searching my pockets for a handkerchief. Then, suddenly I would turn away, sneeze, and turn back with a massive length of snot swinging from one nostril. Of course, it wasn't really snot, it was wet cling-film, but it always got a big reaction from the other customers, especially if they were eating. I decided I'd try this on stage, and then wrote some sneezing material to precede it. I suppose, having already sounded like a twat once in this section, I might as well suggest that this particular bit was an examination of the class-system through the medium of sneezing. It centred on the fact that working-class people, in my experience, do massive great sneezes.

. . . My dad would do about three or four sharp intakes of breath, kind of false starts, before the sneeze actually happened. This gave you a chance to put away your stamp-collection, put the food into tupperware containers, and get the smaller children into hats and mackintoshes before the big explosion came. And when it did, there was no 'hand in front of the mouth' thing. It was just 'AAASHOWWW!' We used to actually surf on my dad's sneezes. (At this point I'd demon-strate, complete with theme from *Hawaii Five-0*.) But then, when I got a bit older, I met some middle-class people. And they're nice and everything, but different. And I was sitting with this middle-class bloke one day, just having a chat, and he said (in a posh accent), 'You know I think I have a bit of a cold com . . . oh . . .' (And then my impression of a little squeaky sneeze like, it has to be said, middle-class people do. I look puzzled.) And I thought, 'What was that? Has he just swallowed a chaffinch?'

OK, I was just finding my way, but it turned out to be the first bit of stand-up I ever did on stage.

I turned up at the gig pretty early. It was quite a big room and I sat on the edge of the stage with my legs dangling, wondering how it would be when the place was full with laughter. One of the other acts, a comic called Andy Feet, was another early arrival. He was a tall, thin, swarthy-looking bloke, I guessed about fifty years old. In anticipation of his performance, Andy Feet wore a smart pale-blue suit, with man-sized footprints made of red fabric stitched to it. There were four on the front of the trousers, and four on the jacket, including one on each lapel. He also wore a massive silver footprint medallion over his shirt and tie. I thought all this was a great idea, but I knew it wouldn't really work with Collins. I'd seen him do a club in Aston, on the same bill as the singer who'd done the Andy Williams number. The centre-piece of his act was an impression of Anthony Newley, so you wouldn't call him topical, but he made me laugh. Now, I was slightly in awe of him. But Andy Feet was nervous. He kept asking me what time the bar would open, and when he finally sat down with a double scotch he told me that he'd had two heart attacks, and had spent some time in a wheelchair after the last one. He also told me that he'd played Vegas, and that Bill Cosby had said to him, 'Andy, when you come back again, we'll meet up and talk comedy.' It was a conversation still pending.

I got the impression that he didn't feel his choice of profession had helped much in the stress department. As he sat, head bowed, looking down past his dangling footprint at the whisky, he seemed like a man with a great deal on his mind. But this was a bloke who earned his living by making people laugh. I couldn't work out what he was worried about.

Eventually, we went backstage and the tables and chairs in the auditorium started to fill up. There were about two hundred punters in. I stood in the wings, waiting to blow 'em away.

My thoughts turned to that mate's girlfriend, the one who'd asked me, 'What's it like to be thirty and on the scrapheap?' It was a fair question. I hadn't done much with my life. I mean, I had a couple of degrees, but I followed them with three and a half years on the dole and I'd spent a large part of my adult years getting too drunk to remember why I needed to get drunk. But through it all, there'd been gags. At the very lowest times, there'd been gags. As I've already said, people had been telling me I ought to be a comedian since I was at infant school. It was the only thing I'd ever been any good at. It was so obviously what I should be doing. How could I have taken so long to realise it? Malcolm came up to me. I was expecting a 'Good luck' but he just said, 'Let's start then.' And I walked out of the gloom into the bright light.

Slight snigger on *Hawaii Five-0*, a laugh on the chaffinch, a laugh and some groans of disgust on the swinging cling-film. I bombed. Not horribly or completely, but to a man who was expecting that, after his opening routine, people from *Saturday Live* would be chartering helicopters in order to get to Icknield

Port Road in time for the second half, it was a major shock. I honestly couldn't believe that the crowd weren't on their feet. I mean applauding rather than leaving.

Before the show I had been completely calm and confident. Now, as I stood in the wings watching the first act, The Nice People, get laughs, I was filled with dread. I couldn't do it after all. I'd been kidding myself. I was just shit, and I had to go out there again and again and again. My next routine was, worryingly, a slightly more experimental piece about the X20 bus that went from New Street station to Stratford-upon-Avon. I suggested the bus was named after the Stingray character, X-Two-Zero, Titan's evil henchman, and began to riff on this very unconvincing theme. This was fraught with problems. For a start off, this was just before reminiscing about kids' TV really took off, and very few people in the audience seemed to know who X-Two-Zero was. Also, everybody who knew the bus, which was maybe a quarter of the audience, referred to it as the X-Twenty. Most of the two-hundred-strong crowd had heard of neither the puppet nor the bus and, although they weren't openly hostile, they were starting to lose faith in me, fast.

Dying on your arse, as comedians tend to call it, is, as you might expect, a pretty grim experience. And it doesn't take much to start the terrible ball slowly rolling. A comedy act is a bit like a long street, with the jokes as lampposts. I know this is pushing it but bear with me. If you're walking down a long street and you come to a lamppost that doesn't work, it's a bit dark, but not bad enough to cause you to turn back because the light from the next lamppost and the previous one will suffice. However, if the *next* lamppost doesn't work either, then it starts to get really gloomy. Logically it seems wise to turn down another street because, well, you just can't rely on these lampposts any more. Clearly there is some sort of power failure.

It was getting so dark, I couldn't see the end of the routine at all.

As often happens with nerves, I got quicker, and quicker, trying to hurry to the next lamppost before it was too late. I was driving blind, with no headlights, at breakneck speed, and, unfortunately, I was driving the X-Twenty to Stratford.

My best mate, Marino, was in the audience. Pete, who offered me the job at Halesowen College, was in the audience. One of my slightly older female students, who had fantastic, slightly muscular legs and a sun-bed tan, was in the audience. A girl from my drama evening class I was desperately trying to shag was in the audience. And, of course, Malcolm was in the audience. But it was too dark to see any of them. The dying comic is utterly alone. I had come to see myself, from a personal-worth point of view, as funny, and not much else. Now, even that had been taken away.

Comedy without laughs is just someone talking. This is what I became. Andy Feet went OK, but not as well as when I'd seen him previously. The world was upside-down. I started to crumble. I would begin a routine but, if the first line or two failed, I just gave up and introduced the next act. I suppose I was afraid of the dark. Slowly, my terrible evening ebbed away, and when I finally walked off stage at the end of the show, there was just silence. I felt smaller and older. I was back on the scrapheap. As soon as I was in the gloom of the wings, I closed my eyes, took a deep breath, and just stood there. I was a broken man. Then I remembered that I had spent my life-savings booking an hour-long stand-up comedy slot at the next Edinburgh Festival. I was trapped.

I'm in Japan now, and I like it. In Osaka, I saw a Japanese Hell's Angel sitting on his massive bike at the traffic lights. He wore a helmet that had 'Fuck the World' written on it, but he didn't look like he really meant it. When Phil took his photo, you could tell that he stayed especially still in order to be helpful. The Japanese are incredibly polite. I know everybody says this – well, everybody except old POWs – but it's true. It makes the whole place seem really safe. I know 'Fuck the World' doesn't seem all that polite, but I'm not sure that English translations are ever quite right over here. Everything comes out sounding a bit like modern poetry. I saw a girl wearing a t-shirt that said, 'Lay low until they consider you more highly.' If only she'd been at the Portland Club. More confusing, since we're in Japan, was another girl's t-shirt, on the railway platform in Osaka. It said, 'Turn soft and lovery every time you have the chance.' Now, of course, it could have meant 'lovery' as in like a lover, or, alternatively, well, I suppose it could have been a Japanese post-modern ironic take on Benny Hill.

We went to meet a schoolteacher in Shimizu, whose school has produced a stupid amount of professional footballers, several of them internationals. He was a very still, calm person, not like your average English schoolteacher. He had a manner more like that bloke with the ping-pong-ball eyes in the *Kung Fu* TV series. The one who used to say Grasshopper a lot. (I sense you're giving me that look I got when I mentioned X-Two-Zero, all those years ago.) The schoolteacher was like a sensei, I believe they call them here, a sort of master, a source of wisdom. He said he had a feeling for football, for its rhythms and its special moments. As he spoke, a fourteen-year-old Japanese kid on a nearby dirt pitch swept one sweet thirty-yard free kick after the next round a plastic five-man defensive wall, and into, or nearly into, a goal defended bravely by an unusually tall teenage goalkeeper.

The teacher started talking about football in a very

277

philosophical way. He talked about a thing called 'wa', which seemed to be a kind of extreme form of team-spirit along the lines of being prepared to truly suffer for the good of the team. As another free kick zinged home, he started to lose me a bit. He explained that one of the most important actions in football is inaction, or 'pause'. That moment before something happens. All the great players have this pause, and their movements and non-movements not only employ this pause to its full advantage, but also deliberately fracture the pause in others. I could feel a very fine trail of steam leaving each of my ears. The Japanese word for this 'pause', he explained, is 'ma'. For a brief moment, or pause, I considered telling him the Marmite joke. But I didn't.

Unsurprisingly, I didn't hang around after the Portland Club gig. I had promised the girl from the drama group a lift home in my 1967 Vauxhall Viva, but now the idea of shagging her seemed like it came from a previous life. I no longer had the right to shag anyone. She chatted about everything but the gig on the way home, but it didn't help. Earlier in the evening, I had noticed that her arse looked fantastic in the tight white jeans she was wearing, but as she walked away from the car towards her front door, I didn't even bother to look. I sat there in the Viva, re-living each terrible moment. Malcolm had thought it was hilarious. Not my material, my humiliation, and amidst his uncontrolled giggling, he told my passenger to keep me away from canals on the way home. I turned off the lights and switched off the engine and sat in the dark. Marino, another witness to my disgrace, had the bedsit next to mine, and I didn't want to go home yet in case he was still up. After a while, I could see my breath in the air as the car steadily got colder. Apparently, despite everything, I was still alive.

The next morning I was back in college, teaching again. I entered the building through a side-door because I didn't want to pass the orange dayglo poster advertising the gig. My first lesson was A-level English. Which was a bit unfortunate because the class included the woman with the fantastic, slightly muscular legs and sun-bed tan, and I was hoping to avoid her for a while till I could get some of my composure back. As I neared the open door of the classroom, I could hear her voice, clear as a bell, saying, 'Nobody was laughing.' I stopped, I took a deep breath, I walked in. She looked embarrassed. I think she assumed I would have taken my own life during the night. I looked straight at her and said, 'Wasn't it terrible?' She struggled for a suitable reply, so I went straight into the lesson to get her off the hook. I don't know if she picked up on my strained over-cheerfulness, but I was glad she had turned up. Not because I felt the need to face my demons, or show the witnesses to my nightmare that I had awoken to a bright new day, but because she had fantastic, slightly muscular legs, and she sat at the front desk, where I could see them in all their splendour. I think I was starting to recover.

I went to 7 o'clock Mass in Osaka this morning, at the Cathedral of Santa Maria. As I walked in the back door with Bernie, also a papist, the first thing I noticed was a massive stained-glass window on the side wall showing St. Francis Xavier bringing Christianity to the Japanese. He stood there, in a blue robe, with his arms spread wide. At his side, but slightly behind him, was a man in full samurai-warrior gear, wearing a crucifix. The church was full of morning sunshine.

Bernie and me crossed ourselves with holy water from a massive sea-shell next to the door, and then I followed her to a pew. Dotted around the church were lots of nuns dressed in white, each one standing alone at least five or six feet from the next. I suppose they didn't want to be distracted from their oneness with God, but it meant that in order to get to a seat, you had to pass through a sort of 'nun slalom'.

I was glad Bernie had led the way, because it meant that the fact I'd ended up standing behind a leggy Japanese schoolgirl in a very short grey pleated skirt was purely accidental. Because, and I'm generalising here, Catholic women have a tendency to be better-looking than Protestant ones, this is a regular dilemma when attending a Catholic church. Usually, wherever I go – pubs, restaurants, football matches, public transport, crematoriums – I always like to position myself so that I have at least one attractive woman nearby who I can gawp at in a strictly non-intimidatory way, but in church this just doesn't seem right. I have, accidentally, found myself with a good view of an attractive woman in church, and I don't really enjoy it. I can't help but think of Matthew 5:28, 'But I say unto you, that whosoever looketh on a woman to lust after her hath committed adultery with her already in his heart.' Well, that's no good, is it? Not in a church.

And where does Matthew 5:28 leave all the millions of women I've lookethed on over the years? You can't commit adultery on your own so, presumably, they've all committed adultery with me, without even noticing. Poor Zola Budd.

Anyway, my point is that I try not to commit adultery in this way when I'm in a Catholic church. Which is a shame, really, because I've always thought that a Catholic church is, in fact, a fantastic place to pull girls. There's a black girl who goes to one of my local churches who is absolutely to die for, but I'd never dare approach her in or around church, I mean if I was single, because it seems, well, improper. And yet I know that we already have one massively important thing in common. She would be one of the few girls I've been out with who didn't think my Catholicism was seriously weird. At the same time, even if I saw her in another context, in a bar or something, I couldn't go up to her and say, 'Hello, we go to the same church,' because modern prejudices against Christianity have forced so many of us into the closet that her friends would probably say, 'What's that? You go to church? You fucking weirdo. Don't hang around with us anymore,' and she'd hate me for exposing her. Mind you, I probably wouldn't approach her, even if she was on her own, because I imagine that practising Catholics don't put out. I mean, I know I do, but that's because I'm spiritually flawed.

Nevertheless, there I stood, at seven o'clock in the morning in a Catholic church in Osaka, behind a leggy Japanese schoolgirl in a very short grey pleated skirt, trying hard not to commit adultery with her.

I'd like to add a small technical point here, Japanese schoolgirls in their school uniforms are everywhere in Japan. It's not like in Britain, where school uniforms seem to slowly fade into street clothes as kids get to about fifteen. There are seventeen- and eighteen-year-old girls in school uniform all over the place. This is, it has to be said, a very good thing, especially in regard to socks. Many of these girls wear baggy white socks that look a bit like leg warmers. Phil, who has researched this subject, told me that the girls wear these because it makes their legs look slimmer, and that they glue them to their shins to keep them in place. This sexy-schoolgirl thing has been made worse (or is it better?) by one particular social phenomenon. Because of a Westernisation of diet in recent years, Japanese schoolgirls are much more curvy than older Japanese women. The latter tend to be often beautiful, but also very slim-hipped and flat-chested. Thus, the girls look like women and the women look like girls. I'm keeping out of it, but Japanese blokes must get very bewildered.

The schoolgirl in the pew in front had gone for the baggy white socks, but the effect was spoiled by the fact that her legs were a bit hairy. This was the first hairy Japanese woman I'd noticed. I wondered if, maybe, she was a feminist. But what would a feminist be doing in a Catholic church? In fact, this poor girl had got it bad. She even had thick black hairs coming out of the collar of her skimpy white cardigan. And when she turned to the side, I could see that she also had sideburns, and stubble, and a wig, and was a bloke. I whispered to Bernie, 'This schoolgirl is a bloke,' but she didn't seem at all bothered. I think she was trying hard to be all grown-up and broad-minded about it, but I was really shocked. Thank God I hadn't committed adultery on this occasion. It would have been a double whammy.

Now, don't get me wrong. I don't have anything against blokes dressing up in women's clothes if that's what they like, but a middle-aged man in a schoolgirl uniform? In church? Maybe he had in mind Matthew 18:3: 'Verily, I say unto you, except ye be converted, and become as little children, ye shall not enter into the kingdom of heaven.'

Then it came to the bidding prayers. These are prayers in which the congregation join together to pray for others: the heads of the church, the poor, the sick, and so on. The first of these was read by a nun, in Japanese of course, but there was a pamphlet which had the prayers translated into English. Her prayer was 'Send messengers of love and compassion to countries suffering from drought and hunger, into slum areas, and among the poor and neglected.' And we all replied, 'Lord, your kingdom come.' Then an old lady read a prayer, 'Send messengers of peace into army barracks, weapons factories and rocket warehouses, strongholds of rebels and private armies. And so we pray.' Amidst the response, I thought, 'Wow! That's what I call a prayer.'

Then the hairy transvestite spoke. I stood, mouth slightly open, as a middle-aged man in a schoolgirl uniform offered, in a voice deeper than mine, this prayer to God: 'Lord, send messengers of tenderness to the dead-end streets, the furnished or unfurnished rooms of the lonely, and the attics of the abandoned in our cities. And so we pray.' My 'Lord, your kingdom come' was said with a tightening throat. I imagined him, lonely in his furnished or unfurnished room, a figure of fun to most people, but embraced by this small Catholic community happy to encourage his active participation in the Mass, regardless of his bizarre appearance. I felt humbled and slightly ashamed. I suppose I had dismissed him as a freak, but he was, it seemed to me now, a brave and very honest man.

Japan is eight hours ahead of Britain, so when you're next out, living it up, at eleven on a Saturday night, remember that, in a Catholic church in Osaka, there's a middle-aged man in a schoolgirl uniform and wig, listening attentively amidst the whirr of electric fans to the word of God, and offering up his prayers for the lonely and the abandoned.

Malcolm had got me a second gig. This was an amazing thing in itself, but there were two things about it that made it even more amazing. Firstly, it was back at the Portland Club, and secondly, I was getting paid. Fifty quid for half an hour. I was to supply the comedy for the club's New Year's Eve Extravaganza. After my grim debut at the same venue, I decided that I would write a completely new set, and even chuck in a few old mainstream gags to get the audience on my side. I was glad I was going back to the Portland. It was like getting back on the horse that had thrown me. It would exorcise the devils that still lingered after December 9th.

When Malcolm and me arrived on New Year's Eve, the

party was already in full swing. All the audience, which ranged from twelve-year-olds to old-age pensioners, wore paper hats and blew little cardboard trumpets that made a high-pitched shriek. The DJ was playing sixties classics and everybody looked like they were up for a good time. I had learned a lot from my first gig. Now it was time to put those lessons into practice.

I stood in the wings and listened as the DJ faded out Herman's Hermits' 'I'm into Something Good' and told the audience that I was a 'very funny local lad'. Then, in a much louder voice, he said, 'Ladies and gentlemen, Chris Collins,' and I bounded forth, on to the stage, to much applause and cheering. I went straight into my brand new opening gag: 'I bought my girlfriend a lovely engagement ring for Christmas, but she dropped it on the floor and the dog ate it. And we've been just going through the motions ever since.'

How quickly an audience can turn from summer to autumn. There was mainly silence and some groans. Not just casual groans, but groans of profound disappointment and indignation. I hurried on to the second lamppost. 'The manager told me to keep it short and sweet tonight, so I've spent the last half hour sitting in a bath full of ice-cream.' Silence, except for a couple of cardboard trumpets. No groans. This was good. I was on an upward curve, but the street was still very dark. I decided to try and engage the audience on a more personal level. I turned to a bloke at a table near the front. 'Just think, mate,' I said, 'in an hour's time, it'll be 1988. Doesn't time fly when you're going bald.' I think he said, 'Fuck off,' but I couldn't hear him over the shrill chorus of the now-deafening cardboard horn section. I looked into the wings. Malcolm, the DJ, and the manager of the club, were standing, shoulder-to-shoulder, frantically gesturing me towards them and mouthing 'Come off' with a look of desperation in their eyes. I turned back to the audience. The tenor trumpets had been joined by a baritone chorus of booing.

I knew a few old gags which involved animals, and had written some stuff on a similar theme, myself. This, I felt, would turn them round. 'I'm going to tell you my ten favourite animal jokes,' I said.

'Oh no you're not,' said a voice from the back.

'No, honest, I am. And you'll really like these.'

I could just make out an 'Oh no we won't' over the booing and trumpeting. I looked into the wings again. Three grown men had passed through asking, continued through pleading, and had now reached begging. They really wanted me to come off. I turned back to the crowd. A little frail old woman stood at the front of the stage. She looked up at me, shook her head in disbelief, and then, slowly and shakily, made her way to the toilet. 'Well,' I said, still trying to get the crowd on my side, 'I don't think she'll see another strawberry season.'

I had to hang around in the bar to get my fifty quid. I'd decided against joining in with the 'Auld Lang Syne'. These people were old acquaintances that I really felt should 'be forgot' as soon as was humanly possible. As I stood there, with people pointing at me and sniggering, and that was just Malcolm, a young girl of about eleven came over and said, 'Excuse me, I thought you was alright but my dad thought you was shit.' It was my first-ever review.

On the drive home, Malcolm, predictably, was merciless, but I just couldn't accept that the dream was over before it started.

My first death had been a polite, quiet affair, with a lot of personal anguish but a minimum of fuss, but this second demise had been an act of group-savagery. I had been flayed alive. I never wanted to go through that again. So, I had two choices: get out, or get better.

I've been back in England for just under a week, and I spent today de-Carolining my flat. Yeah, we finally split. One of those mutual things you hear about. I guess you saw it coming. Even the tabloids had started to refer to it as our 'on-off relationship'. Not good.

We split on Saturday night, just after the results of the *Stars in Their Eyes* Grand Final. Such is the back-drop for modern tragedy. And it got worse. As we spoke of broken hearts and rubbed away our tears, Des O'Connor was interviewing Bradley Walsh about his days as a redcoat.

We were two people pulled apart by love and rage. Even as she screamed at me I noticed how beautiful she was. The argument, as usual, was about almost nothing. She told me that earlier in the week she had been chatted up by Jerry Springer, which pissed me off. And I told her that, co-incidentally, he had chatted up my previous girlfriend, which pissed Caroline off. But, of course, that's not really what it was about. For the last six months, we haven't needed much to start a row. In fact, 'start a row' isn't quite the right phrase. It's been like one long row that never got switched off. We just pressed the pause-button, so it was easy to resume at any moment. We had a love like cancer. The more it grew, the more pain and suffering it caused. But it *was* love, and I miss her already.

I said I didn't want any contact at all. No texts, e-mails, nothing. We've had too many commas. We need a full stop. I'm not sure that 'staying friends' ever really works. I don't think two people can have a normal friendship if they know what each other's genitals look like.

I've just realised that there's a horrible amount of mixed metaphors in those first couple of paragraphs. I suppose I'm just trying to work this out as I go. I had a feeling that writing about it might be therapeutic, but it isn't, and it's not doing my prose style much good, either.

Anyway, another door closes. We talked about staying together forever and having babies and stuff, but that's all gone now. As she left, she offered me one piece of advice. Get a girlfriend who's deaf. Funny to the last. She could be a fuckin' nightmare but she made me laugh, and she had the softest skin I ever touched.

So now I'm taking down photos from the cork-board, removing sweet messages from the fridge, and pulling knives out of the wall, making my flat look like it never knew her. I've even tuned my radio-alarm into another station. Hearing her voice as I lie in bed would be too much. We'd been together nearly a year. It doesn't sound that long, but I can't remember how it feels without her. Well, I'll soon find out.

And it's July, at least two months before I can even think about finding someone else, because they've all got suntans and, well, you remember Jerry's advice. Not that someone else feels like an option at the moment. I fuckin' hate Venice.

There was a pub on the Hagley Road, not far from the Birmingham Oratory, called The Ivy Bush. On one Saturday every month, its upstairs room was the home of the 'Ha Bloody Ha Comedy Club'. It specialised in alternative comedy and attracted a young, hip audience of students, ex-students, and generally broad-minded Brummies. Malcolm got me an unpaid ten-minute slot there in the January of '88.

I decided I needed a completely new image. I was very skinny at the time as a result of running eight miles a day, and so I got some little, round National Health specs, incorporated my guitar into the act, and billed myself as 'The Rockabilly Charles Hawtrey'. (You know, that skinny guy with the glasses in all the *Carry On* films.) When I turned up that Saturday night, the room was absolutely heaving. I was on just before the interval. I walked up to the microphone, looked at the crowd, and felt totally at home.

'I took my driving test this week. I had a really polite examiner, which, to be honest, confused me a bit. Instead of just telling me what to do, like my instructor does, he said stuff like, "Would you like to turn left here, Mr Collins?" Well, I thought it was optional. (Laugh.) He said, "Would you like to turn left here, Mr Collins?" and I said (miming as if to turn left and then thinking better of it), "No, I don't think so. (Big laugh.) There's a bit of a nasty junction down the bottom, there. (Laugh.) I nearly killed some fucker last week." (Laugh.)

Oh, joy of joys. They were laughing. They were really laughing. I felt my confidence rise up like one of those massive waves that big-time surfers ride. I was a comedian. I wasn't getting paid and I was only doing ten minutes, but I was a comedian. Anyone who doubted that only had to listen. During the interval, people were coming up and saying how much they liked my stuff. I was so happy.

A few days later, I was in a club in Moseley when I noticed a really stunning woman, skinny but with big tits, looking at me and smiling. Eventually, like after about forty seconds, I went over. 'I saw you at The Ivy Bush last Saturday,' she said. 'I suppose you get fed up of people telling you this, but you're brilliant.'

As I left her place the following morning, I knew, at last, that I had found my true vocation.

My publisher asked me to put in something about love. This worries me, talking about 'love'. Pop singers do it all the time, usually without even noticing because they're concentrating on the tune and making decisions about their next sensual body-shape. Comedians are supposed to be above that sort of thing. You remember those 'Love is . . .' cartoons that were always stuff like 'Love is . . . buying her flowers for no reason'? I was asked to do one once, for a Valentine's Day something-or-other. Mine was 'Love is . . . just about the only four-letter word I don't use during sex'. It's my job to undermine all that single-red-rose, teddy-bear-in-a-'I-Heart-You' t-shirt bullshit. And to really talk about love, I mean properly, in terms like you don't get at the card shop, well, that's for novelists and poets, not for comics. Comedians are supposed to be below that sort of thing.

Despite all this, because my publisher is so keen on the idea, I'm going to give it a go. On Love. I once found an old diary of mine from the eighties. There was only one entry. On January 3rd it said, in a version of my handwriting that suggested the intervention of drink, 'There can be no true love without the fear of losing.' I don't remember what caused me to write this, but I still think it's true. As soon as that fear subsides, there is a short period of bliss, steadily undermined by complacency and ordinariness. How long can you sit atop a mountain before you start to miss the climb?

I never reached that easy bliss with Caroline. We didn't fade, we snapped. We watched it happen. We saw the individual strands pinging, one by one, but we couldn't do anything about it, except brace ourselves for the fall. This was a different end for me. Harder, because I hadn't finished loving her.

But my usual ending, quiet, with a steady hand, is even scarier. It gives love a kind of built-in obsolescence. You love until you drive out the doubts, you take a breath, you turn around, you realise that love went with them. It sounds sort of cyclical, doesn't it?

Some people ask me why I bother. I'm on telly, why don't I

stay single and free and dine only on fresh meat? Of course that has its thrills. Not knowing what you're going to see at the unpeeling of underwear is breathtakingly exciting, feeling different lips against your skin, hearing a different sigh, smelling a different smell, tasting a different taste.

But what about the shared moments you re-live together, over and over, and the utterly unhelpful hot drinks you make when they're ill, and the way your mouth opens slightly when you hear them fumbling for keys and know they'll soon walk through the door, and the way you say 'Let's put the light off. We can still talk', and you both know you'll be asleep in thirty seconds? What about all that? What about knowing what her lips will feel like against your skin, and aching in anticipation of it? What about fucking someone, quick and hard, in a hotel toilet and desperately caring about them at the same time. That's what love is, but it doesn't fit on a teddy-bear's t-shirt. And even as I write, I can't remember how all that fades, or what it feels like when you gradually become aware that the shadows are lengthening. I know it feels bad enough to make me pretend it's not happening, but it's not shocking and sharp like a sudden fall. Either way, in my experience, it ends.

OK, I did it. I talked about love. I think I'm better at nob-jokes.

Malcolm decided I should try my act in London, so he booked a weekend of 'open spots' for me. All ten minutes, all unpaid. On the Friday night, I drove down from Birmingham after college and did a gig in a club in Notting Hill, run by Tony Allen, an alternative comedy legend. He had been on the bill the night the Comedy Store opened, and was known as The Godfather. He was very nice to me but I didn't go very well. After the gig, because I didn't know anyone in London and couldn't afford a hotel, I drove till I found a quiet street and slept, or at least lay with my eyes shut, in my Vauxhall Viva.

The following night I did a club called Drummond's, near Regent's Park, run by a bloke called Ken Ellis, who had done a lot of TV work with Noel Edmonds. There were about twelve people in the audience and, as the night slowly progressed, one after another, they went up on stage and did a spot. It turned out that only five of the people there were actually paying punters. Again I didn't go very well. After the gig, I drove to another quiet street and once again laid down my weary head in the Vauxhall Viva.

On the Sunday, I drove to Camden and bought a very fine brown-leather flying jacket with the fifty quid I had been paid for New Year's Eve. I reckon I could have got the bloke to go as low as forty quid, but I was very keen to spend my exact fee on the jacket. I needed to feel something warm and lovely had come out of that terrible experience. Obviously, it wasn't as warm and lovely as what had come out of my Ivy Bush gig, but then the jacket didn't give me a sexually transmitted disease.

On the Sunday evening, I had my last gig of the weekend, at a club near to the Blackwall Tunnel. The club was called The Tunnel, and when I was on the London comedy circuit, everybody had a terrible tale to tell about it. This is mine. The Tunnel was run and compered by a comic called Malcolm Hardee. Yes, the same bloke who tipped me off about *This is Your Life*, ten years later. He was a chubby, affable bloke with thick horn-rimmed specs and greasy black hair. He usually wore a scruffy old suit covered in cigarette burns and beer-stains. Malcolm always said that he had the second biggest testicles in showbiz, second only, he once told me, to Jenny Agutter's dad's. Well, I never saw Mr Agutter's, but Malcolm's were enormous. I know, because he used to get them out on stage, fold his penis into a sort of nose, and do a fabulous impression of General Charles de Gaulle. On that fateful Sunday night at The Tunnel, Malcolm closed the show by having a piss from the front of the stage. It was that kind of club. But the real star of The Tunnel was the crowd, or, more precisely, that part of the crowd that did the heckling. It was the heckling that brought in the people, not the acts.

For example, if a comedian called Jackson was having a bad time, the crowd would start calling 'Cab for Jackson' till he got off. Sometimes, the heckling didn't even require words. Comics would get hummed off. The whole crowd would start humming loudly until the poor devil would just give up and walk offstage. Then Malcolm would come on and say something along the lines of 'Well, he was shit. Nice bloke but shit. That bloke who was on earlier and went very well, he's a cunt.'

They say that Jim Tavare, a comic who was also to be part of that plan to tip me off about *This is Your Life*, once opened his act at The Tunnel by saying, 'Hello. I'm a schizophrenic,' and someone shouted, 'Fuck off, both of you . . .' Anyone could die at The Tunnel, and anyone did. Every comic I had spoken to that weekend had warned me about it.

I had one routine that had been going relatively well. It was about Skippy the bush kangaroo. Yes, I was still flogging the kids' telly theme. The routine was fairly standard stuff, centred around the fact that Sonny Hammond, the little kid who was Skippy's best mate, could understand everything Skippy said even though the only noise the kangaroo made was 'Tut, tut, tut, tut, tut'. This gave me a chance to do my Aussie accent and a bit of kangaroo miming. Here's kind of how the routine went:

. . . so Skippy would come bounding in and go (I stood, crouched, with my limp hands at chest-level, kangaroo-style, for all Skippy's bits), 'Tut, tut, tut, tut, tut.' And Sonny would say:

'What's that, Skip?'

'Tut, tut, tut, tut, tut.'

'Helicopter crash?'

'Tut, tut, tut, tut, tut.'

'Forty-seven miles north-west of Walamaloo?'

And, even as a little kid, I'd think to myself, 'Bollocks.' I bet what Skippy is saying isn't anything to do with a helicopter crash. I bet he's saying kangarooey-type things like (back into Skippy-pose):

'Excuse me, could I have some leaves please?'

'What's that, Skip?'

(Very big sigh.) 'I said, could I have some leaves please?'

'Helicopter crash?'

(Looking all around.) 'Where?'

'Forty-seven miles north-west of Walamaloo?'

(After a long pause with puzzled expression.) 'What the fuck are you talking about?'

So, anyway, I began this routine on that Sunday night at The Tunnel. Just as I started getting into it, a bloke shouted, 'It was Flipper.' Flipper, you may recall, was a dolphin in another kids' TV series.

'No, mate,' I replied, keeping very calm. 'It was definitely Skippy.'

'Listen,' said the voice, now sounding much more threatening, 'it was fackin' Flipper.'

I panicked. I tried to see the routine through, but change Skippy to Flipper as I went along. So I had Sonny come down the ranch-house steps and say:

'Ooo! What's that strange wheezing, slithering sound? Oh, it's you, Flip.' I then stuck in another elaborate mime: Australian schoolboy picks up slippery, wriggling dolphin. After much struggling, I thrust my index finger down the air-hole on top of his imaginary head, to keep him still. 'They hate that,' I explained. Then, at last:

'What's that Flip?' Now my mime had switched from kangaroo to dolphin, with hands acting as flippers.

'Click, click, click, click, click.' (Y'know, as in the sound a dolphin makes.)

'Submarine crash?'

Shortly afterwards, the crowd started shouting 'Malcolm' – the compere, not my manager – and he stepped in like a boxing referee to stop me from taking any further punishment. I drove back to Birmingham that night and was back in college at nine on Monday morning.

Malcolm had entered me for a talent contest at a place called the Phoenix Club in Cannock. It was a small, dingy place, but I was impressed by the fact that the front of the bar was covered in fake leopardskin. It gave the place a sort of a Vegas feel. I suppose there were about forty punters in there, all eager to see the stars of tomorrow. The winner would go through to the Grand Final, in Wolverhampton. The show was hosted by a chunky comic stroke singer, who was billed on the poster as Marty Miller, 'The man with the golden voice'. He opened the show with a light operatic number, which I think was Renee and Renata's 'Save Your Love', told a few quick gags and then brought on the first of the turns. The act before me was a big fat woman who sang 'Don't Cry for Me Argentina', looking like some sort of chiffon mountain. No one seemed to mind that another woman, three acts earlier, had sung the same song. I went on and did ten minutes and went pretty well. By now I was writing new stuff every day. The obsession was starting to kick in.

During the interval, Marty Miller came over for a chat. 'You've got something, son. I don't know what it is, but you've got something,' he said. I was very flattered. 'You won't win, but you might well come second.'

'How do you know I won't win?' I asked.

'Well, we've got a ringer in.' I had no idea what he was talking about. 'He's a semi-pro. He wouldn't come if we didn't promise him Wolverhampton.' I was shocked. Just a few months in and I was already face-to-face with showbiz corruption. Marty was nice to me, though. He was very drunk, but he was nice to me. 'What you need,' he explained, 'is a sure-fire opening gag, something that can't fail. Then they know you're funny. I always start with this.'

He told me his sure-fire opener:

I picked up this bird the other night and when I got her back to my place and took me prick out, she said, 'Who ya gonna satisfy with that?' and I said, 'Me.'

'You can't use that though, that's mine,' he explained. I felt really privileged. It was like a sort of comedy master-class. Years later, I got some more advice from a helpful comic. I suppose this next tip shows how my career had progressed. I had done a storming set at one of the top clubs in London, Jongleurs in Battersea, and I was getting a lift back, in a BMW, to Malcom Hardee's house, from a comedy-magician called Keith Fields.

Keith was a nice bloke but very business-minded as comics go. He was the first comedian I ever saw with a mobile phone. I was doing alright but I was still very new. 'Frank,' he said, as we got nearer to Malcolm's place, 'you're going to do well in this business, very well.' Again, I was flattered. 'And I'm going to offer you one bit of advice.' I was all ears. Keith was quite successful, and I felt that one pearl of wisdom from him could be a crucial piece in my comedy jigsaw. He paused for effect, and then went on, 'When you buy a BMW, and you will, make sure you get one with power-assisted steering.'

As I chatted to Marty, the old guy who managed the place walked past breezily and said, 'We could have filled the London Palladium with the bill we've got on here tonight.' He hadn't seemed to notice that this bill couldn't even fill the Phoenix Club, Cannock.

The semi-pro, a middle-aged crooner, did Barry Manilow's 'Copacabana'. When he said, 'She was a showgirl,' he did that thing that blokes used to do in the sixties to represent a sexy woman. Y'know, when you use both hands sliding downwards to mime an hour-glass figure. The crowd whooped. Oh, I had so much to learn.

By now, I was getting friendly with a student called Lisa, the dark-haired girl who had sat under the orange dayglo poster a few months before. I was thirty-one, she was seventeen. Clearly, I was born for the showbiz life.

Maybe I should take some time out here to talk about young women and me. Caroline was twenty years younger than me. My previous girlfriend was about the same. (I don't know if you believe in Freudian slips, but I just had to correct that 'previous' because I mis-spelt it as 'pervious'. Oh, dear.) In fact, my last four relationships have had that kind of age difference, but I didn't plan it that way. The fact is, most thirty-something women or even, God forbid, forty-something women, are in relationships. There just aren't many older properties on the market.

For some reason that I'll let you guess at, thirty-something women often get really angry with me for going out with young women. They always ask what I find to talk about to a girl of that age. But what can I talk to thirty-something women about that I can't talk to girls in their early twenties about? There's been so many TV programmes about the seventies just lately that the thirty-something women have lost their trump-card.

At the same time, one of the unpleasant side-effects of going out with girls in their early twenties is that guys come up and start shaking my hand and saying stuff like 'You lucky bastard', and this just makes me feel unclean. The fact is, when I was in my early twenties, I couldn't get women in their early twenties because I was ugly and not on television, so I've got a lot of catching up to do. And, anyway, they're just firmer, now leave it.

Let me take some time out to tell you about Lisa. She was, like Celine before her, well into Indie music and black clothes. She once persuaded me to completely shave her head, which I did, with a t-bar razor that got caught on a mole and pared off a strip of skin like I was peeling a potato. She took this with an indifferent shrug, which was how she took most things when I first knew her. Her dad had walked out when she was fourteen, and I think she'd decided that emotions were a kind of disability, but she had big dark eyes and a dirty laugh and everybody liked her. One night, I was, as usual, off to a comedy gig, and asked her how she was planning to spend her evening. After listing three or four potential activities, including, visiting friends and going to the gym, she said, 'But

I think I'll stay in, sit on me big fat arse, and watch television.' I don't know if you find women like that outside the Black Country. Eventually, after much deliberation, she decided that a bald head was too extreme and so grew it into an orange mohican.

Although Lisa wasn't actually in any of my classes at Halesowen, she was still a student of the college, which made things slightly problematic. She used to skip cookery classes to see me. I used to think about that a lot after we got married, especially at meal-times.

She wasn't very keen on my comedy career and wouldn't come to gigs because, she said, she didn't want to watch me suffer. I once managed to drag her to a club in London, but just before I went on she walked outside and sat in the car. I suppose it's a bit like going out with a boxer. I did persuade her to come to another gig, though, on a Saturday night in Coventry city centre, but as we wandered around trying to find the venue I was doing, dodging gangs of marauding drunkards, she said, 'I'm sick to death of your stupid fucking comedy,' and I didn't try to get her along to any more gigs for quite a while.

In fact, my stupid fucking comedy was going quite well. London Weekend Television were starting a series for new alternative comics, called *First Exposure*, and Malcolm got me an audition. When I say it was for new acts, I mean acts that had, in the main, been around for a few years but hadn't yet done any telly, not for new new acts like me, but I thought there was no harm in giving it a go. I drove down to the rehearsal rooms in Kennington, South London, and did my act in front of four people including the producer, Juliet Blake, sitting at a table in what looked like a massive school hall. They laughed. As I drove back, I was desperately trying to not get carried away, but I thought it had gone pretty well. They asked me if I was in Equity, the performers' union. I said I wasn't and they said they'd sort it out. Now, why would they have said that if I didn't have a chance?

Sure enough, on June 28th, 1988, two hundred and two days after my first-ever gig, I made my television debut. I know comics are supposed to have years of struggle and all that, but this was one of those 'right place, right time' things that happen to lucky people. Of course, the producers liked the idea of a wet-behind-the-ears Black Country lad appearing with all the stars of the London alternative circuit. I had novelty value. And I was funny-ish. The recording was at the Theatre Royal, Stratford East. I spent most of the day chatting to a bloke called Hank Shanks, who told me that he had chosen this as a stage-name purely because it gave the compere the chance to say 'Thanks Hank Shanks' at the end of his act. The compere that night was Arthur Smith, who sat in one of the lovely old theatre boxes and did his intros from there. Arthur is a truly funny comic, and the author of perhaps the finest piece of observational comedy I ever heard: 'Whatever happened to white dog shit?' On that night, he forgot my name during the intro, and had to stop and think for a bit before it finally came back to him. I bounced on, looking positively thrilled to be there, and did the sneezing routine, complete with my old swinging cling-film gag, as a closer. It all went pretty well. The show didn't exactly open a lot of doors for me career-wise, but just getting on and getting laughs was a massive boost for my confidence. I also got a cheque for £149.69. That was it. I had placed my foot on the bottom rung of the 'Highest-paid Man on Television' ladder. Only thirteen years to go.

When I watch that show now, only for research, you understand, there's one thing that always makes me wince. As the audience applaud at the end of my set, I say, with Uriah Heep-like humility, 'You've been very kind.' I think this highlights a problem that was holding back my act at the time. I was a bit too desperate to be liked. The most important thing for a comic, I think, is to 'find himself' onstage. To know who he is and why he's there. A comic, like I've said, needs a point of view, and I hadn't found mine yet.

My main problem, at this stage in my career, was that I couldn't get enough performance time. My hour-long show in Edinburgh was only two months away and I had put together about fifteen minutes of slightly shaky material so far. I needed to work at my act on a regular basis.

There was a very strange pub in nearby Tipton called Mad O'Rourke's Pie Factory. It was the first theme-pub I ever saw. The theme they had chosen was, well, abattoir, I suppose, with phoney cows' heads and other animal parts making up the bulk of the decoration, but the most talked-about aspect of the pub was its catering. They sold these enormous 'Desperate Dan Cow Pies', complete with horns made of pastry, that were a challenge to even the greediest bastard. People came from all over to try the pies and get arseholed on one of the many real ales they had behind the bar. It quickly became a Black Country must-see. And it had an upstairs room.

So, Malcolm and me opened a comedy club at the Pie Factory. We got two acts from London up every week, I hosted, and if any locals fancied an open spot, we stuck that in the mix as well. Nick Hancock, Jo Brand, lots of people who went on to do really well, played the Pie Factory at that time. Nick Hancock, probably best known as the host of BBC's *They Think it's All Over*, is a man not known for his sophisticated social niceties. He's very competitive and a bit grouchy, but he took the time to give me a lot of praise and encouragement one night at the Pie Factory, when stuff like that, from an established London name, meant a lot to me.

I was writing my bollocks off, forming a habit that I've never shrugged off. If I could spend thirty or forty hours a week drinking, I didn't see why I shouldn't spend fifteen hours a week trying to write gags. Stand-up seemed to be justifying all my wild years. I thought I'd wasted my time, chasing rough birds and getting pissed, but now it all turned out to have been research. More and more of the things that had happened to me got shoved into my comedy sausage machine, and came out the other end as neat little sausage-shaped routines.

Of course, an autobiography is the ultimate example of turning life into work. Speaking of which, I think I should make a point about this book.

When I read all this back, especially the journal stuff, it actually sounds like I lead, and have led, a very interesting and eventful life. Well, that's how it reads to me. There might actually be people reading this who are slightly envious. Well, listen, if your only knowledge of football was *Match of the Day*, you might think that it was all about goals and near-misses. It isn't. Most games have quite long patches of dead time when everything is bogged down in midfield and no one can put two passes together. Well, it is at the Albion, anyway. *Match of the Day*, or its equivalent on ITV or Sky, is a highlights package. They take out the shit and just give you the good stuff. Though it might sound like I've spent most of the duration of this book swanning around premieres and award ceremonies, driving Bentleys, and jetting off to Venice, Korea and Japan, the fact is I've spent most of the duration of this book shut away in a room, on my own, writing it. Besides, I'm forty-four and single. Who'd envy that? Yeah, OK, put your hands down.

I don't know where that speech came from, but we'll move on. The Pie Factory gave me a chance to try stuff, loads of stuff, every show. The thing was, we got the same people in all the time so I had no choice other than to keep giving them new material. I suppose I wrote about twenty minutes every week. I don't want to reveal too much of it to you now, because I'd like you to think I was a lot better than is actually the case, but this is the truth of it:

Hello, my name's Christopher Collins, which, as some of you may have already worked out, is actually an anagram of 'willing cocksucker'. Well . . . it isn't quite an anagram of 'willing cock-sucker', but one feels that it ought to be.

As you may have guessed, I also work as a children's entertainer, but when I'm doing that, I have to have a chirpy, cheeky, children's entertainer-type name, so I don't call myself Christopher Collins. Besides, a lot of them little kids wouldn't know what an anagram was.

So when I'm doing kids' parties, I call myself 'Berdum-Berdum the Clown', because kids make that noise, don't they, 'berdum-berdum'? (Wait for response that doesn't come.) Well, you've obviously never run one over.

I was sitting in that cemetery, next to St. Philip's in Colmore Row, when this tramp came and sat next to me. And I tried to ignore him and concentrate on my sandwich, but he was scratching the old scrotum and tugging the old penis . . . and eventually I said, 'Look, will you just get your hands off me?'

I had a friend who worked with tramps in Wolverhampton and he told me that the main cause of anyone becoming a tramp is a broken heart. That's sad, isn't it? I wonder how long that process takes. Does a bloke get in from work one night and his girlfriend says, 'Listen, Geoff, I'm not gonna lie to you. I've met someone else. It's all over between us. I'm sorry but I'm leaving,' and the bloke says, 'Oh, God . . . I just can't . . . look . . . you haven't got ten pence for a cup of tea, have you?'

Anyway, I'd like to finish my act . . . and who wouldn't?

When the Pie Factory gig was totally full, Malcolm and me still lost fifty quid a week each. So, after a couple of months, we knocked it on the head, and headed for Scotland.

Edinburgh '88 was not a massive success for me, box-office-wise, but it was a major turning-point in my career. I did two weeks at the hundred-seater Calton Studios, from 12.45 to 1.45 p.m., at two quid a ticket and, on August 18th, 1988, I got the following returns (I know because I have kept the Return Form to this day).

Venue sales – 0
Fringe Office Sales – 0
Comps – 0
Total in audience – 0

It was, to be fair, my only blank sheet of the run, but my record attendance was only twelve, and over the two weeks I averaged about four. The show before me in that space was a kids' show. They got two people in during the whole week's run, and they were close friends of the cast. Every day, when

I arrived, they'd be sitting around in clown outfits and jolly-face make-up, moaning about how much money they were losing and trying to work out how the rot could be stopped. It couldn't.

I got two reviews during my two-week run. A newspaper called *Review '88* said, 'He is a very ordinary, lad-next-door type of character, with a fairly sound repertoire of jokes, but he desperately needed an atmosphere to get himself and the audience going – something which a dingy bar upstairs in the Calton Studios doesn't provide at one o'clock in the afternoon. Stick him in the corner of a busy pub, heaving with drunken revellers, and I'm sure he would go down a storm.'

And the *Festival Times* said, 'His inexperience as a performer lets him down slightly. He never manages to move far enough away from the nice bloke approach to bring out the best in his material. He's worth watching though, and with a bit more experience and slightly bigger audiences, he could be very good indeed.' Not bad for an hour-long show from someone who'd only been doing comedy for nine months. Meanwhile, the 'nice bloke approach' was about to go out of the window. The Students' Union building at Edinburgh University had a venue known as the Fringe Club. Acts of all types, musicians, poets, comics, would go there and do a bit of their Edinburgh show for free, as a sort of a taster so that people who liked it would go and pay to see the full show at a later date. The crowd could be very horrible, pouring beer on the acts from above, throwing paper aeroplanes, and generally being abusive.

When I turned up for my spot, that's what they were like. Acts were leaving the stage in a state of shock. I was shitting myself. As it got to my turn, I could hardly breathe, I was so scared. Then, thank God, that which I like to call my 'Oh, fuck it' factor kicked in. I asked a friend for a cigarette, I hadn't had one since I'd stopped drinking, and walked on stage with an expression not a million miles away from the one that Jack Nicholson had when he chopped down that door in *The Shining*. Though, I say it myself, I was fuckin' unstoppable. I was belting out my usual stuff with a swagger that gave it new life, improvising, having a go at people in the crowd and dealing with hecklers like I'd been doing it for years. I wanted to be a comic, and these fuckers weren't going to get in my way. And after a while, I realised they didn't want to, they just wanted to hear me being funny. I fucking stormed it, got my first-ever encore and left the stage a new man. I had found my point of view: Mouthy Brummie, who couldn't give a fuck. It was a slightly distorted version of my personality, but I can't say it was a totally false one.

Funny, isn't it? Just remembering that gig seems to make me swear more.

I'm worried you're missing the journal bits. I figured that now I've actually become a comic in the story, you wouldn't need my regular showbiz injections to keep your interest. I know playing to zero people in a bar in Edinburgh isn't, strictly speaking, what you'd call 'showbiz', but bear with me and we'll see how it goes. To be honest, I'm worried that I took too long to get you to this point, too much wilderness years and not enough razzmatazz. Oh, fuck it. You might as well finish it now you've come this far.

When I got back from Edinburgh, I found that my Equity membership had come through. An Equity card was still quite a prestige thing in those days, but there was one problem. I had to change my name. There was already a Chris Collins in Equity, a northern club singer, if I remember rightly, and they didn't allow two members to have the same name. So, just as I was starting to think Chris Collins was finally becoming a comedian, I had to stick him in a drawer and find a new identity.

To be honest, this was not such a big deal to me. My parents, for some weird reason, always called us kids by our second names. At school I was known as Chris, my first name, because that was the name on the register. So when mates called for me, they'd say to whichever of my family opened the door, 'Is Chris in?' and the answer would be, 'Yeah, I'll call him. GRAHAM!' So another name here or there didn't make much difference. The question was, what name should I choose?

At first, I fancied 'Wes Bromwich' but I thought this might be a bit too parochial. Thank God. How would you have fancied going into a bookshop and asking for a copy of *Wes Bromwich* by Wes Bromwich? I don't think so.

Then it hit me. When I was a kid, my dad was the captain of a local dominoes team (we were a very sporting family). Every week I'd watch him take a load of names, written on little bits of white card, from an old Strepsils tin, and pick his team. There was one name that always stuck in my mind. I used to go on to my dad about how much I liked it, but I'm sure he just thought it was little kid's nonsense. Now was my chance to take that name for my own. Thus, I became Frank Skinner. I'll never know why the name fascinated me so much when I was a child, but I've still got the tin, and the bits of white card.

A few years ago, someone sent me a photo of Frank Skinner's grave. I don't know if it was the same bloke, but the inscription reads 'Peace after pain', which I like a lot. It's now on the cork-board in my kitchen, where all those pictures of Caroline and me used to be. Peace after pain.

Oh, for goodness' sake. I've got to stop being so bloody melodramatic about my split-up. I'm sorry, it's just that I'm at that odd, 'What do I do now?' stage that people go through when they're immediately post-relationship. I just feel like a bit of a Billy No-Bird. But I'm desperately trying to avoid all those predictable things that just-got-single people do, stuff like joining a gym, phoning up your exes, and wanking so much that your cock drops off. Anyway, I won't mention it again. Back to the name-change.

And so it was that the next time I strode on stage and grabbed a microphone, I said, 'Hello, my name's Frank Skinner, which, as some of you will have already worked out, is, of course, an anagram of 'skunk fucker'. Well, it isn't quite an anagram of . . .'

Malcolm suggested I could run a comedy workshop at the college on Monday nights. If we could get a dozen people who wanted to be comics, and give them the benefit of my massive experience, then we could finish the course with a showcase performance, hosted by me and helped out by a couple of pros from the London circuit. He'd got the idea from a play he'd seen, *Comedians* by Trevor Griffiths, but the difference was that, in the play, the bloke who ran the workshop had been doing comedy for about thirty years. Our version was more a case of the near-sighted leading the blind. I justified my role as comedy-sensei by telling myself that these hopefuls would be better off with someone who could still remember his first, faltering steps into comedy, rather than someone who had left his early days far behind him. I mean, I'd be shit at running a comedy workshop now. If anyone showed promise, my advice would be 'Do a couple of eighty-date tours and then get your own chat show.' Hopeless.

Anyway, we advertised the course and the response was really good, not only from potential students, but also from the media. All the local papers and telly were interested, and even the *Guardian* wanted to come and watch a workshop in action. We filled up the twelve places straight away, each of them paying £31 for the privilege. The theory was that stand-up is made particularly difficult by the fact that you have to do all your rehearsals in public. Actors have a few weeks, locked away with a director, to get it right before they show their stuff to a paying audience. This gives them the chance to leave a lot of the shit in the rehearsal room. The comic just walks out there and does it, and if it goes badly it's kind of awkward to ask the audience for a de-briefing.

Our plan was to get in a video camera so people could watch their own act and say what they thought about it. Then me and the rest of the group would offer our opinions, all done in a friendly and mutually supportive environment. And every week, the homework would be 'Get funnier'.

Then, on the Saturday morning before the course was due to start, I picked up a nasty injury whilst washing my hair. I was leaning over the sink in the communal bathroom at my bedsit in Ravenhurst Road, when my back went. I mean really went. I was holding on to the sink to keep upright, and the shampoo was running down into my eyes and mouth. Lisa, who had moved in a few weeks earlier, mainly because there was no room for her at her mom's new place, just stood and looked at me. Four hours later, I was lying on the floor of my room, full of pain-killers, watching *Grandstand*. There was a sort of a newsflash. Apparently there'd been a bit of trouble at the Liverpool–Forest Cup semi-final at Hillsborough. I watched, still in agony, as the commentary team gradually realised that people were dying. Bodies were being carried on advertising hoardings, and laid on the pitch. Any human being that watched it would have been moved, but for a football fan, it was inexpressible. It was the first time I'd cried for years. But this was to be a big week for crying.

The next day, a couple of friends of our Nora's turned up at the door. (I didn't have a phone.) My mom had been taken to hospital. It sounded serious. My mate Paul drove me there. It was the hospital where my mom had given birth to me, thirty-two years earlier. The nurses gave me some injections for my back, and a walking stick. For five days, as the country was wrapped up in the aftermath of Hillsborough, I watched my mother slowly die. I arrived, each day, with my pockets full of Hubba Bubba bubble gum. If I thought I was going to break down, I just shoved a couple of pieces in my mouth and breathed through my nose, and it went away. I didn't want to cry in front of her, or my dad, for that matter. I did cry at home, suddenly, with no warning, mid-meal. Poor Lisa, she looked at me in shock with tears dripping off my chin and food falling out of my mouth. She just didn't know what to do.

My dad wouldn't accept that all this was happening. He kept saying that she'd pull through. I sat at my mom's bedside, remembering all my childhood hugs and goodnight kisses. I held her hand and leaned in towards her. She told me that she loved me, and I told her that I loved her. I had lots more to say, but I felt like she knew anyway. There was an Indian doctor there and my dad said to him, 'Hey, do you know who this is? It's Frank Skinner.' Of course, the doctor had no idea what he was talking about. I had only just got around to telling my parents about my comedy thing. I never told them anything much about my life after I moved out. They didn't even know about Lisa, the woman I was living with, until I turned up with her at my mom's deathbed. They didn't know that I'd gone back to the Church. I wanted to be all independent and free. But I didn't want this.

Then on Thursday, April 19th, I watched the priest read the last rites, and she was gone. I leaned over for one last kiss. The pain in my back didn't seem very important now. I kissed her soft, warm face. I recognised the familiar feel of it against my own. All my life, I had associated that kiss, that soft cheek, with love and caring and security. All my life. I touched her hair and looked at her face for the last time. And then I hobbled out of the room.

You know, it's hard, when you're reading back through your book, and doing corrections and re-writes, and trying to make the whole thing presentable, because grammar and punctuation, even the words themselves, seem pointless when you've got tears dripping off your chin.

The comedy workshop was quite a hit. The group were an incredibly varied lot. There was Tom, a fifty-nine-year-old ex-brewery worker who told comical stories about the war and wanted to specialise in doing old people's homes; Ron, a retired British Leyland foreman who wrote Stanley Holloway-type monologues, including one about a haunted house that had about seven puns on the word 'ghoulies'; Suzanne, a busty club-singer who talked about the horrors of marriage; Terry, a trendy systems analyst from Land-Rover, who did mainly politics and PMT; and Evo, who developed a special-needs-type character called Norman.

Evo, six-foot-three and sixteen stone, did a few open spots as Norman. He would turn up in character, with bad clothes, unnerving stare, and mysterious carrier-bag, and genuinely scare the punters before he went on. He then dumped the character-comedy, became a working magician, and now makes a balloon-animal second to none. Shame about Norman, though. A special-needs magic act is something I would pay to see.

I have no idea what happened to the rest of them, but week after week, they turned up, did their stuff, and talked comedy. The showcase was, as you might imagine, a bit of a curate's egg. Malcolm Hardee, one of the London special guests, made the audience squirm with guilt when he told them that Tom, who had just gone down quite badly, was dying of cancer. It was a complete lie. But one very interesting thing happened during that workshops period. One night, out of the blue, Jasper Carrot turned up. Apparently he'd met the college principal on a train, and the conversation had turned to the comedy workshops. The idea had fascinated Jasper, so he made the forty-five-minute drive and dropped in to check it out. He stayed for about three and a half hours, listened to all twelve acts, and offered advice and encouragement to all of them. I decided that night that, if I ever got to be a top TV comic, I'd remember my roots and try to be a nice bloke like Jasper. Oh, fuck it.

A new alternative comedy club had started in Birmingham. It was called the 4-X Cabaret, named after the sponsors, Castlemaine 4-X lager. It took place on Thursday nights in, inevitably, a room over a pub: the Hare and Hounds in King's Heath. The show was hosted by the same double act who'd run and hosted the club in the Ivy Bush, where I'd done my third-ever gig and pulled the skinny bird with the big tits and the venereal disease. They were a nice pair (the double act, I mean), but they didn't have much time to write new stuff together, so the audience, many of whom were regular attenders, soon got a bit over-familiar with their material.

I got booked to do the 4-X and had a bit of a stormer, so much so that the brewery phoned Malcolm and asked him if he'd like to run the club with me as the regular host. Thus began one of the happiest spells of my comedy career. I've won awards, had hit TV shows, and got laid in the changing room at Bloomingdale's in New York, but none of these were quite as joyous as the twenty months I spent hosting the 4-X Cabaret. If I could ever get across, in a TV show, the specialness that permeated those 4-X nights, I'd be the highest-paid . . . oh . . . well, anyway, I'd be more successful than I am now.

Of course, you couldn't do it. One of the great things about the 4-X was that it was profoundly local. I used to do gags about Bearwood Fruit Market, the mad bloke with the long scarf who hung around the Hagley Road, and the nearby chipshop that sold bright-orange chips. I wrote more export-able material as well, but I found the fact that I put so much effort into writing gags I knew I couldn't use anywhere else in the world was incredibly liberating. We didn't need London or telly, it was fuckin' party-time every week, and most of us lived close enough to walk home afterwards. I used to get so adrenalined-up at the gigs that when I got home, I'd watch old boxing videos into the early hours just to bring me down slowly. Because King's Heath sold out its two-hundred-seat capacity every week, we opened a second 4-X club, at the three-hundred-seater Bear Tavern in Bearwood on Wednesday nights, and that sold out as well. So then we took the show to the Fleece and Firkin in Bristol on Tuesdays for more wild nights. There was no holding us. Malcolm started a fourth club called Pillar Talk at Cheltenham Town Hall on Monday nights. It was another smash.

So this was my schedule: Monday – Cheltenham, Tuesday – Bristol, Wednesday – Bearwood, Thursday – King's Heath, and then, at the weekend, I would do every Friday and Saturday in London, often three or four twenty-minute sets each night, jumping on and off tube-trains and often turning up as the compere was just getting ready to introduce me. I usually did only one London gig on a Sunday. Lisa felt more confident about watching my gigs by now, but I wouldn't say we were spending a lot of time together. Especially as I had to find the time to write half an hour of new material every week, including specially tailored bits for Birmingham, Cheltenham and Bristol.

At first, I tried to combine all this with my lecturing job, but I had recently been given a one-year full-time contract at the college, and it was all getting a bit too much. Then something happened which made me decide I didn't want to be a lecturer any more. One Sunday night, somebody fucked the college goat.

I'm sorry. I felt that just had to be an end-of-paragraph. But it's true. People whose houses overlooked the college playing-fields had phoned the police and said that a man was having sex with the caretaker's goat, which was tethered there. By the time the coppers turned up it was all over, but the next day, everyone at college was talking about it and the CID had been called in. There was one obvious suspect, a local bloke who was known for being particularly weird. Let's call him Nick. He did all his own tattoos, badly, and had a habit of jumping on a complete stranger's back, without warning, and aggressively demanding a piggy-back. In the case of the goat, this habit had obviously got totally out of hand. The caretaker, under-standably upset by the incident, said that the goat would have to be put down, because he wouldn't want to drink her milk after she'd had sex with Nick. It says something when a man fucks a goat and people are worried about the goat catching something.

Now, the English department at Halesowen had quite a strong politically correct contingent. One woman in particular had had a bit of a go at me because I once held a door open for her. I thought this was a little extreme, but I didn't say anything because I didn't want to be seen losing a fist-fight to someone in floral leggings. I wasn't one of these bitter anti-feminists. One of my best friends, Olga, was an extreme women's-libber, as I still like to call them, but she also had a heart of gold and a sense of humour. This woman at college was certainly a bit short on the latter.

I'd come up against the politically correct lobby on some of my London trips and I found the whole thing a bit crap. Of course, women had taken a lot of shit over the years and some things needed to be put right, but I once got hissed at the White Horse pub in Brixton, which was, of course, full of white middle-class people, because I used the phrase 'my girlfriend'.

'Oh,' said some woman, who almost certainly had a job with the word 'community' in it, 'so you *own* her, do you?' It wasn't the kind of heckle you'd get at the 4-X.

The big deal for comedians on the London circuit in the late eighties was the comedy section of *Time Out*, a local listings magazine. Every week the comedy specialist, Malcolm Hay, would write a little profile of a circuit-comic. Every Tuesday, comedians would flick through the new edition to see if it was their turn. In late '89, it was mine. After pointing out that I lacked originality and went for 'easy laughs', he closed by saying: 'The positive reaction he got recently at the Comedy Store to a spoof quote by a reviewer about his routine ("I laughed my bollocks off", Fatima Whitbread) was a reason for despair.'

Now who's getting the bad review here, me or the audience? The fact was, when I hit the London circuit there were a lot of comics doing stuff about Thatcher and ecology and things, but I wasn't interested in all that stuff. (Though I admit I did get the whole 4-X audience to dance and sing 'Ding, dong, the witch is dead' the night Mrs Thatcher resigned.) I liked gags about shagging and football, and, at the end of the day, so did most of the audience. Some people saw me as a backlash, but if I was, it was an accident. I was a working-class bloke from the Black Country. Why should I pretend to be anything else? In my opinion, I was definitely non-sexist and non-racist. The problem is that some people hear a topic come up and their politically correct siren goes off before they've actually stopped to hear how that topic is being treated. One socialist London comic described me as 'symptomatic of the New Right', but for fuck's sake, I was doing nob-jokes, not invading Poland.

Anyway, I'm straying from the point. I was talking to my colleague in the floral leggings about the caretaker having the goat destroyed. 'Typical,' she said. 'Some male can't control his libido, and the innocent female has to pay the penalty.'

'Yeah,' I said, 'maybe you should start a Goat Support Group.' It was a nothing line, she didn't really react, and I forgot about it. A few weeks later, I was called into the principal's office and he explained to me that there had been an official complaint about my goat remark.

On Friday, January 19th, 1990, against the advice of hecklers everywhere, I finally gave up my day-job. Suddenly, I was a full-time professional comedian. That night I went to Sainsbury's with Lisa and we combed the shelves for half-price offers and 'eat within the next twenty minutes' stickers. I had explained to her that things were going to be tough. I had ten gigs lined up for the last twelve days of January, and another twenty-five lined up for February. We'd probably be OK.

The 4-X gigs were going from strength to strength. We were even getting ticket touts outside. One visiting comic described it as being like a 'Frank rally', but most of the acts seemed to have a good time. One exception was Sean Hughes, now a regular on BBC's *Never Mind the Buzzcocks*. Sean, an Irishman, was a very good stand-up, and he was booked to close the show in King's Heath with a half-hour set. I introduced him and then wandered off into the corridor to have a fag. I was still smoking on stage at this point. I wanted to quit, but the brilliant Scottish comedy-magician, Gerry Sadowitz, a man who would sit with me in the back-bar of the Comedy Store talking comedy into the early hours, and saying very supportive things about my act, advised me against it. He reckoned that my comic timing had become reliant on the rhythm of my smoking. If I lost the ciggie, Gerry maintained, the whole thing could collapse like a house of cards.

It turned out he was wrong, but I loved the way he talked so intensely about comedy. I was in a Montreal theatre in the summer of '91 when Gerry got thumped on stage by a French-Canadian punter enraged by an act that had begun, 'Greetings, moose-fuckers', and gone on to describe how smelly French people are.

Anyway, Sean Hughes at the 4-X. About ten minutes into his set, Sean began a bit about the IRA. Now I'd seen this routine before, and I knew that it very cleverly avoided all the pitfalls of talking about such a touchy subject, and was, in fact, really funny and not offensive. However, Birmingham, at that time, was not a good place to do IRA material. The Birmingham pub bombings in the early seventies had hit everyone very hard. It was a horrible time, and the memory lingered, as it probably will for many years to come. I had drunk in the two pubs that were blown up, and, like a lot of people, I knew it could easily have been me that night. Consequently, two blokes went off at Sean, gave him a load of abuse and, when they felt they had had their say, noisily stormed out, shoving their way past me in the corridor. Sean was understandably a bit thrown, and when he finished, although he got good applause, there was a tense atmosphere in the room. When it gets tense in a comedy club, it is the compere's job to release the pressure-valve a bit. 'Well,' I said on my return to the stage, 'what happened there? I was standing in the corridor having a fag and two blokes came past, shouting about somebody called Iris Hunt.'

The crowd at the 4-X were generally top-notch, but it could get a bit lively at times. I was doing a routine about bouncers one night, saying I resented someone in a tan-leather bomber-jacket and a red dickie-bow telling me I couldn't come in because I wasn't dressed properly. The massive blonde-haired bouncer from the pub downstairs, who had sneaked up to watch the show, took exception to this. He walked on stage and got me in a friendlyish bear-hug. 'I suppose this is what Fay Wray felt like,' I said to the crowd. There was a laugh, but they were clearly worried in case this very big man didn't appreciate being compared to a brutish, ignorant giant ape. 'Don't worry,' I said. 'He won't get it.' He didn't.

I was still getting bits of telly, guest spots on comedy shows and the like. On one occasion, I did the local debate show, *Central Weekend*, hosted by Nicky Campbell. I did five minutes of stand-up about a pilot who, that week, had been sucked half out of a plane when the window in the cockpit shattered. He wasn't badly hurt. I even showed a picture of him sitting up in his hospital bed, and said that when he was fully recovered he should come and get his tunic off my satellite-dish. It was a squeaky-clean routine and it went really well but, once again, people who heard gags about a potentially touchy subject, in this case, a near air disaster, didn't hang around to hear what was actually being said. The show got a hundred and thirty-one complaints, including one from local MP Edwina Currie, and one from the head of the airline.

During those twenty 4-X months I felt myself becoming more and more at home on stage, till the line between on and off became very blurred. When I did that first gig at the Portland Club, I thought I could just go on and be like I was with my mates in the pub and everyone would be pissing themselves. I was very wrong. So then I became Mr Please-like-me, trying far too hard to get the crowd, all five of them, on my side. After the university Fringe Club epiphany, I became Mr Fuck-you, almost resentful of the audience for having made me act like Mr Please-like-me. It was pay-back time. On stage, I was arsey and quarrelsome. Now the pendulum, having swung high in both directions, had settled back where I started. At the 4-X, I became me with my mates in the pub again, but this time it worked. I had found my point of view and it was basically just me. Me, with some of the dials turned up to ten, and others down to two, but, essentially me.

I think a lot of this comes down to the fact that I did hours and hours of compering during that 4-X period. The compere's job is a very underrated one. I've been to a lot of comedy clubs where they don't really bother with it. The bloke who runs the club will often just get up and introduce the acts with no attempt at patter or performance. Sometimes they will use a very inexperienced comic, because they come free or very cheap, to fill the compering slot. I've even been at places where nothing happens between acts except an offstage announcement. This all seems very wrong to me. A good compere is the bridge between the audience and the acts. He's a bit of both and a bit of neither. At the 4-X, it was like I was out with a bunch of mates, and during the course of the evening I would introduce them to a few funny new friends I'd met in London. At the same time, I was doing material which kind of made me a bit of an act myself. But, because I'd brought these professional comics to see them, anything funny I said felt like a bit of a bonus. Often I'd go up to do a link I'd written and something would happen, or someone would say something, and I wouldn't do any material at all, just improvise stuff around this new theme.

All this gave me the confidence to mess about on stage, and developed in me the need to talk to the crowd, to engage them. Stand-up is not a spectator sport, it's a participation event. The audience, indisputably, is a crucial part of the evening. If you watch a dress-rehearsal for a play, or a band sound-checking, it's not very different from what you get when there's an audience there. Stand-up doesn't work that way. The crowd is everything. If any young stand-up comes up to me and says, 'How do I get better?' (OK, maybe it's happened three times in ten years), I say, 'Compering.' Unless, of course, they already have loads of stage presence and good material, in which case I say, 'Quit now, you'll never make it.'

Don't get me wrong, I'm hardly the comedy oracle, all I'm saying is that my personal comedy journey to my current position (which I would describe, without being too 'Aw! Shucks' about it, as 'Comic who is fairly well-known, and who some people think is funny and some people think is alright, but not as good as Blah! Blah!') was massively influenced by compering all those 4-X Cabarets.

Now I did warn you that when I talk about comedy, I always disappear up my own arse, so I'll close this bit with a quote from a Brummie journalist called John Kennedy, writing about the 4-X in a local mag called *Brum Beat* in 1990. This should make everything a lot clearer:

'Take one Frank Skinner, an Excalibur forged in the mighty furnace of Oldbury's creative fury . . . a Theseus, treading boldly through the labyrinth of trivia ready to slay the half-man, half-bullshit Minator of mainstream comedy.'

In March of 1990, Malcolm got a phone call from Sandy Gort, Steve Coogan's manager. Steve was a fairly well-known impressionist, who'd done a lot of the voices on ITV's satirical puppet-show, *Spitting Image*. He was going to do a show in Edinburgh that August, and he wanted me to be his support act. Furthermore, there would be a national tour to follow, sponsored by Cutty Sark whisky. It all sounded great but there was a slight hitch. A woman called Judith, who worked at the Pleasance Theatre where we were to perform, had heard tell of my act and said, 'Frank Skinner will play the Pleasance over my dead body.' As I didn't walk around much on stage, this wouldn't really have been a big problem. If you're gonna make an omelette . . . Anyway, in the end she relented and the deal was done.

Meanwhile, I was still doing the London clubs at the weekend, sleeping on people's floors and sofas, friends I'd met on the circuit. One comic who gave me a regular settee-slot at his place in Islington was a guy called Patrick Marber. Patrick was one of the circuit's top turns, with an act which had a lot to do with a suitcase of silly props like plastic ears and toy trumpets, and a lot to do with Patrick's ability to improvise. When I virtually stopped doing the circuit in 1992, I more or less lost touch with him. The next thing I knew, he'd become a big-time playwright, director and actor, in the West End, at the National Theatre, and on Broadway. I wonder who sleeps on his settee nowadays.

One Saturday night I was at the Red Rose Club and the performance-poet from Manchester, Henry Normal, was on the bill. Henry seemed a bit edgy in the dressing room. He explained that he had been having talks with Channel Four about doing a comedy show set in a theatre, a bit like the *Muppet Show* but with humans, so you'd get real acts on stage and a sort of sit-com going on behind the scenes. The saucy blonde-bombshell comedienne Jenny Eclair was up for a regular part in it as well.

The woman from Channel Four was in the audience that night and Henry was feeling nervous. At the time, there were always dressing-room conversations going on about TV ideas and projects. Television companies were really getting into the alternative comedy thing. I think they liked the idea that when they hired a comic they automatically hired a writer as well, and that his gags would tend to be 'his gags', not ones that he'd heard someone else do at a working men's club in Salford.

I loved comedy-circuit dressing rooms. Once you established yourself as a circuit regular, they were a joy to inhabit. Because the same comics did so many gigs, there were always people on the bill who you knew really well. Jack Dee would come in, his motorbike helmet under his arm, having sped from a gig on one side of London to a gig on the other. He was all jeans-and-jumper in those days, no flashy suits, but already dead-pan and dead funny. Eddie Izzard might be having an incredibly intense conversation with another comic about why some rooms suited comedy and some didn't. Steve Coogan would be telling someone how much his designer sport-jacket had cost, and getting all excited about a new pair of tan-leather driving gloves he'd seen in *Big Fast Car* magazine.

It was a real comedy community, with everyone having stories about weird gigs in weird places like, for example, Bungay, where Malcolm Hardee, I think just to be awkward, had started a club. This particular line of chat would usually end up with someone quoting that part of the comic's code that says, 'Never do a gig in a place where they still point at aeroplanes.' Then there'd be stories of student gigs, getting sucked-off by an Economics fresher in a phone-box in Bolton, or seeing a stage-hypnotist make a female volunteer describe having anal sex, in front of 700 students at a May Ball in Scotland. It was heaven. And every now and then, one of us would get up to do his twenty minutes, and the 'Have a good one's would echo around the room, or an act would return from the stage and everyone would ask, 'How was it?' In the tiny Comedy Store dressing room, the trivia quizzes and anecdotes would occasionally be punctuated by someone getting up to have a piss in the sink in the corner of the room.

Anyway, back at the Red Rose, Henry said, 'Have a good one,' and I walked towards the stage and, boy, did I have a good one. Though I say it myself, it was an absolute belter. Within a few days, Malcolm had a phone-call. How would Frank like to be a regular character, and co-write an eight-part Channel Four series, with Henry Normal and Jenny Eclair?

Things were really happening. The 4-X and Pillar Talk gigs were fantastic, I had an Edinburgh show and tour lined up, I was about to do my first TV series, and I'd only been doing comedy for just over two years. What could possibly spoil my fantastic year?

I'd been a bit worried about my dad. He'd never really got over my mom dying and I'd watched him slowly crumbling since she'd gone. There was no more searching for timber, no more trays of seedlings. His garden, for the first time in my life, was overgrown and neglected. The only gardening he did now was tending my mother's grave, which he visited every day.

He had always been a robust, barrel-chested bloke who liked to have a good drink before deciding whether he fancied a punch-up or a sing-song. Even in his sixties, I remember him coming home one night, after a few pints, with his right hand swollen and bruised. I asked him what had happened. He explained that a bloke had approached him and asked if he knew the time, so my dad hit him so hard in the face that the bloke went over a garden wall. This, to me, seemed an over-reaction. I asked him why he'd responded so violently to someone asking him the time, but all he said, enigmatically, was, 'Ah, I've seen that trick before.' I wondered what kind of conversation was going on at the other bloke's place.

One Sunday afternoon, Lisa and me turned up at my dad's house for tea and a chat. It was about two in the afternoon. As we walked towards the front door, I noticed that the *Sunday Mirror* was still in the letter-box. I felt my stomach go into a knot. I rang the bell over and over but there was no answer. I walked across the lawn and looked through the front bay-window. I could see my dad, dressed in a suit and tie, sitting on the settee. 'Please God,' I whispered, 'let him just be sleeping.' My brother Keith lived just around the corner, so we went to his house. I don't know exactly why. I suppose I needed some family with me. I told Keith what had happened and the three of us walked back to my dad's. Keith and me went around the back of the house and decided to break a window. As I was the smallest, I clambered in. Keith distinctly told me to walk straight down the hall past the door leading to the front room where I knew my dad was sitting, and let him in. Then we would go into the front room together. I jumped down from the window and was in the kitchen. My heart was beating hard.

I started to walk down the hall. I stopped at the door to the front room. I could see Keith trying to peer through the frosted glass of the front door to make sure I came straight through, but I had to see my dad. I walked in. He was sitting there. He really looked like he was sleeping, like he was just sleeping. Then I touched his hand. When I kissed my mother just after she had died, I was reminded of all the times I had kissed her and she had kissed me. All that warmth and love. My dad's hand was hard and cold, like stone.

He was my hero and now he was gone. I cried like only an orphan can cry. I could hear Keith, outside the house, banging at the door and telling me to let him in, and he could hear me, inside the house, crying for our dead father. All through Keith's tears and Lisa's hugs and the policewoman's stupid questions, all I could say, over and over, was 'I just want him to be alive. I just want him to be alive.' He'd been so strong, so big and loud and funny and more alive than anybody. But not just lately.

He had died of a heart attack earlier that morning, one year and seventeen days after my mother. They don't use the phrase 'broken heart' on death certificates. Often, when my mom and dad had an argument, he would throw the brakes on, half-way through, and say, 'Well, anyway, there's only one thing I want. If you die on the Monday, I want to die on the Tuesday.' In many ways, that's exactly what happened.

On the night of his funeral, I did a gig at the Fleece and Firkin in Bristol. I'm sure no one there would have suspected a thing. Once I was back on stage, I felt a lot better. I knelt in the Catholic church in Stourbridge the following Sunday and prayed for help. When I was a kid, I had watched TV footage of an astronaut walking in space. I remember thinking what it would be like to do that and have the cord break, to be left floating in dark nothingness, totally isolated, totally alone. I had been thinking about it a lot since my dad had died. How could I get rid of that feeling? How could I replace that bond? Then I got it. Of course, I'll get married and have babies of my own. I told Lisa. She was shocked but sort of went along with it. I told my priest. He suggested I thought it over. What's the rush? But I had made my mind up. I was thirty-three. I would marry my nineteen-year-old girlfriend on September 29th, 1990, Jerry Lee Lewis' birthday.

The Edinburgh show with Steve Coogan was a great success for me. To be honest – and Steve is very open about this – I blew him off the stage most nights, which, in the end, I think was the best thing that ever happened to him. Steve is an incredibly talented bloke, but he was a lazy bastard. He was making so much money out of easy voice-over jobs that he never took the time to work on his act. Our Edinburgh show, and the resulting tour, was the kick up the arse he needed. As he's won about fifty awards in recent years, I don't suppose he's too bitter.

He was a joy to work with, a naturally funny bloke who would have me rolling around his kitchen floor just by pulling faces and doing funny voices. Although the reviews tended to say nice things about me and negative things about him, I never got the slightest hint of resentment or malice from him, in Edinburgh or on the tour.

The show was simple. Basically, I would do the first twenty-five minutes, storm it, introduce Steve, and then he would do half an hour of material he'd been doing for about six years, a lot of it on national television, which he was clearly bored with. We'd close the show with a song we'd written, called 'It's Over Now', a sort of Hope and Crosby spoof, and that was that.

On tour, we did mainly student gigs, all offering half-price

Cutty Sark whisky to the kind of kids who could get drunk on half a lager. To be fair, it was always going to be easier for a dirty-mouthed, heckle-if-you-dare comic like me than a subtle, clever character-comic and impressionist like Steve, but he was much richer and better-known than me, so fuck him, I thought to myself.

After a tour gig one night, as me and Steve sat nattering in the student canteen, a woman came up and said to him, 'You know, I came here specifically to see you, but he was much funnier.' Then again, on another occasion, a much better-looking woman came up and asked Steve to sign a poster. After he'd done so, he passed it to me, but she snatched it back. 'No, thank you,' she said to me. 'I don't want yours.' I remember thinking that being in a comedy double-act must be a bit of a nightmare.

I got married in St. Mary's Roman Catholic Church in Vivien Road, Harborne, at five in the evening. My best man was my old drinking-partner, Shane, and Steve Coogan did a couple of readings from the Bible. Happily, he resisted the temptation to do Jesus as Ronnie Corbett, or anything of that sort. The disco was about as West Midlands as you can get. There was a sort of DJ double-act, two fat blokes with moustaches, who both wore those baseball hats with false hands on the top that clap when you pull the strings. And they pulled the strings a lot. Lisa and me had the first dance, to Elvis singing 'Love Me Tender', and the rest of the night was all Black Lace and 'Hi Ho Silver Lining' with the volume turned down for the chorus.

My wife and I spent the next day, Sunday, sitting around reading the papers and getting the confetti out of our hair. The honeymoon had to be put on hold. On the Monday morning, I set off for ten days of touring with Steve. My 'stupid fucking comedy' couldn't be put on the back-burner, especially if it was going to pay for the new house we fancied and all those kids I was planning to bang out.

We filmed the Channel Four show in June 1991. It was called *Packet of Three*. To be honest, although we had a great time making it, in front of a live crowd at the Wakefield Opera House in West Yorkshire, it didn't really work. I had had my usual dreams of earth-shattering success, but it didn't happen. We had some decent guest turns, with early TV appearances for Harry Hill and Al Murray, a whole show based around the Reduced Shakespeare Company, who performed the Complete Works of Shakespeare in ten minutes, a French stunt-motorcyclist, and a sixty-five-year-old yodelling accordionist called Billy Moore. We just never managed to successfully marry the onstage and backstage stuff.

Henry was the manager and host of the fictional 'Crumpsall Palladium', Jenny Eclair was the usherette, and I was the teddy-boy caretaker. The script had its moments, but not too many of them, although I did enjoy the almost vaudevillian nature of some of the writing:

FRANK: I met this gorgeous bird last night, so I invited her back to my place for a game of cards.
HENRY: Poker?
FRANK: No, we just had a bit of a snog.

During the filming of *Packet of Three* I started to get panic-stricken about my very sudden decision to marry, buy a house, and have children. It all seemed to have happened in a bit of a blur. I decided that when I went home, I'd suggest to Lisa that

327

we pull out of the house-deal and wait for a while before making any decisions about kids. It was all very tough on her. I'd railroaded her into a marriage she wasn't at all sure about, just because I didn't want to feel like an orphan anymore. My professional life was faltering – one bad TV series can finish someone for good – and my personal life was even worse. To complicate matters even further, I was becoming slightly besotted with a woman who worked on *Packet of Three*. Her name was Jane.

I'll always feel bad about the way I treated Lisa. She was a young, funny, and lovable girl, and I let her down badly. When I told her about my decision to slow things down a bit, she lost faith in me and we drifted apart fast. We tried going to Relate, the relationship counsellors. I'd never tried anything like that before. The counsellor told us to be totally honest in that room because everything was totally confidential, so I opened my heart and spoke more openly about myself than I ever had before. But there was no saving our marriage. When I got married, especially considering the Catholic Church's teaching on divorce, I thought it would be forever. Ours lasted ten months. We had fucking cake left.

Malcolm advised me not to do Edinburgh in 1991. He reckoned I would be better off going down to London and cashing in on the fact that most of the top turns were up in Scotland.

At the time, my working relationship with Malcolm was going about as well as my relationship with Lisa. I didn't feel he was really coping very well with the increase in workload. He'd taken on some other acts, Tim Clark, a regular compere at Jongleurs, Alan Davis, who became a star in BBC's *Jonathan Creek,* and Caroline Aherne, who was destined for great things with Mrs Merton and *The Royle Family,* so he was doing pretty good. But I wasn't happy. I didn't feel very 'managed'. I once drove all the way down to Battersea for a gig at Jongleurs, only to find that someone had got the dates mixed up. On another occasion, I got a lot of grief from one promoter for not turning up for my gig the previous weekend. I'd known nothing about it.

We had lots of crisis meetings. At one of these, I suggested that Malcolm should perhaps hire a secretary to look after the nuts and bolts of the business while he could take a more general overview. I was being diplomatic. It's not easy to tell an old mate, especially an over-twenty-stone, bad-tempered one, that you think he's messing up. He dismissed my secretary suggestion by saying, 'I think attention to details is one of my strengths!' This was the last response I had expected. I remember telling David Baddiel what Malcolm had said. Dave's response was, 'I think he's got the word "details" mixed up with the word "sausages".'

I bumped into Jon Thoday at a comedy club. We had become friendly at the Montreal Comedy Festival, where I had gone down pretty well earlier in the year. He was absolutely astonished when I told him that Malcolm had advised me not to do Edinburgh. Two days later, he phoned Malcolm to suggest that Avalon could, with his permission, promote a Frank Skinner one-man show in Edinburgh, with Malcolm and me working out a financial arrangement between us. Avalon would do all the work, accommodation, posters, venue-booking, leafleting, the lot, and take fifteen per cent of the box-office. I suggested that I would pay Malcolm a further fifteen per cent of whatever I earned.

Malcolm was very keen.

So, off I went to Edinburgh. I was to play the Pleasance Cabaret Bar, the same room where I had decided to become an alternative comic at the 12:12 Cabaret, four years earlier. On my poster it said 'From Channel Four's "Packet of Three"'. By now the first few episodes had gone out, and the response had not been great. One critic wrote, 'May God forgive everybody involved in the making of this Texas-sized turkey.' It was quite a setback. Maybe a good Edinburgh might put me back on the right track. My poster also said, 'Don't miss this outstanding natural comedian', the *Independent*. It was a completely fictional quote that Avalon had made up to give me some extra cred.

The opening night felt very different from my first Edinburgh stand-up show, three years earlier. The 4-X, I believed, had prepared me for anything, but my one doubt was whether or not I had built up enough material. Obviously, in twenty months I had written loads, but lots of it would never work in Edinburgh. It was a bit too Birmingham, both from a local references point of view, and from a 'Brummies laugh at dirty jokes but sophisticated festival-goers don't' point of view. Anyway, I put together a routine that I thought would work and hoped that it would fill the hour. The show started and I was going great. Eventually I realised I was about half-way through my material. I looked at my watch to see how long I had done. It was fifty-five minutes. Phew! I had loads of stuff to spare. I felt the weight lift off my shoulders. In those days I always performed in a leather biker-jacket, t-shirt and jeans. I liked to perspire a little onstage. It made it look like I was working. The cabaret bar was hot, sweaty and heaving most nights, but I liked seeing the condensation running down the walls. It made a nice change from the cold emptiness of the Calton Studios.

Now I was really rocking. About half-way through the run I got fed up with doing the same stuff, so I did the other half of my joke-store. That all went down great as well, even the really dirty stuff I thought I'd never get away with outside of my 4-X circuit. There was one routine I tried as an act of bravado one night, fully expecting a bad reaction, but it got exactly the opposite response. I'll run it by you, but it's against my better judgement. The problem with quoting stand-up, or any kind of verbal comedy, in a book is that so much depends on the tone, delivery, facial expression and body-language of the comic. If stand-up worked as well on the page as it does on the stage, I would have bought a fax machine years ago and saved myself a lot of petrol money. Nevertheless, here's the bit I'm talking about:

Now one thing I've always tried to do in life is to put other people's feelings first. For, example, sometimes, when I'm just about to perform oral sex on a woman, I'll notice just a tiny piece of toilet-paper. Not a large, just a tiny, piece, like a cloakroom ticket tucked behind a lapel. Now, in those cases, I don't point and go 'Urrrrrgh! Guess what?' No. I eat it. Yes. Put other people's feelings first. I've eaten fuckin' rolls of the stuff over the years. Doesn't bother me.

And the odd thing about that routine was not so much that it went well with an arts festival crowd, but that I could always tell by the sound of the laughs that it was the women in the audience who really went for it. The laughter was like a cheer at a hockey international, a good octave higher than normal. I don't have an explanation for this, but it was definitely, night after night, true.

Pretty soon a whisper was going round the Pleasance. Lots of the Perrier panel had been in to see my show. Let me explain this. The Perrier Award is, or was in 1991, the most prestigious award that a British stand-up comic can get, bar none. It's kind of like the stand-up comedian's Oscar but more so because they only give one a year. It is decided by a panel of so-called comedy experts and the odd token punter, and, though they may deny it, it's what every stand-up at the Fringe is dreaming of. At that time, the five nominations were announced half-way through the second week, and the winner was announced on the Saturday afterwards, giving them a further week to sell out every night on the strength of their achievement. The word on the street was that Jack Dee was an odds-on certainty to lift the silver bottle that year.

I was sharing a flat in Edinburgh with the American comic, and now film and TV sit-com star, Denis Leary, who was doing his *No Cure for Cancer* show at the Assembly Rooms. I had met Denis at a gig in Windsor months before and at the Montreal Festival in June. We got on really well, chiefly because we both liked sport, John Wayne, *Columbo*, TV Westerns and each other's acts. A magazine called *The List* had done a survey to find 'The Filthiest Man on the Fringe', and Denis and me had tied with 26 out of 30. I scored Sexually Explicit: 9, Lavatorial: 9 and Sick: 8. Denis lost a point on Lavatorial but made it up on *Sick*. Bill Hicks came a close second with 25, and the Australian Doug Anthony Allstars third with 24. I felt like I was flying the flag for good old British smut. *The List* said of me, 'Max Miller would have been like this, if he'd come from Birmingham and had a much filthier mind.' What a compliment.

The funny thing was that Denis and me also had the filthiest flat in Edinburgh. We found a great fish and chip shop and a great pizza place, and that was us sorted. Soon the chip-papers, pizza-boxes and dirty cups were everywhere. It was two joyous weeks of blokiness until Denis flew home. We would hire videos to watch in the early hours, but it always seemed to be

Goodfellas, *The Godfather*, or *The Wild Bunch*, and then we'd spend the days talking about women and sport. This was exactly what I needed after my marriage break-up: bloke-therapy. For the third week, Denis was replaced by Dave Baddiel, and a very strange American musician called Mitchell Zeidwig, who arrived wearing two pairs of shades. I remember sitting in the kitchen, baring my soul to Dave about my marriage, while Mitchell stood eight feet away, balancing the ironing-board on his chin.

Anyway, on the second Wednesday, I was leaving the flat around lunchtime, to have yet another crisis meeting with Malcolm, when the phone went. I had been nominated for the Perrier Award, along with Jack Dee, Eddie Izzard, Lily Savage, and an American kids' entertainer called Avner the Eccentric.

That afternoon, Malcolm and me finally parted company. We were both slightly teary. It seemed like a long time since that first night at the Portland Club. We'd had some rows but a lot of laughs. People tell me that he doesn't speak too well of me nowadays, but him and me shared a fantastic adventure and he'll always have a place in my heart.

A few years later, a journalist from the *Mirror* told me that Malcolm had been very talkative about my drinking habits, marriage, and other murky areas of my past. Journalists often lie about these things in order to get a juicy quote in response. I hope he was lying about Malcolm.

At that time, the convention was that the Perrier winner was surprised at the end of his show by the entire Perrier panel storming the venue and presenting the trophy onstage. I finished my show on that Saturday night, and there was no sign of them. Oh well, it was as I'd expected. To be honest, in the inside pocket of my biker jacket I had a 'Congratulations' card that I intended to fill in as soon as I found out the name of the winner.

I took my bows and walked to the dressing room, with the

audience still applauding as I went. I was getting ready to leave when the stage manager came in. 'Frank,' she said, 'they want you back on stage.' In the distance I could hear a voice on the microphone, 'Ladies and gentlemen, we have a very pleasant duty to perform here tonight . . .'. I walked back on to a massive cheer, and they gave me a bunch of flowers, a bottle of champagne, and the little silver bottle on its wooden plinth. I handed the champagne to a bloke in the front row who I'd been taking the piss out of all night, and then I left to a hero's applause. One of the panel asked me if I'd like to phone my family to tell them I'd won. I explained that not only would my family not have heard of the award, they almost certainly would not have heard of the product. Another panellist told me that what had really swung it for me was that all the Perrier panellists have to watch the nominees again, after the nominations. They all sat through four shows they'd seen before and then came to see me. By a fluke, of course, I'd changed my material because I was getting bored with it. When they turned up and saw a whole new show, they decided that I was the man.

That night, I went up on to Arthur's Seat, that tall, majestic hill that looms over the old town, and, underneath the twinkling stars, fucked the arse off a woman I'd met. Her original request was a bit more unusual, but I explained that I couldn't because they'd taken it back to be engraved.

Two days later, the *Guardian* said, 'Skinner is the nearest thing to Bernard Manning to win the Perrier Award. He has taken the traditional Northern working men's club act, and subtly re-invented the genre as something fresh and right on.' I think I preferred being a Theseus.

Having lost my manager, I spent the rest of the festival wondering where to find a new one. Avalon was the obvious choice, but everyone on the comedy circuit told me they were the evil empire, so I was a bit wary of joining them. The broadsheets would occasionally run a feature about Avalon's 'no-nonsense approach' to comedy promotion, usually accompanied by a picture of Jon and his business partner, Richard Allen-Turner, looking like the Kray twins. The alternative circuit had a kind of hippyish attitude to ambition and success. They were slightly dirty words. Any comic who appeared to be in any way career-minded was viewed with at best suspicion, and at worst downright scorn. There was one comic named Mike who people were always slagging off because he'd done a couple of telly shows and taken to wearing a suit and tie.

To be honest, I kind of agreed with this prevailing attitude. One thing I didn't like about the Montreal Festival was the lobby of the Delta Hotel, where all the acts were staying. It was always full of American agents in designer suits, on their mobiles talking loudly about gameshow deals with KFRRDTY, or one-off specials for WXTJO. The British comics, wearing badly chosen shorts and ankle-socks, would all sit around the same table, smoking and drinking tea, and taking the piss out of these tossers. I didn't want a flashy manager who sold me like he was selling toothpaste. At the same time, I really wanted to stop worrying about whether I was heading to the right gig on the right night, and whether the other acts on the bill were getting paid three times more than me for doing the same job.

Seamus Cassidy, the then Channel Four Head of Comedy, told me that if I signed with Avalon he wouldn't want to work with me again. For a still relatively new comic, this was quite a big deal, but I didn't want a broadcaster to pick my manager. One thing I liked about Jon was that he didn't seem scared of anybody. A lot of managers and agents are so thrilled that they're talking to broadcasters and signing fancy contracts that they worry more about upsetting the TV people than they do about fighting their act's corner. I knew I wasn't equipped to deal with some of the tricky fuckers who run telvision, so I thought it might be a good idea to get my own tricky fucker to do it for me.

I asked, in turn, every Avalon act, including Dave Baddiel, what they thought of the company and, especially, Jon Thoday. Of course, as is traditional, they all moaned about expenses and the like, but every one of them said that, to be honest, they thought Jon did a great job, and that his main priority was always his acts. When I got back to London, I decided to throw in my lot with the evil empire.

I know what you're thinking. 'What does he mean, "back to London"? I thought he lived in the Black Country.' Well, after my marriage went bust, I just wanted to walk away from everything. Lisa was living with friends by now, and I left the flat and all its contents, and drove out of town. Most entertainers move to London because it is the centre of Britain's showbiz universe, but I just went there to escape. I asked Jane, the woman I'd met when working on *Packet of Three*, if I could stay with her. She thought it was a bad idea, but I talked her round and suddenly I was living in London N1.

This is, I think, a fair and accurate account of what happened to me in 1991.

Alternatively, one could suggest that I got a bit of success and a bit of telly, dumped my poor young wife who'd stuck with me through the hard times, and replaced her with some fancy London bird who worked in telly. And then dumped my old mate and manager, who had been with me from the very start, and replaced him with the most despised, ruthless and cynical comedy agency in Britain. I think if you've read the book this far, you've earned the right to decide for yourself.

*

In November, I was back in Birmingham, doing a sell-out show at Birmingham Town Hall, one of my regular haunts for watching bands back in the 1970s. It was a really special, local-lad-makes-good occasion. Even Lisa turned up to congratulate me in the dressing room afterwards. Then she asked if she could have a quick word outside. I stepped on to the landing, right next to the stage, and she asked me for a divorce. She left, and, after a quick 'ma', I stepped up on to the big empty stage, and stared into the big empty auditorium.

The divorce was a horrible drawn-out process. I desperately wanted to treat Lisa fairly, but my lawyer kept trying to rein me back. Lisa and me and our lawyers finally ended up, two years later, in the Birmingham Magistrates Court. I was told that, although I needed to attend the hearing, I wasn't allowed to say anything. The magistrate said he felt that my final offer to Lisa, a £15,000 lump sum, was 'extremely inadequate'. This was at a time when I earned about £40,000 a year. He said she was unemployed, with no savings and no source of income, and it was only right I should give her enough money to make a fresh start.

I felt really misrepresented and demanded to speak. My lawyer got very agitated and warned me against this, but I felt I had the right to defend myself. The magistrate gave in and sat back to listen to my explanation. I said I was sad that my marriage to Lisa had failed and that I had chosen a lawyer from the list of 'Family Lawyers' I had been given, because I was told that this would reduce the chances of a messy divorce and help ensure that Lisa got a fair settlement. I told the magistrate I was ignorant in all these matters. I didn't know what a 'fair settlement' was. If, I went on, the magistrate told me what he believed was a fair sum, I would write a cheque for that amount here and now, and hand it over to Lisa.

The magistrate looked stunned. He said he had been in the

job for fifteen years and he had never heard such a speech. It was a real shame, he said, that a marriage that had produced such sentiments hadn't worked out. All this conversation went on in front of Lisa and the two lawyers. The magistrate said he thought that £30,000 was a 'fair' settlement, so I wrote the cheque and handed it over. My lawyer had gone purple. That was on the Friday.

Two days later, Lisa was in the *Sunday Mirror*, saying how horribly I'd treated her and quoting loads of stuff that I'd said in those 'totally confidential' counselling sessions at Relate. The headline was 'My Half-Time Sex with Fantasy Frank'. She said that, on one occasion, we'd been watching football when the half-time whistle blew, and I'd immediately turned to her and suggested that we squeezed in a quick shag before the second half. Well, so what? It was a televised game, we weren't on the fuckin' terraces. I think it makes me sound quite loving, and remember, these were the days when the half-time interval was only ten minutes long. I'd get two in now. There'd even be the opportunity to change ends.

A year later, she was in the *News of the World*, telling a similar tale but with a bit of extra spice, which I imagine was added by the journalist. In this version, I would only have sex if there was football on the radio, and after we'd done it, I'd run around the bedroom, kicking a football and shouting, 'Skinner has scored.' If anyone accused me of that now, I could bring in Mr Keepy-Uppy as a character witness. He'd testify that I could never get all the way round the bedroom without losing possession to an inanimate object.

And then, in late 2000, Lisa spoke to the papers again, this time the *Sunday People*. She would soon be able to list her profession as 'columnist'. Having used up all the true stuff in the first two stories, she moved into fiction. She claimed I had tricked her into taking a lump-sum divorce settlement and that our relationship put her off sex for life. She had two children and one on the way. She also stuck in a personal message to Caroline, telling her to get out fast before I ruined her life as well. Here, hold on a minute . . .

Anyway, I guess she got her own back. In my defence, I was devastated by my parents' death, and I stupidly thought that marriage would make everything better. As the balance of power was heavily weighted towards the rising TV star, I suppose she had to use what methods she could. I got a bit pissed off after each of her articles, but I still wish her well. After all, what is this, or any other autobiography, but an elaborate kiss-and-tell. Maybe one day she'll forgive me my mistakes. She might as well, she's running out of Sunday papers.

Following my Perrier success, and despite my move to Avalon, Channel Four were very keen on a second series of *Packet of Three*, but they felt that some changes needed to be made. Their first suggestion was a bit of a shock. They wanted to get rid of Henry. I thought this was unjust. The first series had been a flop, but it was hardly Henry's fault. The show just didn't work. And anyway, if they dropped Henry, who would host the show? They had a suggestion. Me.

Their argument was that it was a waste to have the Perrier winner on the show and not let him do any stand-up. This was really difficult for me. First of all, Henry was my mate and I didn't want to stab him in the back, even though Channel Four insisted that they would do the show without him whether I hosted it or not. Secondly, my now girlfriend, Jane, was set to produce the new series. I didn't want people thinking that I'd got the job because my bird was running the show. It was all a bit grim, but I did want to do a second series and prove the critics wrong.

First Lisa, then Malcolm, now Henry. That's what it felt like. What should I do?

I hosted the second series. It was re-titled *Packing Them In*. Henry moved on and began concentrating on his writing. He became a top-notch writer on the award-winning *Mrs Merton Show* and also on the award-winning *Royle Family* series.

Packing Them In died on its arse.

When *Packet of Three* was slowly going down the plughole, the Perrier Award turned up and saved my comedy bacon. How was I going to get out of this one?

I got asked to appear on the BBC satirical panel show *Have I Got News for You?* Y'know, I like those little introductions I've started slipping in just lately – 'the BBC satirical panel show', for example. Maybe I could make a feature of them. I should try something like 'the disjointed, disappointing variety show *Packing Them In*, hosted by 'the ruthless, back-stabbing, gone-all-la-di-da Perrier Award winner, Frank Skinner'. Actually, maybe I'm being a bit harsh here. *Packing Them In* wasn't all *that* bad.

I have to stop for a moment. Throughout this book I have tried to be completely honest, even if it hurts, but now I'm doing something else. When that Henry Normal thing happened, I felt a bit uneasy at first, but I never felt like I was doing a bad thing. I spoke to Henry while it was all going on, and he seemed totally fine about my part in it. So there's being honest, and there's that Catholic hitting yourself with a cat-of-nine-tails to try and prove how pious you are. Oh, I don't know. Maybe this is another one for you to call.

Anyway, I got asked to do *Have I Got News for You?* which was at the very peak of its popularity. The show was made by Hat-Trick Productions, at that time the Man United of independent television companies, certainly as far as comedy was concerned. Hat-Trick had tried out another panel show earlier that year, called *The Brain Drain* and I had really rocked on one of the episodes. One question was 'What never happens in movies but you wish it would?' I said that when, in Robin Hood films, Robin and his merry men, dressed all in Lincoln Green, leap from the Sherwood Forest trees to ambush the Sheriff of Nottingham's men, I wish, just once, one of the baddies would point at Robin and say, 'You just wait till autumn.'

Anyway I must have impressed someone because I ended up on the very prestigious *Have I Got News for You?*, and went really well, so much so that I was the first guest to appear twice on the same series. These two appearances were very important for me. Suddenly *Packing Them In* was forgotten and I was on the up again.

Even twice-bitten Channel Four were still showing faith in me. They were planning a series called *Bunch of Five*. The idea was based on the old BBC *Comedy Playhouse* format. The series would consist of five sitcom pilots, and the one that went down best would become a series. The five included *Dead at Thirty* by Paul Whitehouse and Charlie Higson, *The Weekenders* by Vic Reeves and Bob Mortimer, and *Blue Heaven* written by and starring me. Guess which one got the series?

Blue Heaven was about an unemployed West Midlands bloke in his early thirties called Frank Sandford (played by me, obviously), who still lived in Smethwick with his parents. My dad was played by John Forgeham, who I remembered as Jim Baines in *Crossroads*, and Paula Wilcox, who I had fancied for about thirty years since she was in *Man About the House* and *The Lovers*, played my mom. In fact, she was still pretty stunning, which is the last thing you want from someone playing your mother.

I took the name Sandford from Teddy Sandford, an old Albion player, and the whole series was my sort of love-letter to the Black Country. It was mainly shot on location around Oldbury and Smethwick, and the scripts included lots of incidents from my life, including Celine and the earrings, and Fez asking at the Social if it was where you got the free money.

In the show, I was half of a pub duo called Blue Heaven. The other half, my onscreen mate Roache, was played by the Irish actor Conleth Hill, a good Catholic boy who became one of my closest friends. I spoke to the camera, mid-dialogue, like Michael Caine in *Alfie* and there was no laugh-track. It was sort of like *The Grimleys*, but with jokes.

To be honest, if you'd asked me a few years ago what I thought of *Blue Heaven*, I would have said it was no more than a fair try by an inexperienced writer, but six months ago, a fan at a stage door gave me all six episodes on one VHS. I was really chuffed because I didn't have any of it on tape, and the next night Conleth and me watched the whole series, straight through. I didn't remember any of the gags seven years on, so it was like watching someone else's stuff. As a great athlete once said, I laughed my bollocks off. It was the funniest sit-com I'd seen in ages.

I know this sounds terrible, but it's a problem I have. When I was in that Edinburgh flat with Dave Baddiel in 1991, we watched a TV show called *Edinburgh Nights*, hosted by Tracey McLeod. Tracey was a friend of Dave's and I had got to know her during that Edinburgh. She was one of the unfortunates that I would sit down and tell about my broken marriage. I remember explaining to her that I was still upset but I wasn't crying anymore. I called it my post-blart stage.

Anyway, that's by the by. Dave and me were watching

342

Edinburgh Nights, mainly because I was on it. They did a short interview and, as usual, I sat looking at myself and thinking, 'Fuck off, Baldy.' Then they showed about five minutes of my stand-up. I laughed like a big fool. Dave was amazed. 'Why are you laughing?' he said. 'You've heard all the jokes before.'

'Yeah,' I said, 'but I'm doing them so well.'

I know it's not a story that shows me in a great light. I just thought I'd add egomaniac to my ever-growing list of self-abuse. Self-abuse? No, I must get on. The fact is, I'm a very good comedy audience. I laugh at other comics so why shouldn't I laugh at me? Besides, I once read that my all-time comedy hero, Stan Laurel, used to laugh like a drain at Laurel and Hardy movies. That made me feel a lot better.

If something's funny, I laugh at it. If it happens to be my gag, so what? I've had to read this book through a few times before publication, and I always laugh at the line about someone fucking the college goat. Even though I know it's coming.

While I'm in the mood, I should tell you something else about myself. I'm not very good at watching my shows with other people. I spend too much time watching their reaction. Sometimes they don't laugh where I think they should, and then they talk over really good bits. I once switched off a video of the previous night's *Fantasy Football* after one of my friends had talked over a really good gag, and said, 'Well, look, obviously no one's interested in this so let's just talk.' I was half-joking, but only half. Stop looking at me like that. If ever you see me on the tube, and you're reading this book, my advice is start looking enthralled.

Anyway, there was one bit on the *Blue Heaven* tape when I really laughed. I was talking to a barmaid about my brother, Brian. He had murdered somebody, and she'd seen the whole thing.

BARMAID: Ooo! It was amazing. He just walked through the door with a gun in his hand.
FRANK: It was a revolver, wasn't it?
BARMAID: I don't remember what kind of door it was.

Every episode I, or at least my character, would bump into my old Asian mate, Prem, (Nadim Sawalha), who was also unemployed. His last job was working for BT as 'the Asian bloke who answers the phone when you dial a wrong number', but they had made him redundant and replaced him with samples from old Peter Sellers records. Prem would always offer a piece of Eastern-sounding philosophy, which never sounded quite right, like:

Life is like a goldfish. It may sparkle and shimmer but, if you look closely, there is usually a long piece of shit hanging off the back of it.

The series passed by virtually unnoticed. I was starting to wonder, how many unsuccessful TV series could I make before broadcasters lost faith in me? The answer was quite a lot, actually.

In August 1992, I went back to Edinburgh with a brand new stand-up show, then took that show on a national tour with Al Murray as my support. I suppose we played around thirty dates. In '91, I'd done a post-Perrier tour of around twenty dates. In '94 I did a sixty-date tour, and then, in 1997, a one-hundred-date tour, culminating in a show at Battersea Power

Station in front of five and a half thousand people, which was, at the time, according to the *Guinness Book of Records*, 'the World's Biggest Solo Comedy Gig'. I know because I've still got their official certificate on my wall. Maybe I should get that Return Form from the Calton Studios in 1988, and frame them together, so every time I walk past, I can 'treat those two imposters just the same'.

Anyway, the reason I lump these three big tours together is because I think I should say a bit about my tours in general.

Firstly, apart from the chat show, which I'll discuss later, when I do stand-up nowadays, I do it as part of a national tour, usually in venues that seat between one and two thousand people. Whether this is, at the end of the day, a good thing, I don't know. There is part of me that thinks stand-up belongs in a poky little room above a pub, rather than a plush two-thousand-seat theatre (or, indeed, in Battersea Power Station, with the show projected on to two enormous screens on either side of the stage). But I also think that a two-thousand-seater theatre can feel just like a room above a pub, when the force is with me.

On tour, the show opens with a support act who does about twenty minutes, then there's a short interval, and then I come on and usually do about an hour and a half. Sometimes, I wonder if this is too long. It sounds a lot, doesn't it? People do seem to laugh all the way till the end and ask for an encore, but it could be that they'd be just as happy with an hour. Then the show would take less time to write and I could tour more often. How am I supposed to know? Oh, anyway, what do you care about this? Honestly, sometimes this stops being a book and just becomes chit-chat.

Anyway, when I wrote the material for the Perrier show, I didn't know I was doing it. I was just writing stand-up for the 4-X and then Edinburgh came along and I thought, 'Well, I can use all this stuff I've already got.' Now I have to aim my writing deliberately towards a long theatre show. This means, if I fancy it, I can write quite long routines. One review of a show I did in 1994 said that I'd done nineteen minutes on football, and twenty-three minutes on anal sex.

In this case, I feel the subject somewhat dictates the duration. With football, I have to allow for the fact that some audience-members may not be knowledgeable about the game, so some time is taken up by explanation. Anal sex is a similar case. The latter routine is slightly longer than the football stuff because I also need time to discuss the health issues. I always make a point of telling the women in the audience about the, in my opinion, hare-brained theory that anal sex is dangerous. I try my utmost to be completely objective in this, explaining that, if they wish to discover whether it is indeed dangerous, they should ask around their female friends, nip in the Citizens Advice Bureau, or even phone up *This Morning*. After all, it's best that the woman doesn't leave such enquiries to the last minute. She's hardly likely to get an unbiased response from a man with a bottle of Johnson's Baby Oil in one hand, and his nob in the other.

So, if a club gig is like a degree, a tour gig is like a Ph.D. I have more scope to specialise.

At the same time, a funny gag is a funny gag and they all get in on that merit. Not that it's my choice. I have the most reliable editor in the world, the audience. When I'm preparing for a tour, I write about twenty-five minutes of new stuff a week, a target I've stuck to since the days of the Pie Factory. Naturally, some of this will be shit. I have to find out which and get rid of it. If thy shit jokes offendeth thee, pluck them out. So, I'll do a couple of circuit gigs a week to try out my new twenty-five minutes and then, depending on the response, I'll split the stuff into three categories.

Firstly, God willing, there will be some jokes that get good laughs. These go into the drawer marked 'In'. Secondly, there will be some jokes that go quite well but not great. These go into the drawer marked 'Potential'. As I've said before, my jokes are like children to me, I want to give them a fair chance. This is why I try virtually all of the new stuff at least twice. Maybe I delivered a new gag badly and didn't do it credit; or maybe it's not right in its present form, but it could be slightly re-written into a better gag. If one of these methods works, the gag gets transferred into the 'In' drawer. Thirdly, there are the gags that die on their arses. I mourn them, briefly, and then bury them in the drawer marked 'Shit'. I don't literally have drawers for these gags, obviously, but that's how I split them up.

After the gigs, I'll scribble a note next to each gag, signifying its allotted drawer. Incidentally, all my stand-up gags are written free-hand. Everything else I write, sit-coms, sketches, this book, is written on a computer, but that just doesn't feel right with stand-up. I've never really worked out why. Perhaps it's simply that I was writing stand-up before I owned or knew how to operate a computer, and old habits die hard.

But sometimes I think it's because stand-up has such a special place in my heart. It was seeing live stand-up that inspired me to go into comedy in the first place. It was stand-up that I was writing in my dirty bedsit in Ravenhurst Road, and if I hadn't been writing that stand-up I wouldn't be moving into my two-million-pound house in North London next week. All through my career, it's been the constant, the one link between the beginning of the journey and where I am now. And I'll tell you something, when it works, it's the best fucking feeling in the world. Yeah, OK, I get a bit romantic about stand-up. Still, you get the picture.

The tour-show building process is something of an emotional journey. You'd think that some bloke off the telly who turns up to do a gig in a room above a pub would be holding all the aces, but it doesn't work like that. When I appear at those circuit gigs, I'm on the bill with comics who are doing material they do every night. It's slick and, what's more, they aren't worried about forgetting half of it. I go up there, people settle down to watch the amazing famous bloke, and all I have with me is my completely new and unfamiliar stuff that might possibly be total shit. This, it has to be said, gives the whole experience a bit of edge.

Putting tours to one side for a moment, I also perform new stand-up at the beginning of each *Frank Skinner Show*, and I use the same method to build that material. But because it's a topical television chat show, trying out the stand-up in circuit clubs gets even trickier. Firstly, the material is all based on that week's news. If ever you try topical news stuff in a comedy club, you soon realise that no one actually knows any news at all. Well, maybe the really big stories, but that's it. Then, on top of that, it's only worth trying material I can get away with on telly. So, for the first time in my career, I'm the clean act on the bill, and sometimes my written-for-telly stuff sounds pretty tame when the previous act has been shouting 'Cunt!' for the last twenty minutes. I mean as part of his act, not as part of my introduction. Now how in the world am I supposed to compete with them and their easy laughs?

Either way, the main thing about this perform-and-then-prune process is that it's the audience who make almost all of the decisions. I show them what I've managed to come up with that week, and they identify the good stuff. When I was preparing for my '97 tour, my regular try-out places were The Spot Club in Covent Garden on Tuesday nights, and the Oranje Boom Boom in Soho, on Wednesdays.

One Tuesday at The Spot I died on my arse. I kind of hid the fact with some ad-libbing mainly about the fact that I was going badly: 'You know that when the *Titanic* sank, there was an orchestra in the main ballroom, who kept playing as the ship was going down. This is what it would have been like if there'd been a comedian on instead.' When this got laughs I stuck with it, making it up as I went along. I asked them to imagine the *Titanic* comic, trying to save his act like I was now trying to save mine. 'Are there any fish in tonight? (PAUSE.) Well, give it five minutes.' It enabled me to leave on a laugh, but I knew it was only cosmetic. I didn't sleep much that night. Comedy is like a little bird on your shoulder. One day, for no reason, it could just decide to fly away.

The next morning, I went to Budgen's to get some milk and a newspaper. At the checkout, an old lady recognised me and said, 'Oh, you're that comedian, aren't you?' I had to stop myself from saying, 'Well, actually, I'm not sure that I am. I used to be a comedian. I used to make people laugh and all that, but now, I can't actually do it anymore so no, I am not that comedian. I used to be, but now I'm not.'

Had I said this, I think the old lady might have been slightly alarmed, and it wouldn't really have helped me much either. So, instead, I smiled and chatted, paid for my things, and then went home and re-worked and re-worked the previous night's shit material. This was totally against my usual practice. Stuff that has gone that badly would normally have been straight out, but I had a point to prove. When I went on stage at Oranje Boom Boom that night, none of the sixty or so people in the audience had any idea how significant the gig was to me. In my head, it was more important than Battersea Power Station. And I fuckin' stormed it, with a re-vamped version of the previous night's rejected goods. I was back. I suppose it looked like just another day at the office.

Anyway, eventually, the 'In' drawer fills to the top, and then I go on tour.

For each town on the tour, again learning from my 4-X days, I add a bit of local stuff, produced by scanning the local papers, reading guide books, and, on the day of the gig, checking out the town centre and any local landmarks. I also keep an eye on the national news so I can add topical stuff to the mix. On the '97 tour, I was able to cover the Louise Woodward verdict and the Gary Glitter scandal, hours, or, in Woodward's case, minutes, after the stories broke.

But news can cause you problems. I was due to start that '97 tour in Jersey, on a Wednesday. On the previous Sunday, Princess Diana died. Ticket sales just stopped. It's easy to be cynical now, but at the time, it really felt like the whole nation was in shock. I had a sold-out gig in Southend on the following Saturday. Now it was to be the night of Diana's funeral.

The manager at Southend asked if I wanted to pull the gig. I asked if it was definitely sold out. He said yes. I said no. Besides, if I could do a gig on the night of my dad's funeral, I wasn't going to let this stop me. I watched the grim ceremony on telly in my Southend hotel room. There were tears in my eyes. Diana had been around for a long time, in the papers, on the telly; I'd got absolutely arseholed on the day-off-work I got for her wedding, she was part of my life. I know this all sounds a bit over-the-top, but they were strange times. Imagine, in five years' time, telling someone how worked up you got about *Big Brother*.

That night, I walked on stage at Cliff's Pavilion, Southend-on-Sea. You could feel the tension in the air. It was like following Sean Hughes at the 4-X multiplied by about twenty. I had made my decision. It was, I felt, possible to do jokes about what had happened, without making fun of her actual death. I went for it:

'In case you're wondering, I did watch the funeral, and, I'll be honest with you, I cried. I really cried. I kept thinking about that flower-shop I sold, three months ago. I wouldn't mind, but I invested the money in a land-mines factory. Elton John, he was good. I'm really glad he did that 'Candle in the Wind' song, really glad. I kept thinking he might completely misjudge things and do 'I'm Still Standing'.

They laughed, the mood changed, and we were off.

So, that's touring. Well, except for one crucial topic that I feel an obligation to cover. Sometimes, I find myself on tour when I'm single. In these circumstances, I feel duty-bound to, how can I put this, fuck anything that moves. I'm not saying that this is a good thing, and I'm not saying that it's something that I'm proud of, but then I'm not exactly proud of the fact that I imagine, in quite a lot of detail, whilst on the toilet, that I am generally acknowledged as the greatest footballer in the world. But I still told you about it.

I'm not a good-looking person. I've struggled to get girls for most of my life, and then, suddenly, I win the casual-sex lottery by getting famous. Imagine how that feels. Becoming a celebrity is like suddenly becoming handsome. It's alright for Robbie Williams or Brad Pitt. They were always used to women paying them attention, with little or no effort required on their part, but for me, it's like I suddenly found a magic after-shave that draws women towards me. I really want to use it up before it evaporates. Obviously, it doesn't work on all women, but then I haven't got the time to shag ALL women.

Suddenly, the ugly duckling has turned into a swan. OK, not the best-looking swan you've ever seen. In fact more like just a bigger duckling, but still with the long neck and some of the stateliness and that. And it is in the context of touring that I am truly able to flap my wings. Imagine how it feels, for a man who had to kill himself to get so much as a slow-dance in a Birmingham nightclub, when a beautiful young woman not only agrees, at once, to spend the night in his hotel room, but, gesturing towards the dressing room fruit-bowl says, 'And why don't you bring along a couple of those bananas?'

And, better still, they were both for her.

I think I need to make a point here. This is not payback time. I'm not suddenly getting revenge for years of rejection. I mean, let's be philosophical. I think I appreciate my job more because of the shit jobs I had in the past, and I appreciate my *Guinness Book of Records* certificate more because I've got my Edinburgh Return Form, and so I appreciate an upturn in my popularity because pulling girls used to be like pulling teeth. And, joking aside, the improvement is not as dramatic as I'd hoped, but it *is* an improvement and, just occasionally, it's like being 'cute in a stupid-ass way'. Besides, they get a good story to tell their mates, and I don't begrudge them that. I went out with a TV presenter a few years back, and, whilst watching her on a particularly jolly, all-round-family-entertainment game-show, I still recall the very special pleasure I got from nudging a mate and saying, 'I've fucked her up the arse.' I imagine James Hewitt makes similar remarks every time he passes a souvenir-mug stall.

I met one woman, nineteen years old and dressed from head to toe in black PVC, in a club quite near my hotel. Within fifteen minutes we were in bed. She had so many piercings, so many metal rings and rivets, that we had to shag next to the window so that I could keep an eye out for lightning. She was beautiful, and it was a fantastic night. At one point, she said, 'I'm often attracted towards older men.'

'Yeah, and magnets,' I replied. I don't think she got it. It seems to me that most people become quite serious when they're having sex. I don't. And, yes, I have wondered if that's what I'm doing wrong.

But, anyway, too much metal. Her vagina, as it clanked open, looked like one of those wallets people use to keep their keys in. I must admit, it put me off a bit. I approached cunnilingus the way, as a child, I approached a Christmas pudding that I knew had got silver threepenny bits in it. She was a very likeable person, though. As I get older, I find a woman's personality becomes more and more important.

I have tried the odd threesome. This is really not all it's cracked up to be. On one occasion, the women involved both swooped in for oral sex at the same moment, and there was quite a nasty clash of heads. One of them was actually too shaken to go on. Also women, especially when they've been drinking, are inclined to squabble, even if one of them is having intercourse at the time. I can remember two women I was with in a hotel room suddenly marching off into the bathroom to have a big row. Well, who needs it? And whispering and sniggering is another turn-off in this situation. It always makes me think I've got something on my bum.

When I was still with the BBC, I wrote a sitcom pilot called *Heavy Revie*, about a heavy-metal star, played by me. It never went to series. As I've said before, even Homer nods. I made the main character, Frank 'Heavy' Revie, a slightly tragic, still-single Brummie in his early forties. Ergo, I was able to take lines that I'd used when chatting with my tour manager or support act during a hotel breakfast, and give them to him. Here he is, talking to his brother, Dennis, after it's been discovered that Frank has had a threesome with two eighteen-year-olds:

*

DENNIS: It's the morality of it. You're forty-one. And there were two of them at the same time.

FRANK: Well, I don't think an eighteen-year-old girl should be alone with a man of my age.

DENNIS: My point is, it might be legal but it's still a scandal.

FRANK: But there's no logic to that. If I'd had sex with a thirty-six-year-old, no one would have minded. Surely it's only the difference between a pint and two halves. Anyway, if you're going to take a woman back to your hotel room, I think it's nice if she's got somebody to talk to.

There was a woman who used to write to me on a regular basis, very obscene letters suggesting all the disgusting things we could do if we ever got together. Some of her plans for us even made *me* blanch, but I wrote her off as a nutter and thought no more about it. Then, after a tour-gig one night, there was a message from a fan asking to meet me backstage. This woman, small, blonde and curvy, came in, I'd guess she was in her early twenties, and started chatting in a very normal, friendly way. Then she said a couple of things which reminded me of the letters, not crude or sexual things, just a couple of turns of phrase. I sensed that this was deliberate. I got slightly edgy. Steve, my regular tour-manager, was still on stage telling people how to roll up wires, or whatever it is that he does, and I felt slightly exposed. I reckoned this was the sort of woman who could pull a bread-knife if she didn't get her own way. Anyway, I got brave and confronted her about the letters. She admitted she'd written them, but said it was just a silly phase that she was going through, and she wouldn't be doing it anymore. Then she asked if she could spend the night with me. I actually laughed. 'Listen,' I said, 'I don't mean to be un-friendly, but you are a nutter. I don't trust you, and there is no way in the world that you are going to spend the night with me.' She seemed slightly hurt by this and said that she wasn't a nutter and that she would never do anything to harm me and that if I'd just spend one night with her, she'd tell nobody, and I'd never hear from her again.

I was amazed at her perseverance. 'Look,' I said, 'for the last time, there is no way in the world that I am going to spend the night with you.' At this point, she lifted up her t-shirt and showed me her tits. I said, 'And I definitely wouldn't hear from you again, you say?' She nodded. And then I took her back and shagged the shit out of her.

Now, to talk of these things may well prove to be unwise. It could be, now that evidence of my sleazy past is exposed, I'll never get another girlfriend as long as I live. But this previous behaviour was just a silly phase I was going through, and I won't be doing it anymore.

It's weird. When I was asked to write this book, I spoke to Caroline about it, and told her that, if I wrote it, I felt I should be really honest. I explained that this might mean the book would include things about me which she might well find upsetting. She said that I should write what I want to write, that I should tell the truth, and she would handle it as best she could.

I chose these particular incidents because I think they give a reasonable flavour of life on the road for the single man. I admit that, although they're true stories, I've highlighted the humorous aspects in order to make them seem slightly less sordid. Whether I've succeeded in that, I don't know. Still, I kept my promise to myself and told the truth. But, I'll be straight with you, I don't know if I'd have put these stories in the book if Caroline and me were still together. Oh well, every cloud . . .

I was at a party once, bending some bloke's ear about

touring, not the sexual side of it but the thrill of playing two-thousand-seater halls and staying in flashy hotels. I realised I'd gone on a bit, so I thought I'd better ask him – his name was Nick – about his job. He looked, to me, like a bank clerk. 'Oh,' he said, 'I'm in a band.'

'Really,' I said. 'Will I have heard of them?'

'I don't know,' he said. 'They're called Pink Floyd.'

Since then, I've been a bit wary about telling people about what touring is like. Will any pop stars who read this section please forgive me if I sounded like a know-all? I know I'm pretty small-time compared to some.

And, if any woman reads it, and thinks I sound like a sad, dirty old pig, who has abused his celebrity by using it to seduce beautiful young women, I give the defence's summing-up speech to Frank 'Heavy' Revie.

FRANK: I mean, I'm no oil painting, I'm aware of that, but I'm famous, and that gets me in. If it wasn't for famous people, all the beautiful people in the world would only shag each other. They'd form some fabulously attractive élite and people like me would be nowhere. We'd be stuck with all the other ugly people, rutting in our own filth like pigs. Banging out one ugly kid after the next, while the beautiful people stroke each other's unblemished skin, and close the window to stop the smell coming in. No, Dennis, it's my duty to stop that segregation happening, and, by glory, I'll infiltrate as many of those bastards as I can. Yes, two at a time, if I have to. Shag the beautiful, Dennis. So few of us ever get the chance.

Of course, he's just a fictional character.

In 1993 I got my first taste of hosting a chat show, or, at least, co-hosting one. *Late Night With Wogan* got me on a few times to co-host with Terry; they even sent me on trips to Euro-Disney, and also Los Angeles to interview Robin Williams. I never got on a plane till I was thirty-four, for a belated honeymoon in Italy, and now, at thirty-six, I was virtually jet-set.

It was great working with Terry. Younger readers might not realise it, but Terry Wogan was, for about eight or nine years, probably the biggest name in television, and now I was sitting at his side as we interviewed the likes of Jeff Goldblum and Quentin Tarantino.

Terry would call me into his personalised dressing room at Television Centre, with the wooden carving of him playing golf in the corner, give me little cigars and tell me stuff about telly being 'chewing gum for the eyes' and how I shouldn't worry too much about what I said, because viewers hardly ever listen. I was never sure whether Terry really believed this incredibly dismissive view of television, or if he just pretended that he didn't care as a way of coping with criticism. Maybe he was just being kind and thought that playing down the importance of the show would put me more at ease. Or maybe he was just bored. He'd already interviewed most of the guests two or three times before on his early evening chat show, and he'd lost a bit of interest. However, when Terry spoke about radio, his face lit up, and all the cynicism disappeared. Clearly that was his first love.

I wonder if Terry talks about me like this, but with the word 'radio' replaced by the phrase 'anal sex'? How expertly this book combines the poetic and the crass! Maybe I should have called it *Blank Verse and Bell-Ends: the autobiography of Frank Skinner*.

Either way, I was incredibly wide-eyed and enthusiastic, and I really gave the Wogan show my best shot, ploughing through all the clippings and trying to find questions that the guests might not have heard before. This, however, led to an incident that left me feeling slightly more cynical about the world of television.

One night, the guests were George Best, Cliff Richard and Sister Wendy Beckett, the nun who did those art-appreciation programmes. Sister Wendy had been in a closed order for years so had had little or no contact with the outside world. I don't think she really knew who any of us were. Anyway, I had read in a magazine interview with Cliff that he disapproved of women priests. It was just one line and I think it had slipped past virtually unnoticed, but it was right up my alley. Half-way through the interview, I asked him about it. He looked edgy, but admitted that he did not believe women should be priests because there was no biblical precedent; all the disciples were male. Sister Wendy was outraged. She said all the disciples were Jewish, so where does *that* leave biblical precedent? She went on to say that she hoped a time would come when people would be no more shocked by a woman priest than they would by a woman doctor or a woman teacher. The audience applauded. I thought this was great television. The Catholic nun in her seventies, more broad-minded and forward-looking than the pop-star.

However, when I watched the show go out the following night, my question and Cliff's answer had been removed. In the broadcast version, Sister Wendy, suddenly, out of the blue, started talking about women priests, for who knows what reason, and, get this, they had even stuck in a shot of Cliff, nodding his apparent agreement as she spoke.

I don't know why this happened. Your guess is as good as mine. But I decided if I ever had a chat show, I'd want to have a say in what got cut and what stayed in.

*

Things weren't going too well with Jane and me and we decided it would be better if I moved out. I phoned Dave Baddiel and asked if I could sleep on his sofa for a couple of nights until I found somewhere more permanent. I stayed for five years.

The time I spent living with Dave was one of the happiest of my life. It was like those two weeks with Denis Leary in Edinburgh, but it lasted one hundred and thirty times longer. When I first moved in with Dave, he lived in a very grotty flat in Kilburn, north London. Shortly after I arrived, he went on tour with Rob Newman and left me on my own in the flat. Within a few hours of his departure, I found a flea on my arm from his cat, Zelda. I hated cats and I wasn't that keen on fleas. I found some flea spray, completely soaked an armchair in it, and stayed on that till Dave returned. The flat was full of videos, but I presumed they were just old movies and tapes of Dave's TV appearances, so I didn't bother watching any of them. Little did I know that my flea-proof fortress was surrounded on all sides by tape after tape and hour after hour of relentless hardcore pornography.

To be honest, I hadn't seen that much pornography in my life. Years earlier, a friend in Birmingham had dragged me along to the Taboo Cinema Club, where you had to sign a membership form stating that you were not a member of Her Majesty's police force or The Festival of Light, but it wasn't long before my mate regretted taking me along. As soon as I saw the first film's title, I started giggling. It was called *Stuffed Arseholes*. 'Is this the menu?' I said, loudly, expecting to get laughs, but getting only a hard elbow from my mate. For the rest of the programme (the films showed from midday to midnight, but you were given a ticket with a time on it, and only allowed to stay for an hour), I couldn't stop giggling. My mate said, in a bit of a huff, that he would never take me to a pornographic cinema again.

Now, I'm not one of those blokes who pretend they only watch pornography for a laugh. That's not true. I only watch pornography in order to masturbate, and as I couldn't really pull that off, so to speak, in the crowded Taboo, I was forced to watch the films as if they were, well, films. If you do that, they soon become ridiculous. Dave, however was a connoisseur. He would no sooner have suggested that we watch pornography together than fly in the air. We worked out a very civilised rota system. It gave Dave the lion's share of the viewing time, but that only seemed fair, considering that he owned the property and, indeed, the pornography. However, when we discussed the various films, *Pissing Party*, *The Bottom Dweller*, *Buttman's Moderately Big Tit Adventure*, usually at meal times, we made a remarkable discovery. Dave and I liked exactly the same moments in each movie. When I watched a new batch of porn, I could tell instantly what tapes Dave would like, and what bits on those tapes he'd like best, and the reason I could tell was because his views tallied so exactly with mine. It was slightly scary.

If you think this sounds like a commonplace, get a friend to watch a pornographic film that you have already watched, and I bet you differ on what bits you like best. Hold on, this could be the new *Mr and Mrs*.

Incidentally, even when I used porn for its proper purpose, it could still, occasionally, make me laugh out loud. In, for example, the aforementioned film, *The Bottom Dweller*, featuring Roscoe Bowltree, there is one great piece of dialogue:

ROSCOE: Hey, Marty, I've got my finger in your wife's ass.
MARTY: Try not to get anything on the carpet.

When, six months later, Dave announced he was moving to a

very posh flat in Tanza Road, Hampstead, me and the porn and, unfortunately, the cat, moved with him.

Meanwhile, I managed to fit in another couple of TV series, this time for BBC1. Like my three Channel Four efforts, they bombed. I think my appearances on *The Brain Drain* and *Have I Got News for You?* had led people to think that a panel show was the right vehicle for me. I was re-united with Terry Wogan on a prime-time moral dilemmas show called *Do The Right Thing*. Terry hosted and I was his naughty sidekick. Two guest panellists and me would be shown a short film depicting someone facing a moral dilemma, and we had to say what we'd do. I, of course, always kept the money and shagged my best friend's wife. The show got a second series, but I didn't fancy it so I jumped ship.

Then I did another prime-time panel show called *Gag Tag*. Devised by my mate Tracey McLeod, the idea was to break down the barriers between mainstream and alternative comedy by having teams combining comics from both schools and getting them to complete various comedy tasks. So, we might be given a classic gag-format, and then have to produce some examples.

I'd get a line like 'I wouldn't say my wife was ugly but . . .', and then I would say, '. . . she walked on to the set of *All Creatures Great and Small* and Christopher Timothy put his arm down her throat'; or '. . . she lay down in the garden and the cat buried her'.

I was one team captain, Bob Monkhouse was the other, and Jonathan Ross was the host. Jonathan was already a mate of mine, so I was looking forward to working with him, but Bob was an unknown quantity. A few weeks before we recorded the series, I met an old Birmingham mainstream comic called

Dave Ismay. He said to me, 'I hear you're going to be working with the master.' I thought I'd got a part on *Doctor Who*. Turned out he was talking about Bob. The following week, Bob invited me to have lunch with him at his club. He was totally charming, and when I told him I'd broken my watch by accidentally putting it in the washing machine that morning, he reached into his briefcase, took out a flashy gold Seiko, and gave it to me. I was well chuffed, not because it was a flashy gold Seiko but because it was Bob's.

He is a pretty rare thing in a British comic of his generation. He doesn't do the 'a bloke went into a pub' type stuff. He is much more like his American contemporaries, clever and sharp, and making everything sound like it happened to him. Don't be fooled by the crappy game shows, Bob Monkhouse is our Bob Hope.

I was also really impressed with his knowledge of comedy. He had all the videos and tapes of my TV shows, knew all about the various alternative comics and their material, was a bit of an expert on silent film comedy, fifties American comedy, British comedy since the war and, oh, you name it, if it's comedy, Bob Monkhouse will have three books, twelve tapes and thirty anecdotes about it. A journalist once asked me about the watch. I said it was like Bob: 'The timing's impeccable, but it's gone a bit of a funny colour.' I'm not sure that Bob took it in the spirit that it was intended. Mind you, he once introduced me as 'a man that hasn't let success go to his clothes', so that makes us quits.

Nevertheless, I didn't feel that *Gag Tag* really worked, and I ducked out of the second series of that as well. I needed a TV hit and I needed it soon. The door of opportunity was starting to slowly swing shut.

BBC Radio Five asked Dave and me if we'd each like to manage a fictional football team on a new show called *Fantasy*

Football League, hosted by Ross King. The show was based on a postal game, where you picked a team of footballers from the Premier League. We did the show a few times, talking a little about our hand-picked teams but mainly just chatting about football.

After a few appearances on the show, Dave and me became convinced that it was a good idea that would be even better suited to telly, especially if we were hosting it. We could still have 'guest managers', celebrities who liked football, but we could also have funny clips and sketches, and all sorts of things that wouldn't work so well on radio. Most importantly, we could do on telly what we did every day in the flat, sit watching football and taking the piss. Accidentally, we'd been in rehearsal for this show for the last year.

Dave knew a guy, yes, Jewish, who he felt could produce the show. He was called Andy Jacobs. We met up and Andy thought it was a great idea. The BBC gave us a small amount of cash and we made a pilot with guest managers Nick Berry and Shelley Webb, wife of the England international Neil Webb, and no set. The whole thing looked terrible, but it was funny. We showed the pilot to BBC2 and they said they liked it. Then they said they'd like eighteen episodes, and my latest attempt at making a good TV show was up and running. This time it was *Fantasy Football League*.

I remember the pre-publicity for *Fantasy Football League* was all centred around Dave in a sort of 'New vehicle for David Baddiel, also features Frank Skinner' sort of a way. I felt this was fair enough. Dave, with Rob Newman, had had cult hits on TV with *The Mary Whitehouse Experience* and *Newman and Baddiel in Pieces*, and had sold out Wembley Arena with their live show. It was them that inspired Janet Street-Porter to say 'comedy is the new rock 'n' roll'. I was a good stand-up who did bad television. I think a lot of Newman and Baddiel fans saw me as a sort of Yoko Ono figure who broke up the band, but I reckon they would have split anyway. Besides, I thought it was nice for Dave to be the good-looking one for a change.

It was decided, by Jon Thoday, BBC2 and us, that we wouldn't do loads of publicity to promote the show. It was felt that it would be better to leave our new project to quietly find its feet, to be a slow-burner. That's a luxury you can afford when the series is eighteen episodes long, three times longer than most new comedy series. This took the pressure off us while we found our way around the format. The director was Peter Orton, who'd done *The Last Resort* with Jonathan Ross and *Vic Reeves' Big Night Out* with Reeves and Mortimer. We recorded the shows on Thursday nights at Capital Studios in Wandsworth, edited through the night, with Dave and me in every edit, and the show went out at 11.15 p.m. on Fridays. *Fantasy Football League's* theme tune was an instrumental version of 'Back Home', that first single I'd bought twenty-four years earlier.

The set became a crucial part of the show. It was based loosely on our living room at Tanza Road, with football books and memorabilia, the adjoining open-plan kitchen where Statto dwelt, and, of course, the sofa, and I soon felt as at home on the set as I did in the flat. Well, except we never worked out a rota.

The guest managers on that first series included Peter Cook, Bob Mortimer, Sue Johnston, Lennox Lewis, Roddy Doyle and Basil Brush. Basil, then operated by Ivor Owen, was, as you may know, a puppet, which posed problems we didn't have with the other guests. Ivor, now, sadly, dead, had been with Basil from the beginning. It was strange to meet this frail old man, who spoke with what was basically Basil Brush's voice. In rehearsal, it was discovered that the hole that had been sawn for Basil in the kitchen work-surface wasn't quite big enough, so we rehearsed with Ivor's old man's hand sticking up eerily out of the counter. As Ivor could still be heard doing Basil's voice, it made the whole experience a bit unnerving. When we finally got Basil fitted in place, Ivor got uncomfortable in the box under the table that he was hidden in, and withdrew his hand. I had grown up with Basil Brush, and watching him now, minus Ivor's hand, slowly imploding before my eyes made me feel like crying. When we finished the recording that night, poor Ivor was in agony. His knees had locked as he knelt in his box, and four of the crew had to lift him out. It was like carefully unpacking a sculpture that's arrived at an art gallery.

We soon made one of the major discoveries about *Fantasy Football League*: football people will do stuff you never thought they would do. There was a famous old football moment, captured on TV, when Luton Town narrowly avoided relegation, and their manager, David Pleat, ran on the pitch in his seventies beige suit and did a funny little skipping, running dance. We got Andy Jacobs to phone David Pleat and ask him if he'd come and recreate that dance in the studio. He not only said yes, but that he still had the exact same outfit in his wardrobe and would be happy to wear it. On the night, we showed the old clip of Pleat's dance and it got a good laugh, then we moved on to something else. Ten minutes later, the doorbell went. We opened the centre-stage front door, always a scene of much coming and going, and Mr Pleat skipped in. He did a complete circuit of the studio, past the bemused guests, and then skipped out through the door again. It absolutely brought the house down.

One interesting thing about this is, when I describe Pleat's dance as a 'famous old football moment', I mean famous amongst hardcore football fans. It was hardcore football fans who were our target audience. We never talked down to them or bothered to explain an obscure football reference. If you didn't know about football, that was tough. But the amazing thing was that loads of non-football fans watched it. People would stop me in the street and say, 'Well, I'm not really into football, but I love your show,' and I'd say, 'But don't loads of the gags go over your head?' and they'd always reply something like 'Oh, yeah, but it doesn't seem to matter.'

Andy Jacobs was our secret weapon. He was only a little man, with glasses and a moustache that gave him a slight Groucho Marx appearance, but his knowledge of sport, acquired partly from working in sports TV and partly from just being obsessed with sport, was phenomenal. Football, however, was his speciality. He would watch the games and football-related programmes on the telly and spot the most obscure and wonderful things. He'd put all these moments on one VHS tape and then bring them round the flat for me and Dave to see. We'd pick the ones we liked and they went into the show. We'd also spot the odd clip ourselves, but Andy was the man, and not only in the clips department. He'd come up with ideas for guests, subjects for the aforementioned 'Phoenix from the Flames', and discovered Statto. Me and Dave were the star strikers, Statto and the soon-to-be-recruited Jeff Astle were the creative midfielders, but Andy was the midfield dynamo, the boiler room, the Jewish Roy Keane.

Our rock-solid, vastly experienced central defender was Peter Orton, the director. Pete was only in his late forties, but he'd worked on everything from *Blue Peter* to *Penn and Teller*, and had an air of done-it-all confidence about him. Sometimes this was frustrating. Dave and me would have an idea and Peter would look at us in a 'now let me explain something' kind of way and I used to get well wound up. But whatever we asked

Peter for – special effects, spoof styles, unusual camera-shots – he always delivered. His direction deliberately gave the show a live feel, that rough edge that made it feel slightly chaotic, but he still managed to catch every unexpected, unrehearsed moment on camera. Peter and me argued about almost everything at first. When he was pissed off he looked like Michael Douglas on vinegar, but I soon came to respect him and his solid, steadying influence on the show.

The audiences were unbelievable. They came from all over Britain, to Wandsworth on a Thursday night, wore footie shirts, waved scarves, chanted for Statto, and, most importantly, laughed. They were a real supporters' end, our Kop or North Bank.

On Show Sixteen I closed with a song. It was nearly the end of the football season and Albion had three games to avoid relegation. I stood up as we neared the end of the show and sang a version of 'I Believe', which explained why I loved the Albion and how I still had faith in them. It could have been embarrassing, but it was from the heart and our football-mad audience understood and went with it. At the end of it there was massive applause, and three Albion fans I hadn't even noticed in the audience ran out and hugged me like we were all family. It was a special moment for me when some fans turned up at the next Albion game with a banner that said, 'Frank Skinner. We believe.' A girl at the refreshments stall that day told me her dad had cried when he heard the song. And no, not because he was a musician.

All previous football TV programmes had offered the opinions of ex-players, or journalists, but now it was the fans' turn. For years, football supporters had laughed at bad players, enjoyed horrible tackles, and developed a weird nostalgia-based folklore, but it had remained strictly an oral tradition. Then, in the eighties, football fanzines rose up, putting these gags and alternative, fan-based views of the game on paper. Now football fan culture had a voice on national television. David Thomas, in the *Daily Telegraph*, described the show as 'one long celebration of the free-masonry of football fandom'.

The second series stuck with the same format as the first, but introduced Jeff Astle as our close-the-show crooner. The new set of guest managers included Elvis Costello, Jo Brand, Nick Hancock, Paula Yates, Patsy Kensit, Alan Hansen and Nick Hornby. Nick Hornby, of course, was the writer of *Fever Pitch*, a book about the life and times of an Arsenal fan, which had become a bestseller. Some journalists were saying that *Fever Pitch* and *Fantasy Football League* had both made a significant contribution to football's new mega-popularity, particularly among Britain's middle classes. Dave, Nick and me, all university graduates, had suddenly made it OK for the Hampstead set to talk about Francis Benali instead of Francis Bacon, and write about Paul Gascoigne instead of Paul Gauguin. Obviously, I felt terrible about this. I never expected to be blamed for football going posh, a phenomenon I was, and am, incredibly suspicious of. Only recently, I had started to think that maybe the old days of football hooliganism weren't, in fact, such a bad thing. At least the boot-boys kept posh people and, of course, girls away from the grounds. Now, it seemed, I was ushering them in.

The other thing that always came up when *Fantasy Football League*, or just *Fantasy Football* as everyone now called it, was discussed was the phrase 'New Lads'. I had first heard this term used about Newman and Baddiel a few years earlier. Again, it was a case of the middle classes hijacking something which had always been largely associated with the working classes. Traditionally, lads, as in 'lads' night out' or 'one of the lads', referred to someone who was male, working class, under thirty-five, and liked shagging women, playing and watching football, getting pissed and fighting.

The New Lads, like New Labour, were a sort of laundered version of that. They were middle class, under thirty-five, liked shagging women but only if they used a condom, and made it clear in advance that this was just sex so that no one was being exploited, playing football in a trendy 'five-a side in the gym followed by a quick drink in a local bistro' kind of a way, watching football in an 'England matches on Sky, season ticket at Arsenal' sort of a way, getting quite pissed on bottles of beer with slices of lime in the top, and fighting, but only in kick-boxing classes at their swish health club.

Despite this, I was often described as the archetypal New Lad. I was forty, nouveau riche, had a season ticket at an Endsleigh League Division One club I'd supported since I was in liquid form, couldn't play at all, was a practising Roman Catholic teetotaller, and hadn't had a fight since I stopped drinking ten years earlier. OK, I liked shagging, but one swallow doesn't make a summer. (Mind you, it can certainly make an evening.)

Anyway, I must have been a New Lad because it was in all the papers.

The third series of *Fantasy Football*, in 1996, was extra-special because it was tied in to the whole 'Three Lions' thing. But just before Euro '96, after years of taking the piss out of footballers, something happened that we hadn't seen coming. On May 22nd, the headline on the back page of the *Sun* was 'Skinner and Baddiel wrecked my career'. It was an interview with Nottingham Forest striker Jason Lee, who claimed that our jokes about him on the show had destroyed his confidence, created an unfairly negative view of his abilities, and inspired an open season of scorn and abuse from football fans wherever he played.

We had done a sketch, earlier in Series Three, which had me playing Lee's club manager, Frank Clarke, and Dave playing Lee himself. The sketch included clips of some terrible botched goal-opportunities by the player, and the main comic thrust was that Jason missed everything. He missed a tea cup with a sugar cube, a waste-bin with some rolled-up paper, and so on. It was typical *Fantasy Football* stuff. Dave's make-up included a hair-do that incorporated a pineapple. Jason's tied-up dreadlock-style hair looked a bit like a pineapple. I believe a chant pointing this out was already doing the rounds of Premiership grounds where he played. So that was it. We did the sketch, it went well, we forgot about it. But the audience didn't. We got a massive response from viewers. Week after week they sent in pineapple-based sculptures, a photo of a pineapple-roofed house they'd seen on holiday and so on. So Jason Lee, with his crazy hair and his inability to score, accidentally became something of a running gag.

But we made one large mistake. It's one thing to take the piss out of Peter Beardsley, or Gazza, or Alan Shearer. These were extremely talented players, with massive self-confidence, who couldn't give a shit about leg-pulling, but Jason Lee was different. He wasn't, by Premiership standards, quite good enough. This, I suppose, must have led to all sorts of doubts and insecurities and so the running gags, to him, must have felt like a cruel vendetta.

Dave and me felt bad about Jason being so hurt and we wrote to him to make friends and invite him on the show, if he fancied it. We never got a reply. The papers were full of it that week. We'd overstepped the mark, they said: when does comedy become cruelty? There was even a vague hint by one broadsheet journalist that the jokes, or at least the ones about his hairstyle, were racist. John Barnes, God bless him, defended us on this charge, but did say that the continued ribbing of Lee probably did go a bit far.

A few months later, a documentary called *Footballers' Wives* showed Jason and his missus watching tapes of the show and generally slagging us off.

I have never deliberately tried to upset anyone with my comedy, well, not professionally, anyway. I was genuinely sorry Jason took it so badly. Mind you, when he eventually shaved his hair off, he was photographed in the *Sun*, holding a pineapple just above his shaven head and talking about his new look as a 'kiwi-fruit head', so I think he learned to cope.

Some of you might ask what gave me, a self-confessed shit footballer, the right to take the piss out of any player. Well, I'm a football fan. It's my job.

The fourth series, I can't bring myself to call it the last, saw some drastic changes. We had switched to ITV, the show was centred around the World Cup rather than the Premiership, we were on three or four nights a week, and we were live. It still seemed to work, maybe even better, but I missed the domesticity of the old show. The World Cup is lovely, but British club football is what I really like.

Still, *Fantasy World Cup* did produce my favourite-ever headline. On June 14th, 1998, the front page of the *Sunday Sport* led with 'Three Lions stars hire lesbo porn girl'. Unfortunately, it was just a reference to the fact that one of the guests on the series was *Emmanuelle* star Sylvia Kristel.

The series opened with a bang, but one that was much more enjoyable for the viewers than it was for us. Brigitte Nielsen, the big-titted six-foot blonde from Denmark, Sylvester Stallone's ex-wife, was one of the guests. I don't know if she was pissed or what, but she was wild as the wind. As soon as she came through the door, she grabbed me in a massive bear-hug. Then she started shouting in Danish and attacked Dave with a

Danish pastry. Dave asked her if the silicone had gone to her head. We were under siege and the gloves were off. Brigitte grabbed Dave's hand and stuck it down her top so he could check if her tits were silicone or not. He was really going for it by now. He asked her why Sylvester Stallone had divorced her. She said why don't you ask him. I had a little gadget I often used on *Fantasy Football*, a button under the coffee table that, when I pressed it with my foot, made the phone ring. When Brigitte suggested we ask Stallone why he divorced her, I pressed the button, and picked up the phone. 'Yeah,' I said to the imaginary *Rocky* star on the other end, 'we guessed.' But there was no stopping Brigitte. In the end, as she stood waving her arms and shouting at the audience, you could quite clearly hear me say on air, in what Dave described as 'the most complete breakdown of accepted chat-show etiquette ever seen on British television', 'Oh, sit down, Brigitte. You're making a twat of yourself.'

Dave and me wrote and starred in seventy episodes of *Fantasy Football*. After five failed attempts, I finally got my hit TV series. If only I'd lived closer to Arthur's Seat.

The success of *Fantasy League* on BBC2 rekindled BBC1's interest in me. I was keen on trying a chat-show format, having enjoyed my time on *Late Night with Wogan*.

The Frank Skinner Show began in the Autumn of '95. It was produced and directed by Marcus Mortimer, a highly experienced comedy director who had a sort of aristocratic playboy manner about him, and who looked unnervingly like the golf legend Jack Nicklaus. Marcus had been engaged to the posh-totty sex symbol Fiona Fullerton but, unfortunately, wouldn't give me any of the details.

I wanted the chat show to be different from the usual

Hollywood-star-plugging-his-film type of affair, so we combined famous names with non-celebrities, or 'people-guests', as chat-show bookers call them. Thus, on the first show, we had the Sheriff of Nottingham (yeah, the real one), the late Charlie Kray (brother of the more-famous twins), Buzz Aldrin (the second man on the moon), and Neil Armstrong (not the first-man-on-the-moon one, the giant-leek-growing one).

It had its moments. When Charlie Kray explained that he'd done several years in prison for disposing of Jack the Hat, I said, in a journalistic tone, 'Charlie, when you say you went to prison for disposing of Jack the Hat, let me just clear up one thing for the audience. Jack the Hat wasn't just a hat, was it? It was actually a bloke.'

'Oh, yeah,' replied Charlie, taking me totally seriously. 'He was a bloke, not a hat.' I could have hugged him.

The show lasted half an hour and began with five minutes of stand-up from me, and also had a couple of sketches. There were six shows in that first series. The guests included Ivana Trump, Marvelous Marvin Hagler, Myra Lewis Williams (the woman who had married her cousin, Jerry Lee Lewis, when she was thirteen), a dog psychiatrist, a couple who'd trained a chimpanzee to do sign language, and Drew Barrymore's mom.

To be straight with you, although that first series had its moments (the three 'Best Of . . .' compilation programmes were great), I wasn't really happy with it. I was writing the stand-up and the sketches and planning the interviews and editing with Marcus, so I had to take the blame, but it just wasn't right. Still, the BBC thought it showed real promise and commissioned a second series.

Marcus went off to do the very successful BBC comedy-drama, *All Quiet on the Preston Front*, and I had a new producer, or rather two – Jilly Hafenrichter and Juliet Rice, the sister of Anneka. They were from a documentary background, having made those *Hollywood Men*, *Hollywood Women* and *Hollywood Children* films for ITV. They were the kind of slinky brunette, slinky blonde combo that had worked so well for Abba, but they were much more than just pretty faces.

The second series was, in the main, much better than the first. Guests including Eddie Izzard, Tony Blair, and heavy-metal legend Ozzy Osbourne, but we still stuck with the non-celeb idea and included a woman from Birmingham who'd streaked at a televised snooker match, a Japanese inventor who'd invented biscuits with holes in the middle for watching telly through, and a man called Paul Sayce.

Paul was heavily tattooed, mainly with images of significant people and places from his life. He referred to his body as his 'inky diary', and agreed to have a tattoo of me put on or near his bicep. He still had the bandage taped over his sore arm when he walked on, but when it came off, there I was, next to his ex-wife. I sometimes wonder if people from my past ever think of me. I bet Paul Sayce fuckin' does.

The BBC had extended the series to nine shows, but half-way through we hit problems. The broadcasters felt that the show was straying towards bad taste. Firstly, in the stand-up. It had been in the papers that charities for the deaf were not getting their fair share of lottery money. I claimed that a spokesman for the lottery had said, 'Well, if they don't answer the phone . . . .' This got several complaints. Secondly, in the sketches. There was, at the time, a TV advert for IKEA in which several housewives threw floral-patterned curtains and furniture out of their windows and dragged them into a skip as they sang a song called 'Chuck out the Chintz'. I parodied this, but with them singing 'Chuck out the Chimps', and including several scenes of chimpanzees flying out of bedroom windows and even, in one case, being finished off with a baseball bat. This got a lot more complaints and, in fact, a spokesman for the BBC was asked to defend these items on a *Right to Reply*-style TV show. He just apologised and said it wouldn't happen again.

I was pissed off. There had also been several complaints about the Japanese inventor, all along the lines of 'I don't know how you could have one of those people on after what they did during the war'. Were we also supposed to apologise for that? One of the problems about having a public-funded broadcaster is that anything you do can be described as a waste of licence-payers' money. On ITV, it's not like that. When did you ever hear anyone complaining about a waste of advertisers' money?

Everyone who buys a licence has the right to an opinion. Fair enough, but the only people who ever bother to phone in are, in the main, angry and confused sex offenders who live alone in desolate high-rise flats, or terrified, valium-popping old spinsters, whose dead pets lie decaying all around them. Are these the people whose opinions programme-makers should be listening to?

Anyway, it got worse. On the show that followed the 'Chuck out the Chimps' controversy, I apologised profusely for the sketch and then said, slightly under my breath, 'Thank God I didn't do that version set in Chinatown.' Then I sat down and introduced the first guest, 'No stranger to contro- versy herself. Ladies and gentlemen, Rose West.' The band (I'll come to them in a minute) played 'Go West' and the audience applauded. I pissed myself. Not only did they believe that Rose West was coming on, but they applauded her! I sneaked through the under-the-breath remark, but the Rose West bit was cut. On the next show I interviewed a married couple who were swingers. Y'know, they went to fetish clubs and bondage parties and had group sex with other like-minded couples. We had no graphic details and no swearing, but it still had to go. Then there was Mr Methane.

Mr Methane, a very tall thin man in a tight lime-green lycra body-suit and a lime-green mask, was a stage-farter. At the end of the show, I launched into the Phil Spector classic, 'Da Do Ron Ron'. When it got to the bit where they sing 'Da Do Ron Ron', the camera cut wide to reveal, on a table at my side, his legs raised high, Mr Methane. He provided the 'Da Do Ron Rons' as only he could. Yes, he farted them. As this duet continued, the audience were, many of them, literally in tears of laughter. We played it totally straight, which, of course, made it even funnier.

Admittedly, I had cracked up earlier, but only because while we waited to begin, Mr Methane did an enormous, completely unrestrained and tuneless fart, in the same way, I suppose, that an operatic tenor might clear his throat just before he begins to sing. I wasn't expecting this and I just lost it. The BBC insisted that the duet was cut, and I was on my final warning. The headlines in the paper included 'Clean it up, comic warned', 'Frankly, who needs good taste', and 'Beeb pulls plug on bum notes'.

Now, I am aware that even if I worked for days, honing and polishing a joke until it was technically flawless, it is impossible to create anything deliberately that is as intrinsically funny as a loud fart. However, I have always felt that jokes about farting are almost always unfunny. Even to hear a comic use the word 'fart', for some reason, always makes me cringe. I don't even like reading it here. But Mr Methane was pure music-hall, like a sword swallower or a contortionist, and the audience, still my editors-in-chief, absolutely loved him.

I am not a 'dangerous' comic. Like I've said, I have no desire to be shocking or controversial, just funny. I'm not saying I was right in all of these instances, but I do think my duet with Mr Methane should have stayed in.

Anyway, the series still did pretty well without him, I

learned my lesson, and the BBC forgave me and commissioned a third series.

Some months later, I got an e-mail from a friend of mine, Janet McLeod, who lives in Melbourne, Australia. She had been watching an awards ceremony on Australian TV, where Phil Spector was getting a 'Lifetime Achievement' award. Halfway through his speech, the famously eccentric Mr Spector suddenly started going on about the shabby way that 'artists' were treated nowadays, and launched an attack on 'the British comedian, Frank Skinner' who had, Speco explained, taken a work of art and desecrated it by turning it into a duet with a stage-farter. Listen, Phil, you have your 'Wall of Sound', I'll have mine.

When Lianne Croft, the snooker streaker, was on the show, she said, 'I drove up to the tournament in my knackered old Maestro. Oh, am I allowed to say "knackered old Maestro"?'

'I should think it's alright,' I said. 'I've got four of them over there.'

I was referring, of course, to my house-band, 'The Skinnerettes'. These four ageing musicians, Bob Rogers on guitar, Ken Penney on keyboard, Ron Seabrook on bass, and Ronnie Verral on drums, were the great discovery of Series Two. They were put together (Yes, they're a 'manufactured' band, like The Spice Girls) by my musical director (Oh, I love being able to say 'my musical director') Richard Thomas, and they have been on the show ever since. They accompany any songs, play the guests' walk-on music, and appear in sketches playing everything from Eminem's homeboys to, well, The Spice Girls. Not bad for four blokes with a combined age of nearly six hundred.

The songs they play to get the guests on are all carefully chosen. (My favourite combination was Aled Jones coming on to the Manics' 'If you tolerate this, then your children will be next'), but the Skinnerettes always make them their own.

The drummer, Ronnie Verral, is something of a legend. As well as playing with loads of big jazz and TV stars over the last fifty years, he was also the man who played the drums for Animal on *The Muppet Show*.

But what I love best about the Skinnerettes never makes the screen. In rehearsal, whenever there's an enforced break, I'll start singing, usually an old standard, maybe Glenn Miller's 'Chatanooga Choo Choo' or Frank Sinatra's 'I've Got You Under My Skin', and, gradually, I'll hear the Skinnerettes working out the key and smoothly gliding in underneath my vocal. Y'know, if there was no *Frank Skinner Show*, I'd happily pay them to come round my place, and we could spend the whole day just doing that.

Shortly after that second series of *The Frank Skinner Show*, Dave hit me with a bombshell. He announced that he was going to live with his girlfriend, Sarah, and it was time for me to move out. I always knew this day would come, but it still hurt. I had lived with Dave for five years. I never managed to live with any woman for two. My marriage only lasted ten months. In our time as flatmates we only really had one nasty row. In a game of Trivial Pursuit, I asked Dave what Elizabeth Taylor historical epic had lost so-and-so millions at the box office. Dave said, '*Antony and Cleopatra.*' I said this was wrong. The film was called, simply, *Cleopatra*. Dave protested. After some debate, I explained that if Dave didn't want to play the fucking game by the fucking rules then he could stick the fucking game up his stupid fucking arse. Dave walked out of the room and there was a terrible silence for some time. In case you're thinking that I over-reacted, I should point out that it was a 'pie' question.

There were, inevitably, rumours that Dave and me were gay. Two single blokes, over thirty, sharing a flat, people are bound to talk, aren't they? On one occasion, I was leaving The Ivy, a very celeb-heavy restaurant just off the Charing Cross Road, when I bumped into a gay television celebrity. We chatted and he said, 'You know, I always thought that you and Dave were an item.' I explained that this was not the case. 'Well,' he continued, 'I always thought you were. In fact, I'll be honest with you, I've had more than one wank on the strength of it.'

I moved out of Tanza Road in May, 1997, and into a flat about ten minutes' walk away. Shortly afterwards, Dave bought a house about five hundred yards away from my flat. He moved in with his girlfriend. A few months later, she moved out. Next week, I move into the house next-door-but-one to him. In about six weeks, he is due to become a father. I had always dreamt that one day, Dave and I might have children.

No, no, I made that bit up. When the story broke, the headline in the *Sunday Mirror* was 'Skinner and Daddiel'. OK, he's going to be a father, but I still got top billing.

I was round his house last night, helping him assemble a Mothercare cot. You should have seen us, two of the world's least practical men, passing each other bolts and screwdrivers, and realising half-way through that we were building some of it the right way up, and some of it upside-down. All we needed was a couple of bowler hats. At one point, I stood, watching him fitting the right bracket in the wrong place, and listened to him talking about the table he'd bought for changing nappies on, and how his insomnia was finally going to come in handy.

My old mate, who'd said I could sleep on his settee for a few days, who'd been shoulder-to-shoulder with me when Brigitte Nielsen ran riot on *Fantasy Football*, who'd shared the terror of that harrowing first episode of *Unplanned*, and who'd stood, with his arm around me, singing 'Three Lions' at Wembley in 1996. I could see the grey in his beard and I imagined how he'd look with his own tiny baby in his arms. Even New Lads have to grow up eventually.

And I looked at him and I thought, 'If ever I have a baby of my own, to hold and to buy things for, there's no way I'm going to let this fuckin' idiot build its cot.'

In 1998, I finally made a series of *The Frank Skinner Show* that I was really proud of. Jilly and Juliet were missing documentaries, so they went back to specialise in that line of work. The new producer was John McHugh, a short, stocky bull-terrier of an Irishman, who was something of a chat-show veteran, having cut his sharp teeth with Irish chat-show superstar Gay Byrne back in the old country. John was slightly scary, but he really knew his stuff and didn't mind telling me if I was talking bollocks. At the same time, he had real faith in my comic judgement and would often take the big risk if he could see that I was really keen.

I had some ideas for the new series. Firstly, instead of a specially filmed title sequence like we'd had on the first two series, I wanted to open the show, in the studio, with a song. I had specially written one for the job. It was called 'Funtime Frankie'. Of course, it's just a light-hearted singalong, but the lyrics have a certain truth about them:

When I was just a boy in school, I always loved to play the fool.
They said it was a childish game, but now I've grown, I'm just
    the same.

That's why when I'm walking out
People always stop and shout
Funtime Frankie . . .

We had a new director as well, *Fantasy Football*'s Peter Orton.
By now, Peter and me had put the early, at-each-other's-throat
days behind us. We even went to Crystal Palace–West Brom
games together. We're mates. Soon, Peter was adding cameras
and changing the set and the whole appearance of the show
improved.

The first show was a Christmas Special, and I had an idea for
a sketch. A few days earlier, I had got out of the bath at my flat
and put on a pair of white briefs, at which point the Venga
Boys came on the radio, so I started dancing in the bathroom,
just in my white pants. Then I saw myself in the mirror. I
absolutely pissed myself. I tried to carry on dancing, but it just
looked too ridiculous. Now, imagine trying to pitch that as a
sketch-idea to your Irish bull-terrier producer.

'. . . and as the Venga Boys continue, I dance in these white
pants.'

'And then what happens?'

But he went with it, and it brought the fucking house down.
When I think of all the time I've wasted trying to write clever
jokes . . .

The guests were great. I explained to country-music
megastar (there I go again, with my little descriptions) Kenny
Rogers what the verb 'to roger' meant, and then asked him
about his fast-food chain, 'Kenny Rogers Roosters'; I gave Eric
Clapton a demonstration of how to play air-guitar; asked
David Essex, when you're in a car with loads of sex-crazed,
hysterical, screaming girls' faces pressed against the window,
what facial expression do you adopt; and, after holding a metal-
detector against Martin Kemp's head to see if it registered the

metal plate he'd had fitted after his brain-tumour operation, (it did), I said, 'You wouldn't get this on *Parkinson*.' And then there was Tara Palmer-Tomkinson.

They say that lightning never strikes twice in the same place, but when It-girl and all-round socialite Tara Palmer-Tomkinson walked on to *The Frank Skinner Show*, I had a flashback to Brigitte Nielsen, just ten months earlier. Again, I don't know what Tara was on, but it wasn't Earth. After some garbled nonsense which made me wonder whether she'd had a snort, a stroke, or just a very posh upbringing, she admitted that she was expecting Frank Butcher, not Frank Skinner, and that when we'd met in the corridor, she thought I was someone from wardrobe. How camp am I? Her eyes were all over the place, she kept standing up and asking companies to send her free stuff, knelt down to demonstrate how her dog kisses her, and suddenly became transfixed by her image on the studio-screen. After stopping to re-arrange her hair and adjust her clothing, she turned to me and said, 'I've just seen myself on the monitor.'

'I haven't said that since I was at school,' I replied. At one stage, she asked me if I was single, and what I was doing after. I was sure she was just kidding, but I explained that we could never be, because she was part of the in-crowd and I was part of the Berni-Inn crowd. Mind you, if she'd been serious, I would have happily shagged her, but only as an act of class-war. The photograph of her, wild-eyed and sitting on my lap, was in every newspaper over the next week. Two days later she flew to Arizona, to go into rehab.

Series Four had one big addition to the show: a commercial break. I had moved, lock, stock, and barrel, to ITV. There was a time – Morecambe and Wise are the example that everyone quotes – when people switched channels and everything turned to shit. The problem then was often that, because people were on the staff of either the BBC or ITV, you had to leave your talented team behind, but in these days of independent production companies and freelance short-term contracts, you just take them along. Of course, it can still all turn to shit, but it can do that at any time for any number of reasons. That's why I wear a gaunt and worried look.

However, for Series Four, I still ended up needing a new producer. John McHugh had been poached, lured away by the offer of an executive post with, you guessed it, the BBC. Honestly, there's no loyalty in this business. He's still my mate, though. I see every lapsed Catholic as a long-term project. Speaking of which, the new producer was another one, Robyn O'Brien.

Now, making *The Frank Skinner Show* is not as piss-easy as it looks. I spend five days in the office writing it, one day rehearsing and recording, and another day editing it, plus an evening when I do two gigs to try out the stand-up.

The good thing about this is, when the new team is assembled, I can make my usual promise that I won't ask anyone to work harder than I do. But Robyn comes fucking close. She is my producer, confidante, big sister, nurse, sternest critic, biggest fan, supplier of fags and tea and all-round morale-booster. She worked on the previous series as one of McHugh's lieutenants and has since produced two *Unplanneds*, which is a piece of piss to produce, and one *Frank Skinner Show*, which is a fucking nightmare. She has to deal with guests pulling out and me asking for complicated last-minute props and researchers being off sick, and me telling her that extra weight she is getting on her upper arms is known as 'bingo-wings'. I know, because I read it in *Viz*. If all this sounds more like a tribute than a description, that's because it is one. Honestly, do you begrudge a woman who works her tits off to help me to make you laugh one measly paragraph?

So, Series Four went great. The guests were mainly chosen because they were women I fancied: Kylie Minogue, Kelly Brook, Bjork, Katy Hill, Sam Fox, Denise Lewis and Debra Stevenson. What's the point of having your own chat show if you can't pack it with crumpet?

Anyway, I'm sure you've heard quite enough about *The Frank Skinner Show*. Fucking hell, we're not far from the end, are we?

There's a lot of other showbiz moments I could have put in this book: my theatre career, acting in two West End plays (*Art* at Wyndham's Theatre, in Charing Cross Road, and *Cooking with Elvis*, at the Whitehall); my success as a stand-up in Melbourne and Sydney in 1997; my appearance on the first-ever *Celebrity Stars in Their Eyes* when, after performing as Elvis Costello, I scared the backstage staff by storming off as the winner was announced, camply screaming, 'Well, they might have stars in their eyes but they've got shit in their fuckin' ears'; and my scooping of the much-respected 'Rear of the Year' award in 1998, but enough is enough.

There is, however, one last professional project that I'd like to tell you about. I'll try and keep it pacey, and concentrate on the off-camera or cutting-room-floor stuff you wouldn't have seen on the resulting TV programme.

It began with a slightly mental piece of extravagance. In 1997, at Christie's, I paid £11,200 for a blue velvet shirt that, according to the accompanying letter, was a stage-shirt worn in 1956 by Elvis Presley. The picture which accompanied its listing in the Christie's catalogue, was of Elvis performing at the Mississippi State Fair, in Tupelo, Mississippi, September 1956. The implication was clear. This was the blue velvet shirt that Elvis wore in Tupelo. This was especially significant. Elvis was born in Tupelo and spent his early dirt-poor days there. In 1956, he had just become a big star. It was a classic local-lad-makes-good homecoming.

Now, obviously, I mean, obviously, there is no comparison between the professional success that I've had and that enjoyed by Elvis. Well, there is, but it's meagre versus mega. Still, a rags-to-riches, local-lad-makes-good story always has a special significance for me. I still think of that Birmingham Town Hall gig in 1991. So I bought the shirt.

Then, after a few weeks, I was looking at some photos of the Tupelo gig, and I noticed that the velvet shirt Elvis was wearing seemed to only have three buttons at the top. My shirt had buttons all the way down. I was gutted. The evidence wasn't conclusive, the shirt in the photos was largely covered by guitar, but it didn't look good. Then I had an idea.

All this was begging for a documentary. I'd travel round America, talking to people who knew Elvis in 1956, and end up meeting Elvis's 1970s bodyguard, Dave Hebler, who had signed the letter claiming that the shirt was a 'stage-shirt worn in 1956'. It would be a dream job, two weeks of pure Elvis. ITV were dead keen, and we signed up Paul Wilmshurst, the bloke who still thinks I'm 'wistful', to produce and direct.

The journey started in Memphis. Well, it would have done, but I got food-poisoning on the plane and had to spend an unscheduled night in Houston, Texas. I was there for less than twenty-four hours but I made one fascinating discovery. If you phone Room 70451 at the Houston Sheraton Hotel, the tune the keys make sounds exactly like the melody-line of 'Three Lions'. This cheered me up, and I was soon feeling well again. Paul had kept me in the dark about the nature of the shoot. I still didn't know if the shirt was the one from Tupelo, where we were going, or who I was going to meet. Nothing. Paul wanted my reactions on camera to be real and spontaneous.

My first meeting wasn't at all what I expected. It was with a sixty-nine-year-old Memphis head-case called Jimmy Denson, 'Jimmy D from Memphis, Tennessee' as he kept saying. Jimmy, white-whiskered in shabby denims and a battered baseball hat, looked like an ex-boxer who had either had too many punches or too many drinks, probably because that's exactly what he was. He'd lived in the same housing project as the young Elvis, who he still insisted on calling 'the baby'. Everything Jimmy said was at ninety miles an hour, very critical of Elvis, and a bit mental. One breathtakingly fast speech went:

'The baby was weak and retarded. He couldn't walk down the street without staring at his feet. In fact, he never raised his head until Dewey Phillips gave him speed in 1954, and then he couldn't sleep for four days. He was a truck-jumping, drug-taking, infantile half-wit, just like his grandmother, Minnie Mae. Her husband deserted her because she was an idiot, with the mind of a five-year-old. She went to my father's church, seven days a week. The author John Grisham has assured me that he will act as my lawyer in a case to show the world Colonel Parker's trickery and Elvis's drug-sickery, and Elvis had to wear a colostomy bag on his last two tours.'

How long before Caroline's talking about me like that?

Then we drove out to meet Marty Lacker. He was one of Elvis's posse, or the 'Memphis Mafia' as they called themselves. He was fat and balding, with glasses, and his eyes looked like they had cried a lot. Talking to him reminded me of talking to an old ex-footballer. He spoke of a special, exciting time that had gone forever, and his tone was coloured by both celebration and mourning, each bleeding into the other.

You know, I could do this for a living.

Marty said that, when he watches a comedian on the telly, he still thinks stuff like 'Elvis would have loved that joke' and he played me a couple of tracks from a Celine Dion album, and explained to me how Elvis would have done them.

I asked him about when the Beatles visited Graceland. He said that, despite stories to the contrary, Elvis got on especially well with John Lennon. Lennon had told Marty he got a lot of invitations to meet stars but usually said no. He was once invited to join Frank Sinatra at his table in a restaurant, but soon realised that Frank only wanted him around to attract young girls. Marty said Frank had tried exactly the same thing with Elvis, back in the fifties. Who'd have thought that Frank Sinatra would need to stoop to such tactics? I wonder what restaurant Robbie Williams eats in . . .

Anyway, Marty thought my shirt could have been the real one, but wasn't sure. Then we went to Tupelo and met the woman who was curator of the Elvis Birthplace Museum. Since the Elvis documentary went out, two or three Elvis fans have taken me to one side and told me that this woman owns the real Tupelo shirt, but, rather than display it at the museum, she keeps it hidden and tells no one of its existence. I didn't know about this rumour at the time. When I asked her about the Tupelo gig she said it was a great day but not as exciting as the birth of her children. Oh, for fuck's sake. I hate it when people come out with that sort of shit.

I remember when Gareth Southgate missed that penalty against Germany. The next day he said he'd been thinking about it, and when you considered all the disabled people in the world it put the whole thing into perspective. And I thought, 'Oh, and that makes it alright, does it?'

Then I drove my Buick Le Sabre out to the deserted fairground where the gig had been in '56. There were a couple of battered old wooden grandstands there. They had been packed with Elvis fans on the day of the show. I sat on the splintered seating with an old guy named Bill, who had been a cop on crowd-control duty that day. He was still dapper, grey hair greased back, but looked like he'd had a tough life. I asked him a lot about the gig but he kept switching the subject to his days as a 'champion old-time-country fiddler'. Obviously, this was fascinating, but I really wanted to know more about that day in '56. Could he remember what Elvis was wearing?

Bill paused for a while, and then explained that, in competition, you were only allowed to play tunes from what he called 'the old-time-country-fiddling bible', *1001 Fiddle Tunes*. Having completely given in, I said to Bill it was a pity that he hadn't brought his fiddle along with him, so that he could have given us a tune. He said he didn't play anymore because he had low blood-sugar.

Then I drove to Nashville to meet Jimmy Velvet, an old friend of Elvis and an obsessive collector of showbiz memorabilia. Or at least he had been till he'd had to sell a lot of it to pay for his recent divorce. Jimmy took me to a massive warehouse where he still had Elton John's platform-boots and feathered hat, Christopher Reeve's Superman outfit, John Travolta's white suit from *Saturday Night Fever*, Liberace's mink bedspread, Jackie Gleason's Rolls-Royce golf-cart, and a hat that had been made for John Wayne, with a note that said, 'This crown is too damn small. OK for museum or something. John Wayne.'

Jimmy, all gold rings, perfect teeth and grey quiff, spoke a lot about the shirt and said that it was in worryingly good nick for a 1956 garment, because velvet doesn't normally age that well. I liked Jimmy a lot. He had all the energy and sparkle of a man who had recently left his wife for a much younger woman.

Then I drove out to see Lamar Fike, another member of the Memphis Mafia. Lamar reminded me of a sixty-year-old version of my ex-manager, but with a southern drawl. He was a big fat man. So much so that, when we were filming him, we didn't need to mark where he was previously standing because you could still see the indentation in the carpet. No kidding.

When I showed him the shirt, he began talking about Elvis and clothes. He explained that Elvis never bought people clothes. Instead, he bought people cars, 'because he always knew what size they wanted'. Lamar was not a fan of Elvis's ex-wife, Priscilla. I said she was beautiful. He described her as 'biologically fortunate'. He also talked about how Priscilla was fourteen when Elvis fell for her: 'Hell, he'd got underwear older than that.'

Lamar said the shirt was definitely the one from Tupelo and that he'd sign a letter to say so. 'I'm a walking authenticator,' he declared. He left me with one last story, of how he was stricken with fear when a plane he was on with Elvis ran into turbulence. Elvis asked him why he was so scared and Lamar replied, 'I don't want to die in a plane crash with you. I don't like the billing.'

That night, I drove through dense woodland on the outskirts of Nashville till I arrived in a house in Blueberry Hill Lane, the home of Elvis's old guitarist, Scotty Moore. My heart was thumping when I heard the front door begin to open. Scotty was a lot thicker-set than he had been in the fifties, but still with the same haircut and a nose that couldn't make up its mind where it wanted to go. I was totally star-struck. I began by thanking him for his guitar-playing on 'Mystery Train'. I said it was the best record ever made. He looked genuinely chuffed. We chatted, about the shirt and other stuff, but as I came to leave, I did something I don't think I ever did before in my life. Maybe it's because he was a musician, I don't know, but as I said goodbye to him, I unironically used the expression 'man'. 'You changed the world, man,' I said. He looked kind of shy.

'Yeah, so I've heard,' he replied.

And so the journey went on. In Las Vegas, I met The Jordanaires, Elvis's old backing singers, all in suits and matching hair-pieces. They got me to put the shirt on, and then, I'll never know where it came from, I started to sing an old Elvis gospel number, 'Peace in the Valley':

> Well I'm tired and so weary,
> But I must travel on,
> For I know there's a voice, calling me.
> Well, the morning's so bright,
> And the land is alight
> But the night is as dark as the sea

Just as I reached 'weary', this rich swell of voices lifted me up until I felt like I was floating on a cloud. It was The Jordanaires, joining in like the Skinnerettes do when I sing an old standard, and like they themselves did when Elvis held impromptu gospel sessions around the studio piano. I think I knew then that Elvis had worn this shirt. It was an almost supernatural moment. I felt closer to my life-long hero than I had ever felt.

£11,200 was starting to feel like a bargain, even though I had waived my fee for the documentary so that we could afford to go all the places we wanted to go.

I finally met the slightly scary karate-black-belt former-bodyguard, Dave Hebler, in a car park near the beach at Santa Monica. He looked kind of old, but when I put my arm around his shoulders, he felt like he was made of granite. He said he'd told Elvis about a fancy-dress party he was going to, done up as Elvis, and Elvis had walked into one of his cavernous wardrobes and come out with an armful of clothes, including the shirt, and told him to take his pick. He couldn't recall any mention of 1956, even though he had said so on the letter. I pressed him on this but he could hardly recall the letter, let alone the gift thirty years earlier. In the end, he wrote me a new note of authentication. I found it very moving. It said:

To Frank,
You fucking paranoid fool, you. Enjoy the shirt – it's real.
Best wishes
Your new friend
Dave Hebler

I know this last section has gone on a bit, but that documentary meant a lot to me. Just think of it as being like when your mate feels the need to show you ALL of the photos from his dream holiday in one go. As I said to a journalist just before the documentary went out, 'It's always great to work on something you're really passionate about. I've done a football show, I've done an Elvis show, now all I need is a show about anal sex and I've got the hat-trick.'

I just bought the *Daily Mirror*. Across pages four and five it says, 'Exclusive: Comedy star's lover reveals why they broke up', and then there's a headline that's nearly half a page: 'Frank spent a lot of time making me sad . . . he was just too old.'

There are some lovely photos of us, wrapped up in each other and kissing. There's that smile that made me forget to breathe. There's that bracelet I bought her. She tells the journalist, Polly Graham, that she's off to Genoa this weekend, to watch Watford with her friend, the one who visited me and Dave backstage when we were doing *Unplanned*.

As the *Mirror* puts it: 'With a defiant gesture she added, "You'd better ring the Genoan bars and tell them to get some extra vodka in. In spite of everything I'm still up for a girlie night out. You know me, Polly, I just love to have a good time."'

All this sounds like a logistical nightmare to me. Just getting hold of the phone numbers will be bad enough, but then trying to explain to various Italian barmen, over the noise of clinking glasses and Europop, in what I'm guessing will be indifferent Italian, why the arrival of one woman will require an unscheduled trip to the cash-and-carry, well, it doesn't bear thinking about. I just hope Polly knows what she's taking on. I know I didn't.

I'll quote you one last bit: 'To be honest, I need to go out with some people my own age. I'd forgotten how young I was because I was concentrating on being so grown-up and domesticated.'

I wish I hadn't let my publisher talk me into writing that bit about what love is. It sort of celebrated domestic realities like making hot drinks for your poorly bird and talking in the dark. Turns out I was boring the arse off her. What a berk I am. Still, everything in the book represents how I felt at the time of writing and I'm not changing it now.

I'm going to the Albion tomorrow, it's a pre-season friendly against Sunderland. I'll be all self-conscious about the *Mirror* article and make a fool of myself by trying too hard to look sprightly and youthful. Still, you'd better ring the Albion refreshment stall and tell them to get some extra tea in. You know me, Polly, I'm a middle-aged alcoholic. I just love to have a good time.

And all this from lips that used to say, 'I love you.'

Oh, don't mind me. I have to have a quick wallow before I bounce back. I have, of course, a classic opportunity here to give you the cautionary tale that is my side of the story, but you know I won't. Ours was a very public, tabloidy, *OK*-magazine-type love-affair and, as my mate Jack always says, 'If you dance with the crocodile, you have to be prepared for what happens when the music stops.'

I wouldn't mind, but only yesterday I broke my pledge of non-contact and sent her one last e-mail, thanking her for all the good times and wishing her happiness for the future. She said she'd spoken to the *Mirror*, but only to tell them what a nice bloke I am. It's Birmingham Magistrates Court all over again. Speaking of which, there'll be champagne corks popping round my ex-wife's house tonight.

Oh yeah, I almost forgot. That's how famous I am.

Well, that's about it. That's my life. I thought I'd better write it all down now, in case I start drinking again. That option is never far from my thoughts. I sometimes think of doing a one-off West End show called *Frank Skinner Starts Drinking Again*. I imagine myself strolling on stage, glass in hand, as they play that old cowboy number, 'Back in the Saddle Again', and steadily getting smashed in front of an appreciative crowd. Maybe if the book bombs.

Speaking of the book, I'm sure there are parts in here where I've sounded cocky, or grand, or even downright unpleasant, but I'm not going to go back through it, cleaning myself up. I've really tried hard to tell the truth because I think, in a book like this, that's important. Like Polonius said, 'This above all: to thine own self be true, And it must follow, as the night the day, Thou canst not then be false to any man.' At the end of the day, I'm just an ordinary bloke. I know that, because I still say 'Whoops!' about nine or ten times when I watch *You've Been Framed*. But I think the life of an ordinary bloke can still be, in a way, sort of extraordinary.

Thanks for sticking with it. Whoever you are, friend, family or stranger, the next time we meet, you'll know more about me than I know about you, so that's good, isn't it? That gives you the upper hand.

It took six months to write, so if you've taken longer than that to read it you need to question your commitment. By now, all being well, I will have moved on to the next project, my ex-wife's response in the tabloids will have bought her a new kitchen, and Caroline will be lying on a beach somewhere with a Genoan bloke in his early twenties. Still, it's better than Jerry Springer.

I hope our Nora is still speaking to me, and I hope I haven't put off any woman who could have been the great love of my life. Who knows, maybe the woman who could be the great love of my life needs to have read this and still think I'm OK. After all, this is what she'll be getting. I'm not really ashamed of anything in here, well, except the stripy blazer on the cover, but I just borrowed that for the photo-shoot. Honest. So, anyway, maybe I should start carrying copies around with me, and handing them out to attractive women in bars.

This book could end up being the longest chat-up line of all time.